JAMES MAY'S
TOY STORIES

24 Hour re

This book is to be returned
above, but may be renewed u
demand. Ask at your local libra

Please note that charges are made on

JAMES MAY'S

TOY STORIES

James May

with Ian Harrison

CONWAY

everybody who joined in

First published in the United Kingdom
in 2009 by Conway,
an imprint of Anova Books,
10 Southcombe Street,
London W14 0RA

Produced in association with Plum Pictures Limited,
33 Oval Road, London NW1 7EA

British Library Cataloguing in Publication Data:
A catalogue record for this book is available
from the British Library

10 9 8 7 6 5 4 3 2 1

ISBN 9781844861071

Reproduction by Rival Colour Limited, UK
Printed by Butler Tanner & Dennis, Frome, UK

www.anovabooks.com
www.conwaypublishing.com

The following brand names, trademarks and logos are reproduced with kind permission:
Plasticine: Flair Leisure Products plc
Meccano: Meccano
Hornby, Airfix and Scalextric: Hornby Hobbies Limited
LEGO®: The Lego Group

CONTENTS

WHAT REAL TOYS MEAN TO ME

I once said, in an earlier programme I made, that the story of toys is the story of everything, and that if some bearded archeologist of the year 3000 wants to know what life was all about in the 20th century, all he has to do is dig up the toy-box.

The truly great toys are incredible historical records of a richness that has not generally been appreciated. They are a mirror of the technological developments and social aspirations of their eras.

Today's video games are actually pushing the boundaries of digital possibility, and, in their own time, Airfix kits showed just how amazing the new-fangled science of plastic injection moulding was. Scalextric celebrated the widespread embrace of the motor car and sent the train set into gradual decline, just as the real railways were left to rot in favour of investment in roads. Meccano, though it seems fantastically old-fashioned now, was once a way by which small boys (girls had yet to be admitted in those pre-war days) could emulate the work of the great engineers who had made Britain an industrial superpower, and thus ultimately succeed them.

And that's something else that old toys tell us and that isn't really found in the study of Art Deco furniture or portrait painting; they were intended for children, so they indicate how we thought the future would turn out.

Until now, though, my curiosity about old toys was largely academic. I saw them as an unexplored conduit to the past. But then I thought about this a bit harder. There is obviously something deeply valuable in this activity we blithely dismiss as 'playing'. Psychologists have told me of the value of Lego in repairing traumatised or injured minds, and physiotherapists might point you to a lump of Plasticine as a means of exercising a rheumatic hand. Architects and automotive engineers have long used constructional toys as a means of trying out ideas in miniature.

> "The truly great toys ... are a mirror of the technological developments and social aspirations of their eras."

Walk into the Early Learning Centre today and the boxes of supposedly 'educational' toys will be covered in proclamations about how they encourage role playing, stimulate the development of hand–eye co-ordination, and other things designed to make parents feel better about buying them. But toys, and especially constructional toys, have always been educational. Most of what I know about DC electricity was learned from Scalextric, and Newton's equations of motion make much more sense if you can see how they help you to win.

Toys can be sociable, too. A toy I genuinely and unashamedly love is the train set. Mine is packed away in the loft, and usually comes out only at Christmas. But when I set it up, I discover that it's a great focal point for the community, and that neighbours I·don't even know knock on the door to ask if they can have a go. Mulled wine and shunting parties have become something of an annual fixture in the May household.

There's something else, too, and this is what formed the kernel of the TV series. As a child, with an open mind, our ambitions for our toys were enormous. No one can have looked at a box of Lego and not wondered what would be possible with an infinite supply of the stuff. But resources were always limited, because toys were packaged to a price to satisfy grown-ups, not in accordance with the vision of the eight-year-old James May.

So what if I could have ten miles of Hornby track, instead of just enough for a figure of eight? Or three million Lego bricks, instead of just half a bucket full? Or enough Scalextric track to go round a real racing circuit, rather than just enough to make a vague representation of one on the carpet? It was time to supersize toy culture, and in doing so lay to rest some enduring toy-related frustrations that millions of us must have suffered.

"toys are a frail thread connecting us to the joy of childhood"

To be honest, I imagined that *James May's Toy Stories* would be a sort of popular science and history series. But as each project progressed, something unexpected happened. Toys asserted themselves as a force for good in the world, and drew together thousands of people who needed to exorcise some deep-rooted urge to play with stuff, but who were scared to admit it. Toys allowed people to shed inhibitions and daily cares, to put aside the stultifying drudgery of working and paying mortgages and shopping in supermarkets. I suppose this was inevitable; toys are a frail thread connecting us to the joy of childhood, when none of that stuff mattered.

As an unknown man working at Legoland told me, 'The day we stop playing is the day we start getting ready to die.'

Page 2: My much-loved old Scalextric Mini Cooper from the 1970s.
Page 7: A selection of my treasured toys.

FLYING SCOTSMAN

9

J.MAY.09

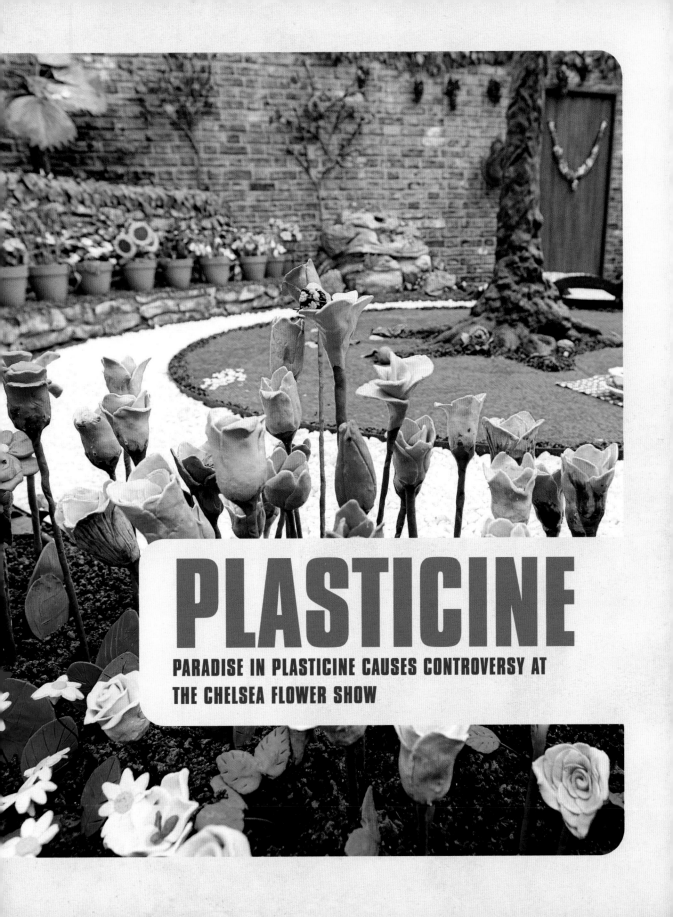

PLASTICINE

PARADISE IN PLASTICINE CAUSES CONTROVERSY AT
THE CHELSEA FLOWER SHOW

WHY PLASTICINE?

I never really played with Plasticine as a child. I'm not really an arty person, I'm a techie person, so Plasticine wasn't really my thing. As an adult I discovered it was invented by an art teacher, not as a toy but as an artists' modelling material, which proved my childhood instincts correct.

I'm not really a gardener either, so for me personally the idea of making a Plasticine garden for the Chelsea Flower Show is by far the most alien of the challenges in this book.

Left to my own devices I would never have dreamt of including Plasticine in my selection of boys' toys because my first thought was that it's hopeless; you can't do anything with it. But whilst it doesn't have interconnecting components like the other constructional toys in my selection, it is something that you can make things with. And when my producer suggested creating a Plasticine garden I took on the challenge and discovered that my first thought was wrong – in fact, Plasticine is brilliant, you can do anything with it. When I made a Plasticine apple I was, like Cézanne, astonished by it. I had a real sense of achievement. And when I made my first Plasticine flower I ran round the house in the throes of a mystical, spiritual experience.

> "Plasticine is brilliant, you can do anything with it"

The reason I didn't engage with Plasticine as a child is because I never liked working with soft materials. I never made anything out of fabric (because that was for girls anyway) and I found Plasticine too soft and indeterminate. When I made balsa wood gliders the bit I always struggled with was covering them with tissue-paper, because you couldn't measure it and cut it and shape it with a tool like you can with wood. You had to nip it and tuck it and *massage* it into position, and I just wasn't very good at that. I had a similar problem with Plasticine, until I started thinking about it in engineering terms; that is, until I started evolving techniques for achieving what I wanted.

So for me, the Plasticine experience was more craft technique than artistry. There's artistry in being able to look at something and think, 'How can I do that in Plasticine; how can I make it look like something without it actually being that thing,' but in the main I found it was a craft and manufacturing skill.

I don't think William Harbutt, the inventor, would be offended by that assessment (if he was still around to pass comment). He was an artist but he was also an educator, and he saw Plasticine as an educational tool – the 3D equivalent of pen and paper. He saw it as quite a worthy thing, expanding the

realms of education by engaging the hand, the eye and the mind (which was quite a revolutionary thing in those more traditional book-learning days), and he marketed it towards schools and middle-class parents. So I'm sure that whether I engaged with it as an art or as a craft would have been OK by him. It wasn't until after World War I that Plasticine was mass-marketed as a toy, and even then the bulk of sales still went to schools and art colleges.

Plasticine is obviously still popular with small children but I think it's one of those things that they never make the most of because nobody really shows them what can be done with it. As I discovered when I started making the garden, you need a few basic techniques, and unless you manage to work them out for yourself or somebody shows you, you feel that you've exhausted the potential of Plasticine quite early on. But I think the garden shows just what can be done with Plasticine when you've mastered the techniques – and marshalled the manpower.

Despite the fact that I don't like the feeling of Plasticine on my fingers, and the fact that I still don't think I'm particularly good with soft materials, I did find the experience of sitting in my kitchen trying to make a Plasticine daffodil remarkably satisfying. In fact, it got to about 10.30 p.m. and I realised I hadn't even been to the pub. I suddenly panicked and thought, 'God, I need a drink,' but of course I didn't need one because I was playing with my Plasticine.

But I went anyway.

And there's the rub – I went anyway. The Plasticine daffodil had made me veer off my usual path but it hadn't stopped me reaching my usual destination. Likewise, the garden as a whole – creating it was a pleasant diversion but it didn't cause some Damascene conversion that made me abandon my faith in proper constructional toys and become a convert to soft materials. It didn't make me think I'd missed out on a vitally important part of my childhood. To be honest, by the time the garden was complete I'd had enough of Plasticine to last me several childhoods.

FROM COTTAGE INDUSTRY TO GLOBAL SUPPLIER

When builder John Harford moved into a house on Alfred Street in Bath in the early 1990s he knew nothing of the historic events that had taken place in the basement of his new home. He suspected that there were rooms beneath the house but the ground level floors had been extended over the access to the basement, so he was taking a calculated risk about whether the lower rooms would be suitable for renovation. When he opened up the floor he was mystified to discover an array of equipment, including work benches and mixing vats, and a slightly tacky, pliable substance covering parts of the floor. Given that the house had no garden he was even more mystified to discover a heavy-duty garden roller. 'It was a bit of a time capsule really, as if all this equipment had just been left there from 100 years ago.'

It was not until a decade later, when a television researcher contacted him to ask for permission to film in the house, that Mr Harford discovered his assessment was correct: the basement was a time capsule, and the equipment had been left there almost exactly a century earlier by William Harbutt, who invented Plasticine in that very room in 1897. The vats had been used for mixing Harbutt's experimental ingredients, the garden roller was used for squeezing water out of the resulting paste, and the tacky substance was in fact some of the world's first Plasticine – handmade by the inventor and still malleable almost a century later.

ABOVE: William Harbutt invented Plasticine in the basement of his family home in Alfred Street, Bath, in 1897. Look carefully: you can see some in his beard.

Not knowing the significance of this dusty and innocuous-looking equipment, or of the unidentifiable substance on the floor, Mr Harford cleared out the equipment, scraped up the Plasticine and disposed of them. But while the tools may be lost to posterity, a remarkable story survives: the story of how artist William Harbutt invented Plasticine in his Alfred Street basement and then turned a small family business into one of the world's first global suppliers. Within a decade of its invention Plasticine was being produced in the nearby village of Bathampton and distributed throughout the British Empire.

As Stuart Burroughs, curator of the Bath at Work Museum, observes: 'One can imagine someone picking up one of the early boxes of Plasticine in Canada and reading "Made in Bathampton, England", and imagining that Bathampton was a great chemical town where they were mass producing Plasticine in huge quantities. But in fact it was made in a small mill in a village high street, surrounded by open fields.'

The story of Plasticine's extraordinary rise to popularity is inextricably entwined with the story of William Harbutt. And who better to introduce William Harbutt than chief modeller Albert V Blanchard, who worked for Plasticine from 1906 to 1963. Three years after his retirement Blanchard prepared some 40 pages of handwritten notes recording his memories of Harbutt, the factory, and the manufacturing process. He describes Harbutt as 'a man of medium build with a long grey beard and a club foot ... As an employer Mr Harbutt was very easy going ... He was a non-smoker and a teetotaller. I once saw Mr Harbutt talking to three of his employees and each had a club foot.'

This last observation seems a surreal addition to his notes, but Harbutt's club foot was clearly a distinctive feature. It was the result of a skating accident at the age of 16 in which he broke his hip and was bedridden for two years, after which he was left with one leg permanently shorter than the other. Little else of Harbutt's childhood is recorded except that he was born in North Shields, Northumberland, on 13 February 1844, the seventh of eight children, and that after recovering from his skating accident he moved south, graduating with a Medal of Honour from the National Art Training School in Kensington (later the Royal College of Art). In 1874, at the age of 30, he moved to Bath to take over as headmaster of the Bath School of Art. Once there he found the committee too set in its ways to accept his progressive ideas, so within three years he had left to establish his own art school – the Paragon School of Art – and to act as a private art tutor in local schools.

ABOVE: Multiple self-portrait of William Harbutt. Harbutt became very interested in experimental photography after striking up a friendship with the pioneering photographer Fox Talbot.

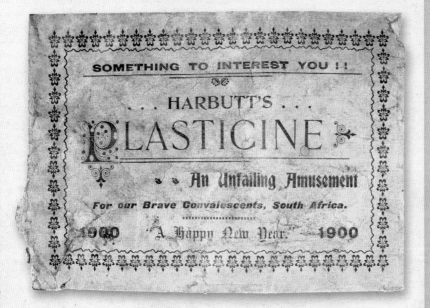

SOMETHING TO INTEREST YOU !!

... HARBUTT'S ...

PLASTICINE

An Unfailing Amusement

For our Brave Convalescents, South Africa.

1900 "A Happy New Year." 1900

LEFT: Within a decade of its invention Plasticine was being made just outside Bath and shipped as far afield as Australia, Canada and the USA, making the tiny village of Bathampton famous throughout the world.

The fact that Harbutt was a trained artist and practising art teacher was crucial to the invention of Plasticine, which he conceived not as a toy but as a professional artists' modelling material. Working in clay presented problems for his students. It was heavy and difficult to sculpt, and students would often find that their clay had dried out over the weekends or holidays so that it was impossible to work with on their return. So Harbutt decided to create an alternative that would mould like clay but which would not dry out.

From Alfred Street to the Old Flour Mill

To accommodate his ever-growing family (Harbutt and his wife Elizabeth went on to have a total of 12 children), Harbutt moved in the 1890s to Alfred Street, where he continued to run an art studio. It was here, in the basement of his new home, that he began experimenting with various recipes for his new modelling material. The original formula for Plasticine was lost in a factory fire so it is impossible to know what ingredients Harbutt mixed in the basement at Alfred Street but it would have been similar to those used in later years. That is, roughly: 65 per cent bulking agent or 'whiting' (the factory used farina and later gypsum); five per cent lime; ten per cent petroleum jelly and ten per cent lanolin, with small quantities of various other ingredients including sulphur. When the ingredients are mixed the lime reacts with the acids in the liquids, stiffening the mix and causing the paste to heat up as the chemical reaction takes place.

Albert Blanchard remembers William's daughter Olive telling him that Harbutt would combine the ingredients in a bucket (the 'vats' discovered a century later by John Harford), mix it by hand with a large egg whisk, and then roll out the mixture on the floor of the basement using a 130 kg garden roller. Other accounts state that the whole family would assist in kneading the mixture by hand and that an anonymous retired soldier had the job of pushing the garden roller, which was used to squeeze out the moisture before the Plasticine was left for several days or weeks to mature.

Harbutt succeeded in creating a satisfactory version of his now legendary product in 1897, at the age of 53. At first he made his new modelling material in small quantities purely for his own students but soon other artists began to hear about it and Harbutt began supplying some of them with Plasticine.

ABOVE: Plasticine began life as both a serious modelling material and a way of making yourself a new head.

BELOW: One of the earliest packs of Plasticine. In those days Plasticine was available, to paraphrase Henry Ford, in any colour you like, so long as it's grey.

Harbutt's own children (and no doubt those of the other artists) were fascinated with the new material and, to quote Albert Blanchard, discovered 'the joy of making, breaking and re-making countless things with this almost indestructible, ever-plastic "Plasticine".' Harbutt realised that there might be a market for Plasticine both as a modelling material and as a toy and he began to look for ways of manufacturing it in greater quantities. He acquired a second studio in Milsom Street, Bath, where the matured Plasticine was taken from Alfred Street. There it was moulded into slabs using wooden spatulas similar to those once used in butter-making and then cut to size and packed ready for sale. Harbutt began by advertising locally and supplying small quantities to local art shops but the reaction from the trade was not as enthusiastic as that of his fellow artists and his children. As an unknown product it was caught in a vicious circle: it did not sell well so art shops were reluctant to stock it, and because they were reluctant to stock it it did not become well known.

This was where another of Harbutt's skills came to the fore – his knack for presentation and marketing. Initially he had produced Plasticine only in grey, like the clay for which it was intended as a substitute. But as he developed his product for the market he began adding colours to the mix and created a three-colour pack of red, blue and yellow Plasticine in a pack known as The Complete Modeller – a product which remained in the Plasticine range for many years. Despite these efforts sales remained slow, and Blanchard records that Harbutt had almost resigned himself to the fact that Plasticine might always remain 'a hobby or a sideline' to supplement his work as an art tutor. But when a friend alerted Harbutt to the fact that a new publication called *The Royal Magazine* was about to be launched, Harbutt took the risk of spending £5, which would then have been a vast amount, to place an advert. The advert offered a 1lb pack of Plasticine for 1/6,

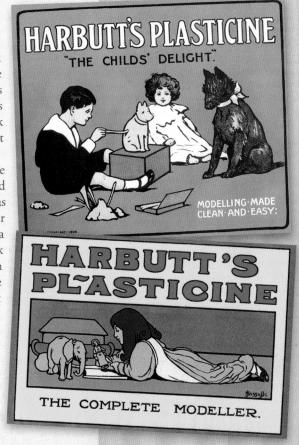

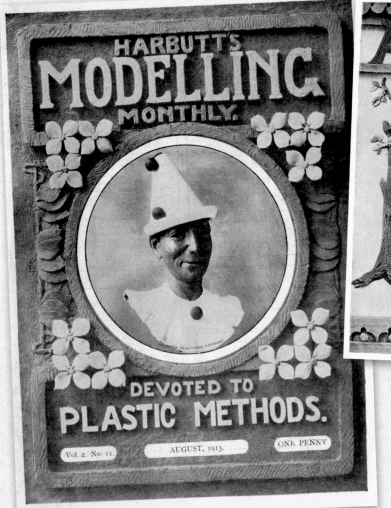

LEFT AND ABOVE: From 1911 onwards *Harbutt's Modelling Monthly*, later *Harbutt's Modelling Magazine*, was a right rollicking good read.

postage paid. Harbutt was unsure whether the outlay would be worthwhile but the response was astonishing: orders flooded in and his entire family was roped in to help pack and dispatch unprecedented amounts of Plasticine.

More importantly there were several trade orders, including one from London art supplier Chapman & Hall asking for 50 kg of Plasticine. Presumably Harbutt supplied this in small batches, because he was still making Plasticine as a cottage industry in his two studios. Nonetheless, Chapman & Hall must have been pleased with the result because not only did they start placing regular orders but they also suggested that Harbutt produce a handbook of instructions. This was so successful that Harbutt followed it in 1901 with a booklet entitled *How To Use Plasticine as a Home Amusement*.

To artistic and inventive success Harbutt now added business acumen. He knew that in order to sustain Plasticine's initial success he must expand, and that meant finding new premises in which to produce it on an industrial scale. Harbutt was shrewd enough to realise that the old flour mill at Bathampton, two miles outside Bath, would be ideal – not only were the mill and its outbuildings large enough to house the factory but it was close to the Kennet and Avon Canal, Bathampton's main street and the Great Western Railway. These communication links would later be vital for bringing raw materials to the factory and shipping the finished product around the globe. But, despite the growing popularity of Plasticine, the banks saw it as a risk and would not lend him money to purchase the mill. Nonetheless, Harbutt persevered and managed to secure a loan from artist John Wilson, one of his relatives in the north of England. He bought the Old Flour Mill for £2,000, and on 1 May 1900 factory-scale production began in what was to be the home of Plasticine for just short of 83 years.

Albert Blanchard describes the Old Flour Mill as 'a five storey building with a "cat head" projecting from the fourth floor on the north and south sides.' (A cat head is a nautical term for the strong beam projecting from the bow of a ship to support the weight of the anchor; Blanchard uses it to describe a room cantilevered out from the side of the factory with a trap door for hauling materials up and down. On the north side the cat head projected over the canal.) Blanchard continues: 'The walls were of local stone and very thick. The purchase included a very fine old house known as "The Grange" in which the Harbutt family now lived.'

It was here, at the characterful Old Flour Mill, that production of Plasticine was transformed from a cottage industry into a global enterprise.

Producing Plasticine

Albert Blanchard recalls that the first improvement in production methods was that instead of turning the 'egg whisk' by hand a small gas engine was used. This would power two machines that turned extra large whisks in two separate vats. Coke to power the gas engine was delivered by barge along the canal, and the finished product was taken to the railway station once a week on a hand truck. As production increased the egg whisks and buckets were replaced by a revolving drum and the hand truck was replaced by a horse and cart.

Blanchard has left for posterity a detailed description of the manufacturing process. The first stage was to prepare the lime:

A cartload of rock lime was delivered. This was placed in a wooden trough (about 5' x 2'2") which had a trap door at one end with an arrangement for opening and closing it. With the trap door closed and the trough half full of rock lime it was sprayed with water from a hose. Some time after, the trap door was lifted with only a sheet of perforated metal to prevent the solid matter coming out. This allowed the surplus water to drain away, and in time the lime in the trough was of the consistency of soft butter. At this stage the soft 'putty lime' was shovelled out and placed into a covered pit, ready for use when required.

ABOVE: The company's 75th anniversary publication, *The Plasticine People*, describes the Old Flour Mill as being 'full of odd little staircases, rough wooden floors, curiously fashioned doors and tiny windows peering out of the thick walls solidly built of local stone. Not to be compared with the pleasant airy premises of today [1972], but a building with a decided character of its own.'

BELOW: Two views of the inside of the Old Flour Mill during the 1920s.

Meanwhile the other ingredients were being prepared. Blanchard describes two types of distillate, which made up the greasy element of the mix. These were lanolin and strearic acid, both by-products of the wool industry. Lanolin is a waxy substance that occurs naturally in sheep's wool (the word comes from the Latin lana, wool, and oleum, oil) and stearic acid is a solid fat. These distillates were supplied to Harbutt's by woollen mills in the north of England, where it was recovered from washed fleeces by distilling the run-off from the washing process – the washing agents could then be reused while the lanolin and stearic acid went to make Plasticine. Blanchard records:

> The distillate was of two kinds known as 'hard' and 'soft'. Each was melted in a separate iron or copper vessel by means of an ordinary household gas ring raised by a couple of bricks to get the gas flames closer to the vessel.
>
> The dry ingredients were sulphur and farina [cereal flour]. These were mixed in a revolutionary cylinder, then liquid distillate was added, both 'hard' and 'soft', but a much bigger amount of 'hard'. The 'putty lime' was then added but as water and oil won't mix the result was a cylinder of tiny crumbs. If any particular colour was wanted it went in at this mixing stage. The ingredients in the revolving cylinder became quite warm when thoroughly mixed.
>
> The crumbly mixture was now placed into a metal bin with holes in the bottom. After draining for a day or two the 'crumbs' (as they were called) were put through a machine to squeeze the water out which was caught in buckets by the machine. The result of this was a paste [which was extruded from the machine in the form of] 'worms'. The next stage

ABOVE: Plasticine gift tag.

BELOW: 'Barred-out' Plasticine was left to mature before being sent to the pug mills (opposite page).

was to place the 'worms' in wire trays which were taken to the top floor to dry by heat and air – all the windows were taken out on this floor. If time allowed the material had to dry for six months but as trade improved this time was reduced.

In due course the dry worms were taken down to the ground floor, chopped into ½" or ¼" pieces and mixed with farina and vaseline. It was then ready for extrusion in the ordinary way.

After extrusion, the finished Plasticine was sent to 'Rainbow Alley' – so called because of the bright array of colours that were stacked together at this stage for packing. Blanchard does not mention sulphur, which was an ingredient of Plasticine until the 1950s. It was dropped from the formula after a fire at the factory, during which the firemen had to wear breathing apparatus due to the sulphur fumes. Afterwards, Harbutt's experimented with removing the sulphur and found that it made little difference to the end product so it was permanently removed.

As time went by there were other changes to the formula. Gypsum ('whiting') was used instead of farina and the stearic acid and lanolin were replaced by distilled tallow fatty acids (DTFA). Blanchard calls DTFA 'a cheaper kind of distillate', implying that it was introduced for reasons of cost, but William Harbutt's great-grandson Terry remembers that DTFA was introduced at the behest of the marketing department, who felt that if the public discovered Plasticine contained a waste product from the wool trade they would stop

ABOVE: Steve Giles (top) and Keith Gosling, who regularly won the competition for the fastest workers on the pug mills.

BELOW: Harbutt's markets another variation on the Plasticine theme.

buying it. (This despite the fact that lanolin is used in expensive cosmetics, ointments and soaps.) Ironically, if the public knew the origin of the alternative they might have been even more likely to stop buying Plasticine – DTFA is distilled from the carcasses of pigs, cows and sheep when they have passed through the rendering houses after butchering. The end products of rendering include nitrogen, bone meal and fats, the last of which are distilled into DTFA. The marketing department felt that this would be more acceptable, possibly because it was a by-product of a food process rather than an industrial one.

The introduction of DTFA may have suited the marketing department but it created problems in the production process because the chemical make-up was different depending on which animal it came from. Terry Harbutt explains:

> If it was all cow then it would be a certain type of mix but if it was, say, cow and pig we would have to vary the amount of greases and the amount of lime that would go into the mix. We would be given a breakdown of the chemical constituents of every new batch that came in but we still had to make up a small batch and then do what we called a drop test. This was done with a penetrometer, which meant dropping a needle into a little cone of Plasticine – how far it penetrated would give a reading of the relative consistency. High numbers meant it was too soft, and required more stearine in the mix, while low numbers meant it was too hard and required more petroleum jelly.

BELOW: At 'Rainbow Alley' the different colours of Plasticine were packed together, each layer separated by cellophane, and then put into a jig where they were cut to the required length using a piano wire. This wire would cut enough for 40 or 50 small packs at a time, which were then sent to the packing room where they would be boxed up for sale. During the 1970s the boxing process too was automated, and at busy times the factory would run a double shift, producing about 70 tonnes a week of Plasticine. Most of it ended up in the carpet.

At first the DTFA was delivered to the factory as solidified fat, in 45-gallon oil drums. Terry Harbutt remembers, 'We used to have to open the drums and then put either electric heaters or steam heaters on the top. The heater would gradually sink through the DTFA until the whole drum was liquid. Once it had liquefied the men would dip a bucket in to transfer it into the mixing machine. My father, Jack Harbutt, initiated the modernisation of that process so that the DTFA was delivered as a liquid in heated tankers and pumped straight into our heated tanks.'

Although the formula had changed by the 1960s, the basic production process remained the same. Pumping the DTFA into one of four mixing machines was a modern improvement on Blanchard's description, but even in Terry Harbutt's day the lime and the whiting would be put in manually by slicing a bag open on the top of the mixing machine and tipping the contents in. Once mixed, the paste would then be 'barred out' – that is, taken out of the mixing machine, formed into bars (the equivalent of Blanchard's 'worms') and stacked in wheeled bins. The bars were then left for a week or two (far less than in Blanchard's day) for the chemical reactions to cease and for the Plasticine to dry.

After 'aging', the bars were transferred to any one of four pug mills, where they were chopped up, remixed and then extruded through a grooved plate which created the ribbed strips of Plasticine that millions of children remember peeling off one at a time. As the strips came out of the pug mills they were cut into approximately three-foot lengths and stacked on boards, which were then taken to the packing area, 'Rainbow Alley'.

Blanchard laments the introduction of whiting and DTFA, asserting: 'The paste made in the early days was far better than the material made today [1966] – it was slightly softer, very clean and altogether very pleasant and easy to use for very large or the smallest of models… It was much easier to get a fine 'finish' to a model – today's paste is comparatively dry and does not easily respond to finger work in modelling.'

This opinion is not simply that of an old-timer objecting to change – as Plasticine's chief modeller, Blanchard writes with a depth of knowledge and experience. Blanchard created countless models for demonstration and publicity purposes, and his performances often attracted large crowds to the Harbutt's stand at trade fairs, where he would quickly and masterfully model cartoon-like heads, faces and animals for the amusement of the assembled crowds. During World War II his skills were even called upon to provide a model for the Allied attack on Zeebrugge.

When the formula was changed Blanchard was asked to report any differences that the changes made to modelling qualities of Plasticine, but he found that he was very unpopular when he reported that the new formula was inferior. 'It seemed as if I was making trouble for someone if I complained, and lacking in my duty to the firm if I did not.' He acknowledges that the changes were a huge success from a business point of view and, he writes, 'As the present generation has never seen and does not know the world's best modelling material, everybody is happy.'

ABOVE: The product of 'Rainbow Alley'. From the late 1930s Plasticine became available in 12 colours, rather than just clay grey. This 12-colour 'Corona' pack was first introduced in the late 1950s.

An Historic use of
Harbutt's Plasticine.

A MODEL THAT HELPED TO WIN THE BATTLE OF VIMY RIDGE.

The following extract appeared in the *Daily Telegraph* of April 16, 1917. A similar notice also appeared in the *Times*, *Daily News & Leader*, *Globe*, *Daily Sketch*, *Evening Standard*, and many of the great provincial dailies.

BATTLE OF VIMY.

THE STORY OF A MODEL

HOW IT HELPED VICTORY.

BRITISH HEADQUARTERS (France).
Sunday.

Comparative trifles may determine great destinies. The victory on Vimy Ridge may well prove one of the decisive events in that progress of the war on the Western Front. To say that this victory is directly associated with a pretty little model sounds almost like meaningless levity. Yet I have it on the authority of one who is beyond question qualified to speak that such is the case. And to every visitor of commissioned rank to this Headquarters goes forth the stereotyped question: "Have you seen our model?" It is a scale reproduction of the landscape of which the Vimy Ridge is the central feature, and the hand that fashioned it is that of a consummate artist. The material of which it is moulded is **PLASTICINE**, and the colouring is done with vivid realism. You see the general verdure of the landscape, the alternate chalky and earthy tracery of the whole trench systems, the network of roads and tracks, the railways and streams, and, most important of all, the contour of the ridges, spurs, gullies, and plateaux, all reproduced with amazing fidelity in precise proportions. Every mine crater is reproduced, and every belt of wire shown as it existed before the terrific bombardment which preceded the infantry attack.

This work of months was executed from aerial photographs, from maps, and direct observation. Local knowledge was largely requisitioned, and the author of the model gladly acknowledges the assistance he received from the Mayor of Vimy, himself a keen sportsman, with an intimate knowledge of the country. Over this Lilliputian landscape Staff officers of high rank pored for hours on end, and officers and non-coms. from the Canadians and British units which were detailed for the assault were coached in their parts on this wonderful model. Much artillery plotting was done over this fantastic plan. It deserves to be placed in some monumental niche, for beyond all question it contributed to a degree which it would be difficult to exaggerate to the splendid victory so often schemed upon its surface.

The story of that imperishable adventure was unfolded to me by the Staff officer as we bent together over the model. He traced exactly the development of the attack, pointing out the dispositions of our own and the enemy troops. While I do not know that his profoundly interesting account leaves me much to add to what has already been written about the capture of Vimy Ridge, it did bring home to me very vividly the immensity of the achievement. There was great danger of a prompt counter-attack from the north-east, where the Germans were in strength, and a glance at the model rendered it clear that the key to the position was Hill 145. This the Army Commander clearly realised from the outset. As a matter of fact, so admirably was the whole thing schemed and carried out that the cost was extraordinarily light.

It is very interesting to learn that a study of the captured ground has, thus far, confirmed the accuracy of the model above described in every detail. I was even shown the slight depression in the ground where our gunners had failed to reach the wire entanglements.

Reuter's Special Service.

The London Letter of the *Birmingham Daily Post*, April 17, 1917, contains the following—
"A suggestion has been heard here to-day that the fine colored Model of the Vimy Ridge, constructed by "our Officers to assist the work of its capture, should be preserved in the Museum of the Royal United "Service Institution, Whitehall."

HARBUTT'S PLASTICINE Ltd., Bathampton, Bath.   London Office and Show Rooms, 34-40 Ludgate Hill, E.C 4.

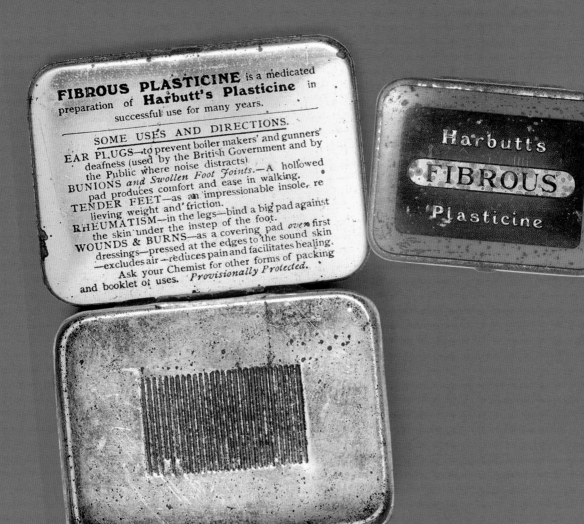

FIBROUS PLASTICINE is a medicated preparation of **Harbutt's Plasticine** in successful use for many years.

SOME USES AND DIRECTIONS.

EAR PLUGS—to prevent boiler makers' and gunners' deafness (used by the British Government and by the Public where noise distracts)

BUNIONS *and Swollen Foot Joints.*—A hollowed pad produces comfort and ease in walking.

TENDER FEET—as an impressionable insole, relieving weight and friction.

RHEUMATISM—in the legs—bind a big pad against the skin under the instep of the foot.

WOUNDS & BURNS—as a covering pad *over* first dressings—pressed at the edges to the sound skin —excludes air—reduces pain and facilitates healing.

Ask your Chemist for other forms of packing and booklet of uses. *Provisionally Protected.*

Harbutts FIBROUS Plasticine

Historic Uses of Harbutt's Plasticine

Plasticine was put to many uses during World War I, in connection with gas masks, military hardware, the modelling of battleground terrain and even field dressings. On 28 August 1914 – less than four weeks after Britain joined the war – Harbutt filed a patent application for 'an improved plastic composition which shall be solid, tenacious and

LEFT: During World War I, Plasticine's chief modeller Albert Blanchard created detailed models of theatres of war for the armed forces, including Vimy Ridge, which was celebrated in the national press.

homogenous in structure and applicable to a variety of uses.' In layman's terms that means Plasticine mixed with a fibrous material, such as lamb's wool or cotton wool, to make it stronger and more binding than modellers' Plasticine. Harbutt's patent points out that because it contains sulphur Plasticine is antiseptic, and that his improved version could be rolled into sheets and used for bandages and field dressings. The patent continues: 'It forms a very efficient ear stopping for gunners to prevent deafness in ship turrets and forts and for boilermakers using percussion tools. It is also applicable in the resetting of broken and fractured limbs.' The result was Harbutt's Fibrous Plasticine.

Life at the Old Flour Mill

William Harbutt was a generous and popular employer who organised annual outings for his employees and created a convivial atmosphere at the factory. If the weather was good Harbutt would occasionally send everyone home early to enjoy the sunshine, and in hard winters he would extend the lunch break to allow his employees to skate on the frozen canal. He made the family boat available at lunchtimes for employees to go out on the canal, and one of the best-remembered factory traditions was the annual outing. Employers, workers and their families would be driven en masse to Henley or Maidenhead for a four-hour cruise along the Thames by steamer. Terry Harbutt and his sisters went on several trips with their father Jack. One of the traditions Terry remembers is that everyone would write their seat number on the tyre of the bus ('using Harbutt's chalk, of course') and the person whose number was nearest the ground when the bus stopped would win all the money in the kitty.

Harbutt's generosity extended to local charities and he even gave over part of the factory premises as a club-room for the people of Bathampton. He was a member of the Parish Council and the Board of Guardians, and in 1907 he stood for election to Somerset County Council, stating to his would-be constituents: 'I ask you to send me to the Council not to rule but to serve, having no belief in the birthright privileges of a governing class.' By all accounts this manifesto was a genuine reflection of his views and his actions, rather than mere politicking, and it is reflected in the way he ran his factory.

According to Albert Blanchard, when World War I broke out in 1914 Harbutt was vocal in his opinion that Britain should have remained neutral so that British industry could profit while other nations concentrated on the war effort. 'However, he did not hold this belief for many weeks, but went on a recruiting campaign over a wide area locally. When young men from Bathampton finally enlisted, as volunteers, he gave each one a golden sovereign as a parting gift.'

MR HARBUTT KICKED OFF.

ABOVE: A 1911 London Festival of Empire Pageant medal, awarded to William Harbutt for Plasticine's contribution to 'Arts and Education'.

LEFT: Blanchard recalls the male workers playing impromptu ball games during their lunch break: 'the girls doing the fancy packing and the one office girl were always spectators if the weather was fine. Mr Harbutt took a keen interest in these games (football, cricket or hockey) and would sometimes spend a quarter of an hour watching the antics of his enthusiastic workers playing the game according to rules made up on the spot. There were times when the game was ending in a draw; then Mr Harbutt would extend the dinner hour to see if we could not find the winner. During the fierce hockey games windows were often broken but this did not worry the boss. He would simply say, "Tell the carpenter to renew it before tomorrow's game."' This illustration by Millar Watt dates from 11 September 1920.

From the very beginning Harbutt travelled to promote Plasticine. Albert Blanchard remembers: 'In the early days I had to do much travelling with Mr Harbutt to demonstrate the uses of Plasticine in schools. Generally it was three or four demonstrations per week each in a different town. This meant much riding in a horse-drawn cab, as well as trains.' As the business expanded, and Plasticine was sold around the globe, so the travel was extended and the variety of venues widened to include trade fairs and exhibitions. In 1908 Harbutt and his daughter Olive went on an extended tour of Australia, New Zealand, Canada and the US, during which they gave more than 140 demonstrations in less than 12 months. Meanwhile, the factory in Bathampton was run by William's sons Noel and Eric.

After World War I Harbutt, now in his 70s, continued travelling to promote Plasticine. In 1921, en route to New York for one such promotional tour, he caught a chill which proved fatal – the chill developed into pneumonia and Harbutt died in New York at the age of 77. His body was embalmed and brought back to Bathampton, where he was buried within sight of the factory.

ABOVE: Plasticine was well received in schools, as it brought glorious colour to a world that was otherwise still black and white. In this image the flowers on the left are bright yellow and red.

Plasticine after William Harbutt

Three more generations of Harbutts continued the business, updating the machinery and the production process and diversifying the range of products. They also ventured into the world of character merchandising as early as the 1930s, producing modelling kits in association with Disney and Enid Blyton. Business continued to improve, and sales reached new heights immediately after World War II when, after years of grey austerity, children were delighted at being able to play with this brightly coloured modelling material. From the 1950s onwards the appeal of Plasticine was widened yet further by the production of modelling kits in association with further licensed characters including Sooty, Basil Brush, Noddy and Camberwick Green.

Business was booming and Harbutt's was even acquiring other companies. But then, disaster struck. In 1962–63 Harbutt's again updated its machinery, but instead of improving production it was to have an unexpected and disastrous effect. An electrical fault in the new equipment – which was designed to carry molten wax to the mixing machines – caused a fire in the early hours of one frozen morning in February 1963. The fire brigade arrived to find the fire hydrants frozen and the canal covered with a thick sheet of ice. By the time they had broken through the ice to feed their pumps the fire had gutted the old part of the factory. The newer buildings were saved but the 200-year-old flour mill was completely destroyed. With it went much of the production machinery and countless artefacts and records, including the original formula for Plasticine and scores of models, Plasticine pictures and early samples.

Amazingly, production restarted within three weeks, although it was a year before the rebuilt factory returned to full production. Temporary huts were

'*Plasticine*' for peace and pleasure,
children have pleasure, parents have peace'

**Harbutt's Plasticine Limited
Bathampton · Bath · England**

LEFT: The real reason no one smokes a pipe any more is that it's impossible to get a good one going unless the children are fully occupied. Plasticine was the answer to the pipe-smoker's prayers.

BELOW: The palette-shaped window in this Plasticine packaging is a subtle reminder of Plasticine's origins as an artists' material.

erected in the grounds and managed to bridge the gap until a modern labour-saving factory rose from the ashes of the Old Flour Mill, under the leadership of works manager Jack Harbutt. Jack's son Terry remembers his father saying that the firm lost only five per cent of normal output during the year of rebuilding: 'A lot of our competitors said they would help us and keep us in business by making our product for us.' When asked why competitors would help out a rival firm he explains, 'Harbutt's was a well-respected family company. Members of our family were always in the Fence Club, which is the top echelon of the big toy fairs at Earls Court, Harrogate, Nuremburg. The Harbutts were always very well liked and it was almost like a gentlemen's club. They didn't want to see us wiped off the market so they came along and helped us make our Plasticine and other products.'

And so Harbutt's successfully overcame one major disaster, but worse was to follow. For another decade business seemed to continue well, and in 1972 Harbutt's celebrated its 75th anniversary – counting from the invention of Plasticine in 1897, rather than the founding of the limited company in 1912. But behind the scenes things were amiss. The

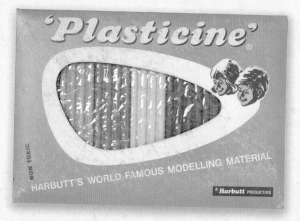

'*Plasticine*'

NON TOXIC

HARBUTT'S WORLD FAMOUS MODELLING MATERIAL

A *Harbutt* PRODUCTION

company was diversifying too fast and too widely, to the detriment of its core product, and was acquiring other businesses without sufficient planning or thought. By 1976 Harbutt's had gone into the red – even though Plasticine was still doing well – and the company was sold to Berwick-Timpo Ltd.

Jack Harbutt, who disagreed with the acquisitions at the time they were made, later wrote: 'We were forced to sell the company after having lost over half a million pounds in a short period through the purchase and running of companies that should never have been purchased or kept running after the second year of acquisition… This is when under a democratically run business, the majority vote of either the directors or shareholders is not always the right course for the future of a company or those depending on it.' Jack, who was given just half an hour to clear his desk after the takeover, described the fiasco as: 'a happy story of a small family business that was expanding gradually and solidly until a few misguided members of this same family became too eager and greedy for growth.'

Berwick-Timpo ran Harbutt's as a going concern but when they too went into liquidation Harbutt's was bought out by Peterpan Playthings. Production was moved to Peterpan's Peterborough premises, and on 3 March 1983 the gates of the Bathampton factory closed for the last time after nearly 83 years of production.

Peterpan Playthings continued to produce Plasticine but in very small quantities. The brand then went through a series of ownership changes as Peterpan Playthings became part of Bluebird Toys and Bluebird Toys was taken over by Mattel. It was sold to Humbrol Ltd (famous for its Airfix kits and model paints) and then, in 2005, Flair Leisure licensed the brand from Humbrol and relaunched Plasticine. A year later, when Humbrol went into administration, Flair bought the Plasticine brand outright. It is now available in 24 colours, including bright neon hues, and the formula has undergone another major change with DTFA being replaced by a mixture of oils and waxes. Plasticine is currently made in Thailand, which Terry Harbutt sees as the ultimate irony: 'Flair are having Plasticine made overseas and shipping it in, whereas we used to make it here and ship it all over the world.'

ABOVE: Harbutt's started producing modelling kits of licensed characters as early as the 1930s in association with Disney and Enid Blyton. In the 1980s the stable of Plasticine character kits expanded to include Aardman Animations' famous duo Wallace and Gromit.

Plasticine record breaker

On 10 August 2008 Plasticine became a Guinness World Record holder when the longest Plasticine sculpture was created at the Museum of Childhood in London. The sculpture – a snake called Sandy-Lucas – used 77.9 kg of Plasticine and measured 426.55 metres long. Over 1,000 children and their parents took part from as far afield as Arizona and Australia. The world record took place over three days with each person contributing his or her individually sculpted part of the snake. Although shaped like a snake, its record was for 'longest Plasticine sculpture'.

PARADISE IN PLASTICINE

My entry for the Chelsea Flower Show was upliftingly entitled *Paradise in Plasticine*. But standing wearily among the Plasticine flowers at 8 p.m. on the dreary, rainy Sunday evening before the show, with the garden still not finished, it felt more like *Hell on Earth*. I found myself asking the question that countless others have asked me since – why did I decide to create a 35 m² garden out of Plasticine for the world's most prestigious flower show?

The answer is that I didn't – I simply agreed to it because it seemed like a good idea at the time, insulated as I was from the January chill in the warmth of my local pub. Now, on a cold, wet, supposedly spring evening five months later, it didn't seem like such a good idea. It seemed like a terrible idea. But there was a chance that the Queen might be visiting the garden the next afternoon so I and my team carried on for another hour (until we were turfed out of the showground), frantically putting the finishing touches to the garden and making a royal Plasticine posy, just in case.

When we returned the next day the hard work that some 2,000 people had put into the garden was vindicated – in the morning sunshine, in a prime corner spot by one of the main exits from the central marquee, it looked superb. The Plasticine vegetation swayed gently in the breeze and the flowers glowed with the luminescence of an Emil Nolde watercolour (more about him later).

Not everyone approved, of course, but I was proud of it. We had succeeded in what we'd set out to achieve – a community artwork on a huge scale that showed just what could be done with Plasticine if you have enough of it (2,255 kg in 24 colours, to be precise). The question was, would the Royal Horticultural Society consider it good enough to win a medal? All the early indications were that the answer would be no.

More than 157,000 people visited the Chelsea Flower Show, and millions more saw it on television and online. A fair proportion of them must have seen *Paradise in Plasticine* but very few can have imagined the trauma – sorry, the journey of discovery, the exploration of my inner self – that led up to it.

Creating a Plasticine garden may look like child's play but, in fact, it's bloody hard work.

And it all began in a cellar in Bath.

BELOW: You could almost see the glint of pride in the eyes of William Harbutt, inventor of Plasticine, a bust of whom presided over the whole scene.

Through William Harbutt's cellar door

J.R.R. Tolkien once said that 'cellar door' was the most marvellous-sounding phrase he knew. But that's not why my journey began in a basement. Before I started on the garden I wanted to know how Plasticine is now made. The obvious thing would be to go to the factory, but that's in Thailand and the budget wouldn't stretch that far. So instead I went to Bath, where I spoke to the inventor's great-grandson, Terry Harbutt.

Equipped with a camping stove, a set of weighing scales, a couple of buckets and Terry's handwritten notes on the Plasticine formula, we descended into the basement of his great-grandfather's former home in Alfred Street. And there, in the very room where William Harbutt invented Plasticine in 1897, we made some of our own. We had enough ingredients to make 2.5 kg of the stuff – only just over 1/1000th of what we would need for the garden but enough to get a feel for how Harbutt first made Plasticine 112 years earlier.

Mixing the original ingredients by hand was extremely hard work, which made me realise why, within three years of inventing it, Harbutt had moved production to a factory just outside Bath where machines could do all the hard work – another example (as if one were needed) of the triumph of manufacturing over the craft tradition.

Before leaving we secreted some of our home-made material in the basement as a permanent memorial to the birthplace of Plasticine, and Terry marked the occasion with a brief speech subtly adapted from the original *Toy Story*: 'For Posterity and Beyond!'

Our brief foray into the origins of Plasticine was enough to convince me that it was a suitable material for making flowers but, sitting in that basement, I couldn't help wondering whether William Harbutt would have approved. But I needn't have worried – Harbutt conceived Plasticine as an artists' modelling material, and making flowers and other organic forms was exactly the kind of

BELOW: Making Plasticine with Terry Harbutt, the inventor's great-grandson. First we melted roughly equal quantities of distilled animal fats and petroleum jelly over the camping stove then mixed it with powdered cement colouring and 2 kg of gypsum (aka whiting). The result was a brown, sticky, greasy syrup. But then we added the vital ingredient – lime. This started reacting with the other ingredients, making the mixture stiffer and quite hot from the energy of the reaction. Then suddenly, magically, the gooey mixture transformed itself into something that was recognisably Plasticine.

thing it was intended for. In fact, Harbutt began publishing booklets explaining the possibilities of Plasticine as early as 1900, and some of the earliest instructions were for flowers, leaves and trees. The difference is that the trees in Harbutt's literature were tabletop models, no bigger than a bonsai – mine would be full size, and I had significant doubts about whether a full-size Plasticine tree was going to stand up. To solve that problem I needed to talk to an expert on modelling clay, and I found one at Aardman Animations, the birthplace of the Oscar-winning duo Wallace and Gromit.

May morphs modelling material

I wanted Aardman to tell me how to make a Plasticine tree that would stand up on its own because I was dead against the idea of using a wire support. But when I asked them for their top tips on modelling clay the first thing on the list was 'use a wire support'. Modelling clay may be malleable but it has no strength. A flower stem won't support its own weight, let alone that of the flower on top. So Aardman recommended making stems by rolling the modelling clay around a wire (or 'armature' as it's known in the trade). The tree was of another order altogether – the armature for that would need to be a steel frame, with wire mesh for the leaves.

I thought this was cheating but Aardman were having none of it. Their character Morph – who first hit our TV screens in 1977 in the children's series *Take Hart* – is made entirely of modelling clay but he's only about four inches high. Wallace and Gromit, on the other hand, have sophisticated jointed steel skeletons, which are then clad in modelling clay. I was sorely disappointed to discover that the loveable duo are not made entirely out of modelling clay but Aardman told me they simply wouldn't support their own weight – without their armatures Wallace and Gromit wouldn't even be able to stand up, let alone keep Shaun the Sheep under control or chase Were-Rabbits round the countryside. So I came up with an unofficial rule for the garden – we could support things with armatures because that's what professional modellers do, but all the texture and all the detail must be Plasticine.

Aardman were very helpful but they were also quite… let's say 'realistic' about the possibility of making a Plasticine garden for Chelsea – they said it couldn't be done.

Actually, it wasn't quite that bad.

They said it couldn't be done *in time* unless I got a lot of people involved, and that there would be a lot of heartache along the way. They were right on both counts, but I didn't know that at the time. So, determined to prove them wrong, I went to the local poncey kitchen shop, bought myself a pasta mangle, like the one I'd seen them using to roll out their Plasticine, and started putting into action some of the techniques I'd learnt.

TOP: Aardman's Wallace reveals what he keeps under his modelling clay. 'Gromit, fetch me clothes, lad, they can all see me armature…'

ABOVE: Roses are red, but in Plasticine they could easily be blue.

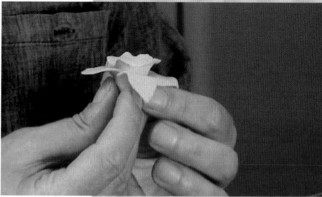

The first thing I made was an apple, and I was very pleased with that. I used a polystyrene ball as an armature to save Plasticine and make it lighter. I carved round the top of the ball to create the dimple for the top of the apple, then I rolled the Plasticine into sheets using the pasta mangle. After a while I discovered that wetting the Plasticine with a weak solution of washing-up liquid stopped it sticking to the rollers, which meant I could roll it even thinner. Then came the clever bit: having made a lighter shade of green by mixing green and white Plasticine, I discovered that if I put both shades through the mangle at the same time they blended but they didn't completely mix – they came out with gradations and variations of shade which looked just like an apple. So I carefully applied that to the polystyrene ball and put it in the fruit bowl. When my girlfriend got home from the pub she didn't notice it, so it must have been a thoroughly convincing apple. Or she just hadn't bothered to look.

It seemed quite Biblical to be making the apple first – and before anyone writes in, I know the Bible doesn't specifically mention that the fruit of the Tree of Knowledge was an apple but if an apple is good enough for Classical tradition it's good enough for me.

But one apple doth not a garden make. I was going to need flowers. Lots of flowers. So I set about making a daffodil by modelling individual petals and joining them all together. It took me about 20 minutes, and that was when I realised the enormity of the task – there was no way I was going to make thousands of flowers in just a few weeks at 20 minutes each. I needed more advice, and this time from someone who knew specifically about making flowers. So I went to see actress Jane Asher. Why ask an actress about making flowers? Because she now runs a cake-decorating business, and that means she spends a lot of time making flowers out of icing. But could she make them out of Plasticine?

Yes, very easily. The principle will be the same as modelling icing. I haven't played with Plasticine since I was about four years old but when I first started cake-making I tried to make the icing into a Plasticine-like texture, so to go back to the original material would be very simple. There are different ways of making flowers. You can mould them bit by bit, which can be very

ABOVE: Sitting in my kitchen making a Plasticine daffodil, wondering what tomfoolery of the fates had brought my previously blameless life to this point. Then I went to the pub.

BELOW: The incomparably lovely Jane Asher in her cake shop. I discovered, rather too late, that cake decorators are already possessed of the skills needed to make perfect Plasticine flowers. I wish I'd known that earlier. There are a lot of things I wish I'd known earlier.

beautiful but it's quite time consuming. You can pipe them, which would need quite a bit of practice, or you can roll out a sheet of icing and cut them out with cutters, which might be very good for you if you're making them en masse. There are cutters for every kind of flower you can imagine.

And that was it – the solution was so obvious I couldn't believe I hadn't thought of it earlier. But that's because I've never made a cake. And because I was thinking about it in engineering terms. I'd been working out the 'development of the shape' – as they call it – and cutting out individual elements to fix together. But what I should have been doing was seeking out a cake-maker and buying some cutters.

Using cutters was much, much quicker. I made a leaf, a sunflower and a pansy in seconds. I discovered that if I wiped the cutter with a silicon wipe it wouldn't stick to the Plasticine, which meant I could cut out 15 daisies in quick succession. And I thought, fantastic, that's 15 daisies – now all I have to do is work out how to make about 100 an hour. And that was when I decided to rope in the children of Stockwell Park School in London.

But now something else was worrying me.

When I was in her shop Jane had asked me whether I had the right colour Plasticine to make all these flowers and I'd told her I wasn't worried whether or not the colours were authentic. The whole point of a Plasticine garden is that it's a fantasy land. It doesn't carry the baggage of nature's cussedness when it comes to colours, size and which plants can grow in proximity to each other or flower at the same time – there are no seasons in Plasticine. I was quite pleased with my proclamation but Jane was a bit more down to earth: 'I think it'll look terrific, but how do you think the RHS are going to feel about this garden that's breaking all the rules of nature, with things flowering at the wrong time and in the wrong colours?'

As things turned out, it was quite a prescient question.

BELOW: With a stack of cutters, and the inquiring minds of the pupils of Stockwell Park School, we'd have paradise knocked out in half an hour.

The design conundrum

My knowledge of horticulture can be summed up in the Latin phrase *Buggerum allus*. So at the same time as learning about Plasticine and perfecting my flower-making techniques I was also undergoing a crash course in flower arranging and garden design. I don't have a garden myself so I'd never really thought about how to lay one out. That doesn't mean that I don't like gardens – I think gardens are wonderful things, but I like to walk through them and look at them and then go to the pub. So the idea of designing my own garden was a bit like the idea of making my own Plasticine – I was going to need help from an expert. And that expert was Judith Blacklock, who runs a flower school in Knightsbridge.

Judith made me realise that while I *thought* I knew what a flower looked like I'd never really looked properly. In fact, not only are they all different sizes and colours, they're different shapes as well. 'You have to divide them into round shapes or linear shapes or spray shapes,' Judith told me. 'Once you're mixing your flowers, putting the different shapes together is what makes a good composition. Shapes are absolutely crucial, and round shapes are particularly important because they hold the eye and stop the design looking fussy and messy.'

She also stressed the importance of foliage. 'If you've got a base of green all the other colours will work and hold themselves together. When people think of flowers they tend to think of the flowering heads and they forget that stems are green and leaves are green and that they too belong to the flower. Foliage pulls all the other colours together that would otherwise look confused.'

And my third big lesson was about relative scale. Judith said that as a rule of thumb no flower in a group should be more than twice the size of the one next to it. 'So you don't put a hydrangea with a snowdrop. But if you are going to use very small flowers with a big flower you group the small one so that it becomes more important and makes the scale work. A hydrangea and a single snowdrop would look silly, but a hydrangea and a group of 50 snowdrops will work better in terms of scale.' She added that in a real arrangement I'd have to keep the flowers in season (snowdrops being a spring flower and hydrangea late summer) but of course I didn't need to worry about that because there are no seasons in Plasticine.

ABOVE: When I met Judith Blacklock at Covent Garden Flower Market she showed me lots and lots of flowers, which seemed sensible enough. Except that I already knew what a flower looked like and I couldn't work out how seeing lots of them in one place was going to help me design a garden. But Judith could. And she's terribly nice.

LEFT: With some reluctance, I attended Judith's beautifully scented flower shop, where I was to learn how to make a 'hand-tied bouquet' and discover the value of incorporating green foliage in my final garden design. My first attempt at flower arranging looked like the work of a man who takes old motorcycles apart and fails to put them back together again, but the second one, seen here, was considered pretty good. Judith was even generous enough to say I had some aptitude for flower arranging. I wish she hadn't. She's just told me in this picture, and look at the expression on my face.

They were three very important lessons, but I wasn't done yet. Following a trip to Judith's flower school, where I learnt to make a 'hand-tied bouquet', I was now fully equipped for creativity. But designing my garden was going to be as much to do with art as horticulture so I thought I'd better have a look at how flowers and gardens have been portrayed in art through the ages. I went to the National Gallery and I was particularly struck by Van Gogh's *Sunflowers*. I was also inspired by some old postcards I had of Emil Nolde watercolours because his flowers are so vivid they seem to glow – and there was no doubt that the colours in my garden were going to be vivid. I also liked the fact that, being an Expressionist, Nolde's flowers are not realistic. They look like flowers but not quite like flowers, and it struck me that that was a good starting point for the garden. There was no point pretending that my Plasticine flowers would be real because they wouldn't; they'd be Plasticine.

RIGHT: Van Gogh painted seven versions of his famous *Sunflowers*. He wrote to his brother Theo: 'I am hard at it, painting with the enthusiasm of a Marseillais eating bouillabaisse… I am working at it every morning from sunrise on, for the flowers fade so quickly.' These ones certainly look as if they were suffering from the heat.

OPPOSITE TOP: My 'spit painting', created by blowing edible ink through a straw.

BELOW: Another inspiring reference point was *Flowers*, by the German Expressionist Emil Nolde. I came across his work years ago in Berlin while InterRailing round Europe.

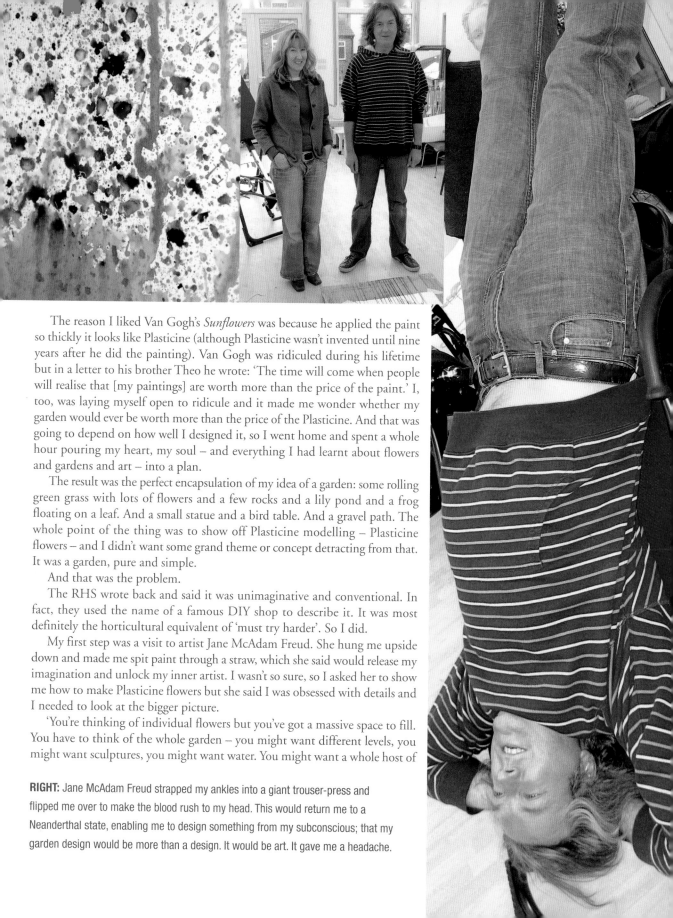

The reason I liked Van Gogh's *Sunflowers* was because he applied the paint so thickly it looks like Plasticine (although Plasticine wasn't invented until nine years after he did the painting). Van Gogh was ridiculed during his lifetime but in a letter to his brother Theo he wrote: 'The time will come when people will realise that [my paintings] are worth more than the price of the paint.' I, too, was laying myself open to ridicule and it made me wonder whether my garden would ever be worth more than the price of the Plasticine. And that was going to depend on how well I designed it, so I went home and spent a whole hour pouring my heart, my soul – and everything I had learnt about flowers and gardens and art – into a plan.

The result was the perfect encapsulation of my idea of a garden: some rolling green grass with lots of flowers and a few rocks and a lily pond and a frog floating on a leaf. And a small statue and a bird table. And a gravel path. The whole point of the thing was to show off Plasticine modelling – Plasticine flowers – and I didn't want some grand theme or concept detracting from that. It was a garden, pure and simple.

And that was the problem.

The RHS wrote back and said it was unimaginative and conventional. In fact, they used the name of a famous DIY shop to describe it. It was most definitely the horticultural equivalent of 'must try harder'. So I did.

My first step was a visit to artist Jane McAdam Freud. She hung me upside down and made me spit paint through a straw, which she said would release my imagination and unlock my inner artist. I wasn't so sure, so I asked her to show me how to make Plasticine flowers but she said I was obsessed with details and I needed to look at the bigger picture.

'You're thinking of individual flowers but you've got a massive space to fill. You have to think of the whole garden – you might want different levels, you might want sculptures, you might want water. You might want a whole host of

RIGHT: Jane McAdam Freud strapped my ankles into a giant trouser-press and flipped me over to make the blood rush to my head. This would return me to a Neanderthal state, enabling me to design something from my subconscious; that my garden design would be more than a design. It would be art. It gave me a headache.

things. There has to be some symmetry, some balance, and if you just go for a standard garden it won't work. It'll look pedestrian. You need to be more creative with your overall conception of what a garden is.'

I tried to think creatively but it was difficult with all that blood in my head. All I could think was that if it was too abstract the Queen would not be amused. But I have to admit that when I got home and tried again my next design was quite imaginative. It did have levels and water and symmetry and balance. And it had a sculpture. On the perspective drawing (see pp. 42–43) there was a sinuous Henry Moore-ish thing, which remained part of the design until I had the bright idea of commissioning Jane to make a Plasticine bust of William Harbutt instead. By that time there were only three weeks left before the show, and Jane normally takes between three months and two years to complete a sculpture. But she managed it, and when she delivered it she told me: 'I was in heaven working in Plasticine, it was so nostalgic. I worked in a way I've never worked before, with absolute speed – on a mission. The spirit of William Harbutt flowed into the thing immediately.'

So that was the design sorted but there was still one more hoop to jump through: the application form. The questions were deceptively simple but somehow my answers kept transforming themselves into philosophical treatises on the meaning of Plasticine. Seemingly the spirit of William Harbutt was flowing into me, too. Or perhaps it had more to do with the spirit of William Grant. For instance: 'Describe the purpose or theme of your garden, including its intended use.' My answer:

> *Paradise in Plasticine* is in essence an artwork, imitating nature and inspired by it but free of the restrictions that it places upon a real garden, rather in the way that Picasso in painting a guitar was not constrained by the requirement accurately to portray something that could make music. The garden will be botanically faithful but need admit no let or hindrance to its bounty on the grounds of season, climate, geographical location or anything else that nature, in her cussedness, contrives to place in the way of all plants and flowers being able to co-exist in perfect harmony.

Next question: 'Indicate whether the garden has structures and what purpose they serve. Mention the boundaries of the garden.'

> In this garden Plasticine can be regarded as the paint, and the garden's contours and fixed structures as the canvas. Rocks, plinths, trellises and the surface of a pond form an arena in which artistry can flourish unfettered.

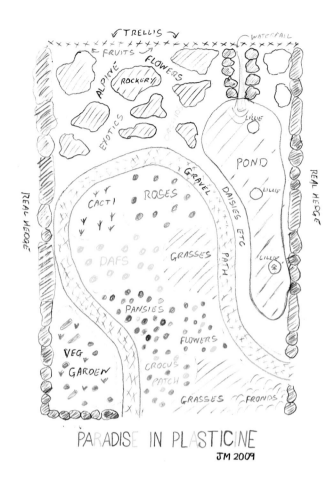

PARADISE IN PLASTICINE

JM 2009

ABOVE: My first design, which was rubbished by the RHS. Some elements of this made it through to the final design – the path remained roughly the same shape, and the vegetable patch and the rockery both appeared in the Chelsea garden. But I must admit that after my visit to Jane the redesign (see pp. 42–43) was much more sophisticated, especially as I secretly paid a graphic designer to draw it up for me and colour it in.

I then had to describe the type of soil and the aspect and prevailing conditions of the garden. That was easy:

There is no soil in this garden, and the aspect and prevailing conditions are of no consequence because everything that grows is not actually growing at all but is in fact Plasticine, inert and lifeless, except in art.

This time the response from the RHS was positive. I was in! Now all I had to do was build the bloody thing.

How does your garden grow?

The children of Stockwell Park School were fantastic – well, most of them – but it soon became clear there was no way they were going to manage 6,000 flowers in just a few weeks. I'd also persuaded a group of Chelsea Pensioners (from the Royal Hospital in whose grounds the Chelsea Flower Show is held) to make some Plasticine poppies, which seemed highly appropriate. And they did produce some admirable specimens, but it wasn't going to be enough.

I needed to do something drastic. I needed to find a gathering of thousands of people who all had a sufficient interest in gardens to be persuaded to make some flowers. Fortunately, I knew just the place – I would set up a 'Home and Garden Theatre' at the Ideal Home Exhibition. Thousands of people would be visiting the exhibition, and if I could persuade even a fraction of them to make a flower each I'd have enough. The theme of the event was 'James May Needs You' and we ran it like a military operation. Thirty-four tables were set up for groups of six people, each equipped with a bottle of talc, a rolling pin, a ruler, 20 armatures and 20 small blocks of Plasticine in various colours. Some people made four or five flowers each and we ended up with more than 2,000 flowers to add to the ever-growing garden.

Meanwhile, at the construction workshop in Twickenham, things were beginning to take shape. We built a low plywood stage, roughly five by seven metres, on which the entire garden was drawn out in thick black marker pen. Then we made the contours of the rockery out of polystyrene blocks cut with a hot wire and artfully 'cragged' to make it look more rock-like. I particularly enjoyed cutting into the 'rock' to give it undulations and strata, effecting two million years of erosion in a couple of seconds with a hot wire.

Next it was a question of creating all the elements to complete the garden. First up was the centrepiece – the all-seasons tree, which had four branches: one bare, one bearing blossom, one in fruit and one with turning leaves. The basic shape was created with a wire armature in accordance with 'The Rules', but all the texture and colour and gnarlyness was created with warmed-up Plasticine smoothed on and moulded by hand – by baby-oil-covered hand, to prevent it sticking and dragging.

TOP: Me hanging a recruiting poster at the Ideal Home Exhibition. To be honest, the slogan originally read, 'Your country needs you to make flowers out of Plasticine', but one of my researchers spelt 'Plasticine' wrongly so I had to cut the bottom off. He was executed.

ABOVE: At first the Chelsea Pensioners thought I was the long-haired reason why national service should be reintroduced. But they warmed to the task and produced some damn good poppies.

ABOVE: At the Ideal Home Exhibition we ran workshops at which I would demonstrate techniques for making crocuses, tulips, orchids, buttercups and hibiscus, and then people would sit down and make as many as they could in an hour. Before the event I was worried that no one would turn up, but in the end it was mobbed – we had five sittings of 200 people and they were all full. Most of the people who came seemed quite normal.

The tree was to stand in the centre of a circular lawn and for that to happen we had to work out how to make Plasticine grass. I seriously considered cutting out individual blades of grass until I worked out that we'd need about 100,000 of them to cover the lawn, so we'd have to find something quicker. There were various suggestions for improvised grass-making tools, ranging from spaghetti makers to garlic crushers, but in the end we discovered that the best method was to push a variegated green Plasticine through the artists' mesh that we were using as an armature for the tree branches. That produced masses of very fine, short blades of grass, but even using that technique it took three people an entire day to make one square metre of grass. The result was a good approximation of a close-cut lawn but it wasn't quite perfect, so we decided that once everything was transferred to Chelsea we would disguise the bald patches with daisies, toadstools, windfall apples, fallen leaves, a picnic and, of course, Jane Asher's splendid Plasticine cake.

Once the base of the garden had been transferred to Chelsea and the tree was safely in place we were able to start planting the thousands of flowers that we had amassed. The soil was made on site from a mixture of black and brown Plasticine, using a scrabbling tool ('the scragger') which is normally used to clean up concrete walls – this would shred the Plasticine into a perfect facsimile of a rich and well-wormed soil. And like good landscape gardeners we scattered the edges of the lawn, the flowerbeds and the vegetable patch with bark chippings, which were made from brown Plasticine using an ordinary household cheese grater.

So the only surface element of the garden that was not made of Plasticine was the path, which had to be made of gravel in order for people to walk on it. The path was one of the few things that had survived from the original design, and it meant my visitors at Chelsea would be able to walk into my mystical garden, experience it, and be transported to some other, Plasticiney, world. They would wend their way round and emerge from the garden back into the real world wondering if it had all been a dream. Very Lewis Carroll.

Those visitors, of course, would include not only my invited guests but also the dreaded RHS judging panel.

LEFT AND ABOVE: The fruit and veg of our labours, plus some flowers. Everything except me is Plasticine, even that incredibly convincing soil.

Paradise in Plasticine

1   Dwarf Mountain Palm

2   Aubrieta

3   Trellis covered in grape vine

4   Pots of pansies, poppies and
    crocuses etc.

5   Irises, crocuses and roses

6   Lawn

7   Dwarf Mountain Palm

8   Trellis covered with climbing rose

9   Canna lilies, Red Hot Pokers and
    orchids

10 Crocuses, irises, snowdrops and
    pansies

11 *Viburnum davidii*

12 Statue/sculpture

13 Canna lilies, Red Hot Pokers, orchids
    and Helicona

14 Herb garden

15 Trellis of honeysuckle

16 Vegetable garden with sweet peas,
    cabbages, carrots and lettuces

17 Aubrieta

18 Irises

19 Fountain and pond with lilies and fish

20 Bullrushes

21 Trellis of hop vine

22 Rockery with alpines, including
    Helianthemum 'Ben Fhada', *Hebe*
    odora 'Summer Frost', *Tropaeolum*
    and *Hypericum olypicum*

23 Pots containing crocuses, poppies,
    pansies and cactuses

24 Fig tree

25 Aubrieta

26 Box hedge bush with berries

27 Grape vine

28 Rose climber, honeysuckle and ivy

29 *Licula spinosa*

30 Dwarf Mountain Palm

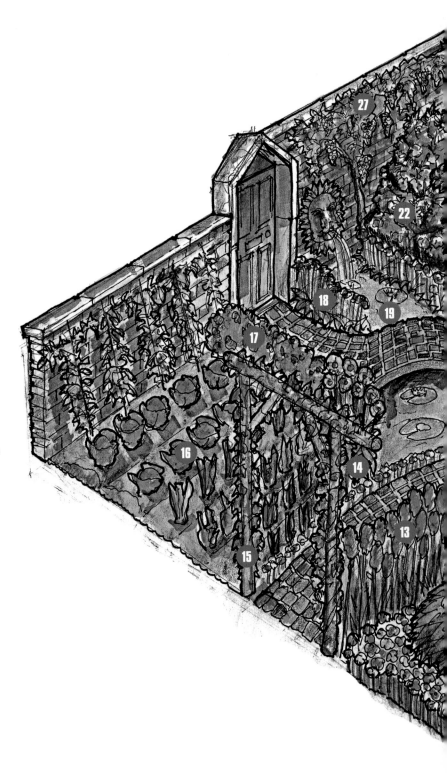

Work in progress

My second design was much more creative than the first but it was still a work in progress. Sharp-eyed Plasticine fans will notice that several elements were adapted or cut before the grand unveiling of the garden. The Henry Moore-ish sculpture was replaced by a bust of William Harbutt, the path became gravel rather than brick, the trellises disappeared and the tree morphed into an 'all seasons' tree.

MAKING YOUR OWN PLASTICINE FLOWERS

Here is how you, too, can amaze yourself with your untapped artistic potential.

YOU WILL NEED:

Green Plasticine
Yellow Plasticine
Orange Plasticine
White Plasticine

Copper wire
Wire cutters
Flat surface

How to make a buttercup

Roll a ball of green Plasticine 1 cm in diameter. Roll this out into a thin sausage, so it measures 5 mm wide. Form a hook at one end of a 15-cm length of copper wire. Wrap the Plasticine around the copper wire, from just below the hook to 5 cm from the bottom end. Smooth with fingers.

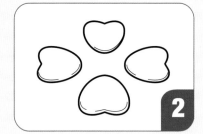

Roll four 1-cm balls of yellow Plasticine. Flatten to form a heart shape.

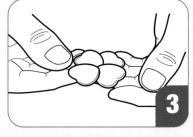

Place the four petals flat on the table into a flower shape, overlapping slightly.

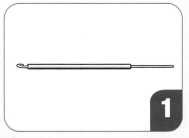

Roll a 1-cm ball of yellow Plasticine and gently push it into the centre of the petals. Wrap a very thin sausage of orange Plasticine around the yellow ball. Flatten a small green ball of Plasticine and add to top of flower.

Use a tool to stipple the other colours into the flower bud.

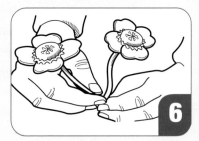

When happy with effect, push flower head on to stem.

How to make a snowdrop

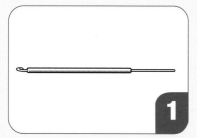

1

Roll a ball of green Plasticine 1.5 cm in diameter. Roll this into a thin sausage 25 cm long. Flatten the sausage, so it measures 7 mm wide. Form a hook at one end of a 30-cm length of copper wire. Wrap the Plasticine around the copper wire from just below the hook to 5 cm from the bottom end. Smooth with fingers.

2

Make three white petals approximately 4 cm long and 1.5 cm wide.

3

For the centre of the flower roll out a flat rectangle of white Plasticine approximately 4 cm x 2 cm. Roll the rectangle into a trumpet shape.

4

Take each petal and space equally around the trumpet to make the flower head.

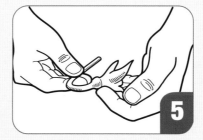

5

Push the head firmly onto the stem over the hook. Roll out a 1 cm x 2 cm strip of green Plasticine and wrap around the join in a bulb-like shape.

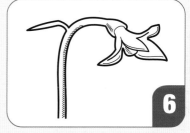

6

Smooth the Plasticine and pinch the ends of the petals to make them thin and delicate. Add one or two small leaves to stem if desired.

It may actually be easier just to grow them.

Judgement Day

The installation was going well and I was starting to think I'd cracked it when I overheard a very experienced Chelsea gardening contractor giving an interview. He said: 'There's not another show on the planet that comes close to the quality that you'll get at this show. There's an awful lot of pressure on designers. For new designers it's a baptism of fire because you're up for a huge amount of criticism and critique. You've got to be very sure of your design, and it takes a certain type of design to create a garden where the public is on the outside looking in. It's not a standard piece of garden design; there's a particular skill to designing a show garden.'

That made me reassess my garden. I went round with Judith Blacklock and looked at some of the other exhibits, and I realised that something wasn't quite right. Mine wasn't a show garden… yet. That was when it really hit home that entering the Chelsea Flower Show was a very different thing from just making a Plasticine garden. I had put too much faith in free-forming when I should have been looking at structure. My garden looked… out of focus. But what could I do at this late stage? As the contractor said in his interview, 'If the Queen's walking down that avenue and you're not finished, well… that's just not an option, really.'

Judith provided the answer: scale and colour.

She had told me very early on not to plant flowers of hugely differing sizes close to each other, and to keep one or two colours together, not to mix them all up. And I hadn't really taken any notice: I'd gone for a fairly random assortment of colours and sizes. But if I rationalised that now, and replanted flowers of similar sizes in blocks of colour, that might pull things into focus.

I was not popular with the team when I suggested replanting but it worked: suddenly the garden looked like a show garden. It was more ordered. It had purpose. I was ready for anything the judges might throw at me…

…except for the thing that they actually did throw at me. On the day of the judging, after months of work and planning, having given me permission to enter a Plasticine garden, the assessment panel (a sort of pre-judgement judgement panel) said that they might not be able to assess the garden because it didn't have any real flowers in it.

Well of course it didn't have any real flowers in it. IT'S A PLASTICINE GARDEN!

If the assessment panel refused to assess it there would be no judgement and no chance of a medal. As the controversy rumbled on through the day they announced that they were prepared to judge my garden, but on the same basis as every other garden. And because 30 per cent of the marks were for plants, and I didn't have any plants, the most I could possibly score would be 70 per cent. Which meant I was starting with a 30 per cent handicap.

Stephen Fry was on my side. He loved it, but one traditionalist certainly didn't. Gardening journalist Peter Seabrook was perhaps my greatest critic, announcing to the world: 'Can you think of a better way to dumb down what was the world's finest showcase for horticultural skills than by introducing Plasticine plants?'

But to me the real absurdity lay in allowing the entry and then penalising it for not having any real flowers. In fact, my original design was for a garden within a garden – a Plasticine fantasy garden framed by a boundary of real hedges. But the RHS said that wasn't good enough, and when I submitted the new idea they agreed I could do the whole thing in Plasticine. And the point is, Plasticine flowers are harmless. They don't spread; they can't be pollinated and they don't propagate.

I had a very good humoured verbal sparring match about it with Chris Beardshaw, one of the world's top gardeners and a former Chelsea judge:

Me: 'What do you think?'
Chris: 'I'm thinking how has the world's finest flower show – with the emphasis on the word flower – allowed this entry.'
Me: 'Because they are the world's finest Plasticine flowers.'
Chris: 'But they're not botanically accurate.'

ABOVE: Stephen Fry, seen here with the Queen's Plasticine posy, appreciated our efforts. 'Even the most dyed-in-the-wool traditionalist should see that what you're doing is celebrating the garden, and that's what it's all about.' A great man.

Me: 'No, but they're botanically in the same ballpark. They're inspired by real flowers. It's an impression – we're not trying to pass them off as real flowers. We're not trying to say, "Ha, ha, fooled you!"'

Chris: 'You're not allowed artificial flowers in a garden at the Chelsea Flower Show.'

Me: 'I contend that they're not artificial flowers because they're not being passed off as real ones. Silk artificial flowers are meant to fool you into thinking they're real. But I'm not suggesting to anyone that these are real flowers. They are a representation of flowers in Plasticine.'

Chris: 'A garden is a little piece of paradise. That's what "garden" means: "enclosed Eden" – paradise.'

Me: 'This is paradise. *Paradise in Plasticine*.'

Chris (smiling): 'If this is your personal impression of paradise, if this is where you think you'd like to spend eternity, then I think you need some help!'

Me: 'Plasticine does last for ever…'

Chris: 'Sadly.'

I think that really Chris quite liked it, he just couldn't bring himself to say so. In fact, most people seemed to quite like it, even if they hated it. I heard one passer-by say, 'Isn't it hideous – in a nice kind of way?' And, ultimately, the judging panel seemed to feel the same way. They marked me down for not having any real flowers but then they awarded me a 'Special Letter' congratulating me on 'an inspiring and creative garden made entirely from Plasticine' and noting: 'The garden is made even more credible by the community who have helped to build it and in particular the RHS would like to recognise the effort made by the schools.'

The letter went on to say that as a result of the 30 per cent handicap the garden had failed to reach the minimum score required for an award. So there was I, trying to decide whether to whip the crowd up into a frenzy and start a revolution or quietly slope off to the pub, when one of the judges surprised me by returning to the garden and announcing: 'We're absolutely delighted with your garden and the RHS therefore has a one-off, specially commissioned overnight, medal for you. Congratulations – it's the best Plasticine garden in the world and the only Plasticine RHS gold medal, so well done. You've inspired us all.'

So, in the end, Stephen Fry was right – they did see that what we had done was a celebration of the garden. And at the end of the week all the negative comments were themselves negated by the fact that *Paradise in Plasticine* won the people's choice award. So thank you to everyone who voted. As I sat there in paradise at the end of the week, I thought, 'How appropriate that here in my fairytale garden we should arrive at a fairytale ending. It's a victory for common sense. It's a victory for gardening. And most importantly, it's a victory for Plasticine.'

ABOVE: The People's Choice Award. The RHS official website stated: 'The winner of the small garden vote was never in doubt. From the moment the vote opened to the minute it closed James May's *Paradise in Plasticine* was way out in front. All the other gardens had a more-or-less equal share of the remaining votes.'

LEFT: The world's first Plasticine RHS gold medal, and almost certainly the last.

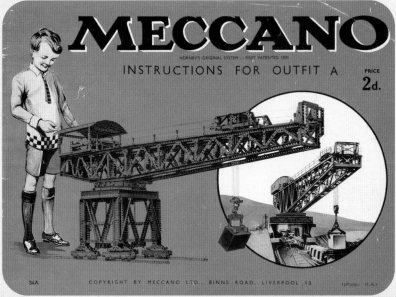

MECCANO

BRIDGING THE LEEDS–LIVERPOOL CANAL

WHY MECCANO?

I didn't really discover the joy of Meccano until my 30s. I never had enough of it as a child to be truly inspired by it; I just had a few bits that had been my dad's or my uncle's. My moment of Meccano discovery came in 1999 when, as a fresh-faced, short-haired journalist, I was commissioned to write an article about it for *The Times* – that's the handsome young journalist in question in the picture opposite.

The Times asked what I thought of Meccano and I said I'd find out whether it had got any easier, because I remember it being quite hard. So I bought an old No. 9 Outfit and borrowed a modern outfit to compare the two. The No. 9 Outfit was very expensive so I decided I would write the article and then resell the outfit. But I liked it so much that I kept it, which means that Frank Hornby ended up costing me about twice as much as I got paid for writing about his invention.

In researching the article I discovered that Meccano is far more than just a toy; it's proper mechanical engineering. Designers and engineers have used it in the development of bridges and buildings and cars, so it has been used in deadly earnest. But it is ugly.

It was already looking fairly ugly and old fashioned when I was a child and it looks even more so in the 21st century, in a world where things are carefully assembled to hide their structure and their engineering. Take a typical mobile phone or computer: its design leaves no real clue as to how it went together or how you would take it apart, and that's why Meccano suddenly looked very outdated; because it wears its nuts and bolts on its sleeve. It's a bit… untidy. In short, Meccano is a very ugly thing unless you make a crane, or a pylon, or the Eiffel Tower – or a bridge.

The Meccano I had as a child wasn't a complete outfit. It didn't have any gear wheels or axles or pulleys, so I had no idea how sophisticated Meccano could be. It was only when I bought the No. 9 Outfit that I realised just how versatile it is – and how much the world has changed since Meccano's heyday. The instructions were aimed at boys aged seven and upwards (no girls; they weren't allowed Meccano in those days) but they were almost impenetrable by today's standards. There were reams of text about ¾-inch shafts and contrates and pinions and lever arms, with only two or three pictures to help you visualise the finished model. But seven-year-old boys understood those things back then because that was the language of the day. Just like people today know about hard drives and MP3 files and how to download things.

The instructions were impressive enough, but making something with it was even more so. I started with a lorry, and I was truly amazed at just how much could be done with this marvellous array of components, which were sophisticated enough to make a genuine three-speed gearbox with reversing and clutch mechanisms. In the old days that's how youngsters would have learnt about mechanisms – by sitting down and making them. And that gave Meccano a very wholesome image as an educational toy.

> "Meccano is serious engineering disguised as a toy"

MECCANO

INSTRUCTIONS for OUTFIT No. 7/8

But was it *fun*? Often when something is described as an 'educational toy' it's not – it's a toy with an educational label attached for marketing reasons. But with Meccano it was almost the other way round. Meccano is serious engineering disguised as a toy, and it's only if you come to it as an adult, or with a genuine sense of engineering inquisitiveness, that it really comes into its own. I think that of the millions of children who ever played with Meccano only about 250 can have really understood it. Meccano is a bit like relativity – everyone buys into it but only a tiny minority really understand it.

Despite all that, as I pointed out in my *Times* article, Meccano has survived two world wars and the decline of Britain as a world power. As such it is a barometer of the state of the nation, and particularly its youth. Ten years ago I wrote that people can argue all they like about whether or not children are stretched as much as they used to be. I thought I had proof that they're not: I had shown that modern Meccano is not half as difficult as the old stuff. And that, I concluded, is probably why we lost the empire.

But I have been made to revise that conclusion by a phenomenally hardworking group of engineering students from Liverpool University. They spent 10,000 person-hours (yes, girls too are now allowed to play with Meccano) building a Meccano bridge that got me across the Leeds–Liverpool Canal, and that gives me hope for the future of Britain. My Bridge of No Return proves that great things can still be achieved with Meccano. And that means that Britain, too, can be great again – if we can find enough nuts and bolts.

MECHANICS MADE EASY

Frank Hornby was a colossus of the toy industry and the creator of three of the world's best-known toys – Meccano, Hornby Trains and Dinky Toys. For nearly four decades, from the patenting of Meccano in 1901 until his death in 1936, he was the custodian of boyhood imagination across the globe. His Liverpool factory has been dubbed 'the Factory of Dreams' and his name is still associated with the best in toy-making more than a century after inventing Meccano, the toy that started it all.

Even before his death Hornby was a legendary figure, partly because of the popularity of the toys he produced but largely because he was a great self-publicist who nurtured and promoted the legend of Frank Hornby in the pages of *Meccano Magazine* (*MM*). He would address his 'Meccano Boys' directly, and in the first edition of *MM* he told them: 'I have corresponded with so many boys about Meccano, and I have got to know them so well, that I have come to look upon every Meccano boy as a personal friend… In future issues I want to tell you of some of the early struggles and experiences I had in gaining opportunities for you to buy Meccano and in getting it manufactured.'

Hornby's version of those early struggles and experiences does not always tally with the versions told by other people. He was prone to hyperbole – in that first issue of *MM* he told his readers that 'More boys play with Meccano than play football or cricket or any other hobby' – and historians have noted that he did not always give others full credit for their part in his success. For this reason there are contradictory stories about Hornby and the origins of Meccano, giving rise to ambiguities, which only add to the mythical status of the man and his invention. The earliest of the contradictions, though, cannot be blamed on Hornby's penchant for embellishing his life story, because it occurred when he was less than two weeks old – officially he was born on 15 May 1863, which is the date on his birth certificate, but it seems that he was actually born on 2 May, the date recorded in the family Bible in his mother's handwriting.

The same uncertainty surrounds the birth (or, at least, the conception) of Meccano. The official story appears in a biography entitled *The Boy Who Made $1,000,000 With A Toy*, originally published by the Meccano Company in New York in 1915. This account relates that Hornby had the sudden

The Largest Gear Wheel in the World. (See page 554.)

VOL. X No. II

NOVEMBER 1925

MECCANO MAGAZINE

The AJAX ILFORD & ROMFORD

FEBRUARY 1925.

MECCANO MAGAZINE

PRICE 3D VOL. X No 2.

GIANT BLOCK SETTING CRANES. (see page 54)

inspiration that was to change his life during a train journey one Christmas Eve in the late 1890s. The biographer, M.P. Gould, tells how Hornby's idea came to him while wondering what to give his two boys for Christmas:

> ...as he rumbled over the bridges, and saw the great derricks and cranes at work in building operations, and saw the wagons and the various machines and the factories along the way, he began to dream how as a boy he had so wanted to build a bridge, how he had wanted to build a crane which could lift things and swing them round and put them down somewhere else… As he journeyed on, he began to wonder how he could make a toy that would amuse his boys and at the same time give them useful instruction that would be valuable to them when they grew up.

As the journey progressed, Hornby supposedly began working out the exact width of the metal strips, how many different lengths there should be, and the spacing of the holes. But his flash of inspiration nearly ended in disaster, because 'he kept puzzling and figuring and working enthusiastically over this problem, until he was almost carried past the station where he was going to visit his family and relatives. Gathering up his things, he hurriedly tumbled out of his compartment… just in time to save himself from a bad fall as the train was gaining headway.'

OPPOSITE, TOP: Frank Hornby looking dapper in court dress.

OPPOSITE, BOTTOM, AND ABOVE: The monthly *Meccano Magazine* was published from 1916 to 1981. Frank Hornby used it to communicate directly with his 'Meccano boys'. In the first edition he told his readers that he wanted to share the story of his 'early struggles and experiences' in making Meccano available. Today he would probably be viewed with suspicion. Sad.

This account was repeated in the January 1933 edition of *MM* and circulated widely on Hornby's death. However, a more prosaic version of the conception of Meccano comes from Hornby's long-term friend A.G. Hayward, who related to Meccano historian and author Jim Gamble how:

Mr Hornby told me himself that he first conceived the idea of Meccano in the very early part of the century when he was a young married man with two small boys… his wife, Clara, had gone out to do the shopping and he was left to do the baby-sitting. It was a miserable wet afternoon and Roland, his eldest son, then about ten years old, had a bad cold and was feeling a bit bored and discontented as children can at that age. The Hornbys could not afford many toys to amuse the children and he got the idea of cutting up an old biscuit tin into strips of various lengths with holes in them, then fastening them together into various constructions using a few nuts and bolts.
He found his own two boys liked the idea and so Meccano was born.

Both accounts centre round Hornby trying to create something to entertain his boys, but it is easy to see which presents the inventor in a more heroic light and would have made better publicity for a growing company. Where Gould and Hayward do agree is that Hornby made the first Meccano outfit himself by hand, and that the dimensions of that first prototype were carried through into production. Those dimensions – the width of the metal strips, the distance between the holes and the thread of the nuts and bolts – have not changed to this day, which means that the original prototype pieces made by Hornby at the turn of the last century (if they still existed) would be compatible with current 21st-century Meccano outfits such as Spykee the interactive WiFi robot.

BELOW: Technical drawings from Hornby's original patent, filed on 9 January 1901. Hornby paid the patent application fee with £5 borrowed from his employer, David Elliott. The patent was published (granted) as Patent No. GB 587/1901.

BOTTOM LEFT: Short-lived gold Meccano, an early foray into bling.

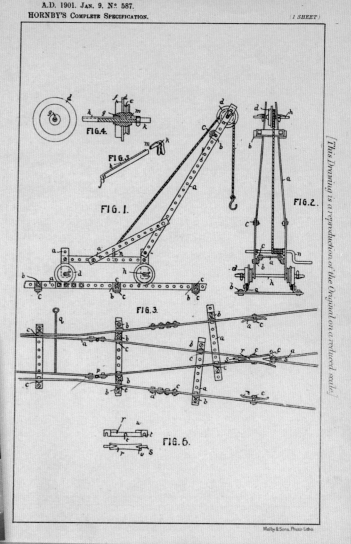

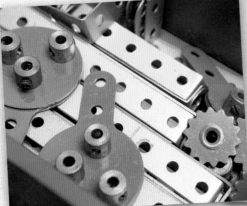

Establishing the Factory of Dreams

Hornby, a 37-year-old Liverpool shipping clerk working in the office of meat importer David Elliott, had long dreamt of being a successful inventor. On 9 January 1901, using £5 borrowed from Elliott, he filed a patent for 'flat strips of strong material perforated with a series of holes arranged transversely along the centre line therein at equidistant intervals apart, in combination with interchangeable pins or bolts and angle pieces.' He called his invention Mechanics Made Easy but it would soon be better known around the world by the snappier name of Meccano.

Lacking the capital to finance a new business, Hornby went into partnership with Elliott and together they began marketing Mechanics Made Easy under the name Elliott & Hornby. At first it was tough going, contrary to numerous accounts that it was an instant success. According to the February 1932 edition of *Meccano Magazine*, 'dealers considered it to be crude and unattractive in appearance, and were very emphatic that it was not in the least likely to meet with a favourable reception from the public.' Elliott and Hornby didn't break even until four years later, when toyshops began to attract interest in Mechanics Made Easy by putting completed models on display in their windows – a marketing idea claimed both by Frank Hornby and by one of the leading wholesalers of the day.

This initial success accelerated rapidly after the name Mechanics Made Easy was changed to Meccano in 1908. Like so many other things, the origin of the name Meccano is uncertain. It was registered as a trademark in September 1907 and used on packaging from June 1908, when Meccano Ltd was established in place of the Elliott and Hornby partnership. Many historians suggest that the name Meccano was coined by company director George Jones (who reputedly came up with the name Dublo for the second range of Hornby model railways some 30 years later). However, Meccano's former advertising manager Harold Owen maintains that Frank Hornby distilled the name from the phrase 'make and know' – which chimes with Hornby's conception of it being an educational toy – while Hornby himself later claimed: 'I decided on the name because it was one that people of every nationality could pronounce.'

ABOVE AND BELOW: Mechanics Made Easy. The original sets were fairly crude, and it was some time before the more sophisticated components such as contrate wheels and universal joints became available. But the fundamentals that made Meccano so versatile – the hole spacing, the shaft diameters – were in place. Note that the strips do not yet have their characteristic rounded ends.

If that was the genuine reason at the time, rather than being imposed retrospectively for publicity reasons, then Hornby's confidence was well-placed – Meccano very quickly became a global product. By 1912 sales in the US had passed the $100,000 mark and sales in France and Germany were so high that Meccano Ltd established offices in both countries that same year. By 1915, less than a decade after the fledgling company had first broken even, Meccano had the largest international sales of any toy in the world, prompting the trade journal *Toy and Fancy Goods Trader* to suggest that there wasn't a civilised country on earth where Meccano was not a household word.

Whilst the *Trader*'s suggestion was clearly ridiculous, as was Hornby's assertion the following year that Meccano was more popular than football or cricket, there is no denying that Hornby's venture had expanded extraordinarily rapidly from its small beginnings. The business had outgrown three premises (James Street, Duke Street and West Derby Road) before moving to the now-famous Binns Road factory in August 1914. That same month Britain went to war with Germany and soon afterwards much of the machinery at Binns Road was seconded to munitions work, with only a limited amount of Meccano being produced on those machines not required by the government.

BELOW: By 1927 Meccano had developed into a comprehensive and highly sophisticated system. This brochure shows most of the basic metal components and what might be achieved with them, given infinite patience and a truly exceptional sense of spatial logic.

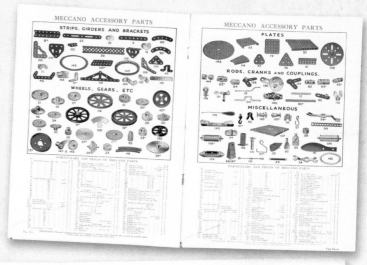

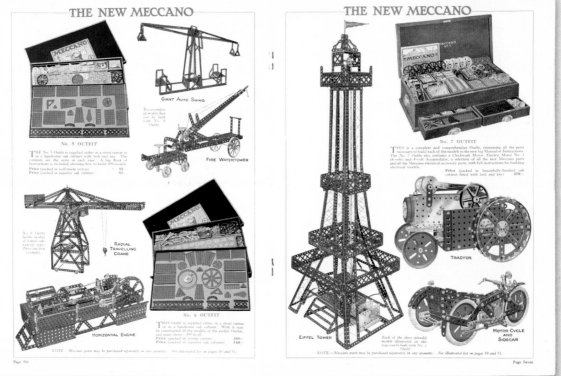

Despite this setback on the toy-making front, Meccano Ltd benefitted financially from the government contracts and made a strong post-war recovery. The inter-war years proved to be the heyday of Meccano Ltd, and during the next two decades Binns Road truly earned its epithet 'Factory of Dreams' as it continued to supply Meccano outfits to boys around the globe and played a vital role in the evolution of Hornby Trains – which started life as a development of constructional Meccano – and Dinky Toys.

A spectrum of outfits

From the outset, Meccano was an expensive toy. One of the reasons that Mechanics Made Easy got off to a slow start was that it cost more than a third of the average labourer's weekly wage. But there was a way of easing the price burden, and a large factor in Meccano's subsequent success is that soon after its inception Hornby began offering a series of outfits of increasing size and variety of components, with Accessory Outfits to upgrade from one to the next. Thus a boy who owned a No. 5 outfit could buy a No. 5A Accessory Outfit confident in the knowledge that he now had a complete No. 6 outfit.

This may have been promoted as a way of ensuring that everyone could play with Meccano whatever the size of his parents' purse, but it was also an in-built marketing device that constantly tempted boys to spend their pocket money on upgrades – each instruction book even showed a selection of models a boy could build if he upgraded to the next level.

Collectors usually identify the period of production of any given Meccano outfit by the colour scheme of the system. Thus the story of Meccano can be neatly divided into a spectrum of historical periods, beginning with Mechanics Made Easy (1901–07) and continuing with the Meccano nickel period (1908–25), the dark red and green period (1926–34), the blue and gold period (1934–42), and so on.

The earliest Mechanics Made Easy outfits were decidedly crude. The metal strips and girders had a tinplate finish, were thin and rather flimsy, and were not rounded at the ends. However, by 1908 the quality had improved considerably and the tinplate strips and girders were replaced by high-quality rolled steel strips and girders with rounded ends, finished in nickel plate and complemented by a wider variety of brass wheels and gears. By the time the name was changed to Meccano in 1908 there were six Mechanics Made Easy outfits; five named A–E and a starter kit called the 'X box', a name which pre-empted the computer game console by almost exactly a century. The five conversion outfits were named X1 and A1–D1. The largest outfit, E, was 'super-sized' compared to the next largest, containing nearly 1,000 perforated strips and a commensurate number of other parts. This trait of having a disproportionately sized outfit at the top of the range would remain a feature of Meccano marketing for almost a century.

TOP: Hornby himself (in the grey suit) at the Binns Road factory. Although plenty of women worked in making Meccano, they were not expected to want to play with it, for Pete's sake. ABOVE: Note how the book of 400 models is free only to boys. Girls are directed to the chapter on vintage Plasticine, where they're allowed.

The change of name to Meccano marked the start of the nickel period, during which the outfits were given numbers instead of letters, with the massive Outfit E becoming Outfit No. 6. During this period the number and variety of components in each outfit was increased, and by 1925 the range of outfits had widened. There were two new outfits at the smaller end of the range (Nos. 0 and 00), and an even bigger outfit, No. 7, at the top. In 1925 Outfit No. 7 retailed at the astronomical price of 370/- or about two months' wages for a skilled worker.

Dark Red and Green

In 1926, the 25th anniversary of Hornby's original patent, Meccano announced the arrival of 'New Meccano'. In fact, it was old Meccano with some of the parts finished in pea green and others in light red – and, confusingly, it marked the start of the 'dark red and green period' (aka the first red and green period). This is because the enamelled red and green parts proved so popular that in 1927 Meccano began producing almost all parts in colour but chose a burgundy red and a darker green instead of the initial light colours.

This period, which lasted from 1926 to 1934, is often heralded as the heyday of Meccano, and it saw the introduction of specialised parts, including rubber tyres for vehicles, ships' funnels, and dredger and digger buckets, all of which made for more realistic models, although they did break with the principle that all Meccano parts should be multi-functional. In addition, there was a wider range of gears, a boiler, improved clockwork and electric motors, an exquisite Steam Engine and the highly complex Geared Roller Bearing, which was the largest and most expensive Meccano part ever produced at 12 inches in diameter and a cost of £1 in 1928.

ABOVE: A built-up bearing like this allows the construction of a truly massive crane.
BELOW: An early Meccano steam engine, 'strongly constructed' (bottom), and a travelling excavator powered by the same.

This period also saw a new outfit at the smaller end of the range (No. 000) and a new departure in the form of the 'Constructor Outfits'. These were made up almost entirely of specialised pieces, which allowed for far more realistic models than the standard perforated plates. The Aeroplane Constructor Outfits, announced in 1931, contained parts for three basic monoplanes and three basic biplanes (No. 1 Outfit) or an additional 16 more advanced aircraft models (No. 2 Outfit). These were followed in 1932 by the Motor Car Constructor Outfits, which had a range of radiator grilles, mudguards and body panels that could be used in various configurations. Clockwork motors enabled the cars to drive and the planes to taxi with propellers spinning. The Constructor Outfits proved very popular but they were withdrawn in 1941, largely because technology had moved on, making their subject matter – biplanes and open touring cars – look very old-fashioned.

ABOVE: Motor Car Constructor used many bespoke parts, which helped to disguise its Meccano origins.
BELOW: The biplane, however, is a bit of a bag of bolts, and of dubious airworthiness.

Blue and Gold

The November 1934 edition of *Meccano Magazine* again announced 'New Meccano' and this time there really was something new to celebrate. Not only had the colours changed – to blue and gold – but there was also a genuinely new departure in the introduction of flexible plates (initially made of fibreboard and later metal) that were perforated only around the edges. This meant that planes, trains, automobiles and ships could be made to look much more realistic: because the plates were flexible it was possible to create curved surfaces, and because they weren't fully perforated the end product did not look as if it had been cut out of a kitchen colander.

At the start of the blue–gold period the ten outfits in the range (previously Nos. 000–7) were again renamed, this time from A to L, leaving out I and J. Not surprisingly this proved confusing for consumers, and in 1937 the range was updated and the labelling of outfits reverted to a numbered system. Outfit 0 (which had been introduced at the smaller end of the range) and Outfits A–H became Outfits 1–9, a system that would remain in place for more than 50 years. At the same time, the famous Outfit No. 10 was introduced as a rationalisation of Outfits K and L. This is sometimes cited as the largest ever Meccano outfit but, in fact, it was considerably smaller than the L set, leaving aficionados divided on the question of whether the red and green Outfit No. 7 or the blue and gold Outfit L was the best ever made.

The blue–gold period lasted until 1942, when production of Meccano at Binns Road ceased due to government requirements for another world war. Production had been gradually phased out over the previous two years, with an announcement as early as the December 1940 edition of *Meccano Magazine* that 'certain Meccano parts are no longer available due to wartime conditions.' Nevertheless, stocks of Meccano continued to find their way to the shops until 30 September 1943, when a government order banned the sale of any new or second-hand metal toys. For two years there was no Meccano available at all – dark days indeed for boys everywhere.

BELOW: Outfit No. 10 is often cited as the biggest and best Meccano outfit ever, but, in fact, aficionados consider that title should go to either the red and green Outfit No. 7 of an earlier era or to the blue and gold Outfit L. It's probably not worth arguing with them, to be honest, because if you thought a Meccano instruction manual was impenetrable, well…

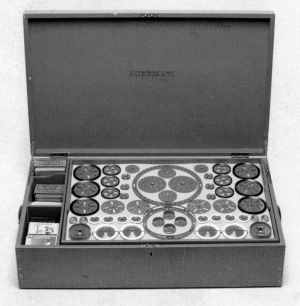

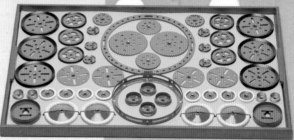

When the war did finally end the world was a changed place. As Meccano historian and author Jim Gamble observes: 'Meccano was of its time. It was conceived and reached its zenith between 1900 and 1945. During that period engineering was angular and mechanical, made from steel, fastened together with nuts and bolts and designed to be taken apart and repaired – and it took time. In contrast, today things are built with compound curves, made from plastics and composites, bonded and designed to be disposed of and replaced – and it has to be fast.'

In a nutshell, before the war everything looked like Meccano – cranes, railway stations, girder bridges and heavy plant machinery – but after the war everything began to look like Lego.

And that was not good news for Meccano.

ABOVE AND BELOW: The No. 10 outfit is, nevertheless, a thing of great beauty and endless intrigue. It is the essence of mechanical engineering in component form, and everything that made Britain great, in a smart lockable box. Costing nearly £20 in 1937, this was a hideously expensive set. Today pristine and complete examples can be worth many thousands of pounds.

Great Exhibitions

Meccano was inspired by the industrial might of Victorian Britain, and by the machines and structures that our greatest engineers laid bare for the delight of the people. Iron paved the way for these Victorian superstructures. The world's first bridge to be made entirely of iron was the aptly named Iron Bridge in Shropshire (detail below right), completed in 1781 long before the Victorian era. Seventy years later Britain hosted the Great Exhibition to showcase the nation's engineering and creative prowess. Housed in the Crystal Palace (opposite), the exhibition attracted over six million visitors from around the globe. The Crystal Palace, made with 4,000 tonnes of iron and 400 tonnes of glass, was erected in London's Hyde Park for the exhibition and subsequently moved to south London, where it burnt down in 1936. Not to be outdone, the French hosted the Universal Exhibition in 1899. The centrepiece was the Eiffel Tower (below), made with 7,300 tonnes of iron. But outdoing them all in splendour and engineering know-how is Liverpool's Bridge of No Return, built in 2009 (detail right).

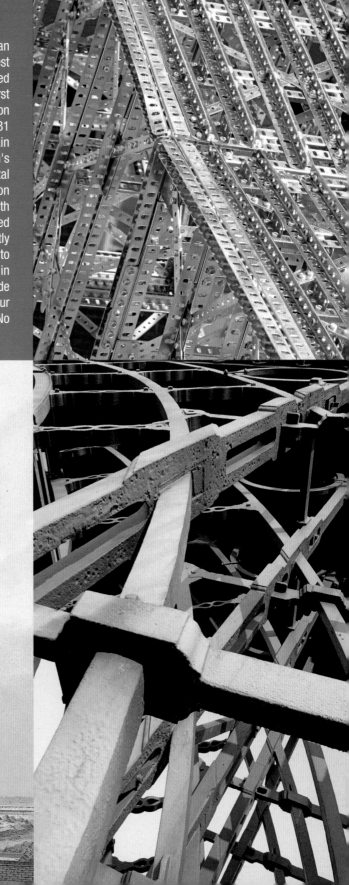

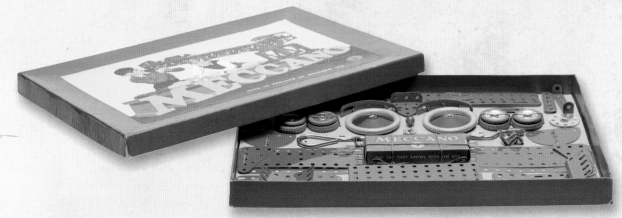

Red and Green Revisited

Although Meccano was not available during the last two years of the war *Meccano Magazine* was published for the duration, and in December 1945, under the headline 'The First Good News', *MM* announced that Meccano would be back in the shops in time for Christmas. The illustrations of the new outfits were of the pre-war blue and gold colour scheme (identifiable in the black and white illustrations by the cross-hatching pattern on the plates) but when the first post-war sets appeared they did so in a new version of an old guise: red and green.

This period is sometimes divided into medium red–green (1945–57) and light red–green (1958–63). Other than these colour changes there was very little development between 1945 and 1963, the only significant innovations being the introduction of 'exploded diagram' instructions and, in 1962, plastic plates that would spring back to their original shape when unbolted from a model, unlike the earlier metal plates. More than 25 new or redesigned parts were introduced in 1962 but these were minor modifications to the system rather than new developments, and in 1963 the trade journal *British Toys* noted that Meccano 'has been made for over thirty-five years without any major change in its design or finish.'

This lack of development, and Meccano's accompanying decline, are often blamed on the complacency of Roland Hornby, who took over as chairman after his father's death in 1936. Under Roland's leadership (or lack of it) Meccano Ltd failed to modernise its products or its manufacturing processes. The former was detrimental to all of Meccano Ltd's brands, and in the case of Meccano itself it was exacerbated by the growing popularity of plastic constructional toys such as Airfix and Lego. The failure to modernise the factory and its working practices was even more crucial, and at Christmas 1962 the *Sunday Telegraph* reported that the products of Binns Road were notable for 'high quality and superb workmanship regardless, it seems of whether [Meccano Ltd] can sell them at a profit.'

Two years later, in 1964, the *Sunday Telegraph* was proved right when Meccano Ltd was bought out by Lines Brothers, the owners of Tri-ang. (Tri-ang was so named because there were three Lines brothers, and three lines make a triangle.) Inevitably, the change of ownership required a change of

ABOVE: A 1958 advert extolling the virtues of Meccano as 'the greatest Christmas gift of all'. Modern advertising standards would no doubt require the addition of the word 'probably'.

VOL. XXXIX No. 12   DECEMBER 1954

MECCANO MAGAZINE

THE JOYS OF CHRISTMAS

1/-

image so Meccano's colour scheme was altered again, this time to silver, yellow and black. Again, this was a merely cosmetic development. The logic behind the choice of yellow and black was that models would look more realistic, and therefore more appealing in those colours given that much of the heavy machinery being used on building sites and in Britain's massive road-building programme was yellow and black.

Blue, Yellow and Zinc

The final colour period of the Binns Road era began in March 1970 when, capitalising on the previous year's moon landing, Meccano underwent a complete modernisation exercise under the slogan 'Meccano for the Space Age'. The colour scheme was rationalised with that of the French factory, which had bypassed the post-war changes and was still making Meccano in blue and gold: the resulting new scheme was blue, yellow and zinc plate. New elements were introduced, including a multi-purpose gear wheel and an electronic control set, new instruction manuals were printed in full colour in five languages, and the packaging was smartened up with the introduction of blue boxes with silver lettering. Trade journal *British Toys* approved wholeheartedly, describing Meccano as 'that great British institution… [which] now looks as if it was born in the 70s.'

These changes also provided an opportunity for some marketing sleight of hand, which still catches out some unwary collectors to this day – outfit No. 9 was discontinued and the remaining outfits 0–8 were renumbered 1–9, giving the impression that prices had been reduced. Collectors beware: a post-1970 No. 9 is essentially a pre-1970 No. 8.

However, even this sleight of hand was not enough to save Meccano from another change of ownership. Lines Brothers went into liquidation in 1971 (albeit not solely due to losses at Binns Road) and Airfix Industries bought the Meccano brand the following year, subsequently introducing various new outfits including the Army Multikit and the Highway and Super Highway Multikits. These outfits proved popular but ultimately Airfix couldn't save Meccano either. After more tinkering with the range of outfits and the colour system in 1978 (dropping zinc and introducing a darker blue and yellow) the gates of Binns Road closed for the last time on 30 November 1979, and the manufacture of Meccano in the UK ceased forever.

Le Méccano

But that didn't mean that Meccano was no longer being made at all. When Airfix bought the British operation in 1972, American toy manufacturer General Mills had bought the French factory, so Meccano was still being manufactured in Calais. After the demise of Airfix in 1981 (closing the Meccano factory had not saved Airfix from liquidation) General Mills bought the toy division, including Meccano UK, from the receivers. Thus General Mills took total control of the entire brand, scrapping all the existing outfits and replacing them with a French-made alternative called Meccano Junior. This, as the name implies, was conceived more as a child's toy than as engineering in miniature for young men.

Meccano then underwent two more changes in ownership, which saw the reintroduction of outfits Nos. 5–10 (which remained in production until 1992), the introduction of the Multi-Models range in 1998, which embraces Frank Hornby's original concept of Meccano as 'Engineering in Miniature',

ABOVE: Meccano embraces the space age, though not very convincingly. Too many exposed bolts and holes.

BELOW: Modern Meccano Eiffel Tower. A bit rubbish. Where's the working lift?

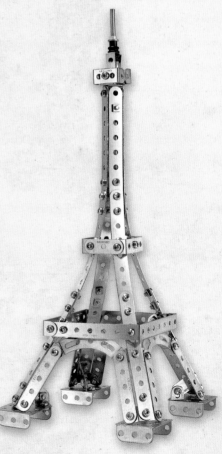

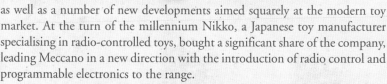

as well as a number of new developments aimed squarely at the modern toy market. At the turn of the millennium Nikko, a Japanese toy manufacturer specialising in radio-controlled toys, bought a significant share of the company, leading Meccano in a new direction with the introduction of radio control and programmable electronics to the range.

In 1977, two years before the closure of Binns Road, author and Meccano collector Peter Randall wrote: 'What appears to be a history of constant change was in fact a long history of very minor changes, and it could be said that Meccano has, in a sense, never changed. Undoubtedly Frank Hornby would instantly recognise his product in the seventies, as most of the original parts are still in the system, unchanged, except for their colour.'

And that was one of the problems – Meccano had not moved with the times. Under French ownership Meccano has been forced to widen its appeal to survive in the modern market. Frank Hornby would no longer instantly recognise every outfit as his product, but modern Meccano does retain some of what Nikko describes as 'the traditional values… that have helped nurture the skills of some of the greatest scientific and engineering minds.' Those values can be found in the Multi-Models range, which Hornby would instantly recognise and whose longevity is testament to the power of classic toys: it has been in production for more than ten years in a market where the typical lifespan of this type of toy is three.

The Multi-Models range shares a brand identity with outfits such as Spykee, a remote-controlled robot that can be made to move, speak, and take still or moving pictures from anywhere in the world via the internet. Spykee's control elements and webcam are housed in a sealed unit which forms part of a reconfigurable robot whose parts are all Meccano compatible. And that means that Spykee can be built into a model using any Meccano part from the last 108 years.

Frank Hornby might not instantly recognise Spykee as Meccano but on closer inspection he would be proud to see that this 21st-century home robotics kit uses imperial measurements for the spacing of the holes and a 19th-century thread on its Whitworth nuts and bolts. And he might well agree that by embracing the technology of its time, and encouraging children to learn through play, Spykee is doing what Mechanics Made Easy did more than a century earlier.

ABOVE: The modern Multi-Models range embraces the tradition of Meccano as modular 'engineering in miniature', but has been scientifically proved to be easier than it used to be, like GCSEs.

BELOW: Meccano for the 21st century: Spykee the reconfigurable robot. If you see one, stamp on it.

MAKING YOUR OWN MECCANO GLASSES

To make your Meccano sunglasses you will need the following pieces. Numbers in brackets refer to Meccano's inclusive parts list.

2 x 11-hole curved strips (89)
2 x 3-hole straight strips (235g)
1 x 4-hole right-angled bracket (12a)
2 x angle brackets (12)
2 x obtuse-angle brackets (12c)
4 x 5-hole curved strips (90)
4 x curved stepped strips (90a)
2 x collars (59)

16 x square nuts (37a)
12 x short-slotted grub screws (69c)
2 x slotted grub screws (69)
1 x coloured plastic sheet

Other sunglasses with fewer sharp edges are available.

1

Loosely assemble four curved strips and one straight strip for each frame and pass the bolts through from the front, but don't attach the nuts yet.

2

Take your coloured plastic sheet. Fold in half and cut roughly to the shape of the frames. Place over your assembled frame, mark the position of the bolts and then make holes with a paper punch or one of those tools for putting extra holes in a belt.

3

Slip the plastic sheet over the bolts and attach the nuts, remembering to include the small angle brackets for the arms.

4

Make up the bridge piece from a four-hole right-angle bracket, two long screws, two collars and two obtuse-angle brackets.

5

Pass the brackets of your bridge piece over the bolts on the inner edge of the frames and add the nuts. Do up tightly.

6

The arms are simply 11-hole curved strips bolted in place. Add extra strips if you have a very big head or if your ears are a long way back. You may have to bend the angle bracket slightly to made the shades sit correctly on your head.

7

That's it – your Meccano sunglasses are complete. The ideal accessory for every discerning young model engineer.

Do not use Meccano sunglasses for driving.

A GAME OF BRIDGE

According to T.S. Eliot April is the cruellest month, so I decided to liven it up by challenging five teams of engineers and architects to a game of bridge. There were no cards involved but the stakes were high: lay your best bridge design on the table for the chance of participating in a world record – the world's largest practical Meccano bridge, sturdy enough to carry me across one of Europe's longest canals. And I didn't mean scaled-up giant Meccano, or concrete painted to look like Meccano; I meant real ½-inch strips of standard Meccano held together with standard Meccano nuts and bolts.

Feeling slightly mischievous, I wrapped up five Meccano kits in brown paper and sent them to the offices of the chosen challengees. Their first test of ingenuity was to find the DVD secreted among the strips, plates, angles, cogs and nuts and bolts. Their next test was to insert the DVD in a player, whereupon I materialised in front of them to issue my historic challenge.

My disembodied self invited proposals for a bridge to span the Leeds–Liverpool Canal at the Mersey Pierhead, right outside Liverpool's most famous landmark, the Liver Building, spanning a distance of 11,047 mm, or 36 feet, 2.88 inches. I stipulated that each submission must be an architectural firework worthy of the location, a structure that reaffirms the excellence of the modular mechanical engineering medium that is Meccano, a bridge that terrifies people with its apparent fragility but amazes them with its enormous strength. It must be modern and progressive and yet celebrate the Victorian origins of this fantastic toy. And most important, it must be a celebration of the greatness of Liverpool itself, which is why it was to be built out of Meccano, a toy that in its day was one of the most famous products to come out of that great city.

In short, I wanted to generate the greatest outburst of collective bridge-building wonderment since Isambard Kingdom Brunel celebrated his success by lighting up a huge stogie in the middle of the Clifton Suspension Bridge – a bridge which, it has to be said, looks as if it was made out of a giant Meccano kit.

One big difference between Brunel's bridge and my own is that mine would be made out of standard Meccano pieces, such as can be found in any Meccano kit. So the question was, would something that was conceived as a children's

BELOW: Our aim was to match the bridge-building wonderment of Isambard Kingdom Brunel's Clifton Suspension Bridge, which itself looked like it had been constructed from a giant Meccano kit.

toy be strong enough to support its own weight and mine across a distance of more than 36 feet? If not, either I was going to get very wet or I was going to find myself on a barge to Leeds. I've never particularly liked swimming – or Leeds – so I was hoping my illustrious bridge designers would come up with something good.

In the meantime, having issued the challenge, I headed north to find out what I could about Liverpool and Meccano. My guide, who met me at Lime Street Station, was an expert in both: Liverpudlian politician, novelist and broadcaster Edwina Currie.

The binning of Binns Road

I had asked Edwina to show me round the city where she grew up because I wanted to put the importance of Meccano in its proper perspective. Sure enough, she confirmed that the Meccano factory at Binns Road had been a major employer, that it had been hugely important for the local economy, and that Frank Hornby had been a generous and paternal boss (he was also, briefly, Unionist MP for Everton). But she also told me something far more interesting – that she had been a Meccano Girl in a world of Meccano Boys.

I was never into dolls. I had dolls when I was about 18 months old and I got bored with them after that. Then someone gave my dad a Meccano set. He was a tailor and someone must have paid for a suit with this set. It was red and green – they started making red and green Meccano again the year before I was born – and I was fascinated by it. My dad and I would sit in the front room and build things, and one of the things that I was most proud of was a working model of the Widnes Transporter Bridge. It was about five feet wide. I had to rig and operate the pulley, and I still remember being really excited that as I turned the pulley it would send the cage all the way across.

ABOVE: Visiting Shropshire's Iron Bridge for inspiration.

BELOW LEFT: Official Meccano instructions for Edwina's beloved Widnes Transporter Bridge, demolished in 1961. Edwina is still with us, thankfully.

(No. 21)   SPECIAL INSTRUCTION LEAFLETS FOR BUILDING MECCANO SUPER MODELS   (Price 2d. Overseas 3d.)

Meccano Transporter Bridge

Suspension type: complete with Automatic Reversing Mechanism for controlling the movement of the Carriage

An L Outfit Model

Fig.1. General View of the Transporter Bridge.

WHEN it is desired to bridge a river the local conditions must of course be taken carefully into consideration before the type of bridge can be decided. Should the river be navigable the bridge must be placed at such a height that it will not interfere with the traffic on the water. But in cases where the river banks are almost on the same level as the river, the construction of a bridge many feet above the water line is not possible, for the cost and inconvenience of building the necessary inclined approaches would be too great. Such difficulties as these have been successfully overcome by the introduction of "transporter"

Published by MECCANO LIMITED, BINNS ROAD, LIVERPOOL 13, ENGLAND   *Printed in England*

I was enjoying Edwina's reminiscence until she mentioned a problem that I knew was probably going to beset my own bridge: 'Our model was quite accurate,' she said, 'but we couldn't get the span in proportion to the height of the towers because we didn't have enough Meccano.'

I knew that whatever design my challengees came up with we wouldn't be able to gather enough Meccano just by buying kits in the shops: I was going to have to make a special order direct to the factory. The problem was that Frank Hornby's Liverpool factory shut down in 1979. At one point during the 1920s and 1930s it was the biggest toy factory in Britain, and in its heyday it employed 2,500 people – 1,500 of them on the factory floor working on no less than 700 machines and machine tools. The employment the Binns Road factory provided, and the income it generated, supported a whole community, so it was no surprise that there was picketing outside the gates when the news broke that it was going to be shut down. But the protests were to no avail, and on 30 November 1979 the gates clanged shut on a legendary era in British toy-making.

When I went to Binns Road I discovered that the factory is now a health club called Total Fitness. But I was really not interested in total fitness, or even in partial fitness. I just wanted to build a Meccano bridge, and I needed to find a factory to make the parts. It made me despair of what's happened to Britain, that something as fantastic as a Meccano factory can give way to a place where people preen themselves in front of mirrors.

So, I went to France instead.

Due to a complicated piece of corporate takeover and trademark licensing, the French subsidiary of Frank Hornby's Meccano Ltd was sold to an American company in 1972. When Binns Road shut down seven years later the American/French offshoot survived, and to this day Meccano is still being made at the French factory. And so I found myself in a largely unknown corner of industrial Calais at the disappointingly small, unassuming, single-storey factory that is the last bastion of metal Meccano – the last outpost of Frank Hornby's once-global empire.

Meccano has been made in Calais continuously since 1959. That may sound like a long time but, to put things in perspective, it will be 2024 before it has been producing Meccano for as long as Binns Road did. And it is a fraction of the size of Binns Road – just 25 people on the factory floor working on a mere seven stamping machines, one powder-coating machine (for painting the parts) and a series of machines for packing the finished kits. There could be no dreams in this factory, which was characterised by the constant thump, thump, thump of heavy machines stamping out Meccano parts, assaulting the eardrums with the noise, pummelling the solar plexus with the vibrations and overwhelming the nose with the sickly sweet smell of lubrication oil. There was something strangely… Victorian about it. In fact, most of the machines were basically the same as the ones Frank Hornby would have commissioned shortly after Victoria died.

But none of that was important. The point was, I managed to persuade them to turn over nearly half of their machinery purely to making strips and angle pieces for my bridge.

So, having secured a supply of raw materials, all I needed was a design. And for that I decided to turn myself into a dragon.

BELOW: There was something strangely Victorian about the Meccano factory in Calais. One machine (top) was stamping out angle girders specifically for the Bridge of No Return while others were continuously sorting and cleaning parts for general sale.

Into the dragons' den

Clearly the only fair way to choose between the designs on offer was to find a warehouse with a spiral staircase, appoint two fellow dragons (Edwina and bridge engineer David Mackenzie) and find ourselves three nice comfortable leather chairs from which to give the challengees a good grilling.

First to descend the spiral staircase were Hayden Nuttall and Adam Miller of global engineering and design consultancy Atkins. They had brought along two designs, Sea Raven and Intensus. The name Sea Raven was inspired by the Liver Birds, which are cormorants (from the Latin *corvus marinus*, or sea raven – clever) and the bridge incorporated a double arch representing both the architectural firework mentioned in the challenge and at the same time the twin Liver Birds. My first question was how on earth were they going to create an arch (which is curved) out of Meccano (which is straight). The answer was that the 'curve' would actually be a series of straight facets, like the side of a 20- or 50-pence piece: the more facets, the smoother the curve. This concept of the facetted curve was something that would eventually make it through to the final design, but in inverted form.

Their second offering, Intensus, was so named because all of the Meccano in it was in tension rather than in compression. This, Hayden told us, is because tension is the most reliable way of carrying force from one side of the canal to the other – which is an engineer's way of saying that Meccano is much stronger when it's being pulled apart ('in tension') than when it's being squashed together ('in compression'). Hayden described it as being a taut structure like the strings of a tennis racket; Edwina remembered it afterwards as being like a giant trampoline.

BELOW: Mackenzie, May and Currie: the bridge judging panel hard at work assessing the pitches.

Next came John Carroll and Josh Woods, two architecture students from the University of Liverpool. Their offering was the Bridge of No Return, which I thought sounded rather doom-laden, given that I was actually hoping to make it home again afterwards. It was an absolutely preposterous idea clearly fuelled by far too much caffeine and alcohol mixed with nowhere near enough engineering know-how. They were students, after all. But there was something about it that I really liked. It was a hybrid of half bascule ('seesaw' or rocker bridge) and half swing bridge, connected by a Heath Robinson arrangement of pulleys and levers, which meant that as the bascule bridge lowered into position the swing bridge swung round to make a complete walkway.

It was a completely crazy idea and I liked the madness of it but I wasn't sure it could ever be made to work. Neither was I entirely convinced that they hadn't arrived at it because they'd simply been unable to decide between a bascule bridge and a swing bridge, and that in desperation they'd linked the two in the hope that no one would notice the discrepancy. But, in that, I was wrong. Together with the third member of their design team, Danny Dobson, they had carefully researched the local area and been inspired by a bascule bridge and a lock gate on the canal, less than half a mile away from the proposed site of my crossing. John Carroll described these moving bridges as 'pivotal structures in the success of Liverpool docks.' It was hard to tell whether or not the pun was intended but the mixed genres were clearly a conscious decision: 'We want to celebrate these historic pieces of Liverpool engineering but at the same time we want to celebrate the essence of Meccano, and that is its playful aspect – the fun, the movement, the flexibility, all these things coming together. So we've taken a lead from historic architectural precedent but it's also about having fun.'

ABOVE: Architecture students Josh Woods (left) and John Carroll delivering their pitch for the winning entry, the Bridge of No Return.

BELOW: The first sketches for the Bridge of No Return were drawn in a kebab shop under the influence of a heavy hangover.

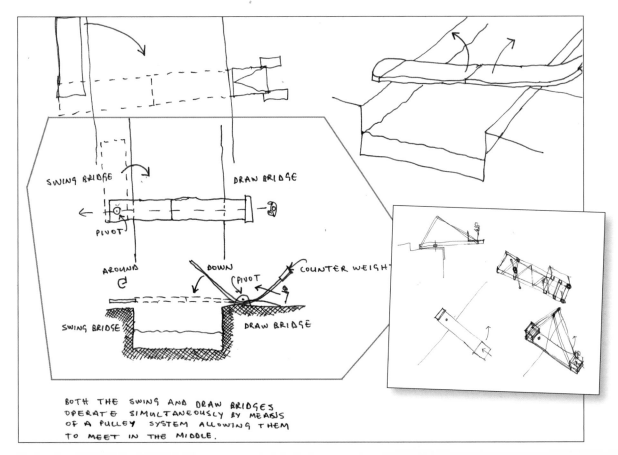

The idea was that as I walked along the bascule section my weight would make that roll into place, which in turn would make the swing bridge close. As I stepped onto the swing section a counterweight would return the bascule to its upright position, at the same time transporting me to the other side of the canal on the swing section. Which begs the question, 'What happens if I want to go back?'

'You can't,' John told me. 'It's the Bridge of No Return. This will happen once only. This is the event – this is celebrating the idea, the toy, the absolute wonder that is Meccano. So it will only happen once and you will have gone on a journey and everyone will live happily ever after.'

I liked it. Particularly when I discovered I was right about the caffeine and alcohol – it had been conceived in a kebab shop, where the three of them had gone to nurse their hangovers after a heavy night's architectural research. Still, mustn't make any decisions until I've seen the remaining three submissions.

Alistair Lenczner of architects Foster + Partners came up with an ingenious Harlequin Lattice Tube Bridge, which was a diamond latticework made of Meccano that would be laid flat on the floor and then rolled into a massive tube – I would then walk through the middle of the tube to cross the canal. As an added bonus it was adorned with an intricate Meccano model of the *Spirit of Liver Love* – a Liver-style bird that would open its plumes when I reached the centre. Ultimately, we decided that rolling up the lattice was going to be too dangerous but we did ask Alistair to produce a *Spirit of Liver Love* to mark the conclusion of the great canal crossing – if I got that far.

Alistair was followed by representatives of the North East Meccano Guild and of the engineering consultancy Arup, who both came up with variations on the box girder bridge. It was very tempting to hand the prize to Arup because theirs was light, efficient and would definitely have worked. But in the end both box girder bridges were a bit too traditional – they certainly weren't architectural fireworks.

So it came down to a choice of two. All three dragons liked the innate and slightly drunken stupidity of the Bridge of No Return but we all doubted that the students had the expertise to make it work. And all three of us thought that Intensus was the best alternative because it was dynamic, clever, good-looking and well thought through structurally.

But we still couldn't quite let go of the Bridge of No Return. After all, Meccano is about mechanisms, and this was a moving bridge. It was also a gag, which is very Liverpool.

So in the end we decided to award the prize to the Bridge of No Return, on condition that the students (John, Josh and Danny) agreed to work with the Atkins engineers (Hayden and Adam) to bring it to fruition. Whether or not that strange brew would work was going to depend on whether there was any common ground between the seasoned professionals, with all their experience, and the slacking, heavy-drinking, hangover-nursing students, with no experience but plenty of optimism.

ABOVE: The original working model of the Bridge of No Return in its three stages of operation. Top: both halves open. Middle: both halves closed to create a complete walkway, with my scale self standing on the swing section. Bottom: me on the swing section being swept over the water towards the bank, on the second half of my journey across the Leeds–Liverpool Canal, a one-way trip at best.

Engineering torment

When I visited the Atkins headquarters a few days later to see if the two teams had managed to find any common ground I realised that there was an interesting circular paradox at work. The students had made a model of a bridge out of Meccano; that's what Meccano was for. And now the engineers were working out how to make that bridge in real life – but out of Meccano. Which meant that we had entered a sort of inner circle of engineering torment from which there might not be any escape.

But in the conference room they were locked together engineering their escape, solving each problem as it arose. Dante would have been proud. There was talk of lever arms, torque, moment, inertia, bending moment, compression, tension, shear, cantilever, mechanical advantage – fantastic words from the lexicon of Meccano model building back in its heyday. And it was a joyful thing to hear everyone taking it so seriously – proper engineers wrestling with genuinely difficult problems.

The three biggest issues to be resolved were the counterweight on the bascule, the pivot point of the bascule, and the Heath Robinson-style mechanism that connected the bascule to the swing bridge.

The problem with the counterweight is that it had to be heavy enough to keep the bascule upright until I was ready to walk across it, and heavy enough to stop it descending too fast as I walked along it. But if it was heavy enough to do that then it was going to make the bridge snap back into the air as soon as I stepped off it, possibly taking my leg with it. The solution was ingenious and particularly apt for a canal bridge – make use of the water. Instead of a fixed

BELOW: The students' model of the Bridge of No Return under professional scrutiny in the Atkins offices from Adam Miller (third right) and Hayden Nuttall (fourth right).

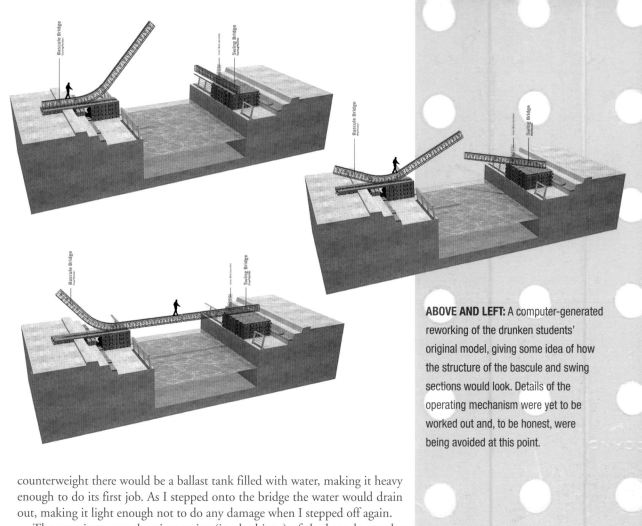

Bascule Bridge
Swing Bridge

Bascule Bridge
Swing Bridge

Bascule Bridge
Swing Bridge

counterweight there would be a ballast tank filled with water, making it heavy enough to do its first job. As I stepped onto the bridge the water would drain out, making it light enough not to do any damage when I stepped off again.

The next issue was the pivot point (ie, the hinge) of the bascule: on the model this was a standard Meccano axle, which is a 4-mm steel rod. But the rules say there must be no giant Meccano, so we couldn't scale up the axle to the required size to support the full-size bridge. This time the answer was a brilliant piece of lateral thinking: don't have an axle at all. Instead, this section of the bridge would become a 'rolling bascule', which means that instead of pivoting on an axle it would take the form of a giant curve, like the rocker on a rocking horse or a rocking chair. And as we'd already seen in the design for the Sea Raven Bridge, a curve can be created in Meccano as a series of facets.

The answer to the Heath Robinson mechanism was equally simple: don't connect the two sides of the bridge mechanically. Apart from the engineering problems in making the mechanism work, we didn't want cables crossing the canal. But I still wanted to make the crossing a self-contained matter, with no need of outside assistance.

This time the solution was electrical rather than mechanical. Instead of the winding mechanism for the swing bridge being controlled by the movement of the bascule bridge as in the model, it was powered by a cordless drill. (I considered that to be an acceptable power source given that modern Meccano kits contain a cordless drill for doing up the nuts and bolts.) That meant that when I reached the middle of the canal and stood at the end of the bascule section I could flick a switch and the swing section would glide out to meet me. Another switch would reverse the drill and the swing section would glide back, taking me with it.

And so, after many hours of intense discussion and calculation, the Bridge of No Return had its engineering pedigree.

Thanks to the combined efforts of the students and the engineers, we now had a witty, celebratory design that was mechanically viable.

But the original question still remained: could it be built out of Meccano – would a children's toy be strong enough to build a bridge that could support its own weight and carry mine across a 36-foot span?

Hayden and Adam went to the Department of Civil Engineering at University College London to find out.

The levitating Porsche

The testing lab all looks very scientific, with the white coats and goggles and minutely calibrated Newton meters, but in fact it's very simple. You put your piece of Meccano in the machine and then pull it until it snaps. Then you put another piece in a different machine and push it until it bends. And that way you find out how strong it is.

Hayden's worry was that all the holes in the strips were going to make the Meccano very weak, but it turned out to be stronger than expected in tension – that is, when it was being stretched. This meant that the weakest link was likely to be the bolts. So he and Adam joined two strips together with a single bolt and started pulling. It snapped when the force reached the equivalent of half a tonne: not enough to build a bridge. Then they tried joining the strips together with two bolts, and that more than doubled the breaking point to the equivalent of 1.1 tonnes, which *is* enough to build a bridge.

But what does a breaking point of 1.1 tonnes really mean?

The next morning I found out what it really means when I looked out of my window and saw my beloved red Porsche hanging in the air from the back of a clamping truck. It was the usual thing – crane on the back of the truck, slings round the wheels of the car – except that the only thing connecting the crane to each sling was four pieces of standard Meccano in two pairs, each pair connected to its partner by two ordinary Meccano bolts.

My car was dangling in the air held up only by a children's toy.

Except that's the thing – Meccano is far more than just a children's toy, and this stunt convinced me that it is strong enough to build a bridge out of. It turned out to be stronger than the engineers expected under tension but very weak under compression, which would not be a problem so long as there was far more tension than compression in the bridge.

The outcome of the testing meant that Hayden and Adam could now engineer a solution and draw up the plans. As soon as those were ready the baton was handed from the University of Liverpool's Department of Architecture, whose students conceived the idea, to the Department of Engineering, whose students and technicians were going to build it.

ABOVE: Adam (left) and Hayden watch a Meccano angle girder being compression tested at University College London. In layman's terms the compression test meant pushing both ends of an angle bracket until it bent, to find out how much pressure it could take.

All they needed now was some Meccano, and that was already on its way over from France. When it arrived it had to be hoisted up to the engineering studio by crane – and a crane is what inspired Meccano in the first place, so there was a very pleasing circularity in seeing it being winched up to the studio. There was also a pleasing circularity in the fact that when it was winched back down again several weeks later it would be a bridge. That was a very uplifting thought.

As I walked away, I couldn't help but remember from my youth that fixing even a few Meccano components together and doing up all those nuts and bolts makes your fingers sore. And we were going to have somewhere in the region of 100,000 parts held together with anything between 30,000 and 50,000 nuts and bolts. So by the time it was finished, after 10,000 person-hours of blood, sweat and swearing, the students and technicians of the Department of Engineering were going to have bleeding stumps for fingers.

BELOW: Meccano actually works best in tension, as it is doing here, with with my beloved old Porsche held up by just four standard strips on each sling. This was Hayden's idea of a good demonstration and a good joke. He still has his head in this picture.

The Bridge of No Return

On the eve of the big day the two halves of the bridge were delivered to the Pierhead and laid out for their final test, to make sure they were still structurally sound after the journey. The bascule was lowered into its cradle and the water tank that would provide the counter-weight was attached. The swing bridge was lowered onto its pivot – amazingly, a standard Meccano 4-mm axle – and the winding mechanism wired up.

Everything worked. Now all we had to do was lift the bridge into position and get a good night's sleep.

First to be lifted was the bascule. The banksman signalled the crane operator and up it came, slowly and majestically rising out of the cradle. And then suddenly there was shouting, people running, and the sickening crunch of 10,000 person-hours of work colliding with the newly installed granite of the Mersey Pierhead.

Attaching the water tank meant that the centre of gravity of the bascule had been raised well above the roll axis – in other words, it was top heavy when it hadn't been before. So when it came out of the cradle it capsized and the heavier end slammed into the ground, buckling the first three feet of the bridge. But at the same time the presence of the water tank acted like a strap, preventing the bridge from twisting all the way down, which would have been a real disaster.

It's an interesting philosophical conundrum – can something be said to have saved a situation when that very thing caused the situation in the first place? The crane operator didn't look as if he was interested in philosophy so I decided not to ask him.

Thankfully, the only damage was superficial, and it didn't affect the soundness of the structure. I reckon you could still have driven a car across it, even after the fall. But I did notice they were a lot more careful about lifting the other bits into place.

BOTH PAGES: The bridge arrives on the canalside in front of the Liver Building. Bottom left shows the ballast tank that caused the bascule section to overbalance.

The next day, as the sun emerged over the Liver Building, the entire site was buzzing with activity – everything was put into place including no less than nine cameras, just to make sure that if I fell in the canal they could film it from every angle. Actually, there was no chance of me falling in the canal because I was in a full body harness attached to the crane that had lifted the bridge into position. And, despite that, I still had to wear a helmet – and a life jacket, even though the canal is only three feet deep. If I did fall in I'd be in more danger of breaking my legs than drowning. Then again, perhaps the life jacket was to cushion the fall.

Ridiculing the safety measures kept me from thinking about my fear of heights, but then it was time to step up onto the bascule. The mounting point was only a couple of feet above the ground, but as I looked across to the Liver Building I saw the ground drop away down to the canalside and then disappear into the chasm of the canal itself. By the time I was over the water my eye level was going to be nearly 20 feet above the canal. And I was going to be walking along a beam that was only just over a foot wide. Thank God we thought of adding a few handholds to the design, however flimsy they may be.

Then I heard Edwina over the PA telling me: 'You don't look up, you don't look down. You just look straight ahead and come to Mummy.'

Come to Mummy. OK. I couldn't let Edwina down. I was going to have to do this. For Edwina, for the students who had conceived and built it, for the engineers who had made it work, for Meccano, for Frank Hornby, for Liverpool. I took a deep breath:

Ladies and gentlemen, behold the Meccano Bridge of No Return. This has taken a lot of time. It has taken a great deal of toil and sweat, an enormous amount or perseverance and self-sacrifice. But most significantly, it has taken a lorra, lorra Meccano.

OPPOSITE: Putting the final touches to the bridge and (centre left) testing the swing section on land to see how rigid it is (not very) before lifting it into place.
BELOW: Addressing the crowd before my crossing. Helmet-cam hangs from my belt.
BOTTOM: Inching forwards along the bascule section as the ballast tank empties. It was quite wobbly.

For too long, for too many generations, this canal has been a hideous rent in the very fabric of Liverpudlian society, separating the people on this side from the people on that side. Today, I hope that that divide will be … er, bridged.

If, God willing, I am successful in my crossing then I shall attain that broad sunlit upland in front of the Liver Building with Edwina. But if I fail then I shall be plunged into a dark abyss, full of quite nasty bacteria. Here goes…

With that, I donned the helmet-cam and gave the signal to release the water from the ballast tank. Slowly, as the water drained out of the tank, the bridge rolled forward onto the first facet of the curve. I took a miniature step forward. One small step for May, one giant leap for Meccano Boys (and Girls).

Minutes passed, then it rocked forward another facet, more minutes, then another. The crowd was getting impatient. 'Think of it as a very slow lesson in physics,' I told them. It didn't help.

The bridge was straining to roll forward but the water in the ballast tank was holding it back. As more and more of the water drained into the canal the bascule rolled forward, facet by facet, until it was horizontal and I was able to walk out over the abyss.

The walkway felt like it was only a couple of inches wide, and narrowing.

And because the swing bridge was still open there was nothing at the end – it was like walking the plank.

But I knew that I had to hold my head up high and walk on.

Finally, after what seemed like an eternity, I was at the end of the bascule section. I flicked the switch on the handhold and the cordless drill on the other side of the canal kicked into life – the swing bridge started to make its graceful arc towards me, stopping exactly in line with the bascule.

It was a triumph! The bridge was complete.

But my journey wasn't over yet.

I stepped off the bascule and onto the swing bridge, releasing the ballast from the front of the bascule as I did so. Behind me the bascule began to rise, making this truly a bridge of no return.

I could no longer go back.

I gripped the handholds on the swing section and flicked the switch to start the drill in reverse. The swing bridge slowly opened again, sweeping me with it across the water. It came to rest parallel with the canal, and all I had to do was walk along it and activate the *Spirit of Liver Love*.

But it was unbelievably wobbly. The day before, when I had tested it on the bank, it had been a couple of inches off the ground and it felt very solid. Now I had a ten-foot drop onto granite on one side and a 20-foot drop into the water on the other. And no handholds, apart from the ones where I stood.

I couldn't move. Everything had gone quiet. Then I realised I just had to do it. I couldn't go back.

Deep breath, sod the wobble, just go. The only thing for it was to walk on, with hope in my heart.

And then, suddenly, I had attained that sunlit upland, and Edwina was unhooking the harness, and the *Spirit of Liver Love* raised its plumage to signal that we'd done it. The engineering students with their bleeding fingers might have spent weeks cursing the architecture students for their kebab shop antics, but we'd done it. We had bridged the Leeds–Liverpool Canal in Meccano. We had produced our architectural firework. We had reaffirmed the excellence of Meccano.

And best of all I discovered that the song is true. Frank Hornby had been with me, the students had been with me, the engineers had been with me, Edwina had been with me – in Liverpool you never walk alone.

OPPOSITE TOP: As I edge forward the bascule drops into position, then I make the leap of faith from the bascule section onto the swing section.

OPPOSITE MIDDLE: Edwina and project manager Sim Oakley look on as I step down from the bridge on to dry land.

OPPOSITE BOTTOM: Signalling the completion of my successful crossing by deploying the wings of the *Spirit of Liver Love*.

BELOW LEFT: As a free man, on the west bank of the Leeds–Liverpool Canal.

BELOW RIGHT: In Liverpool and, owing to the unique way in which the bridge was constructed, with no means of leaving.

SPIRIT OF LIVER LOVE

Alistair Lenczner of Foster + Partners

The idea for a Meccano Liver Bird came about during a train journey from Euston to Liverpool, where I was to present my design proposal for the Meccano bridge. The inspiration for the bird came from a desire to make something that went above and beyond the design brief. Firstly, I wanted to demonstrate the potential of moving mechanisms in Meccano. Secondly, I wanted to create something that could celebrate the successful crossing of the proposed bridge. I knew that the bridge was to be built in front of the Liver Building, so I came up with the idea of a mechanical Liver Bird, with wings that would flap when the bridge crossing was successfully completed.

For my presentation to the *Dragons' Den* style jury in Liverpool, I made a small, fairly crude, Meccano bird with wings that could be moved up and down using a simple push-rod mechanism. Although my proposal for the bridge itself was not selected, the panel liked my bird (christened the *Spirit of Liver Love*) and wanted a fully realised version for the event itself.

I started to explore how a larger three-dimensional bird could be made – something closer to the size of an eagle. I also wanted to include a Meccano wing mechanism, based on the anatomy of a real bird. Luckily, one of Foster + Partners model makers, Rob Sims, had a special interest in animatronics and was keen to help.

I sketched out my vision for the Meccano Liver Bird – proposing that it should be upright on a perch, with a full three-dimensional body, an expressive head, and wings that could fold. It was also to have plumage made of Meccano parts and be adorned with LED lights; one half lit up in red, the other in blue. This additional feature was suggested by one of the judges, Edwina Currie, who was keen for us to include the colours of Liverpool's two main football teams.

On the day of filming, the *Spirit of Liver Love* proved to be very popular with the public – judging from the number of photographs taken of it in front of the Liver Building. When James completed his successful bridge crossing, our bird fulfilled its destiny: the *Spirit of Liver Love* opened its wings as James shouted 'Hello, Liverpool!' Mission accomplished.

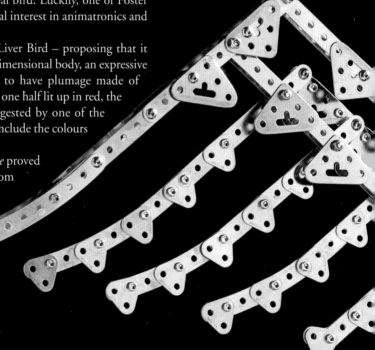

"Hello, Liverpool!"

HORNBY

FULL STEAM AHEAD FOR A GUINNESS WORLD RECORD

WHY HORNBY?

Frank Hornby was a legendary toymaker but you certainly paid for his reputation and expertise. All of his toys were expensive. If you had Hornby-Dublo – like my good friend Oz Clarke – then you were a bit posh, while the rest of us had Tri-ang Railways because they were cheaper. So it's a bit of an irony that the cheap Tri-ang Railways system ended up subsuming the posh Hornby-Dublo system and then taking the Hornby name for itself. And that complicated toy-making takeover means that although I grew up with Tri-ang Railways it was my set – not Oz's – that was the true ancestor of the model railway system now known as Hornby.

I always had a train set as a child and I've never been without one since. At a very early age – probably three or four years old – I was given one for Christmas by my mum and dad. They bought it from my mum's cousin, and it dated right back to the 1950s. It was one of the very first Tri-ang sets, with grey track on a raised embankment, and it had two locomotives: the *Princess Elizabeth*, which was the first ever Tri-ang locomotive, and the Jinty, which over the years proved to be one of the most popular. I also had two coaches, a guard's van, a couple of coal trucks, a flat truck and a signal box. Apart from the track, I still have most of it all these years later and the locomotives still make the occasional appearance when I get my set out at Christmas.

The thing I like about train sets is that they require a great deal of forethought and design. As a toy, train sets are the nearest thing there is to doing the real thing. If you've got anything more than a very basic layout there are endless possibilities for complicated sidings and goods yards and branch lines, and once you've got it set up you have to think ahead in order to get your rolling stock in the right order. I love complex layouts because they can be as sophisticated as a geometric puzzle. You have to work out how to make things get from one place to another, like a Rubik's Cube or one of those children's puzzles where you move the squares around to create a complete picture. Making the layout work, and the locomotives work, and the couplings work is a miniature engineering challenge. But I haven't got any time for scenery.

I use the phrase 'train set' advisedly: I'm not talking about model railways. Train sets are about trains, while model railways concentrate far too much on everything else. I'm interested in the 'working toy' aspect of Hornby rather than accurate modelling, and I get frustrated when people put down two tracks

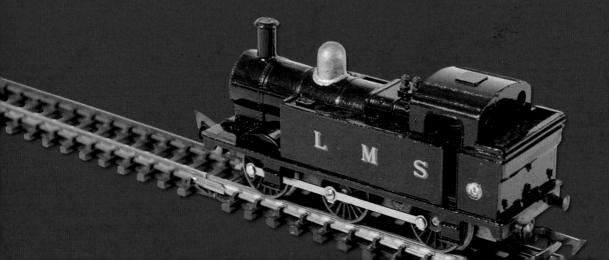

then concentrate on the landscape and the scenery, because that's not railways, that's something else – that's model villages. I'm sure some of them do it because they want to rebuild England the way they wish it was rather than the way it is. Which is an admirable sentiment but it has nothing to do with train sets. Scenery does add something to the train set experience but it shouldn't come at the expense of having fun with trains – train sets, as the name suggests, should first and foremost be about trains.

When I played with my train set as a child – and like most of my toys I never had as much of it as I wanted – I was never bothered about fixing it permanently to a board or making hills and scenery because that to me was a different hobby. I was more interested in making the trains work and making the goods yards as complicated as possible so that I had interesting shunting operations and different ways to send trains. And once I'd got a layout working really well I'd take it to bits and start on a new one, because the fun was getting it all to work and getting the sidings long enough that a line of coal trucks would go into it.

Another of my objections to serious railway modelling is the insistence on only running the 'correct' types of train on a given layout. I'm quite happy to run my *Flying Scotsman* (pictured above) on the same line as my Class 24, even though one is a steam loco and the other is a diesel. The whole point of a train set is that it's a fantasy land and you can do what you like. You can use your imagination; you don't have to be a slave to reality. It doesn't matter if you've got the *Flying Scotsman* running alongside an Intercity 125 and Stephenson's *Rocket* – so what, they're all trains. And anyway, no model railway is ever completely realistic because even with a really extensive, complicated layout the train can never go as far as it goes in real life, even at scale distance, because real railway systems are massive; they cover the entire country. Which is one of the reasons I wanted to build the world's longest train set – because ten actual miles is 760 scale miles, which is almost the length of Britain.

But I suppose everyone's entitled to their opinion.

And whatever your attitude, whether it's train sets or model railways, one thing's for sure; it's not something you grow out of. At Christmas I'll get the train set out of the loft and start fiddling with it and putting it all together and then gradually some of my mates find out and ask if they can come round to play with the train set. Eventually, we end up with half a dozen slightly inebriated blokes, pretending we're not really interested but actually thoroughly engrossed in spending all night driving trains.

"one thing's for sure; it's not something you grow out of"

THE ROVEX/TRI-ANG/ HORNBY CONUNDRUM

Hornby railways have a very complex family tree. The name is descended from Frank Hornby, inventor of Meccano and creator of one of the world's most famous model railway systems, Hornby Gauge 0. Hornby Gauge 0 spawned an equally famous progeny, Hornby-Dublo, but the heritage of the current Hornby system belongs to the distaff side of the family – Rovex-Tri-ang.

What brought these systems together was a marriage of convenience, made on St Valentine's Day 1964 between the well-established Hornby-Dublo and the child bride Rovex-Tri-ang, some 12 years Dublo's junior. When the systems were 'amalgamated' only two Hornby items made it into the new range, and in that sense the development of 'Hornby' railways came to an end then and there.

But just as car marques survive changes of ownership, the Hornby name was kept alive in the form of Tri-ang Hornby, the name given to the new 'amalgamated' system. Six years later the parent company went bust, the Tri-ang name was sold, and the railway system once again became known as Hornby Railways. The circle was complete – but it has resulted in a conundrum that has divided aficionados from laymen ever since.

To the layman, the heritage lies in the marque, and it seems obvious that the present Hornby railways are descended from Frank Hornby's first train set of 1920. But to the aficionado the heritage lies in the continuous development of the range and that, very definitely, is descended from Rovex. If evidence of that were needed, the model railway collectors' bible – *Ramsay's British Model Trains Catalogue* – lists even current Hornby models under the triple-barrelled name of Rovex Tri-ang Hornby.

Most histories – and the Ramsay's catalogue – treat Hornby Gauge 0 and Hornby-Dublo as entirely separate entities from Tri-ang Hornby and beyond. But at risk of infuriating the aficionados, this account will look at the stories behind all three.

BELOW: Contrary to some people's impressions, Frank Hornby did not invent the toy train. This tinprinted German model with soldered details was made by Jean Schoener and dates from circa 1900, some 20 years before Hornby produced his first train set. The needle-sharp snowplough would definitely not pass today's health and safety regulations for a children's toy.

In the beginning: Hornby Gauge 0

The first train set to bear the famous Hornby name appeared in British toy shops in 1920 at a price of 27 shillings and sixpence. Right from the start it had a split personality – the box proudly announced 'The Hornby Clockwork Train' but it appeared in the Meccano catalogue as 'The Hornby Train Set'. It was a gauge 0 set comprising a very basic 0-4-0 locomotive and tender enamelled in one of three plain colours (green, black or red), a single open truck with letters clipped to the side denoting one of three railway companies (GWR, LNWR or MR), and several sections of tinplate track that made up either a circle or an oval. It was a modest start for a name that would soon become world famous but it sold well, largely because it was made by Frank Hornby's already famous firm of Meccano Ltd. Indeed, Hornby later wrote, 'the army of Meccano boys had complete faith in anything turned out by the Meccano factory, and consequently Hornby Trains were purchased without hesitation.'

Frank Hornby described the genesis of this first Hornby Train Set in the June 1932 edition of *Meccano Magazine* (*MM*). He wrote that in 1918 he had been inspired by the shape of a newly introduced Meccano part (No. 108, the Architrave), which gave him the idea of making a Meccano locomotive kit using the new architraves for the cab sides. According to Hornby this kit gave him the idea that Meccano Ltd should begin producing constructional model trains, leading to the

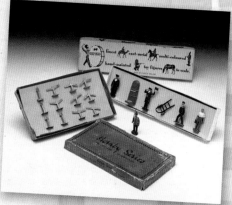

introduction of the Hornby Train Set in 1920. This historic train was held together with standard Meccano nuts and bolts, and although it was supplied ready-made it could be taken to pieces and rebuilt in the same way as Meccano kits, albeit the configuration would always be the same. Frank Hornby cemented the connection with Meccano tradition by telling dealers that 'boys will look upon the Hornby Trains as Meccano models of a new and delightful type.'

ABOVE: Proof, if it were needed, that a train set can be as challenging to operate as a real railway. Here one is being used, in 1953, to teach students the rudiments of signalling and disaster prevention.

Hornby's competitors may not have found them delightful but they were certainly of a new type, the constructional principle being new to model railways. All the model trains of the time were tinprinted – a cheap method of production whereby flat sheets of tin were printed with the relevant physical details and railway liveries, folded into their three-dimensional form and secured to their bases by tabs that were then folded over to hold them in place. In fact, Hornby hedged his bets on the novelty of the constructional principle because at the same time as the Hornby Train Set, Meccano Ltd issued a tinprinted train set copied from the designs of the German toy train manufacturer Bing. However, whilst the Tinprinted Train Set looked much cheaper than the enamelled Hornby Train Set the price difference was only five shillings, which meant that the enamelled set sold much better – so it was clear that the immediate future of Hornby Trains lay in the new, constructional method and not in traditional tinprinting.

Prior to World War I, German manufacturers had dominated the toy train market but now Meccano Ltd was perfectly placed to capitalise on post-war anti-German sentiment and displace the German manufacturers by expanding on its initial success. The March 1921 edition of *MM* promised that 'bigger engines, passenger coaches, new trucks, larger radius lines… will create a sensation in the world of toys next winter,' and the company lived up to its promise in full. By the end of the year the existing enamelled set had bifurcated into the No. 1 Passenger Set and No. 1 Goods Set, while two new sets – the No. 2 Passenger Set and No. 2 Goods Set – were introduced at the top of the range. These four sets incorporated improved locomotives and new rolling stock, such as Pullman cars, dining cars and covered wagons; in addition, 1921 saw the introduction of the first trackside accessory, the Lattice Girder Bridge.

Over the next three years the range continued to expand, and in 1924 Hornby railways came of age. The still-growing range of trains, track and accessories was named 'The Hornby Series', giving the railways an identity of

BELOW: Just a few variations of the popular Petrol Tank Wagon, which first appeared in the Gauge 0 system in 1922.

their own rather than being merely 'Meccano models of a new and delightful type.' The Hornby Gauge 0 system was now a successful brand in its own right.

In its way, 1925 was even more important, being the year of Hornby's first electric train set. The set included the first Hornby locomotive to be modelled on a specific 'real-life' locomotive rather than simply being a generic representation – a coming of age, in fact as well as name. The Hornby Electric Train was modelled on the rolling stock of the Metropolitan Railway, now better known as the Metropolitan Line of the London Underground, which opened in 1863 as the world's first underground passenger railway. It was a clever choice for Hornby's first electric model, because the electric models of Hornby's competitors were almost exclusively of steam trains, while an electric model of an electric train was sure to win plenty of publicity.

Although this first electric train was tinprinted, it did set a precedent for producing accurate models of specific locomotive types, and in 1929 the launch of the 'No. 2 Specials' took the Hornby Series to new levels of realism. For the first time, instead of simply painting the same model in different colours for each railway company, Hornby tooled separate models for each class of railway company locomotive represented: the LMS Compound, the Southern L1, the GWR County Class and the LNER Shire Class. This set the tone for the 1930s, which were the golden years of the Hornby Gauge 0 system and which reached their peak in 1937 – the year after Frank Hornby's death – with the production of the Schools Class locomotive *Eton* and the Princess Royal Class *Princess Elizabeth*.

Eton was designated a No. 4 locomotive, right at the top of the range, and became the most popular of Hornby's 4-4-0 locomotives. But the pinnacle of achievement in the Hornby Gauge 0 system was undoubtedly the *Princess Elizabeth*, a 4-6-2 locomotive that represented a huge technical achievement – for several years the company had maintained that a six-wheel mechanism could not be made, and the engineering achievement in finally doing so was enormous.

ABOVE: The No. 2 Specials took the Hornby Gauge 0 system to new heights. The four No. 2 Specials are: the LMS Compound (top left); LNER Shire Class (lower left); GWR County Class (top right) and Southern Railways L1 (middle right). These were followed by the No. 4 locomotive *Eton* (bottom right), which became the most popular of Hornby's 4-4-0 tender locomotives.

BELOW: Without doubt the *Princess Elizabeth* marked the pinnacle of the Gauge 0 system.

Princess Elizabeth should have marked the start of a new era but in fact it was almost the end of the line for the development of Gauge 0, which struggled on until the early 1960s with no further significant innovations. This was because, from 1938 onwards, Meccano Ltd began to concentrate its resources on another, smaller range of model railways. Sales of Gauge 0 were being encroached upon by rival model railways half the size, so Meccano produced its own Hornby miniature railway system: Hornby-Dublo.

'I double my pleasure with Dublo treasures'

Houses didn't start shrinking in the 1920s but mass production meant that prices were falling and model railways were coming within the financial reach of people who lived in smaller homes than the affluent buyers of the early Gauge 0 sets. As a result various manufacturers, notably Trix, began developing smaller model railway systems which, being half the size of Gauge 0, were known appropriately enough as Half-0, or H0 scale. The competition was serious enough for Meccano Ltd to develop its own miniature system but rather than copying the gauge and scale of Trix, Meccano adopted the prevailing practice of British railway modellers and produced slightly larger-scale models at the same gauge. This was known as Double 0 or 00 gauge, and Meccano's system was launched in 1938 as Hornby-Dublo – pronounced 'dubbelow', not 'dew-blow', being a phonetic description of the scale, Double 0.

Dublo was launched just two years after Frank Hornby's death, leading to suggestions that he didn't approve of this new departure and that his death left the way open for his son Roland, now Chairman of Meccano Ltd, to initiate Dublo at the expense of Gauge 0. However, it seems more likely that the company was responding to changes in the marketplace and that Dublo would have been launched with Frank Hornby's blessing had he still been alive.

Hornby Snr would certainly have approved of the way in which Meccano Ltd improved upon the existing systems rather than merely copying them. With superior diecast locomotives, reliable power supplies and high-quality track Hornby-Dublo soon built up a reputation as a smooth-running model railway system that cost much less than its competitors. Not only that but the speed at which Dublo hit the market was remarkable. Trix already had a full system available so Dublo could not be introduced piecemeal. It had to be launched as a full system, and the inaugural catalogue contained a choice of five locomotives, 12 goods wagons and two carriages. It also included purpose-built brass track, transformers, controllers and accessories – including tunnels, stations, signals, staff and passengers – a remarkable achievement, given that Dublo was decided on in 1937 and available in the shops by the end of 1938.

World War II caused a long hiatus in the development of Dublo, epitomised by the fact that the famous model of the Princess Coronation Class locomotive

TOP: The perennially popular Engine Shed and Signal Gantry, both of which remained in production from the late 1920s until World War II. The Engine Shed was fitted for electric track and had electric lighting.

ABOVE: From Gauge 0 to Dublo: this Hornby-Dublo train set featured the famous A4 Pacific *Sir Nigel Gresley*, which was named after its designer.

Wheel Notation

The three figures used to describe steam locomotives denote the arrangement of the wheels. This system of wheel notation is known as the Whyte system, after the New York Central Railroad engineer F.M. Whyte, who proposed it in 1900. Under his system the leading wheels, coupled driving wheels and trailing wheels are numbered separately. The first Hornby locomotive had no leading wheels, four coupled driving wheels and no trailing wheels (0-4-0); the famous *Princess Elizabeth* had four leading wheels, six couple driving wheels and two trailing wheels (4-6-2).

0-4-0	4-6-0
0-6-0	4-6-4
4-2-2	2-6-2
4-4-0	4-6-2

Duchess of Atholl, which was announced in the 1939 catalogue, did not make it into the shops until 1947. However, once production was back up to speed improvements and developments came thick and fast, including electrically operated points, an automatic coupling system and improved interference suppression to prevent train motors interfering with televisions, which were becoming increasingly common. Developments such as these kept Dublo at the forefront of the market for the next decade, and in 1957 Dublo reached the pinnacle of its achievement with its Castle Class locomotive *Bristol Castle*. This superb model was described by specialist Dublo historian Michael Foster 23 years later as being 'by general agreement the finest mass-produced commercial 00 gauge model locomotive ever produced to this day.'

Bristol Castle was a seminal model in that it blurred the distinction between toy trains and model railways. Until then there had been a significant difference between the two. 'Ready to run' railways were seen as children's toys, while scale model railways were built from scratch by enthusiasts – but now Hornby had released a mass-produced model that was as detailed as anything most enthusiasts could achieve. The introduction of Castle Class marked the beginning of Dublo's golden years in terms of quality, accuracy, detail and performance, but 1957 also marked the point at which competition from Tri-ang Railways began to force a series of changes on Hornby-Dublo, and eventually its demise.

The first forced change was the controversial move from diecast metal to plastic in order to match the level of detail achieved by Tri-ang Railways. This began in 1958 with the release of Hornby's first-ever piece of plastic rolling stock, a 20-tonne bulk grain wagon. Many traditionalists objected to the change but they could not deny that injection moulding allowed for far greater detail than tinprinting

BELOW: Just as Meccano was designed to 'turn boys into engineers', the Hornby Gauge 0 railway system could make a proper signalman of you, and no mistake.

or diecasting. The bulk grain wagon was the first of a series of wagons and coaches to be marketed as Super-Detailed rolling stock – suddenly, details such as doorhandles, hatches, ladders and the gaps between planks were possible in three-dimensions instead of simply being printed on. The Dublo Super-Detailed series had model railway magazines falling over each other to give the highest praise. *Model Railway Constructor* described the bulk grain wagon as being 'as revolutionary and as excellent in its way as the Castle… the detail is exquisite and the neatness of the lettering will be the despair of all modellers who have had to do their own by hand,' while *Railway Modeller* was almost completely lost for words: 'We feel there is little we can add to previous remarks about this series of vehicles – we have virtually exhausted our stock of superlatives.'

Another forced change was the modernisation of track, from the original Dublo three-rail system to more realistic two-rail track in 1959, to compete with Tri-ang Railways, who (as Rovex) had launched a two-rail system in 1950 with enormous success. Typically, the Hornby track improved on its rivals and was roundly praised in the model railway press, but it was blamed by some for the demise of Hornby-Dublo and of Meccano Ltd, which ran into financial problems soon afterwards. Traditionalists claimed that two-rail was the downfall of Dublo because it did not work as well as three-rail; modernisers claimed that it would have saved Dublo but that it came too late, and pragmatists held that the problem was trying to run the two systems side by side in order not to lose existing three-rail customers. Business analysts point to another reason

ABOVE: A rich selection of Dublo treasures: the famous *Duchess of Atholl* train set, which was advertised in 1939 but not available until after the war (top); brick wagon and SR brake van (upper left); the celebrated *Bristol Castle* pulling a composite restaurant car and corridor coach (2nd from top); GWR tank loco pulling various goods wagons (3rd from top); a selection of petrol tank wagons; and the Class 4MT standard tank loco pulling two BR Mk 1 suburban coaches.

BELOW: Hornby-Dublo's super-detailed coaches were among the best in the business, and some enthusiasts are still using them on layouts today. But Tri-ang's cheaper plastic alternatives would help them win the bitter battle for OO gauge domestic railway supremacy.

altogether: Meccano Ltd had failed to modernise its factory or its working practices and many products were being manufactured at a loss.

The result was a bout of panic marketing in 1963, which included prizes of trains or cash to new buyers who could give the judges the best three reasons for buying their set. The winner was 13-year-old Andrew Farthing, whose reasons were: '1. The best buys are Horn-buys. 2. I double my pleasure with Dublo treasures. 3. Their "realistic railway replicas" are the three R's for boys.'

Unfortunately by the time Andrew was announced as winner the best buys were no longer Horn-buys because by then the company had been bought by Lines Bros, the owners of Tri-ang Railways.

A Margate marriage: Tri-ang Hornby

On 14 February 1964 Lines Bros Ltd completed the purchase of Meccano Ltd, putting Lines Bros in control of two of the 'big three' brands of 00 gauge model railways: Hornby-Dublo, manufactured by Meccano Ltd, and Tri-ang Railways, manufactured by Rovex Plastics Ltd. (Two years later Lines Bros turned down the opportunity to buy Trix, the third of the big three.) It was clear that Lines Bros would not be able to sustain two competing brands in parallel but there was a public outcry at the suggestion that they might bring production of Dublo to an end. In fact, Meccano had already done just that: large stocks of unsold Hornby-Dublo had built up at the Liverpool factory and production of new items had already ceased before the takeover.

Lines Bros had a problem: they could not afford to restart production of Hornby-Dublo but neither could they afford to alienate a large swathe of the model railway market by axing such a long-established and highly treasured brand. The answer was to announce that the two brands would be

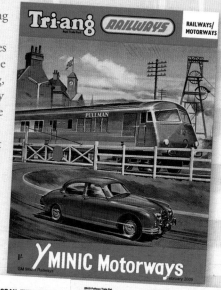

TOP: Tri-ang briefly offered a compatible electric motorway, with excellent vehicle models, as part of its railway system.

ABOVE: Tri-ang, predominantly a toy-maker and committed to modern plastics, was able to offer amazing and relatively inexpensive accessories, such as the coveted Grand Victorian Suspension Bridge. It was also a great innovator. Note that the locomotives feature 'Magnadhesion' for better traction. Cor!

LEFT: The design office at Rovex's Margate factory, sometime during the 1950s.

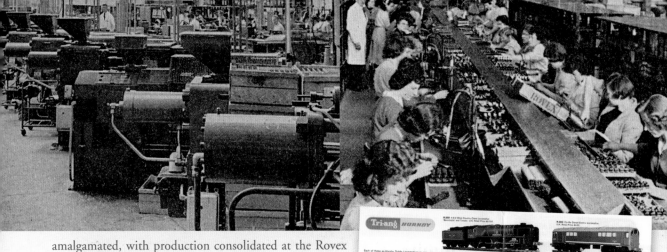

amalgamated, with production consolidated at the Rovex factory in Margate. And so in May 1965, after 15 months of speculation in the model railway press, Lines Bros published a leaflet entitled *An Amalgamation of Tri-ang Railways and Hornby-Dublo*. The title of the leaflet gave the impression that a genuine amalgamation might be on the cards, and its first paragraph stated: 'The two railways will, therefore, be progressively brought together under the name Tri-ang Hornby.'

But, in fact, this was merely an exercise in brand management. The second paragraph of the leaflet revealed the true situation: 'Existing owners of Hornby-Dublo will continue to be able to purchase Hornby-Dublo components while stocks last…' In other words, production of Hornby-Dublo would not be restarted. This was not to be an amalgamation, but a phasing out of Hornby-Dublo.

The amalgamation leaflet listed seven former Hornby-Dublo locomotives as part of the new Tri-ang Hornby range, as well as several former Hornby-Dublo accessories including the Terminus and Through Station Composite Kit. Five of the listed locomotives were offered complete with a Tri-ang Hornby Converter Wagon, which had a Hornby-Dublo coupling at one end and Tri-ang coupling at the other so that Dublo locomotives could haul Tri-ang goods wagons and vice-versa. For passenger trains this was later followed by a converter horse box – a wagon which could logically be pulled as part of a passenger train, thus neatly avoiding the need for converter versions of each type of passenger coach.

But anyone who hoped that the presence of converter wagons meant that Dublo production might continue was disappointed. The locomotives available with the converter wagon remained in the catalogue only until stocks ran out, and the only Hornby-Dublo items that were included in the final 'integrated' range were the terminus/through station kit and the Class 81 Pantograph Locomotive – 'Tri-ang Hornby' was an amalgamation in name only.

Adopting the Hornby name enabled Lines Bros to move forward without alienating most of its new customers, at the same time as linking the kudos of the 45-year Hornby heritage with the relatively young Tri-ang name. But while the Hornby name provided the gravitas, Rovex provided the factory, the expertise, the tooling and the marketing behind Tri-ang Hornby. This meant that the so-called Tri-ang Hornby range was in reality a continuation of Tri-ang Railways and no other. Therefore, the true ancestry of the railway system,

TOP: Inside the Margate factory: injection-moulding machines on the factory floor (left) and the assembly line (right).

ABOVE AND BELOW: The 'Tri-ang-Hornby' amalgamation pamphlet, showing the converter wagon for connecting Tri-ang locos to Hornby-Dublo goods wagons and vice-versa.

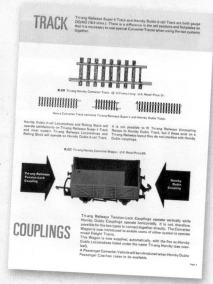

which from now on would carry the Hornby name, dates from 1946, when Alexander Venetzian founded Rovex Plastics Ltd.

Venetzian's Rovex made plastic toys exclusively for Marks & Spencer, and in 1950 he was asked to produce a 00 gauge electric train set based on the Princess Royal Class locomotive *Princess Elizabeth*. This was the same locomotive that had marked the zenith of Hornby Gauge 0 thirteen years earlier, except that the Rovex version was of the *Princess Elizabeth* in black British Rail livery rather than maroon LMS livery. The Rovex version was so popular that Venetzian immediately realised it had the potential to form the basis of a complete system. He didn't have the capital to develop it further but Lines Bros did, and they were desperate to break into the booming post-war market for 00 gauge model railways. So Lines Bros (trading as Tri-ang) bought Rovex Plastics Ltd in 1951, renamed it Rovex Scale Models Ltd, and financed the development of a complete railway system, which was launched in May 1952 as Tri-ang Railways.

The new system included accessories, rolling stock and three locomotives: the *Princess Elizabeth*, a diecast N2 tank locomotive and a Class 3F Jinty tank locomotive, which proved to be one of Tri-ang's (and, later, Tri-ang Hornby's) most popular models. When the original mould tool was retired in 1975 it had produced more than 800,000 body casings, and demand was such that a completely retooled version of the Jinty was launched in 1978.

The new Tri-ang Railways system was an immediate success, and to ensure further expansion Lines Bros built a brand-new factory in Margate, which is still the headquarters of Hornby today. Rovex moved into the new factory in 1954 and two years later – just four years after the launch of Tri-ang Railways – there was a choice of ten locomotives, as well as a commensurate range of rolling stock and accessories. It was a phenomenally fast rate of expansion, and by the end of the decade sales were seriously impinging on Hornby-Dublo. This, combined with the fact that Meccano Ltd's other products were also facing stiff competition (Dinky Toys from Corgi and Meccano from Lego) played a large part in the demise of Meccano Ltd, leading to the buyout by Lines Bros.

A measure of Tri-ang's speed of development is that at the time of the takeover there were 24 locomotive types in the Tri-ang Railways range, compared with 15 in the Hornby-Dublo catalogue. However, only one of the Hornby-Dublo locomotives survived the 'amalgamation', and all subsequent introductions to the Tri-ang Hornby range (with two minor exceptions) were developments of the existing Tri-ang Railways system, rather than of the Hornby-Dublo system.

The 1966 catalogue was the first to carry the name Tri-ang Hornby, and it contained four candidates for the title 'first Tri-ang Hornby locomotive'. One was the Co-Co English Electric Type 3, the first new locomotive to be released after the announcement of the amalgamation. However, this had been designed and tooled by Rovex before the amalgamation and was therefore a thoroughbred Tri-ang Railways locomotive in all but its catalogue date. Released shortly afterwards was the Class 81 electric pantograph locomotive, which is the only Tri-ang Hornby locomotive that incorporated design elements from both systems and is therefore a stronger candidate. The outsiders are the

ABOVE: Lines Brothers, the owners of Tri-ang, had to tread carefully around the sensitivities of Britain's railway modellers following their buy-out of Meccano and the Hornby-Dublo name. This historic 'amalgamation' pamphlet reassured everyone that the new 'Tri-ang-Hornby' range would feature the best of both systems. In reality, little of the Hornby range was used, and what we today call Hornby train sets are really the direct descendants of the old Tri-ang Railways. This is not an opinion that should be expressed in front of die-hard Dublo fans, as they can still become quite heated about it all. It's only a train set.

Hall Class steam locomotive *Albert Hall*, which was announced and developed *almost* entirely after the amalgamation, and the Hymek diesel locomotive which was announced and developed *absolutely* entirely after the amalgamation but, despite appearing in the 1966 catalogue, did not actually make it into the shops until 1967. And the winner of the title 'First Tri-ang Hornby Locomotive' is… a matter of opinion.

The interregnum

In 1971, just five years after the launch of the first Tri-ang Hornby catalogue, Lines Bros went bust. But Tri-ang Hornby remained profitable, despite a general slump in the model railways market – the problem lay largely with Lines Bros' overseas subsidiaries. Therefore, rather than let Tri-ang Hornby be dragged down by the business empire that was collapsing around it, the receiver set up a new company, Pocketmoney Toys Ltd, to keep Rovex trading until a buyer could be found. Richard Lines refers to the period of waiting as the interregnum, and it saw the launch of one of the most exciting Tri-ang Hornby locomotives of all: the revolutionary 2-10-0 Class 9F *Evening Star*.

ABOVE: This Inter-City Express set from the late 1960s actually belongs to me. I'd love to be able to claim that I've had it since I was a boy, but in truth I bought it a few years ago in an internet auction, because I'd always wanted one. Now I have one. This is what's great about being an adult.

BELOW: The real *Evening Star* marked the end of an era for British Rail and the 1971 model marked the end of an era for Tri-ang Hornby, which re-emerged soon afterwards as Hornby Railways. Pictured here is the current version of the 9F, as modified in 1999.

It was ironic (or perhaps appropriate) that *Evening Star* should mark the end of the Lines Bros empire, because it marked the end of an era in its real as well as its model life, being the last steam locomotive to be made for British Rail. For Tri-ang Hornby, as in real life, *Evening Star* was an ambitious project in that the 2-10-0 wheel arrangement made it a technically difficult model to produce. However, Rovex rose to the challenge and the resulting model set a new benchmark for Tri-ang Hornby in the way that the *Princess Elizabeth* had done for Hornby Gauge 0, and the *Bristol Castle* had done for Hornby-Dublo. But unlike its Gauge 0 and Dublo predecessors, this new benchmark presaged not a gradual decline but a revival in fortunes, and posterity would see *Evening Star* as one more ascending step rather than a pinnacle that was never bettered.

Model Railway Constructor described *Evening Star* as 'one of the finest proprietary models manufactured in the British Isles,' which was high praise for the product of a company that was by then in receivership. Not surprisingly, given the reputation of Tri-ang Hornby, a buyer was soon found, and in 1972 Dunbee-Combex-Marx bought Rovex for more than £2 million. The Lines Bros trademarks were sold separately, which meant that the name Tri-ang could no longer be used for the model railway system and so, less than ten years after Tri-ang Railways had subsumed Hornby-Dublo, the resulting system became known as Hornby Railways.

Independence: Hornby Railways

During the 1970s, the newly renamed Hornby Railways thrived under Dunbee-Combex-Marx (DCM), despite challenges from newcomers Airfix, Mainline and Lima in the second half of the decade. The Margate factory was extended and a steady stream of excellent new locomotives and rolling stock were introduced, including the renowned regional and British Rail Mk 3 passenger coaches, the A4, Footballer, Patriot, King and Duchess class locomotives and the hugely popular Class 43 HST (high speed train), aka the Inter-City 125. Meanwhile, behind the scenes, Rovex Models & Hobbies Ltd was renamed Hornby Hobbies Ltd in 1976, further confusing the heritage of the system for laymen.

One of the most notable innovations of the DCM era was a revolutionary new digital control system known as Zero 1. Instead of controlling the locomotives by varying the current passing through the track, Zero 1 locomotives were controlled by a microchip within the locomotive, which meant that in theory up to 16 locomotives could be independently controlled in a single-track section. However, the system as first released was so complicated that scores of Zero 1 control units were returned to the factory, where they proved not to be faulty; the problem was that users simply couldn't understand how to use them. Zero 1 was subsequently refined, and when the idea of electronic control was revisited in 2005 Hornby was careful to make its

**Hornby Train Sets..
..probably the finest start you can give..**
Each set is ready-to-run, excellent value and will give hours of pleasure to young and old

All Hornby sets can be operated straight from the box. No batteries are needed – all sets have mains controllers included. Simply assemble the track, place the rolling stock on it, connect up your plug, switch on, and you're off. Whether it's the exciting APT, the colourful Caledonian or the powerful Western there's hours of fun in every set. And don't forget the clockwork for the younger members of the family.

ABOVE: A 1980s advert for Hornby Train Sets – 'probably the finest start you can give'. No doubt hidden in the side of Dad's armchair is a can of what is 'probably the best lager in the world'.

Digital Command Control (DCC) system as simple as possible. The catalogue entry stresses that 'The days of needing a computer degree to operate a digital model railway have gone,' and ends with a neat summation of the system: 'It's so straightforward… Minimum wiring, maximum effect.'

Despite the continuing success of Hornby Railways, DCM went into receivership in 1980, leaving Hornby Railways once again bereft of a parent company. The management of Hornby Hobbies Ltd managed to secure venture capital for a management buyout, and Hornby Hobbies became an independent company manufacturing a number of brands including Hornby Railways and Scalextric. The new company celebrated its independence by declaring 1981 'The Year of the Locomotive' and introducing seven completely new locomotives to the range, as well as nine new variations of existing models. The seven new locomotives included four that echoed the choice of Meccano Ltd more than 50 years earlier in its Gauge 0 No. 2 Specials: the 00 scale LMS Compound, LNER Shire/Hunt Class and GWR Churchward County Class; the difference from the No. 2 Specials was that the Southern Railway was represented not by the L1 but by the Schools Class, which had been introduced to Gauge 0 in 1937 as a No. 4 locomotive.

In December 1986 Hornby's parent company was floated as Hornby Group plc, which meant that the Hornby name occupied all three tiers of the company hierarchy: Hornby Railways was a brand manufactured by Hornby Hobbies Ltd, which was now owned by the new Hornby Group plc. The influx of

ABOVE: Digital control, old and new. The Zero 1 system (left) was ahead of its time in the 1970s and too complex to be successful but Hornby confidently maintains that the much simpler 21st-century Digital Command and Control system (right) is the future of model railways. I think it might be cheating.

BELOW: The Harry Potter phenomenon hits Hornby – the first batch of Hogwarts Express Train Sets sold out so quickly that extra orders had to be shipped in urgently from the factory in China.

capital resulting from the flotation enabled Hornby Hobbies Ltd to invest heavily in Scalextric and Hornby Railways, and the rate of introduction of new locomotives and rolling stock again increased.

However, competition from Dapol, Lima and (from 1990) Bachmann led to a demand for ever more detail, which was proving prohibitively expensive to produce in Britain. As a result, Hornby made a decision as controversial as the change from diecast to plastic had been in 1958: it decided to outsource manufacture to China. The first totally newly tooled Hornby locomotive to be made in China was the Class 92 electric locomotive, which was released in 1995 as the first in a new series of super-detailed models packaged as Top Link. The level of detail produced in China was far beyond anything possible for the same price in Britain, and the effect on sales was almost immediate, as confirmed by the model railways expert at Hamleys toyshop in London: 'Since they've moved production to China, Hornby have improved their quality greatly, and the collector is now coming into Hamleys for Hornby trains. Collectors who would have bought Bachmann before are now going back to Hornby.'

By the end of the millennium all of Hornby's products were made in China. The last British-made locomotives rolled off the Margate production line in 1999 – the *Morning Star* Britannia Class and a 0-4-0 locomotive to be included in a train set – since when the former factory floor has acted as a distribution centre for the finished models arriving from China. And as Hornby entered the 21st century those models were widely praised. The internet magazine *Model Railway Express* said of the new Princess Coronation Class that 'anyone seeing this model will agree that Hornby are now, well and truly, on the right track,' and of the Rebuilt Merchant Navy Class that it was 'possibly the most detailed proprietary 00 gauge railway model produced for the British market... [it] shows clearly that Hornby intend to take their place again amongst the world beaters in the model railway market.'

It is a position that Hornby intends to maintain, both through the quality and detail of its models and through technical developments such as Digital Command and Control, which Hornby confidently maintains is 'the future of model railway control.' Some traditionalists may see digital control as a gimmick but Hornby sees it becoming standard across the industry as inevitably as – and probably quicker than – electric locomotives replaced clockwork. The aim of most model rail enthusiasts is realism, and digital control brings realism in spades, not only allowing more than one locomotive to run on the same track at the same time, and carriages to remain lit when stationary, but also providing the sounds of the railway, be they steam or diesel engines, guards' whistles or the evocative sound of carriage doors slamming.

Neither Frank Hornby nor Alexander Venetzian could have imagined anything like it, but there is no doubt that both would approve.

TOP: In 2003 Hornby introduced its Live Steam version of the A4 Pacific Mallard, which still holds the world speed record for a steam locomotive. The cutaway illustration in the catalogue shows the electric immersion heater in the tender and the articulated steam pipe, which ducts the steam to the superheater in the locomotive itself. The superheater provides the steam pressure for the double-acting cylinder and piston (above the front bogie) which drives the wheels. Speed and direction are controlled by a separate Speed Regulator.

ABOVE: A present-day Hornby scene. The 'toy trains' have become incredibly realistic.

'10 Tips for more Hornby fun'

By Chris Ellis, editor of *Model Trains International*

1 Collecting or operating? For anyone who does not know it already, some 85 per cent of the world's model railway sales are for British 00 gauge or its international equivalent (H0 gauge) and both run on the same 16.5 mm wide track gauge. This is considered the optimum model railway size, big enough to incorporate every visible detail and compact enough to make up layouts in modest spaces. In engineering and design terms, too, it is better developed than smaller or larger scales with an enormous choice of models available. In addition, virtually all modern 00 or H0 locomotives are very reliable runners. Hornby has the biggest range of British models, but in recent years the Hornby International company has been formed, taking in such European ranges as Jouef (French), Electrotren (Spanish), Lima and Rivarossi (Italian, German and others) all offering large ranges of H0 models. As well as the railway models themselves there is a vast choice of accessories and scenic materials from Hornby, but lots of other companies also offer H0/00 items and accessories, too.

Hundreds of superb models are shown in the catalogues and new ones are released frequently. Very few people would have the space or the money to buy every model produced, but fortunately all of us have our own interests and favourites. Some enthusiasts build layouts big or small, some merely buy the models and never run them, building up collections of the models they like, and others – me included – do a bit of both. They have 'working' locomotives that run on nicely made layouts, and some classic models that rarely come out of the box. There are no rules or regulations in the model railway hobby, so you can more or less go your own way. My main interest is in operating like the real thing, in a modest way, but I've no argument for anyone who just likes owning railway models and does not have any desire other than showing them in a glass cabinet or keeping them in the cupboard. We are all model railway enthusiasts.

2 Layouts and baseboards. The key to good operation is a good firm baseboard. This needs to be properly braced and supported, and how to do it is shown in virtually all the available books on the model railway hobby. If you are a newcomer, one or more of these 'how to do it' books should be an early purchase. Don't be tempted to pin track down on a plain sheet of hardboard or plywood, as some novices do; it will warp and sag immediately with sad results. As all the books will tell you it is best to build large layouts with baseboard sections in modular form. This will make later changes or re-arrangements easier, and very large single-unit baseboards are awkward to handle and heavy to move.

3 Ways of ballasting. Hornby 00/H0 track is robust and realistic, with nicely sprung points, which are very reliable from the electrical point of view. One problem facing the newcomer to layout building is how to add the ballast effect to the track. Experienced modellers prefer to use real crushed ballast, or a granulated cork equivalent, laid around the track and sleepers, then glued in place. This looks superb, but can be messy and time-consuming to do, and particular care is needed around points to avoid gumming them up solid! Hornby help out by offering a foam ballast strip that has recesses for the sleepers. Other firms offer similar ballast strip and also some shaped ballast bases for the points. Carefully laid and pinned down, this looks quite realistic, particularly if you weather the track and 'dirty' the ballast a little with acrylic paint.

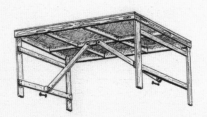

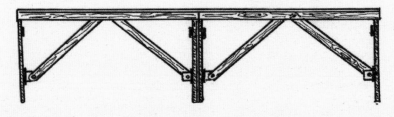

The method I use for giving a ballasting effect to the track is what I call 'Bogus Ballast'. This is nice and simple. Use either Hornby R8066 grey tarmac or R8067 grey granite scenic sheets, cut into ballast width strips, or shapes to match points, and just pin it down under the track as you go along. It gives a ballast effect from the texture of the sheet, but allows you to lift the track or points unblemished if you make track changes later, or need to replace a defective point, etc. Add a few weeds in or along the track from flock powder, and the illusion is given that it is actual ballast. Very few visitors at shows spot that there is no actual ballast. Weathering the track was mentioned above. If you are a beginner this means painting the rail a dirt (e.g. flat earth) colour to look like long-laid track so that the shiny metal of new track is obliterated. The sleepers can also be brushed over to give a dirty stained-wood effect. Be careful not to put paint on the contact areas, and, when the paint is dry, clean any paint from the top surfaces of the rails using a track cleaning rubber.

4 Choice of subject and research. Most of those who take up the model railway hobby are railway enthusiasts already from seeing the real thing or visiting preserved lines or railway museums. We all have our loyalties, often based on nostalgia about the trains we knew as youngsters. With me it is the SR and GWR and the steam and diesel era of British Railways, so the Hornby models I have are Terriers (four of them, in LBSCR, SR, BR, and GWR versions), M7s, and BR Class 20s and 08/09 diesel shunters. I keep to tank engines and short diesels because I only have small layouts, but obviously you can follow your own favourites and there are plenty of railway books, of course, to give you any background information you don't already have about the companies and locomotives of your choice.

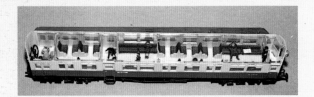

earth, rust, black, grey, etc., lightly applied. Bear in mind that most modern locomotives and stock stay reasonably clean, however, except perhaps for the running gear due to the frequent use of washing plants. If you don't have confidence in your skill at weathering – it needs to be well done – remember that these days Hornby offer a pre-weathered version of most of their locomotives and some of their rolling stock models, and these are certainly my choice when new models appear.

A few extra details can also be added to most locomotives, such as more coal in the tender or bunker, head code discs or lamps, tail lamps, the fireman's pickaxe on top of the coal, and yet more. You can get a lot of ideas for this from loco photos in books.

6 Looking busy. With a few exceptions, most model freight wagons are sold 'empty' and on all too many layouts they stay that way. Just as locomotives lack crews there are whole trains of empty wagons to be seen on layouts. But real railways made their livings carrying freight of all kinds, and this can be depicted in model form too. There are plenty of loads in the Hornby Skaledale range – coal, ore, oil drums, cable drums, tarpaulin-covered cars, and timber – but accessory firms offer a big choice, too, and you can make your own simple loads. Freight depots also need cargo shown as being handled, with some cargo handlers, road vehicles collecting or delivering, and so on. The modern scene is an exception because container wagons are all sold with containers on board, and these are available as accessories, too. You can even get a working container crane and tractor in the Hornby International Lima range to complete a typical modern setting.

To complete the 'busy' look ensure you have passengers, staff, mail bags, parcels, trolleys, and other equipment on station platforms, and don't forget adding drivers and passengers in cars and buses. On quite a few layouts I've seen there are cars with no drivers lined up at level crossings!

5 Adding the extra details. Though a few model locomotives come with crew figures on board, most of them don't. So if you run a steam or diesel model on the track it looks all deserted, running along like the legendary 'ghost train'. Even on a lot of otherwise fine layouts at model shows there are completely empty trains running the circuit. You can transform this 'empty' look to a busy look easily enough simply by adding driver and firemen figures into steam locomotive cabs, a driver (and sometimes a second man) into diesel or electric loco cabs, a guard in a goods brake van, and some seated passengers in the coaches. Immediately, this brings life – or at least model life – to your layout. You can have fun with later models like the Hornby 08 or Class 31, which have opening cab doors, by adding drivers inside *and* leaving the cab door slightly open. This is particularly effective with the 08. Coaches can sometimes cause a problem because some of the more recent models are more difficult to get into, and you may need to do some careful study to see how the body comes off to give access to the interiors.

Very few locomotives or coaches and wagons are seen in the pristine colours of most models, except when they are fresh out of the paintshop. In service, the wheels, running boards, roofs, bodies, frames, and so on, get weather-stained to a greater or lesser degree, and this you can duplicate by careful weathering with appropriate colours such as

7 Visit model railway shows. You can get a lot of inspiration and ideas from visiting model shows. Not only are there layouts of all sorts and all scales operating, but there is also usually a high standard of modelling and operating on display. In addition, there are usually trade stands selling models and accessories, second-hand stands, specialist book sellers, and model demonstrations. So if you see any model railway exhibitions advertised in your area, make the effort to go. Most model railway magazines, too, carry news of exhibitions. Most model shows are organised by local model railway clubs, and these you can join, which is a great way to get a lot of model experience, meet other enthusiasts, and get involved in the big layouts that most clubs have.

8 Read a model railway magazine. Surprisingly, I still come across model railway fans who don't ever read model railway magazines, and even some who hardly know they exist! However, if you want a constant supply of ideas, inspiration, and new product news and reviews buy at least one model railway magazine a month. There are several to choose from and large newsagents, large model shops, and specialist railway bookshops usually stock them.

9 Keep it simple. If you are a beginner and you want a big layout it is better to join a club (see tip No. 7) and assist in their team effort. For home layouts, you can build quite a nice project in as little as four feet of length, up to eight feet or so, depicting a branch terminus or a freight yard, or some variation on this. Plenty of books and magazines give track plans and articles on these sort of layouts and they have the advantage of being easier to build, not too expensive, easy to operate, and not requiring too many wagons, coaches, and locomotives. They are fun, too, and above all don't take up too much space.

10 Don't forget the scenery. Once you've got your baseboard built and track laid you can get on to the fun activity of adding scenery, and let your imagination have full rein. Some beginners keep putting this off, but a bare wood baseboard lacks any sort of realism at all, so take the plunge and have a go. There are plenty of structures and scenic materials available both from Hornby and others. The advantage of scenic work is that you can always improve on it as your skill develops, and there is never an end to the details (lamps, fences, telegraph poles, huts, etc.) you can add.

No model railway layout is ever really finished!

TRAINS AND TEARS ON THE TARKA TRAIL

Monday 24 August 2009 was set to be a historic day. With the help of some 400 volunteers I was hoping to set a new world record for the longest ever train set, stretching 9.89 miles along the Taw Estuary from Barnstaple to Bideford. In my mind's eye I saw this taking place in glorious North Devon sunshine but when I woke up it was raining.

Hard.

So hard, in fact, that I began to wonder whether the whole attempt would be scuppered by the great British weather. It was, after all, an electric train set, and whilst I don't know much about electricity I do know that it doesn't mix with water. That's why hairdryers don't work in the bath.

My spirits lifted slightly when I spied a patch of blue sky on the horizon but when I looked again the low grey cloud had moved in and snuffed it out.

Then, at 07:26 precisely, my good friend Oz Clarke rang and made things even worse. After asking me where I was – 'Standing outside the hotel feeling bloody miserable,' I told him – he launched into an unnecessarily cheerful monologue about how bright and sunny it was in London. I didn't care what the weather was like in London. And neither should he, because he was on his way to join me in Devon.

I felt like Eeyore to his Tigger.

'It's raining here,' I said dolefully. 'Like hell.'

But Oz wasn't listening. He was chattering away excitedly about the fact that he had just left Waterloo Station on the historic route of the now-defunct Atlantic Coast Express, part of which I was about to start recreating in 00 gauge – if the rain stopped.

The plan was for Oz to travel the route of the ACE from Waterloo to Exeter and then on to Barnstaple, bringing with him a Hornby model of one of the Rebuilt West Country Class steam locomotives that used to haul the ACE on this part of the route. The reason he was being so nauseatingly cheerful is that on arrival in Barnstaple his model was due to make the record-breaking attempt – if the rain stopped.

But I had a surprise for him. Oz is a model railway purist, so he would only ever run a Rebuilt West Country Class locomotive on this route because that's

TOP: Clarke calls, making me feel even more miserable about the weather than I did already.

ABOVE: Eagle-eyed readers may recognise my Hornby campaign poster as a modification of the Plasticine one (see page 39). This time the spelling is all correct.

LEFT: The Atlantic Coast Express, leaving Waterloo Station on its way to the West Country. The ACE was hauled on this part of the route by the Rebuilt Merchant Navy Class locomotive No. 35028 *Clan Line*, which was modelled by Hornby in 2000.

BELOW: The route of the ACE from Waterloo to Exeter, with five branches serving Ilfracombe, Great Torrington, Bude, Padstow and Plymouth.

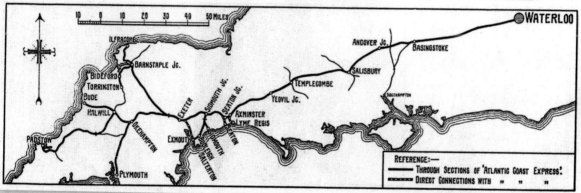

what happened in Real Life. What he didn't know was that his train would be racing against four others, including my ancient and venerable *Flying Scotsman*, which never ran anywhere near this route in Real Life. This would infuriate Oz, but I didn't care – I am not a model railway purist, and this would be my train set so I would run what I liked on it. If the rain stopped.

Meanwhile, Oz was still chuntering on at the other end of the phone. I couldn't bear any more of his cheerfulness so I cut him off: 'I've got to go and build a train set. If the rain stops.'

24 hours earlier...

I can recommend more enjoyable ways of spending a Sunday morning than crawling round on your hands and knees in Barnstaple Station car park. But if you are going to crawl round a car park you need a pleasurable distraction. Mine was my childhood train set, and as I lifted my Hornby Railways *Flying Scotsman* out of its box, still dusty from the attic, I felt a wave of nostalgia wash over me.

'Hello, old friend.'

Still kneeling, I carefully placed the venerable old lady on the track that stretched out across the tarmac. I was supposed to be testing the electrical system of what would, by tomorrow, be the world's longest model railway, but as it turned out there were more problems with the *Flying Scotsman* than with the electrical system.

The *Scotsman* had performed perfectly on my kitchen table but now, on its first outdoor test, it rolled along nicely for about three yards and then stopped dead. Luckily, I had my childhood toolbox with me, and I was amazed to discover that I still knew where everything was. Unfortunately, the problem wasn't simple enough to fix in the car park, so I resolved to take it back to the hotel and mend it later that night. Nothing must defeat my *Flying Scotsman*. I'd rather die.

So it was with slightly gritted teeth that I unboxed my brand-new Bachmann model of a Class 37 diesel and used that instead to test the electrical system. The Class 37 was a concession to the purists because this is what had hauled clay hoppers up and down the Barnstaple to Bideford line between 1964 and 1982, when the line only functioned as a goods line serving the quarry. And I have to admit, despite my preference for the *Scotsman*, that it went like a dream: solid, dependable, weighty and elegant. It rolled imperturbably along the mains-powered section of track and seamlessly onto the battery-powered section. The system worked!

As the Class 37 reached the end of the test track I lifted it off and checked it over. The wheels were still clean: no damage, no dirt.

BELOW: Classic Tri-ang Class 37 diesel loco. The one used in the event, just visible at the left of the picture below, is a modern model by Bachmann.

BOTTOM: My dear childhood friend, the *Flying Scotsman*. Unfortunately it proved temperamental, which meant delving into my childhood train toolbox (left) to try to fix the problem. I remembered what was in each compartment but I still needed reinforcements (right), and in the end I had to take the *Scotsman* back to the hotel for late-night repairs.

This **ELECTRICAL PLANT** on the **LNER** automatically coals "THE FLYING SCOTSMAN" in six minutes

ABOVE: The *Flying Scotsman* is one of the world's most famous locomotives but, somewhat confusingly, 'Flying Scotsman' was the name of an express service as well as the name of an individual locomotive. Sometimes the two names coincided when locomotive number 4472, *Flying Scotsman*, hauled the 'Flying Scotsman' express, as above.

LEFT: This 1932 LNER poster proudly proclaims the benefits of the modern railway system, as trains are loaded with coal from automated overhead dumpers.

I could see no reason why the Class 37 shouldn't make it the whole ten miles – not as quickly as the *Flying Scotsman*, once I'd mended it, but I was confident it would do it.

And so to the warehouse, where all the equipment was being delivered. Hornby supremo Simon Kohler, busy overseeing the unloading of nearly 20,000 pieces of track, looked as if all his Christmases had come at once. 'I've never done anything on this scale,' he enthused. 'The nearest I've come is the toy fairs but even those are nothing compared with this. This is a first.'

Indeed it was – no one had ever before put together a train set on such a massive scale. But, unfortunately, just building the railway would not in itself be sufficient for a Guinness World Record. At least one train had to make it all the way from Barnstaple to Bideford. It didn't have to be a non-stop journey: if any or all of the trains came off the tracks that was fine, so long as they were put back a few feet behind the place where they had come off, so that the entire track had been covered.

We couldn't leave the track or the batteries out overnight so the whole thing would have to be built and run in a single day. To do that we had assigned 81 teams of volunteers, each responsible for a 200-metre section of track and the 12-volt car battery that powered it. The track and the batteries were now being sorted into piles, which would be delivered at dawn by Land Rover to various access points along the route.

Everything was in place, which only left the short-circuiting *Flying Scotsman* to be resolved. When I got back to the hotel I hid myself away and refused to eat until I'd sorted it out, which proved to be several hours, half a bottle of Pinot Grigio and one replacement insulating bush later. It now worked perfectly, and as I waited for my belated chicken tikka massala I reflected that although we were trying to build the world's longest model railway it wasn't the enormity of the thing that was the problem – it was minutiae like the bushes on the *Flying Scotsman*.

And the weather.

Undoing Beeching

Ladies and gentlemen, I'm very sorry about the weather – it's not entirely my fault. You have all come here today to break the world record for the longest 00 gauge model railway in history; slightly under ten miles or, in scale terms, the length of Britain. We are also consummating the desires of many local people who wish to see Barnstaple and Bideford reunited by rail. And today, thanks to your efforts, it shall be.

It was still raining, but our army of volunteers had shown true grit and turned up anyway. Which was a good thing, because if I had to build the track on my own it would take me about eight weeks. My address to the crowd assembled at Barnstaple station was already being relayed down the line to the 350 others scattered along the trail. If all went according to plan – and if it stopped raining – the track would be ready by 13:00 and the trains would be unleashed from the starting blocks.

As I took shelter under a leaking gazebo – the porous variety, which had presumably been erected to keep the sun off – a local journalist asked me why I'd chosen Devon as the scene of my epic attempt. 'Because it's such a nice place,' I answered, 'with such lovely weather.'

Actually, it was because I wanted to use a former railway, and one that the locals wanted to see reinstated. This was partly because the railway

TOP: Unpacking the trains and the track in the warehouse with Hornby supremo, Simon Kohler.

ABOVE: Trying to convince the crowd that it really would 'brighten up' some time in the next few months.

infrastructure would be ideal for running a train set on, because it was fairly flat and level, and partly to make the point that the locals genuinely want the railway reopened. As in so many other parts of the country they resent the way the evil chemist Dr Beeching strode into the political dining room of the 1960s and kicked his way wantonly through the nation's train set, closing branch lines by the score and thus depriving the main lines of their life blood – or, for those who prefer the other side of the coin, rationalising the railway system by closing unprofitable lines. So not only did the former Barnstaple to Bideford line give us a suitable infrastructure but we were also giving Beeching one in the eye and providing a service to the community, all at the same time. Or we would be, if it stopped raining. Which it did, at last, just before Oz arrived.

I was far too happy about the sun coming out to worry that Oz might start gloating that he'd brought the good weather with him. At last, my dream was coming true – I was standing at the beginning of the world's biggest train set attaching the station buildings from which the five trains would depart, and I was doing it in glorious North Devon sunshine. All I needed now was for Oz to arrive with the model ACE and we'd be ready to start.

TOP LEFT: My version of Barnstaple Station standing on the platform of the real Barnstaple Station.

ABOVE LEFT: Gently does it… placing the trains on the track ready for the off.

ABOVE: Simon Kohler checks that everything is in order before the start. Three of the five trains that will attempt the record are visible: from left to right, the Bullet Train, the Class 37 diesel goods train and the Class 42 Warship.

When he arrived a few minutes later, four of the trains were lined up at the platforms of my model of Barnstaple Station, which stood on the platform of the real Barnstaple Station and Oz, as predicted, was horrified by the sight of the *Flying Scotsman*.

'It shouldn't be allowed,' he blustered as he opened the box of his model and promptly knocked my *Scotsman* off the rails – accidentally, or so he claimed.

No matter. The sturdy *Scotsman* was replaced on the tracks, Oz's Rebuilt West Country Class – which turned out to be locomotive number 34045 *Ottery St Mary* in British Rail green livery – was hooked up to three Pullman coaches and we were ready to go. The crowd counted down from ten, the stationmaster gave a long blast on his whistle and I twisted the dial on the controller.

'Onward the *Flying Scotsman*. Go!'

The *Scotsman* crept forward, successfully negotiating the points out of the model station and onto a miniature Forth Rail Bridge that bridged the gap from the real station platform to the car park. The realistic chuffing sound of my 1972 Hornby Railways model was immediately drowned out by the sound of the crowd cheering as the *Scotsman* made its way majestically towards the first corner. It successfully cleared the insulating plates that isolated the mains section from the battery section, rounded the first bend… and ground to a halt.

And they're off. Again...

A toy train goes round a kitchen table layout at about three miles an hour, so we had allowed between four and five hours for the trains to negotiate the ten-mile route and make their triumphant entry into Bideford station, where they

ABOVE: Platforms 1 to 3 of the model Barnstaple Station, with (left to right) the Warship, Oz's Rebuilt West Country Class, aka the ACE, and my *Flying Scotsman*.

BELOW: Oz points out, scornfully, that the *Flying Scotsman* would never have run on the Atlantic Coast Express route and so shouldn't be allowed. But I don't care.

would be fêted at a civic reception by the Mayor of Bideford, a brass band and a male voice choir.

But, of course, it didn't work out quite like that.

It took an hour to sort out the problem in the car park. It turned out that someone who didn't know their left from their right (to put it politely) had set up the batteries with the polarity reversed. This meant that as the *Flying Scotsman* left the mains section behind, instead of meeting fresh power from the batteries it met increasing resistance.

At last, it was corrected, and the 13:00 for Bideford – calling at Fremington, Yelland, Instow and Bideford – finally left at 14:16. Not bad by some rail companies' standards: at least it wasn't cancelled. At least, not for another three minutes. The *Scotsman* crossed the bridge, cleared the insulator, rounded the corner at full speed and then, three feet beyond the place where it had stopped the first time, it ground to a halt again.

This time, with no further ceremony, the venerable lady was retired from the race. I was gutted. After 37 years' faithful service all I could do was to lift it off the track to make way for Oz's ACE. He and the other doubters had been proved right before we'd even left the car park.

Four minutes later, at 14:20, it was Oz's turn to twist the controller dial and the ACE – a superb Hornby model released in 2007, fully 35 years after my *Flying Scotsman* – crept slowly forward.

'Westward Ho!' yelled Oz, but the ACE didn't even make it as far as the *Scotsman*, derailing as it left the model station for the model bridge.

Oz, of course, blamed it on the rolling stock, claiming that they never used Pullman coaches on the ACE. But after being put back on the tracks the ACE edged slowly forwards again and the record-breaking run began in earnest, with the purists appeased by the fact that a model of the Atlantic Coast Express had left first.

It was only when the ACE had negotiated a second mini Forth Bridge, taking it out of the car park, across the road (closed for the day) and onto a cycle path, that the enormity of the task ahead became apparent. The flimsy track snaked away into the distance, its entire ten miles vulnerable to people treading on it, bicycles running over it, dogs gnawing at it and thieves stealing it. Out in the open the miniscule scale of the railway compared to its surroundings seemed totally implausible. A passing dog had a scale height of more than 200 feet. By comparison the train looked puny and yet magnificent, terrifyingly fragile and yet gloriously powerful.

Could a mere toy really make it ten miles along the Taw Estuary to Bideford?

We were about to find out.

As the ACE made its way off down the Tarka Trail I returned to the start to watch Oz send the next train down the line. This was a modern-era reduced Atlantic Coast Express, hauled by a Class 42 Warship diesel locomotive pulling two green British Rail Mk1 coaches. One of the model railway enthusiasts in

ABOVE: The miniature Forth Rail Bridge that carried the model railway from the station platform into the car park. I realise this is geographically a bit wonky but, again, I don't care. The track was much straighter before Oz walked into it.

the crowd called out that this was the most likely model to finish because the steam locomotives, with all their valve gear, have got more potential for trouble. It turned out that he was right about the valve gear but what he didn't know was that there were two trains still to come: the Class 37 diesel goods train that I'd tested the previous day, and our secret weapon – a Hornby prototype model of the new 150-mph Bullet Train, which is just starting in service from Waterloo to Ashford. Now that the *Flying Scotsman* was out of the running, my money was on the Bullet Train.

So, to simplify matters, there were now four trains in the running to make the record, henceforth referred to as the ACE (Oz's steam loco), the Warship, the Goods Train and the Bullet Train.

Having watched the Warship make its way over the bridge and into the car park I jumped on a bike and cycled off down the trail in pursuit of the ACE. No vehicles are allowed on the Tarka Trail so the cameraman and the sound man, Pete and Steve, had improvised a Boadicea-like chariot by wedging two café chairs into the back of a rickshaw which was being pedalled by Charlie, our indefatigable runner. I caught up with the chariot and the ACE a quarter of a mile away, just as the ACE entered the tunnel that took the track under the main road. It was making steady progress, but it was already clear that we weren't going to make it to Bideford in time for the reception: it was travelling at an average of about one mile an hour, and if it continued at that rate it would be after midnight before we reached our final destination.

If we got there at all.

Fremington or bust

Soon after the ACE emerged from the tunnel it slowed down and stopped. Luckily, it turned out to be a simple case of mud on the line – it had just negotiated a dip in the track, where the rain had made the mud and debris collect – and a wheel clean solved the problem. I followed its renewed progress up the incline to the broad sunlit upland where the track opened out onto a glorious vista of the Taw Estuary, and from there I phoned a progress report through to Oz. He had already sent the Goods Train on its way and I warned him to wait a bit before sending the Bullet Train because I suspected it was going to overhaul everything, and we hadn't got to any passing loops yet.

When I cycled back towards the start to check on the progress of the Goods Train it was making slow and stately progress. Unlike the other models, it had not stopped once since the start, thanks to its heavy chassis and the fact that both bogies were powered – but this multi-wheel powering did mean it was much slower than the others. And sure enough, as I admired the elegant lines of the Goods Train, the Bullet Train came tearing round the corner at nearly three times the speed, closing the gap on the Goods Train so rapidly that I had to make a decision: should I move a passing loop from further up the line, to enable it to overtake, or make it wait.

TOP: The Bullet Train and the Goods Train wait for the off.

ABOVE: The only way to keep an eye on all the trains was to cycle back and forth along the route. In the background is the camera crew's rickshaw chariot, valiantly pedalled by Charlie Hyland, my butler.

In the end it had to wait, just as it would have had to do on a real railway. I cycled ahead to recce the passing loop, which was on a stunningly beautiful straight alongside the estuary. I passed the Warship, still going strong, and 500 yards further on I caught up with the ACE at the 1.5-mile point. Progress report: no derailments, and only a couple of stops for cleaning the wheels, but that was merely the equivalent of a coal-and-water stop, which would be necessary for a steam train that had travelled the scale distance of 114 miles.

The passing loop was mounted on a piece of plywood that had warped in the morning's rain, creating a land heave with a scale height of about 20 feet. We weighed this down with rocks from the estuary bank, reducing the heave to about 18 scale inches and allowing the ACE to pass through successfully. The Warship, however, derailed because its coaches were too light. The solution: take them apart, weigh them down with stones, put them back together and send the train on its way. The Goods Train then lumbered into the passing loop and was diverted into the siding to wait for the Bullet Train, which stormed past at 16:41.

Just over half an hour later the Bullet Train had caught the Warship and was shunting it along at twice its normal speed before the faster train was deftly plucked from the track and made to wait again. Clearly the Bullet Train was itching to get ahead, and for my money it would make it into Bideford a good hour and a half ahead of the other trains once it had overtaken them all on the passing loops. In the event, it didn't have to wait until the next passing loop because the ACE derailed, allowing both the Warship and the Bullet Train past. Oz would not be happy.

At the next passing loop the Warship was diverted into the siding but then had to wait while the traction tyres on the Bullet Train were changed, before it came tearing through at 17:38 – at last it was in the lead, followed by the Warship and then the ACE, with the Goods Train bringing up the rear and falling ever further behind.

I cycled ahead to welcome the trains into Fremington, but when I got there I was amazed to hear that the Bullet Train had seized up soon after I left, letting both the Warship and the ACE past. So it was the Warship that was first into sight pulling up the hill into Fremington at 18:38 – four and a half hours behind schedule. At Fremington, the track wound up and down the grassy meadow in front of the former station buildings in a sinuous 0.6 of a mile of tight loops, which provided a spectacle for the patrons of the Fremington Café and, more importantly, ensured that our track would be long enough for the Guinness World Record.

TOP LEFT: Out in the open the model trains looked vulnerable and yet magnificent. The scale speed of the Bullet Train was remarkable but its real speed was still only walking pace.

TOP CENTRE: The Warship waits patiently in the passing loop under military guard while the Bullet Train has its traction tyres changed and then storms past.

TOP RIGHT: Cleaning the Warship's wheels – dirt was picked up from damp leaves on the line.

ABOVE: Passengers on the express train were alarmed by the appearance of giant children through the windows.

The Warship entered the loops in the lead but was almost immediately derailed by a crew member's boot. While I was checking it over the ACE went past, being shunted along by the Bullet Train, which succeeded in derailing the ACE and storming back into the lead. It transpired that the only thing needed to un-seize the Bullet Train's motor had been a bit of oil on the armature and now it was gaining its vengeance for the others having passed it. As it left the loops and continued along the estuary out of Fremington it was followed by the re-railed ACE and then the Warship, with the Goods Train just entering the loops a full hour and a half behind the others.

The Bullet Train would now remain in the lead until the bitter end.

And bitter it turned out to be.

Fremington to Yelland

As I cycled off in pursuit of the trains, leaving behind the bustle, the excited crowds and the stunningly beautiful sunset at Fremington, the atmosphere suddenly changed. The temperature dropped and it seemed eerily quiet. It was after 19:00, which is the time the whole event was supposed to finish – yet we had only covered a third of the total distance.

If the start of this record-breaking attempt had been fuelled by excitement and adrenalin the rest of the journey would be fuelled by grit and determination. I could tell that I was about to find out why world records are not easy to come by, and Roy Castle's song started going round my head. Dedication, that's what you need.

Everyone was getting tired, especially the teams from Buffers Model Railway who were escorting the trains. In the early part of the journey they had walked alongside the trains, dropping to their knees every so often to clean the wheels or oil an armature or place weights in carriages. But now they were spending more and more time on their knees, nursing the trains along through their increasing stoppages and taking them back each time to ensure that they had covered the entire track unaided.

ABOVE: At Yelland the track snaked back and forth in a series of loops on the grassy expanse between the old station buildings and the spectacular view across the river, adding nearly two-thirds of a mile to the length of the track.

BELOW LEFT: A crowd gathers as Maria Husson and Paul Bryant of Buffers Model Railways tend to the stricken Warship. They were destined to spend an increasing amount of time on their knees as the night wore on and their trousers wore out.

BELOW RIGHT: As I cycled away from the bustle of Fremington the atmosphere changed…

For the first time, I really began to wonder whether any of the trains would actually make it. As if to illustrate the point, when I caught up with the Bullet Train at 19:24 it was off the rails again and lying in pieces while the escort tried to mend a loose contact, which was eventually bodged with Blu-Tack. I saw it on its way again and then went back to find the Warship, which I was told was in even worse shape. In fact, when I got there it was the ACE that was in trouble, with a bent piston rod – presumably from over-enthusiastic handling, although I didn't say anything. The bent rod would also have been putting extra strain on the motor, which made me wonder how much longer that would last before it burnt out.

Over the next hour the stoppages became more frequent and longer lasting. The sun had gone down and the cold was draining the batteries (thus reducing the speed of the trains) and causing the track to shrink, which was opening up spaces between the sections big enough to derail the trains. A search party was sent off to find more batteries and three-quarters of an hour later, at 21:00, torchlight revealed the bizarre sight of the Bullet Train speeding along the track much faster than before, with a stone taped to its roof and followed by a length of timber that to scale would have been about the size of the Empire State Building. I'm not sure what the dapper fellow from Guinness World Records would say about this being a standard toy train, but it was certainly ingenious.

The stone had been taped to the roof to weigh down the rear bogie and give the locomotive more grip, because the traction tyres had worn out again. As for the length of timber, closer inspection revealed that it was rigged up to a travelling battery, hanging from the crossbar of a bike that was being pushed alongside. A wire from the battery was fed along the timber to two contacts, which were being dragged along the track behind the train to make a permanent connection. It had been christened the 'perma-connector' and it made a phenomenal difference. Instead of relying on reduced power from a distant battery, the Bullet Train now had its own power source travelling with it and it was now, truly, going like the clappers.

My hopes were revived, despite the news that the Goods Train had now fallen so far behind that it had been quietly retired, which meant that we now had just three chances left at the record.

Nearly an hour later, at 21:57, the Bullet Train arrived at Yelland where some of the original Real Life rails still survived on what had been the level crossing. Our 00 gauge track fitted neatly into the trough of the rails, so here our trains really would be running on the original ACE track. Amazingly, there was still a crowd waiting in the cold and the dark, and as their cheers rang out it felt like a fantastic achievement to have got this far. But it was a sobering thought that after nearly eight hours we were still only just over half way.

Sandwiches arrived, which revived the flagging crew, and then the Warship came through at 22:40, nearly three-quarters of an hour behind the Bullet, bringing with it a rumour that Oz's ACE had burnt out. I strode off into the darkness to investigate, following the gossamer thread of the track that was just visible gleaming in the moonlight.

I returned 15 minutes later with the men who had been driving Oz's Atlantic Coast Express. They had bad news for Oz: 'Unfortunately, we were about 100 metres from where we are now and the little gal has burnt out on us. We've tried everything we can to get her going and we've had to give up the ghost. She's burnt out.'

TOP: As night fell Robert Train of Buffers Model Railways kept a close eye and a useful head torch focussed on the Bullet Train.

ABOVE: The Bullet Train began losing traction so Robert improvised with some tape and a giant boulder the scale size of an Easter Island statue. By the end of its journey it would have several more boulders and a craft knife strapped to its roof.

The news was as plain as could be but Oz refused to accept it. 'How do you know it's burnt out?'

'Smoking like mad.'

'Of course it's smoking, it's a steam train!'

'It's the wrong kind of smoke.'

'Oz,' I said. 'I'm really sorry.'

'You're not gloating, are you?'

'No, I'm not gloating at all.' And it was true. By this time any personal rivalries about the *Scotsman* or the ACE had been wiped out by the immense team spirit that had brought us all this far into the night. 'I think it's very sad – I really wanted the ACE to make it.'

'After all that gutsy effort, all the way from Barnstaple…' Oz sounded close to tears as he looked down at the ACE in his hands. Then he looked up and handed it gently to the team who had been escorting it. 'Thank you for a noble effort. I think you should have this.'

So now it was down to the Bullet Train and the Warship, both of which had already headed on into the darkness.

The bitter end

Rather than following the trains down the unlit track, I went ahead by road to the level crossing at Instow to talk to the crowd that had been waiting there for nine hours for the trains to arrive. Most of them were still waiting, sparklers and flags at the ready, and the historic signal box was crowded with well-wishers. Everything and everyone was ready. All we needed now was a train.

After what seemed like an interminable wait, the camera crew emerged from the darkness in their improvised chariot and the air of expectancy intensified. The camera chariot was now suffering as badly as the trains: the batteries that supplemented Charlie's pedal power were drained and one of the rear tyres was punctured. As the chariot struggled across the road Steve informed us that the Bullet Train was still on the move and only a couple of hundred yards behind them.

But it was to be another three-quarters of an hour before it caught up those couple of hundred yards, and in the meantime the bad news came thick and fast.

First, at seven minutes past midnight, news reached us that the Warship had dropped out. Rumours were rife: some people were saying it had burnt out, others were saying that someone had been over-eager to collect up the batteries and had left it with no power. We eventually discovered that a truck had been following the Warship down the trail, picking up the Portaloos that had been spread along the line for the comfort of the volunteers. The truck had run over a couple of batteries, cutting off the power and scuppering the Warship's chances half way between Yelland and Instow.

So it was now all down to the Bullet Train.

Then, a few minutes later, I saw somebody approaching along the track out of the darkness. But it wasn't the train crew, it was Matt Boulton, the Guinness World Records adjudicator, and he was looking grave.

At 00:11, Matt announced that he could not agree to verify any further progress as a record. 'There's been too much intervention,' he said. 'They've almost got the train in a wheelchair back there. Everybody's willing it on but it's got to the point where it comes off the tracks, it's cleaned, it's put back on, they help it along a little bit to get it going, and then it comes off again. It's

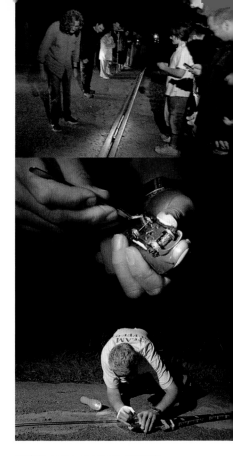

ABOVE: In the end the Bullet Train required so much nursing along that the adjudicator from Guinness World Records said there had been too much intervention for him to verify the record.

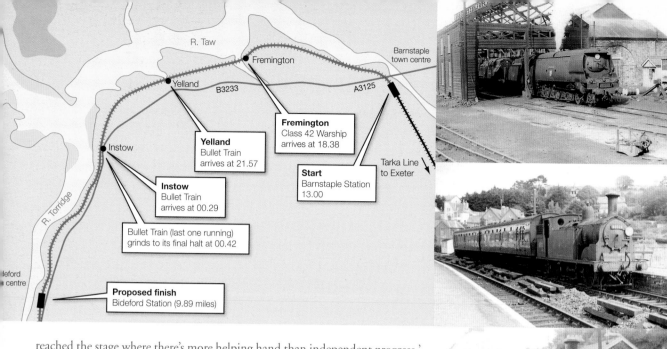

reached the stage where there's more helping hand than independent progress.' I was devastated. All I could muster in reply was: 'OK, fair enough.'

'I feel for everybody who's put in so much hard work,' said Matt, 'but so far as the record's concerned it's over.'

Hearing him say that made me all the more determined to carry on to Bideford, record or no record, for the sake of the people who had put in all that effort to get this far, for the people who had waited all day and half the night to see it pass through Instow, and for the people who were still waiting further up the line.

'OK,' I said quietly. 'Well, we might carry on anyway.'

And as I said it the Bullet Train approached. It was limping along but it was under its own power. As it crossed over Instow's level crossing at 00:29 we could see that it now had a craft knife and several large stones strapped to its roof. It was no longer a proud prototype toy train, it was like something out of *Mad Max*. It passed under the gate at the other side of the level crossing like a wounded animal, cleared the plywood bridge that took it back onto the cycle track and then ground to its final halt.

The faithful escorts gathered round to try once more to revive it, but with the record now gone we all realised it was futile.

I didn't know what to say. I was devastated, as were Maria Husson and Paul Bryant, who had driven the Warship until they were thwarted by the Portaloo truck, and the aptly named Robert Train, who had covered most of the last mile and half on his knees next to the Bullet Train. I pronounced a short eulogy:

That Bullet Train started the day as a prototype model and now, in toy train terms, it's as old as my *Flying Scotsman* was when I tried to set it off this morning. A whole childhood's worth of toy train adventures has passed under its wheels. Look where it came from – not the other side of a board, not the other end of an attic, but a full seven miles across country from Barnstaple. It's worn out, and that is noble.

Time of death, 00:42. The dream was over.

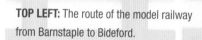

TOP LEFT: The route of the model railway from Barnstaple to Bideford.

ABOVE: The last gasp of steam on the Barnstaple to Bideford line in the early 1960s: (top) the shed at Barnstaple station; (centre) arriving at Instow; (below) Bideford station.

LOCOMOTIVE SERVICING

Hornby and its predecessor Tri-ang Railways have made hundreds of thousands of locomotives since the first *Princess Elizabeth* of 1950, so there's a fair chance you have one in your attic somewhere. And chances are, if you now put it on the track and turn the knob on the controller, it won't work.

This is a source of endless bafflement to people who try to revive ancient train sets, but locomotive servicing really isn't that complex on the older models and the pleasure of seeing your Jinty brought back to life is almost without equal. Actually, a lot of things are much nicer, but it's quite good.

The locomotive is little more than an elaborate means of connecting a simple electric motor to the two wires of a 12-volt supply. Dirt is the main enemy. First check that there is power to the track, which you can do with a light bulb or, if you're posh, a multimeter. I have one that cost a pound from a slightly hooky market stall. Clean the loco wheels. This is best done with the Peco brush and scraper, which can be connected to your transformer and used to spin the wheels against the copper bristles of the brush.

If problems persist, take the body shell from the loco. It will be held on with one or two screws. You will now be confronted by one of three basic types of motor:

1 Open-frame type, in which you can see the rotor assembly and the brushes.

2 'Pancake' type – these are usually in the tender of steam engines or incorporated into the bogie of a diesel. You can't see the working bits but the assembly comes apart when you take out a few tiny phillips screws.

3 'Can' type. These are small and sealed, and can only be replaced.

First, check that the mechanism is not jammed with bits of carpet fluff, dog hairs or similar. Remove them with tweezers.

Before taking anything apart, check that all the wires are connected. This is done with screws, copper tabs or small spade-and-bayonet connectors.

If the touching surfaces are dull, carefully buff them up with a very fine emery board.

The wheels on one side of the loco are insulated from the chassis and current from them is collected through copper wires. Make sure these are clean and touching the wheels.

Current from the wheels on the other side goes to the loco chassis, which is effectively an 'earth'. Here there can be a problem, because old oil on the axles may have dried out and left an insulating coat on them. This can be carefully cleaned away with a degreaser such as Jizer applied lightly with a small paintbrush, but it's probably best to remove the motor first. Avoid pulling the wheels off the steam locos, as they must be aligned exactly during reassembly or the whole thing will jam solid. This is chuffing difficult.

Oil contamination is the most common problem affecting the motors. Over the years, it spreads on to the commutator and brushes (a) and hinders the passage of lovely electricity. Remove the brushes and soak them for several days in a small jar filled with Jizer. Put a bit of Jizer on the end of a cotton bud or pin (b) and carefully clean the commutator. Make sure the slots in the commutator are free of clogged-up cack. If it's there, scrape out very carefully with a piece of fine fuse wire or the point of a scalpel blade. Do not press, or you will burr the soft copper and the motor will run very erratically as a result.

The commutator of the pancake motor can be cleaned by passing a Jizer-soaked tuft of kitchen roll through the brush holes, but if it's really bad you will have to strip the motor.

When everything is clean and dry, reassemble. Now lubricate using either a 'precision oiler' (a sort of oil-filled hypodermic) or tiny drops of sewing-machine oil on the end of a pin (c). Treat axles, connecting rods on steam locos and motor spindles (d, e). Truly minute amounts of oil are required, or you will reintroduce the problem you started with.

Run locomotive and marvel at it. Put back in loft for another 30 years.

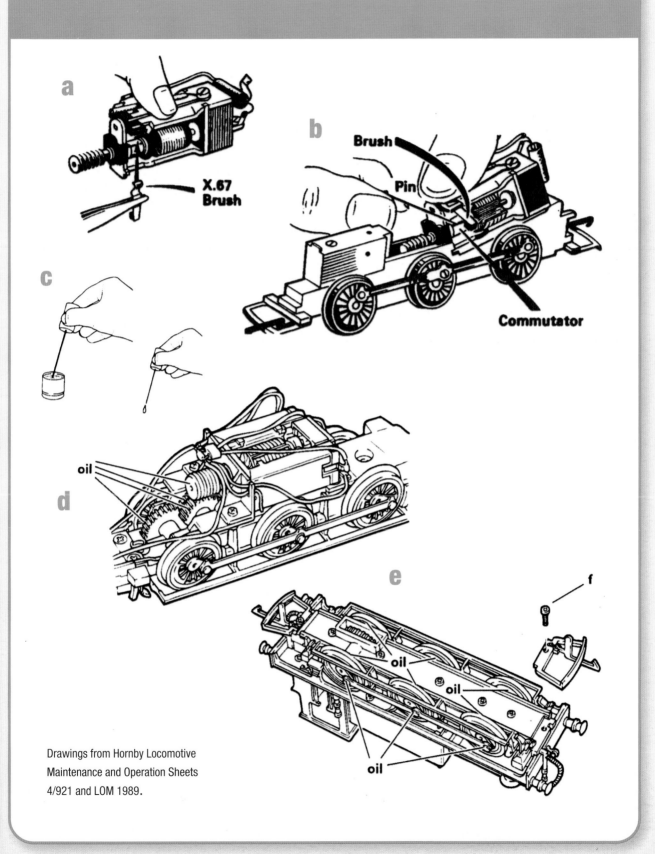

a

X.67
Brush

b

Brush

Pin

Commutator

c

d

oil

e

f

oil

oil

oil

Drawings from Hornby Locomotive
Maintenance and Operation Sheets
4/921 and LOM 1989.

AIRFIX

THE WORLD'S FIRST 1:1 SCALE SPITFIRE KIT

WHY AIRFIX?

For me, Airfix is, without doubt, the ultimate boys' toy. The first thing I proposed for the *Toy Stories* series was to build an Airfix model the size of a real aeroplane, because that's what I'd always imagined doing as a child. And it had to be a Spitfire because – apart from its iconic status as a symbol of the best of British – the Spitfire was the first plane that Airfix modelled and it is still the best-selling Airfix kit of all time.

The Spitfire was also my first Airfix model. I'm not quite old enough to remember Airfix's very first Spitfire, the Mk I (BTK), because that went out of production very quickly, but I did have the Mk IX, which was first released in 1955 and remained in production for some time. I can still remember being given it. When I was about five years old we were staying in a little seaside town and I remember going into a small corner shop and seeing these intriguing looking toys hanging on hooks in the now-famous poly bags. I'd never seen an Airfix model so I picked one up and said to my dad, 'What's this?'

I wasn't being totally stupid – it was a model tank, so the bag was full of very small bits and it wasn't really clear what it was. There was a picture of a tank on the header but my five-year-old self certainly couldn't see a tank in the bag. My dad told me it was an Airfix model and when I asked if I could try making one he said, 'Yes, but don't do that one because that's really fiddly.' And he took it off me and put it back on the hook.

Then he took down the Spitfire and said, 'Do this, you'll like this one more.'

How right he was.

I don't think my dad had ever made an Airfix kit because he was from the era when you made models by hand-carving bits of wood. But he knew what Airfix was and he was pretty keen to have a go at it too. And that was the thing. It may have been made out of new-fangled plastic, and it may not have involved carving the pieces by hand, but Dad could approve of it because it was still a toy that tested your practical skills and exercised your imagination. As Airfix historian Arthur Ward puts it, kit construction is 'a truly interactive hobby. Airfix supply the raw materials and all [you] have to do is bring a modicum of ability, some patience and abundant imagination. The result is always something to be proud of.'

Well, almost always.

But for some reason kit construction engages boys' imaginations more than girls' – and that's not just me being prejudiced, it's a fact borne out by Airfix's sales figures and by my own experience. My girlfriend remembers being terribly disappointed with Airfix because there was a fantastic picture on the box but when she took off the lid all she found was some crumpled bits of plastic. But for boys that's not the point – the picture means that when you start making the model you're in that scene; it isn't little bits of plastic, it's a real aeroplane and you're flying it and there really are bandits at three o'clock trying to shoot you down. And that's something no computer game can do: in a computer game you're tied to the imagination of the programmer but with Airfix the artist's imagination is a springboard for your own.

> "Kit construction is part of the male life cycle."

And as well as firing the imagination there was also the educational aspect. The whole point of making models when I was a kid was that they were supposed to be educational. Not modern, high-falutin', theoretical, hand-eye co-ordination type education. Real education – learning facts about things you wouldn't otherwise have found out about. Airfix was obsessed with historical details and thought everybody else should be too, so all the instruction leaflets had snippets of information or a potted history of whatever you were making.

You might think that as a child the idea that I was educating myself would have put me off, but it didn't. There were always unfinished Airfix models lying around our house because I would get involved with making several at the same time. It was youthful exuberance, excitement, and impatience to make a start on the next kit, and my friends were the same. So the big question is: why aren't 13-year-olds today as excited about Airfix as I was and all my mates were when we were 13? Airfix sales are still high but its market has changed since I was a child: a large proportion of buyers are men in their 40s, like me.

Darrell Burge, Airfix's marketing manager, told me that Airfix is considering developing a simplified range because while adult modellers are demanding more and more detail children are coping with fewer and fewer parts – not because they're less skilful than they used to be but because there are so many other activities competing for their time. Thankfully Airfix is not dumbing down completely. There are no plans for ready-painted, clip-together kits, so there is a place for glue and paint in the future of Airfix. And at least when the simplified range appears there will still be proper kits for those of us who want to relive our lost youth by recreating the glories of the ultimate boys' toy.

Remember: you don't have to grow up. Kit construction is part of the male life cycle. When you reach a certain age you retire to the shed and you return to Airfix. Shakespeare got it wrong with his seven ages of man. Really there are three – Airfix, Adulthood, and Airfix Revisited.

FROM COMBS TO KITS

The name Airfix is almost synonymous with scale model aircraft. The two are so closely related that it's tempting to think Airfix invented the plastic construction kit and that the company was named after the concept.

In fact, neither is true. And Airfix's first kit wasn't even a plane.

The first plastic scale model aircraft kits were marketed by Frog in 1936, a full 17 years before Airfix produced its first kit plane (a Spitfire Mk I). And the name derives from the fact that the company originally made air-filled rubber toys. Founder Nicholas Kove wanted a name beginning with 'A' because he thought it would help his fledgling business if it had a name that would appear near the front of trade directories. 'Air' was the obvious A-word because that's what his products were filled with, and he thought that names ending in '-ix' sounded distinctive. So he put the two together and one of the most legendary names in the toy industry was born – but it didn't make construction kits.

Kove was interested in synthetic materials, and he founded Airfix in 1939 to exploit the market for air-filled rubber toys such as squeezable rubber building bricks. When supplies of latex were curtailed during World War II the inventive and determined Kove simply moved from rubber to plastics. Airfix's first successful plastic product was a utility lighter; then came Airfix baby rattles, and then the product that is the true precursor of the kits we know today – plastic combs. By 1947 Airfix was the biggest manufacturer of plastic combs in Britain. But what is more historically significant than the product, or the volume sold, was the production method. The traditional way to make plastic combs was to cut them out of a solid piece of acetate. Kove could see this was wasteful and time-consuming, so he invested in what was then a very modern piece of machinery: an injection-moulding machine.

Injection moulding enabled Kove to mass-produce combs very cheaply, and it is still the method by which Airfix kits are made today. However, Airfix is now a little more discerning about its raw materials and its finish. Immediately after the war plastics were still rationed so Kove fed his machines with whatever scrap materials were available, ranging (or so the story goes) from unwanted acetate fountain pens to the rubber casing of electrical cables. Kove was even

BELOW: This quirky 1940s plastic chick was one of Airfix's first clockwork toys.

LEFT: As well as injection-moulded plastic combs, Airfix manufactured a range of other cheap, everyday items like these children's scissors.

BELOW: The Ferguson tractor, which was arguably the first kit to be produced by Airfix. However, the first version of this legendary tractor was not a construction kit but a ready-assembled promotional item made at the request of Harry Ferguson so that his sales reps could demonstrate the key features of the tractor.

shrewd enough to keep his raw materials uniformly poor, and when he did manage to get hold of first-grade raw materials he would mix them with second-grade plastics so that his customers weren't spoilt when circumstances forced him to revert to purely second-grade materials.

Airfix celebrated its 60th anniversary in 2009 but this date is somewhat confusing. The company was founded in 1939, 70 years earlier, and first mass-marketed a construction kit in 1952, 57 years earlier.

The reason the anniversary dates from 1949 is that that was the year when Airfix produced what was arguably its first kit – a 1:20 scale replica of a Ferguson tractor. The first version of the tractor was a ready-assembled promotional item but the following year Airfix began supplying the tractor to Ferguson as a 40-part construction kit. However, this was for practical reasons rather than being a conscious move towards the production of kits. Ralph Ehrmann, a former Chairman of Airfix Industries, later recalled: '[We] decided that because the assembled tractor was so fiddly and regularly fell to bits it was perhaps a good idea to actually sell it as a kit of parts and let someone else have the headache of assembling it!' Later still, Airfix decided to sell the kit to the general public and Ferguson, of course, was only too pleased to give its consent to this free publicity.

But the story of Airfix construction kits really begins in 1952 with the *Golden Hind*.

The Golden Hind and the Woolworths connection

The *Golden Hind* has several claims to being Airfix's first true construction kit: it was the first to be conceived from the outset as a construction kit; the first kit to be produced specifically for retail sale; the first to be moulded in polystyrene (the tractor had been moulded in acetate, which is one of the reasons pieces often dropped off); and, perhaps most important, the first to be sold in the iconic 'poly bag' – a form of packaging which was phased out in 1973, to make way for modern 'blister packs', but reintroduced in 2000. As with the supply of the tractor as a kit, the genesis of the poly bag was more serendipitous than planned. It arose because of a dispute with Woolworths over pricing of the kit.

The economic advantages of retailing construction kits were not lost on the managers of Airfix after their experience with the Ferguson tractor: instead of having to pay staff to assemble and paint a finished model, all that was required, to quote Airfix historian Arthur Ward, 'was to insert the moulded frames directly into a box with the addition of a cheap one-colour instruction sheet and some crude decals to boot.'

But Airfix's premier retailer, Woolworths, had made a similar calculation and refused to retail a box of unassembled parts at the same price as they had the assembled tractor. The only way that Airfix could meet the lower price point was to package the kit not in a box but in a polythene bag, with a folded header carrying an illustration of the finished kit on the outside and the instructions on the inside. Like many great ideas, this one was born of necessity and it went on to become an institution. Many are the

BELOW: The original cardboard header for Airfix's first true construction kit, the *Golden Hind* (1952). The real *Golden Hind* was the ship on which Francis Drake sailed round the world in 1577–80. It set sail as the *Pelican* but Drake changed its name part way through the journey in honour of his patron, whose crest was a golden hind.

BOTTOM: 1990s box art: four decades after its first release the *Golden Hind* was still in the Airfix range, now packaged in a box rather than a bag.

collectors who recall taking their pocket money to Woolworths as children and seeing the familiar array of poly bags hanging on the display stand containing the wherewithal for a journey to polystyrene wonderland.

The response to the *Golden Hind* and the other bagged kits which soon followed was phenomenal. Airfix had worried about its margins at the low price point stipulated by Woolworths but it needn't have done. Ehrmann remembers that production runs of the kits were soon in the order of hundreds of thousands rather than the expected tens of thousands; polythene bags were coming down in price; polystyrene dropped in price by about two thirds, and as production became ever more efficient Airfix was making 30 per cent profit on each item.

The choice of the *Golden Hind* was reputedly that of the Woolworths buyer, who suggested it because a ship-in-a-bottle version was selling well in the US. Its success was immediate and over the next few years Airfix produced several other sailing ships to create a Historical Ships range, which was sold both as individual kits and as a boxed set known as the Airfix Armada. The *Golden Hind* has remained in the Airfix range almost ever since, and a new 1:72 scale model of 109 pieces appears in the 60th anniversary catalogue.

Meanwhile, Airfix continued to produce other 'pocket-money toys' but the success of the construction kits had been so great that the company naturally focussed on kits as its core product. Legend has it that Kove was so pleased with sales of the Historical Ships range that he saw no need to diversify into kits of aircraft or vehicles. However, it appears that either this isn't true or his senior managers ignored him – the only kit to be introduced in 1953 (the year after the *Golden Hind*) was an aircraft: the Spitfire Mk I. The following year saw the release of two ships (*Santa Maria* and *Shannon*) and 1955 saw two more ships, a second aircraft (a Spitfire Mk IX) and Airfix's first vehicle (a 1911 Rolls Royce). By 1956 aircraft were already in the majority: by then Airfix had produced eight aircraft, seven ships and six cars.

It was a pattern that would continue. Aircraft soon became the staple of Airfix kits and the area in which the company was to become most famous worldwide – possibly, in part, because the name of the brand gives the impression that aircraft are its core product. In 2009 aircraft dominate the range, accounting for 60 per cent of all Airfix kits. But, as current marketing manager Darrell Burge points out, that still leaves 40 per cent for other areas. 'In fact,' he says, 'if you look just at the smaller kits at the lower price points, tanks sell better overall than aircraft of the same price.' And the 60th anniversary catalogue further dispels the myth that Airfix is all about aircraft, asserting merely that: 'One of the most important parts of the Airfix range is the aircraft category.'

ABOVE: The retooled 1:72 scale Spitfire Mk IA, released in 1979.

BELOW: The *Golden Hind* and HMS *Shannon*, two of the first three ships in the Airfix Historic Ships range. Eight ships of the Royal Navy have been called *Shannon*. The most famous was this frigate, which fought an epic battle with the US frigate *Chesapeake* during the War of 1812, which was the last war (to date!) to be fought between Britain and the US.

Kits in context

To understand the impact that Airfix kits had on modelling it is necessary to consider them in the context of toys at the time. At the beginning of the 20th century model-making still meant creating your own models from scratch. Enthusiasts needed an aptitude for woodwork or metalwork or both, and often owned equipment unlikely to be found in the average household today: soldering irons, brazing irons, lathes, and all manner of woodworking tools, which were used to convert raw materials (sheet metal or blocks of wood) into working models. By the end of the 19th century model railway companies had begun producing metal construction kits of locomotives, and later aircraft modelling companies such as the aptly named Aeromodels began producing kits with partially formed components which modellers had to shape themselves before assembling the kits.

The first aircraft construction kit made up of fully finished components was a Cierva C24 Autogyro, marketed in the 1930s by the British company Sky Birds. It was also the first to be scaled at 1:72, which became a standard scale and remains the most popular scale in the Airfix range to this day. Producing a kit of finished components proved to be a popular innovation – there was a wide market among those who did not have the time, the equipment, the space or the skills required for traditional model engineering – and by 1935 Sky Birds boasted a range of 20 models.

ABOVE: British manufacturer Sky Birds was the first to produce a kit comprising fully finished components. Sky Birds also pioneered the 1:72 scale, which to this day remains the most popular scale in the Airfix range.

BELOW: By Christmas 1936 the British company, Frog, released the first scale model construction kit to be made entirely from plastic.

However, in 1936 Sky Birds was beaten to a more significant first. That Christmas another British company, Frog, released the first scale model construction kit to be made entirely from plastic. Frog, which was already renowned for its flying scale models, named its new range of non-flying, detailed plastic replicas the 'Penguin series' – Penguins being a bird that cannot fly. After the war Frog extended its range to include vehicles and ships, making the Penguin series arguably the true precursor of all modern plastic scale model construction kits.

However, there is one considerable difference between the early Frog kits and their modern descendants: the plastic they are made from. Frog kits were made from a very early thermoplastic known as cellulose acetate butyrate, which often warped and did not age well. After the war, when research and development in plastics were no longer restricted to the war effort, materials improved quickly. Airfix's Ferguson tractor was made of acetate but the *Golden Hind*, released just three years later, was moulded from a far superior plastic: polystyrene. Ralph Ehrmann is in no doubt that Airfix's early adoption of polystyrene was key to its success, telling Airfix historian Arthur Ward: 'There were models on the British market before *Golden Hind* but they were always in acetate, which was hydrotropic and always twisted so that you couldn't make a decent model from it. The fact that polystyrene came onto the market made a lot of difference.'

ABOVE: Exhibitors arrive for the Model Engineer and Aircraft Exhibition at the New Horticultural Hall in Westminster on 19 August 1958. Peter Blanshot cycled to the exhibition from Chiswick with his model of a Staysail Schooner on a trailer. Colin and Leslie Smith, ten and eight, are carrying their father's models of the Fairey Delta II and the Deltaceptor.

From the drawing board to the display stand

In 2009, the injection moulding of polystyrene is still the key part of producing Airfix kits but it is only one part of a long drawn-out process – it can take over a year between deciding to go ahead with a model and that model reaching the shops.

The first step is to design the model, which can take several months. Before the days of computers the designers would execute a series of drawings based either on manufacturer's drawings or on their own measurements, starting with a 'general arrangement' and then moving to a scale drawing which would be broken down into individual components, each of which required a separate set of working drawings. Interestingly, even in the computer age, designing the components is not simply a question of scaling down the originals. Some details are too fine to mould (the molten plastic would simply not reach those extremities of the mould) or too fragile once moulded, and others would look wrong even though they were correct. For instance, the designer of the Airfix Mini revealed that the door handles were 'cheated' because if he had scaled them accurately they would have been 'just a thin wisp' and have looked wrong. 'Your designer's eye allowed you to strike a balance.'

Once the design is completed (whether by computer or by hand), creating the moulding tool can take several more months: this involves cutting the shape of each component into two halves of a mould which, when locked together, leave a kit-shaped gap that will be filled with molten plastic. Only then, when the tools are ready and tested, can the injection-moulding process begin, at which point a torrent of newly moulded kits begins pouring off the production line for packing and distribution. Meanwhile, myriad other pieces of the puzzle must have been completed, such as designing the artwork for the packaging, photographing the model for the catalogue and so on.

But at the heart of the whole process is the injection moulding itself. Polystyrene is a 'thermoplastic', which means it is liquid when heated but completely rigid when cool; thus it can be heated up, injected into a mould and, once cooled, it retains the shape of the mould. Modern thermoplastics replicate the tiniest detail of the finely tooled moulds, which means that 21st-century models can be intricately detailed to a degree that early designers could only have dreamt of, right down to rivets and screwheads at true scale size. The moulds are water-cooled to keep them below the setting temperature of the plastic, which means that once the injection has taken place the plastic sets almost instantly. The mould, which is in two parts, is then opened and the finished article is ejected by a set of 'ejector pins' that push it out of the casing. With early injection-moulding machines the ejector pins would often leave tell-tale circular marks where the plastic had not fully set, but with modern methods this is now a rare occurrence.

Injection, setting and ejection of the plastic takes about 30 seconds, which means that one machine can spew out more than 100 kits an hour. Modellers may not think it very romantic that the kit they spend hours lovingly assembling has been disgorged so rapidly and mechanically from the mould, but they can console themselves with the thought that the real skill and attention to detail has been put in with equally loving care by the designers much earlier in the process.

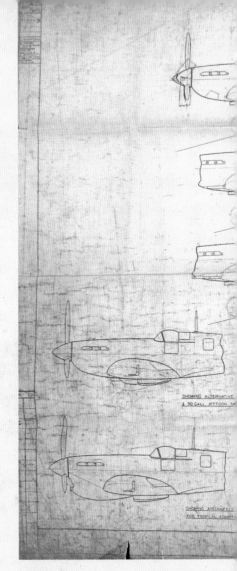

ABOVE: Original technical drawings from Vickers-Armstrong showing the general arrangement of the Supermarine Spitfire Mk V.

RIGHT: Detail of the renowned 1:24 scale Spitfire Super Kit, showing the engine bay.

GENERAL ARRANGEMENT SPITFIR

ROLLS-ROYCE MERLIN 45 ENGINE

VICKERS-ARMSTRONGS LTD SUPERMARINE WORKS SOUTHAMPTON.

34900 SHT 2

The doyen of Airfix artists

In my opinion Roy Cross is the most influential British artist of the 20th century. He must be, given the number of 1960s and 1970s schoolboys who saw his artwork on the Airfix boxes and thought, 'That's what I want for my birthday' – the number of imaginations he fired to believe that, rather than zooming a little plastic model round their bedrooms at arm's length, they were actually flying the real thing. But Roy, who is now in his 80s, is too modest to accept that, telling me: 'Let's just say I'm one of the most exposed.'

I visited Roy at home to persuade him to sketch the artwork for my giant kit. He told me that in his day he would use test mouldings of the new models as maquettes so that he could hold the model at various angles to find the one that would look best in what he called 'that stupid letterbox' – the wide, shallow shape of the Airfix box top. I tried the same thing with a model Spitfire and settled on a view of the underside of the plane as it climbed away from the onlooker. Roy sketched that viewpoint in double quick time and I then had his sketch computer-rendered into the artwork for my historic 1:1 scale Spitfire. The computer-generated artwork was perfect for the model but I still treasure my original Roy Cross sketch.

BELOW: Classic Roy Cross artwork on the packaging of the Blenheim IV (1968) and the Wellington B.III (1958).

BOTTOM: Original action-packed box art for the Boeing B-17G Flying Fortress (1962). There's a lot going on.

ABOVE: Box art for the B25 Mitchell (1965), still in use today as part of Airfix's current range of 1:72 aircraft.

RIGHT: Roy and I discuss artwork for the 1:1 scale Spitfire (2009).

BELOW: The signed sketch that was used to create the box art for my BTK, showing my preferred view of the underside of the plane.

Spitfire BTK

Although the moulding machines and the plastics have improved since 1952, all Airfix kits are made by basically the same process as the first two models: the *Golden Hind* and the Spitfire Mk I. It seems appropriate that the first aircraft construction kit to be produced by such a great British company should be such a great British icon, but in fact it seems that the Airfix model was copied from a model manufactured by the American company Aurora. Former Airfix MD John Grey told Arthur Ward that the 1:48 scale Aurora kit was copied at a reduced scale of 1:72 to produce a mould for the Airfix version, but whether this was done by agreement with Aurora or not is unclear. What is clear is that the Airfix model was copied so faithfully that it replicated a number of significant errors in the Aurora model.

The Airfix kit, which had 21 parts in blue plastic, was released in 1953 and sold in huge numbers. However, this commercial triumph was offset by critical disaster as letters flooded in from modellers and former RAF fitters complaining about errors in the profile, the wing shape, the dimensions and other details of the aircraft. The most obvious error of all, also carried over from the Aurora to the Airfix model, was the squadron code BTK. This had never appeared on a Spitfire but was actually a code used by a Supermarine Walrus squadron, the Walrus being an amphibious biplane. This error has become the stuff of toy-making legend (like Action Man's inverted thumbnail), and although the error-ridden model was soon replaced in the Airfix range it remains important to

BELOW: The very first Airfix aircraft construction kit, the Spitfire Mk I. The model was riddled with errors – including the squadron code BTK – but it has become legendary among collectors.

BOTTOM: Artwork for the 1:24 scale Spitfire Mk IA Super Kit, which 'took the modelling world by storm' in 1970.

collectors. The error was celebrated again during Airfix's 60th anniversary when the code BTK was chosen for the largest ever kit to be constructed on the Airfix principle: the 1:1 scale Spitfire Mk I built at RAF Cosford in 2009.

One of the many modellers to complain about the inaccuracies of the Airfix Mk I was John Edwards, who told Airfix that he could do better himself. Edwards duly became their chief designer and in 1955 he proved that his faith in his own abilities was well founded – Airfix released its second aircraft kit, a much more accurate Spitfire Mk IX, which was so popular that it remained in the Airfix range for more than 40 years (having been remoulded in 1960) and was still present in the 50th anniversary catalogue of 1999. And so, partially due to the inaccuracies of its first Spitfire, Airfix gained a chief designer who was to remain with the company for 15 years (until his early death at the age of 38) and who would become famous throughout the modelling industry for the quality and accuracy of his designs.

One of Edwards' last projects was another Spitfire, the renowned 1:24 scale Spitfire Mk IA, which was released in 1970. This kit – the first in a new range of 'Super Kits' – took kit manufacturing to new heights, and even included a 1.5 volt 'Propmotor' to power the propeller. Arthur Ward is in no doubt as to its significance: 'It took the modelling world by storm. Almost overnight Airfix had set new standards and most of their competitors were left far behind… When the new Spitfire appeared, with its 18-inch wingspan, cockpit, engine and even wing gun-bay detail, modellers rushed to the shops to see how the kit went together.' The Spitfire has remained a perennially popular subject ever since, and in all Airfix has produced 18 different versions with two more due out at the end of 2009.

Until his untimely death, Edwards directed the design of all Airfix kits, not just aircraft, in a range that rapidly broadened from ships, planes and cars to include: model railway accessories (1957 onwards); 1:12 scale historical figures (1959 onwards); railway rolling stock (1959 onwards); military vehicles (1961 onwards), and licensed character models, starting in 1965 with the James Bond and Oddjob diorama. Airfix was on a seemingly unstoppable escalator, constantly improving its range, its quality and its profit margins. At this stage no one could have predicted that before the company's 60th anniversary it would have gone bust – twice.

BELOW: The 1:72 scale RAF Refuelling Set, which added a touch of realism to enthusiasts' airfields. This set included a six-wheel AEC Matador tanker (left), which was used for refuelling heavy bombers, and the smaller Bedford QL tanker (right), which was standard on fighter bases.

Tank firsts

Airfix's first tanks were the Panther, Sherman and Churchill, which appeared in the 1961 catalogue. However, the first real tank was 'Little Willie', built by the British in 1915. An improved version, known variously as 'Big Willie', 'the Wilson Machine' (after one of its co-inventors) and, most famously, 'Mother', went into mass production the following year. At 6 a.m. on Friday 15 September 1916, 'Mother' became the first tank to be used in action, at the Battle of Flers-Courcelette in the Somme. Not everyone was impressed – one aide-de-camp reportedly said: 'The idea that cavalry will be replaced by these iron coaches is absurd. It is little short of treasonous.' He was wrong, of course, and many of the cavalry regiments subsequently became tank regiments. Airfix released its first kit of 'Mother' in 1967, with two new versions following in 2009.

AIRFIX

1:76 WWI MALE TANK

A01315

ABOVE: A 1967 Airfix model of 'Mother', the world's first operational tank.

LEFT: Box art for the 2009 model of the World War I 'Male Tank'.

BELOW: Box art for the Airfix Chieftain tank, first released in 1971.

Boom and bust

For Airfix, the 1960s was a period of constant innovation and improvement during which the company came to dominate the British industry in plastic scale model construction kits. The 1970s saw this domestic dominance extended to the international stage. In 1971 Airfix was awarded the Queen's Award to Industry for Outstanding Achievements in Exports, and in 1976 its international prominence was confirmed by winning America's Top Toy Trophy and a Gold Award for Merit at the Hobby Industry Show in Chicago. The decade was also marked by a series of acquisitions including Meccano, Dinky Toys and Tri-ang, and in 1975 Airfix announced record growth for the ninth year running, with sales hitting as many as 20,000,000 kits per year in 1976.

Such success was made all the more remarkable in the light of the economic crisis the country was suffering. But it wasn't just about business success – in 1976 a critic in modellers' magazine *PAM News* confirmed that Airfix's Super Kits were every bit as good as its sales figures for that remarkable year, proclaiming the Airfix 1:24 scale Junkers Ju 87B to be the best of 1,602 models reviewed: 'There might appear in the shops tomorrow a better kit. But until such time as I can lay my blistered fingers (ever tried opening over 1,000 kit boxes?) on this plastic paragon I stick to Airfix's admirable Ju 87B.'

The 1980s, though, was a different story. Whilst the quality of the kits remained impeccable, and the construction kits division continued to thrive, other parts of the group – including recent acquisitions Meccano and Dinky – were suffering. Exports were also down, all of which added up to disaster for the Airfix group as a whole. As Ralph Ehrmann later explained to Arthur Ward: 'We were terribly export oriented then… The pound went from $1.56 to $2.35 in a matter of about six or seven months and as a result our exports died. Customers did not want to pay 50 per cent more for the same goods as before.'

It was a simple equation and unfortunately there was only ever going to be one outcome. So the 1981 Earls Court Toy Fair, instead of being another triumphant platform for the launch of yet more superlative Airfix kits, became the scene of the announcement that Airfix had ceased trading. A long article in the *Financial Times* laid bare Airfix's woes: losses of more than £2m the previous financial year, the closure of the Meccano factory in Liverpool, unsuccessful attempts at financial reconstruction. But it was the quality of its products that would save Airfix, with Palitoy and Humbrol both bidding to buy the famous brand and continue producing Airfix kits.

In the end Palitoy won and Airfix moved home from south London to Palitoy's headquarters at Coalville in Leicestershire. But not for long. Within five years Palitoy itself was wound up, and in 1986 Humbrol succeeded in buying Airfix at the second attempt. Humbrol recognised that simply producing the best kits was not enough, acknowledging that the company

RIGHT: *Airfix Magazine* first appeared in June 1960 (top) with the subtitle 'Magazine for Plastic Modellers'. Three years later (centre) circulation was still restricted to plastic modellers but by May 1981 (bottom) it was also being sold to human modellers. Despite Airfix's financial problems the monthly magazine was published regularly for 33 years, the last edition appearing in November 1993.

must 'entice and excite new entrants to model making' (which it did by introducing kits such as the 1:16 scale Wallace & Gromit sets in 1999) as well as continuing to satisfy the core modelling fraternity, which it did admirably with hugely popular kits such as the 1:72 scale BAC TSR-2 in 2005. Humbrol also understood from the outset what a powerful force the internet would become in marketing and in communicating with Airfix aficionados around the world.

At Airfix's 50th anniversary, MD Frank Martin said that Humbrol would ensure that Airfix would continue to thrive into the new millennium. That much he achieved. He also said, 'Next stop the Airfix centenary.' That was a little over-optimistic – in 2006 Airfix was on the skids again.

BELOW: Drawing of a converted Lancaster AJ-G, fitted with Barnes-Wallis' bouncing bomb that accompanied Timothy Stevens' article in the December 1960 edition of *Airfix* magazine. This aircraft was piloted by Wing-Commander Guy Gibson during the famous Dambusters raid of 17 May 1943.

Dambusting Lancaster

The Christmas 1960 edition of *Airfix Magazine* carried an article describing how to adapt that year's Series 5 Lancaster kit into the dambusting version of the Lancaster, complete with bouncing bomb. The article pointed out that even in 1960 the bouncing bomb was still military secret, and that the Lancasters used in the famous film had been vetted so that they did not bear too much resemblance to the real thing – all of which meant that the author of the article could only guess at the exact dimensions. However, the article explained, 'It is easy to get a cotton reel which is 1 1/8th inches in diameter, which is approximately the same size.' Inventor Barnes Wallis filed a patent for the bomb in 1942 but for security reasons his patent was not granted until 21 years later, in 1963, bringing the details into the public domain. Thirty years after that, in 1993, Airfix released its Avro Lancaster BIII Special Dambuster kit, which was converted from a 1980 Lancaster BIII mould.

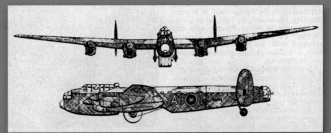

BELOW: The Airfix Avro Lancaster B1 kit, first released in 1958. Before 1958 Airfix had been unable to produce a model of a plane this size because the wingspan was too large for the company's early injection-moulding machines.

Hornby steams to the rescue

The demise of Airfix for the second time in 25 years produced a plethora of puns in the papers. The *Financial Times* went with 'Airfix Comes Unstuck…' and the *Observer* followed suit (going on to say the company's future 'rests on a scalpel-edge'), while the *Daily Telegraph* had Airfix coming to a 'sticky end': 'The engine is on fire, the nose is pointing straight down and, wouldn't you know it, the canopy is covered in glue: after 54 years Airfix was crashing and burning yesterday.'

When Hornby won the race to buy the ailing company the headline writers had another field day, *The Times* leading the way with: 'Hornby steams to the rescue of Airfix.' The *Guardian* followed up with the subtler headline: 'Hornby puts together deal for Airfix.' Again, the mantra for success was the same as in 1981, which was perhaps not surprising given that former Humbrol MD Frank Martin was now CEO of Hornby. The *Guardian* reported: 'The new owners will try to reinvigorate the Airfix business by investing in new products aimed at the younger market and also focussing on traditional products for older fans.'

And so it was: 2007 saw the introduction of the first Dr Who licensed kit, a new departure with a 1:72 scale RNLI Severn Class Lifeboat, a long-awaited Nimrod and a modification to the existing 1:48 scale Spitfire Mk I. The following year Hornby continued this momentum with no less than 13 new moulds: ten aircraft and three licensed character kits in addition to numerous modifications and re-releases. And so, on its 60th anniversary in 2009, Airfix is still going strong despite the ups and downs along the way. The name Airfix may have been coined as a reference to cheap, air-filled toys but the company has long-since evolved to fulfil the meaning that most people attach to the name: the very best in scale aircraft construction kits.

BELOW: In 2007 Airfix introduced the first Dr Who licensed kit, as well as a 1:72 scale model of the all-weather RNLI Severn Class Lifeboat.

'10 Things I Wish I'd Known When I Was 10'

By Chris Ellis, former
editor of *Airfix Magazine*

From my point of view, I was luckier – if that is what you can call it – than most of today's young modellers, by being a schoolboy (well under 10) when World War II was at its height, so I saw and heard all types of warplane, Allied and German, around the clock. We all had spotter's books and read avidly the aircraft magazines of the day. And there was the bonus of 'Wings for Victory' weeks when real aircraft, usually war weary battle veterans, went on display to raise funds for new aircraft. The first aircraft I got really familiar with at one of these events was the Hawker Hurricane Mk I, where the officer in charge of the display – a veteran squadron-leader with an eye-patch – sat in the cockpit and explained all the controls and instruments to visitors who climbed steps on to a wooden platform rigged over the wing alongside the cockpit. I remember at the time being astonished by how big the aircraft seemed compared with seeing it in photographs and flying overhead. Later I made similar 'Wings for Victory' visits to a Spitfire Mk V and a Fairey Albacore biplane torpedo bomber, which was a good deal bigger than the fighters. I have many other memories of those days, of course, including an indoor display of crashed Luftwaffe aircraft, where the rather distinctive and sinister smell of the dope and fuel lingers in the mind to this day. These are just a few highlights from a continuous stream of events which fuelled our enthusiasm and excitement and there was always something new to see. I could, for example, show you exactly where I was standing on the way to school on the morning of 6 June 1944, when an RAF Mustang roared in from seawards, low over the town, and gave us the first glimpse of the distinctive black-and-white recognition stripes on its wings and fuselage, which had been applied to all Allied aircraft overnight for the D-Day invasion.

I mention all this because it leads directly to the first and most important of the '10 Things' – enthusiasm and knowledge of the subject.

1 Obviously, if you were not already interested in the excitement and drama of flight, and warplanes in particular, you would not be buying a model kit in the first place. And it's also true that you could simply assemble the kit, paint it, stick on the transfers supplied, and put it on display. But you get much more out of any model hobby if you study the subject in connection with it. If you are already an aircraft enthusiast you won't need me to tell you this, but if you are a newcomer to the hobby start reading some relevant books and magazines. Try your local public library if your budget is limited and, of course, there are useful internet websites. The Spitfire is a good model to start with and there are plenty of highly detailed publications on the aircraft, though this is true also of other significant types. There are several well-known feature films featuring Spitfires, too, but from a reference point of view the images are not always to be relied on, with such anomalies as the wrong mark, the wrong markings, and bogus squadron codes to confuse those not fully familiar with the subject. However, such films as *The First of the Few* and *Battle of Britain* are certainly good for conveying the historical context and atmosphere of the times, so they are still well worth seeing (and owning on DVD or video). But there are also some good documentary films, too, on important aircraft types and these give valuable detail and information for modellers. In the case of the Spitfire the most useful and interesting video I have is the Thorn-EMI *Spitfire* produced by Garry Pownall, which is superbly comprehensive and includes extracts from instructional films, all the key developments and actions, and ends with a pilot's-eye flight in a preserved Spitfire Mk IX. Get hold of this video and watch it, and I'd be surprised if you did not immediately want to rush out and buy a Spitfire kit!

As noted above, I'm just old enough to remember World War II aircraft in service, and that definitely made me a life-long aircraft enthusiast. But as is well-known, interest in World War II and the equipment of those days has never diminished, and succeeding generations are just as enthusiastic and knowledgeable as the old-timers. There are numerous museums – all the well-known ones – where you can see Spitfires on display really close-up, as well as all the other classic warplanes of past times. And there are numerous air displays each summer where, again, classic aircraft are shown, and flown. You can never know enough or see enough and even I keep coming across new information or new ideas. I go to the Goodwood Revival Meeting each year, mainly to see the historic cars, it's true, but there is always a fine air display as well with the chance to get up close to perfectly restored aircraft. About three years ago the full-size replica of the Spitfire prototype, K5054, was there, something I'd never seen before, and I don't remember the original either! I might mention here that my young grandson, who is the same age range now (5–8) that I was in late World War II, got to sit in the cockpit of a K5054 (and quite a few more aircraft since) and shows the same excitement and interest that I remember from his age. He has also made his first Spitfire kit from the Airfix range, got other Spitfire models, and his own copy of the *Spitfire* video. And he was born in the present century!

So you are never too young or too old to be an enthusiast, and aside from all the foregoing I suggest a scrapbook or ring binder to collect notes, photos, cuttings and so on to back up your interest and, indeed, a camera to take to air shows and museums and, maybe, even to photograph the models you make.

2 Get a proper tool kit together and keep it safe. This may sound obvious, but I've come across beginners who buy a kit – or are given one as a present – find they have no suitable tools and either break off the kit parts with their fingers or never make the model. For the average plastic aircraft kit you need the following: a craft knife with some spare blades, a razor-saw, pointed tweezers, two or three small files, including a round 'rat tail' one if possible, some emery boards, and some fine glasspaper. Additional useful items are an Archimedes drill with selection of fine drills, a small pencil or fine marker pen, and a small screwdriver or two. These extra pieces are most often needed when you are more experienced. While modern kits are highly detailed, there are still older ones around where such details as pitot tubes or radio aerials, etc., need to be added, which is where the Archimedes drill comes in to drill the locating holes. If you come to do any conversion work later you may need to mark out cut lines and so on.

Complete sets of tools are sold in model shops, but all items noted here are available separately at model shops or from stalls at model shows, so you can make up your own choice of tools. Safety is important, so any purchased loose tools should be kept securely in a box. For many years I have used the traditional metal school geometry boxes, which are still sold in stationery shops today.

3 Build up a stock of necessary paints, brushes, and adhesives before you begin. Adhesives are most important for assembly work, of course, and most will be familiar with the tubes of polystyrene cement sold in all model shops. But even more important is liquid poly cement, sold in small bottles, sometimes with a brush built into the lid for

application. Where this is not supplied, use a paint brush kept specially for liquid glue. In general, you can make a much neater job of assembly using liquid poly rather than tube cement. As a basic example, you just hold the parts to be joined correctly aligned and run a brush full of liquid cement along the join. Hold it for a few seconds longer and the job is done without any nasty blobs of cement being squeezed out along the join, as can easily happen with tube cement. Tube cement still has its uses, though, such as cementing 'out of sight' pieces in place where the cement won't be seen, such as cockpit seats on brackets in the fuselage or undercarriage legs into sockets in the wheel wells.

Paint is a material you buy as you need for any given project. Some 'beginner' kits come with suitable paints for the model, plus a brush, which is handy to get you started. Paint is still available is 'plastic enamel', sold in tinlets and covering all the common camouflage colours needed for aircraft models, but the trend of recent years is to use acrylic paints. These are water soluble so brushes can be cleaned in water, making life easier for beginners and youngsters. Brush cleaner (white spirit) is needed to clean brushes used with plastic enamel. Most makes of model paints cover very well in just one coat, but, as with all model work, don't

rush it and be prepared to apply a second coat where needed.

The other item that is useful to have is plastic filler. You might well need this later if you get round to more advanced conversion work, but it is useful, for example, on older kits, where you sometimes find unwanted 'dimples' or rough edges that need filling in. As with tools, keep all paints and adhesives, plus brushes, secure in a box and make sure all lids are tightly fitted so that the paint does not dry out.

4 Don't rush it. With the excitement of getting a new kit there is always an urge to get on with construction right away. But it is much better to take the time to familiarise yourself with the instruction sheet and relate the moulded kit parts to the diagrams. Very often there are sprue charts enabling small parts to be identified by number. Hence leave all the parts on the sprue until needed in the assembly sequence. Cutting all the bits from the sprue before you've looked at the instructions is a good way to lose key pieces and end up frustrated. It may be useful to check out reference books to find the actual

subject of the model (if it's a well-known type) so you know exactly how the finished model should look. Most kits have a slip to return if parts are missing or poorly moulded. Checking out the kit first should enable you to spot any defects.

5 Paint as many small parts on the sprue as possible before you begin assembly. This makes painting much easier. Such parts as tyres, wheel hubs, undercarriage legs, dashboards, cockpit seats, bombs and rockets, crew figures, and so on are much easier to paint while you hold the sprue than trying to do it while holding a tiny part in tweezers. Any gap in the colouring that may arise from the small area where the part is attached to the sprue can be touched up after assembly.

6 Take great care when cutting all parts from the sprue, file smooth the point where the part meets the sprue, clean off any moulding imperfections such as 'flash' along the edges of the part, and ensure all parts align correctly before cementing them together. Very young modellers need adult assistance and supervision here, but it is worth pointing out that there are some simple kits, ideal for youngsters, which largely 'click' together and don't really need any cutting or filing.

7 Some kits have optional parts for two different versions. For example, a recent Airfix 1:48 scale Spitfire kit has parts enabling you to make it up as one of the first production Spitfire Mk Is with the first Spitfire squadron, No. 19, in 1938, or else a Battle of Britain version of 1940. Different props, different cockpit covers, and different markings are included. You need to make the right selection, of course, and I plan to make the 19 Sqn machine from this kit the next Spitfire model I make. With a bit of experience behind you, you can make detail changes yourself to simpler kits, such as cutting the cockpit and setting it in the 'open' position, or cutting out the ailerons and re-cementing them slightly 'drooped', and so on. Photographs of real aircraft, particularly in wartime, can show evidence of worn paintwork, exhaust staining, partly obliterated markings, repair patches, and much else. This is where your references come in, for a modeller with some experience can reflect this sort of thing in the finish of the model.

8 Keep a 'spares' box. Talk to any modeller of some experience and you will hear mention of the 'spares' box. In essence this is any suitable container where you keep all or any parts left over after the model is complete. This might be the optional parts not used in completing the Spitfire kit mentioned

above, any unused crew figures, unused bombs, or whatever. Put any unused transfers from the kit in an envelope. Even the better pieces of sprue can be kept. In no time at all you start to build up a useful stock of spare parts that may come in useful – sometimes years later – for detailing or repairing other models. In other words, don't just ditch all the unused bits when you finish the kit. To the spares box you can also add oddments like wire, pins, plastic studs or anything that looks as if it could be useful for model detailing.

Related to this, most modellers of experience have a stock of card, plastic card, or plastic strip. This can be used later in conversion work, or possibly in scenic work if you set up a model on trestles for having its engine changed, to give just two examples.

9 If any model gets damaged by accident, repair it immediately. It is fatal to leave it for the proverbial 'rainy day', for by then the broken-off parts may well have 'disappeared' or the model has suffered more damage while resting unloved upon a shelf. If you have a well-stocked spares box, of course, you might find you can replace missing parts, but don't count on it!

10 Think about storage. Keeping lovingly made aircraft models neat, clean, and undamaged, and at the same time nicely displayed, is a major challenge in the hobby. Dust and damage are the enemy of models displayed on open shelves or bookcases. Hanging them on cotton from the ceiling is even worse. Don't even consider it. Years ago I bought a cheap four-shelf sliding-glass-door bookcase, added more shelves between the deeply spaced book shelves, and this holds over 100 1:72 scale model aircraft, safe and sound. For smaller scales such as 1:144 and 1:100, old shoe boxes make a safe storage, with tissue between the models. Obviously you can't display them in a shoe box, but the collection takes up minimal space that way. Larger scales, like 1:48, present more of a problem. If you have the room, the bookcase solution is fine, but my relatively few models to this scale I keep in the modern clip-top Useful Boxes, the clear plastic ones that stack.

Take your pick from these ideas, but, above all, have fun and good modelling!

SUPERSIZE SPITFIRE

When my 1:1 scale Airfix Spitfire emerged from Hangar One at RAF Cosford, pulled by the 26 schoolchildren who had assembled it, it looked magnificent. Gleaming in a brief burst of sunshine that cut through the rain, rolling slowly forward to the sound of an RAF band, it was a superb and emotional tribute to a great British icon, one of the world's greatest aircraft. Then the undercarriage nearly snapped off. But that was to be expected – after all, it may have been as big as a real Spitfire but it was still an Airfix model. And at least we didn't fill it with fireworks and blow it up, or shoot at it with giant air rifles, or launch it from the nearest bedroom window.

What I really liked about it was that whilst it looked like a Spitfire – it was the right size and shape, with some amazingly authentic details – it also managed to look like an Airfix model because the colours were a bit too garish, the transfers were a bit too bright, the tailplane was a bit too floppy and the wings were a bit too wobbly. And that's exactly what I wanted: not a replica Spitfire but a 1:1 scale Airfix Spitfire. It had all the signs of the unbridled enthusiasm I remember from my childhood: the way the paint had been slapped on and the pilot had been rammed too hard into his seat and the tailplanes were not quite level. I'm sure there was even glue smeared over the canopy.

Seeing that model come out of the hangar was a childhood dream fulfilled – I'd always wondered what it would be like to build a full size kit. It was also a world record: the first 1:1 scale aircraft construction kit made on the Airfix principle, and the biggest aircraft construction kit in the world by more than ten feet on the wingspan. It felt like a suitably epic way of celebrating the 60th anniversary of Airfix, to create a giant version of the company's most-tooled and most popular kit. Starting with the very first Airfix Spitfire in 1953 – the infamously inaccurate Spitfire BTK – Airfix has produced no less than 18 different versions of this legendary plane, including two highly detailed 1:48 scale kits in 1996 and two 1:72 scale kits to be released in 2009. Indeed, the Spitfire is so closely associated with Airfix that it appears on the covers of both the 50th and 60th anniversary Airfix histories and on the Airfix home page at www.airfix.com.

BELOW: I accidently stuck this Spitfire to my fingertip in 1971, and it's still there.

So what's the big deal? Why is it that even in 2009 – nearly 75 years after its maiden flight – the Spitfire remains probably the world's most famous aeroplane and by far the most popular Airfix kit? Why are we still transfixed by a plane that is chronologically closer to the Wright brothers than it is to the aircraft of today?

To find out just why the Spitfire has become so iconic I went to meet Carolyn Grace, who is the world's only current female Spitfire pilot. And while I was there I persuaded her to let me fulfil another childhood dream – I convinced her to let me fly a genuine Supermarine Spitfire.

Flight of fancy

Back in the 1930s, the Spitfire, along with the likes of Germany's Messerschmitt Bf-109, heralded a new era of fighter design. In an age of fabric-covered biplanes with open cockpits and fixed undercarriages, here was a sleek monoplane with a metal stressed skin monocoque construction, an enclosed cockpit and a retractable undercarriage. It could fly higher and faster than anything before it (349 mph at 16,800 feet on its trials) and was armed with eight guns when all previous fighters had had two or maybe four. And that was just the Mk I – the final version, the Mk 24, was twice as powerful, had five times the firepower, a 25 per cent higher maximum speed and almost twice the rate of climb. To put this truly remarkable machine in context, it replaced a load of clunky old

TOP: A triumph for Thomas Telford School. The 26 schoolchildren who built the Spitfire pull the assembled kit out of the hangar. I'm in two places at once, sitting in the cockpit at the same time as directing operations on the tarmac.

ABOVE: Error writ large. The code BTK was never used by a Spitfire squadron but it appeared on the first Airfix Spitfire, so to celebrate the 60th anniversary of Airfix we repeated the mistake.

biplanes that were basically made out of bed linen and it remained in service with the RAF until June 1957, taking it well into the jet age.

It was of course an instrument of war – a machine for killing the enemy. But it was also a truly beautiful and outstanding piece of design and engineering. And the facts and figures only tell part of the story. It isn't until you've flown a Spitfire – or talked to someone who has flown one – that you really understand what's so special about it. Carolyn Grace explained:

> The Spitfire appeals to all your senses. It sounds wonderful, it looks beautiful and it is superb to fly. The controls are in perfect harmony, and pilots knew it; during the war this was the machine they all wanted to fly. And of course it's British design at its very best. It's an icon that people really do find uplifting. I'm often booked to fly at funerals and I'm told that invariably when I make my third pass and finish with a climbing victory roll people cheer and clap, which is not what you expect at a funeral – the Spitfire just creates that good feeling among people.

BELOW: Box art for the 'Dogfight Doubles' kit of the Spitfire and the Messerschmitt Me 110D, 1975.

BOTTOM: This is an early Spitfire from the beginning of the war. By 1945 its power and armament had changed out of all proportion, but the essential shape remained as a tribute to Mitchell's genius.

It may be uplifting to watch but Carolyn told me it's even more so to fly.

The designer, R.J. Mitchell, was undoubtedly one of the geniuses of our time. He designed the Spitfire to talk to you – if you're really working it hard it lets you know. It's not like other aeroplanes that will just flick out of a manoeuvre; it will tell you that you're just pulling a little bit too hard. With these amazing elliptical wings you can pull in a really tight turn and feel the stall buffet and you know that you're pushing it to the limit so you just ease off a little. And Spitfires were very good in battle because they were so well engineered that they could withstand an awful lot of shooting up.

Mitchell was dying of cancer while he was designing the Spitfire, and he knew that he had less time to live than the Air Ministry had given him to finish the plane. So he finished it ahead of schedule – the prototype made its maiden flight on 5 March 1936 and Mitchell died just over a year later, in June 1937, at the age of 42. He didn't live to see his creation triumph in the Battle of Britain and he could not have dreamt that in 1996 some 80,000 people would turn out to watch a 60th anniversary flight of 13 surviving Spitfires take off from Eastleigh Airport (now Southampton Airport), scene of the Spitfire's maiden flight. However, he did live long enough to ridicule the name that Vickers (Supermarine's parent company) chose for his creation. Mitchell's response when he heard that his plane was to be known as a Spitfire was brief and to the point: 'It's just the sort of bloody silly name they would give it.'

Anyway – enough history. I wanted to find out for myself what Mitchell's Spitfire was like to fly. Carolyn took off with me in the back of her two-seater Mk IX and when we were airborne she gave me control. I was flying a Spitfire! I had dreamt of this since I was a boy. Half of my classmates would probably have chosen to play for Manchester United or something but the rest of us would have chosen to fly a Spitfire, every time. And here was I, actually doing it. It was an incredibly noisy, raw experience but I could feel straight away that this plane was something extraordinary. It felt alive. This was engineering from 70 years ago, worked out by blokes with pencils and slide rules and inspiration, so it was bound to feel a bit primitive. But it was fantastic. It felt like a living, breathing, roaring, panting machine wanting to do its job. Like a husky that wants to pull a sleigh.

When we landed I was speechless. The camera was rolling but all I could do was laugh gleefully and say, 'This is a Supermarine Spitfire and I was flying it. I'm sorry. I can't say anything else. It's a Spitfire. *I flew it.* Have I said that?'

It really was something else. Now all I had to do was go and build one.

A mouse the size of an elephant

Standard Airfix kits are made by injection moulding: by literally injecting molten plastic into a steel mould made up of two halves locked tightly together. When the plastic has cooled, the two halves of the mould are separated and all the components of the kit, interconnected by a sprue, are ejected from the mould. As a child I was aware of the basics of the injection-moulding process but I had no conception of the scale or speed of it. My dad worked in the steel industry so he knew a bit about tool making and I remember him explaining to me that the kit was made in a steel mould called a die, which in those days had to be made by hand. He told me that a die could cost as much as a house, and I remember wondering how it could cost as much as a house when an Airfix model only cost about 48 pence, because as a child I simply couldn't grasp the enormity of the mass-production process. In its heyday Airfix was churning out some 20 million kits a year, and that is a lot of kits – nearly 55,000 kits every day of the year, or 38 kits every minute of every day. It takes some of the romance out of that individual model you've saved up your pocket money for; that fantastic thing that you bought with your birthday money.

To make a complete kit using the injection-moulding process takes a matter of seconds but each piece of my bespoke 1:1 kit was going to be individually moulded in fibreglass, which was going to take a matter of weeks. In fact, my Spitfire, which would be 72 times larger than the original Airfix BTK, was going to take several thousand times longer to mould.

But at least that would make up for the disappointment of discovering that each of my special childhood Airfix kits was only one of identical millions that had been spat off the end of a production line.

Timing was not going to be the only difference in producing a giant kit. There are certain problems that arise if you scale things up without modifying them – for instance, you can't scale a mouse up to be the size of an elephant because its legs would be too weak. That's because not all factors scale up proportionally: strength doesn't increase in direct proportion to weight, and so on. So creating the parts for the 1:1 Spitfire was going to be a very complex process, and to do that I called in a team of experts: Gateguards, a company that manufactures replica aircraft to order. Usually Gateguards build complete airframes for collectors, eccentrics, feature films or for use as 'gate guardians' at airfields, hence the name of the company. Their replicas are so convincing that one of the airfields they supplied had several letters from outraged members of the public saying how disgraceful it is to put a real Spitfire on a pole at the gate. But Gateguards had never made a construction kit, and that is a very different proposition.

Fibreglass gate guardians have been dubbed 'ultimate Airfix' planes but that is actually a misnomer because gate guardians aren't supplied in kit form. In fact, making a complete fibreglass airframe is so different from making a construction kit that Gateguards spent the best part of a week trying to talk me out of it. They said it wouldn't work because to build it as a kit meant there could be no structure inside the fuselage, no ribs, and no spars in the wings. That's fine for a 1:72 or even 1:24 scale polystyrene model but Gateguards said that to do that with a 1:1 scale fibreglass structure would be impossible: the model would collapse under its own weight when it was put together. They were right, of course, but – as we'll see later – a bit of emergency surgery during the construction of the kit soon solved that problem.

The other difficulty was that Gateguards had to remake their moulds so that the wings would split along the leading and tail edges like an Airfix kit – that is, so that the top and bottom halves of the wing would be separate pieces. The mould for a normal replica is split along the line of one of the spars near the centre of the wing, with the leading edge and the tail edge (the front and back of the wing) as separate pieces, which is much stronger and less vulnerable to the weather. On the plus side, using Gateguards' moulds meant that we were going to have something that a genuine Airfix kit wouldn't have. The original cast for the wings and fuselage had been made from a real Spitfire, so the panels of our kit would have ripples and bumps that aircraft pick up over years of use, including the knee indents just below cockpit where pilots had climbed in and out.

But there was one part of the kit that Gateguards weren't going to be able to make for me, and that was the pilot. As a child I always imagined that I was flying the plane that I'd just built. And given that this was my childhood fantasy I decided that the 1:1 plastic pilot in the kit should be made in my own image. As it turned out, that decision led to one of the most unpleasant experiences of my entire life.

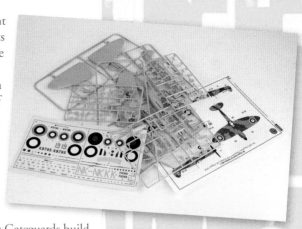

ABOVE: This is a real Airfix model, the 1:48 scale Spitfire Mk I.

OPPOSITE, TOP: Original kit in my hand, I prepare to ask Big Dave of Gateguards the big question. Can he make me a slightly bigger one?

OPPOSITE, BOTTOM LEFT: This is an American P51 Mustang replica. Dave had to finish this one before starting on my Spitfire. That's the rule with Airfix.

OPPOSITE, BOTTOM RIGHT: The first test piece from the quest for less weight. It was a bit floppy, but it was a start.

Face/Off

We couldn't just stuff a shop mannequin into the pilot's seat: it had to be an accurate scale replica of a qualified pilot, so off I went to see Poppy Boden, who makes a living out of casting people's heads, hands, feet, bottoms, bodies and breasts. Now I'm quite claustrophobic – I can't even wear a full face motorbike helmet – so when she described what she was going to do alarm bells started ringing. She said that she was going to encase my entire head in plaster of Paris, except for two small holes near my nostrils. And I was going to have to sit there entombed in this Parisian iron maiden for 20 minutes, until it set.

In the end we settled for casting the back of my head first and then doing my face separately so that I wouldn't be completely encased, but even that was bad enough. First she told me to smile. Smile? The idea of being smothered for almost half an hour in a full-face helmet with no visor didn't make me feel like smiling. And anyway, I wanted my pilot to be steely eyed and combat-ready, just like the Airfix pilots of my youth. But Poppy told me a sombre expression would look lifeless and that I should look as if I was enjoying the flight. Well, it was a Spitfire that my doppelganger would be flying, so a smile was probably allowable…

Once I'd assumed the expression Poppy smeared my face with a warm blue gooey substance made from seaweed, which is designed to cling to the skin and pick up the tiniest of surface details – even individual hairs if you haven't shaved properly. That takes about three minutes to set and it peels off like Copydex. But it's very fragile and it would tear if she tried to remove it on its own so she then applied layer upon layer of plaster of Paris bandage until my head felt about four times as heavy as normal and my head looked – or so I'm told – like an Easter Island statue. Then the room went eerily quiet and I started to wonder if Poppy and the crew had gone off to the pub and left me. Eventually, after what seemed like aeons, Poppy started to remove the cast,

BELOW: We decided to cast the back of my head first and then do my face separately, so that I wouldn't be completely encased. Even that was bad enough.

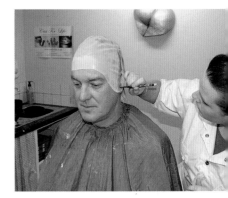

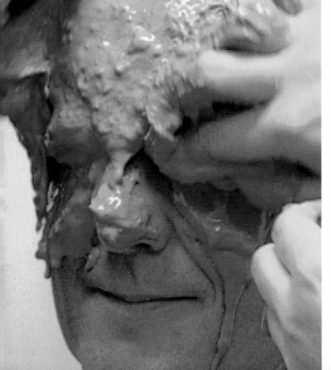

which by that time was clinging to my face like the extraterrestrial in *Alien*. She was pulling and twisting and I was just starting to wonder whether my face was going to come off with it when we finally achieved separation and I found myself staring at a concave version of myself in intricate detail, right down to the smile lines – alright, wrinkles – round my eyes.

All in all, the face casting had been a deeply unpleasant experience but the worst was over. Casting the rest of my body was a relative cinch, especially as the pin that protrudes from the pilot's coccyx to hold him in his seat was going to be added afterwards: I didn't have to have that surgically attached prior to the casting.

Now that the kit and the pilot were in production I needed to recruit some Airfix enthusiasts to build it. I wanted young people, so I could find out whether they were as enthusiastic, committed and adept at Airfix as I was when I was a young person. A school was the obvious place to look, and there couldn't be a better school in which to recruit young modellers than one named after a great British engineer, albeit one who died before the age of flight – Thomas Telford.

Thomas Telford engineers Airfix

The children of Thomas Telford School were great, but they're modern kids and they weren't that excited about the idea of Airfix. Maybe I was being a bit of a hopeless sentimentalist expecting them to be as excited about it as I had been when I was 13, because things have moved on. Life is different now. But I had to get them interested because they were the ones who were going to build the Spitfire. I had to get them Airfix enthused, and I thought I knew of a way. I got them all to build an Airfix tank and then I took them to Northamptonshire to compare their models with the real thing. And to drive the real thing. And to blow up their models with gunpowder. And to shoot at them with air rifles. Destroying your model is a vital Airfix rite of passage, and once they'd done that they were hooked.

BELOW: Another generation is introduced to the joy of the *Golden Hind*. He loves it.

BOTTOM: Tanks are a bit more like it. I only ran over the car to keep the young people amused. I don't really approve.

And so to Hangar One at RAF Cosford, where the giant kit had been delivered by Gateguards and was now being watched over by a plastic effigy of myself in flying helmet and jacket, complete with protruding coccyx pin.

But now I was faced with my first big disappointment. The original plan had been to hang up all the parts on a giant sprue, like a proper Airfix kit, but that was going to require too much engineering so instead we had to cheat. We laid all the pieces out on the floor, arranged cardboard tubes round them to look like a sprue, and then taped everything together. We painted the tubes and the tape to match the blue fibreglass of the kit components and it actually looked very good when filmed from above but I was still disappointed that the pieces weren't attached properly. The first job for the children should have been to cut the components off the sprue with bolt cutters or an angle grinder or even a junior hacksaw, but the tape wasn't strong enough. The pieces came away so easily that it didn't really work. Having said that, once the components began to go together it really was like putting together a giant Airfix kit. While one group started assembling the wings and the undercarriage (using general-purpose silicon in a mastic gun rather than a tube of glue) another group started building the fuselage, which would eventually sit on top of the completed wing assembly.

At this point we discovered another of the problems associated with scaling a mouse up to the size of an elephant. A standard Airfix kit is moulded in polystyrene, which is a high grade thermoplastic that doesn't warp or twist, particularly when used at the small sizes of Airfix models. However, fibreglass

ABOVE: Steely eyed and combat ready? Or just worried about having his head encased in blue goo?

is not so sturdy, especially when used for full size pieces that have been shorn of all internal support structures and transported from Cornwall to Shropshire on the back of a lorry. Just like the 1949 Airfix Ferguson tractor (which was moulded from acetate rather than polystyrene), some of the pieces had shrunk or twisted, so components that had fitted together perfectly in the Gateguards workshop now had to be coaxed into place.

In fact, this was just the sort of complication that had engaged me with Airfix as a child. I would spend ages trimming parts to get them to fit. I didn't just take it for granted that the two fuselage halves go together; I would try them, and maybe trim them for a better fit, or file down the edges and use a bit of filler to get a perfect joint. In our case, as Gateguards had predicted, there were huge gaps where the leading edges of the wings met but a few hours with an angle grinder and a jar of filler had that looking perfect.

However, it wasn't just the look of it – again, as predicted, the scaled-up wings were too weak to support themselves and the scaled-up tailplanes were too heavy to be attached to the sides of the tail assembly without sagging. If that had happened on a 1:72 scale model – which it wouldn't have done, but bear with me – we might have solved it by putting a cocktail stick through the tailplane and a lolly stick through the wings for extra support. So that's exactly what we did – after the surreptitious overnight insertion of a few scaled-up cocktail sticks (ie, box section steel tubes) the wings were self-supporting and the tailplanes didn't sag. Much.

Then came the real test of whether our kit was going to work. It was time to lift the fuselage onto the wing assembly. With a 1:72 scale kit this is a fairly simple process. You just apply glue to both pieces, pick up the fuselage in one hand and the wing assembly in the other, and hold them together. But with a 1:1 scale kit you have to support the wing assembly on trestles in case the undercarriage gives way, lift the fuselage with a heavy duty engine hoist attached to a reinforced steel girder overhead, slide the hoist over the wing assembly and then lower the fuselage ever so carefully, listening to the creaks and groans of the wing assembly as you do so and desperately hoping that it doesn't all collapse in a heap of twisted fibreglass.

Remarkably, it didn't.

Even more remarkably, it was an almost perfect fit. And (with a little help from the trestles) it supported its own weight. A bit of filler round the joins and a little more surreptitious strengthening of the undercarriage with scaffolding tubes, and we were ready to paint our model.

ABOVE: After the insertion of a few scaled-up cocktail sticks the wings were self-supporting and the tailplanes didn't sag. Much. Then, just like I did as a kid, we marked out the camouflage scheme with a narrow line of brown paint. When we started filling it in with wide brushes the whole thing came to life very quickly.

Paint and decals – bringing BTK to life

This was the bit I was never any good at as a kid. I could never get the paint to go on evenly and I couldn't paint straight lines. Then of course there was the debate about whether or not to paint the parts before putting them together. My mate Cookie used to paint all the parts first, so he'd lay the wings and the fuselage out and paint the camouflage pattern on so that it would all line up when he put it together. Whereas I would paint some of the parts – the wheels and the engines and the insides of the cockpit and so on – but then paint the overall scheme on afterwards, which is how we did it at Cosford.

As a child I remember trying to recreate the camouflage pattern that was shown on the box. At first I made the curves in the lines between the green and the brown too gentle – they should actually be quite pronounced. And then I realised that they don't logically follow the surfaces of the plane; some of the brown patches went up the wing and then turned round and came back again with a patch of green underneath. It took me a long time to work that out, but when I started painting my planes like that they looked a lot better. I wanted the Thomas Telford kids to work all that out for themselves, so I took them to look at a few Spitfires and then we held a competition to design the camouflage scheme for our model. There was no fixed scheme for wartime camouflage patterns, so we didn't have to follow a rigid plan to make our model authentic.

The basic wartime colours of the 'temperate land' camouflage scheme were Dark Green (for anoraks, the nearest FS 595B match is 34079) and Dark Earth (30118), which were both introduced in 1936. Gateguards normally use a solvent-based paint closely matched to these colours but we had to find something that would be safe for schoolchildren to use, so we bought several litres of ordinary household emulsion in roughly matching colours: Taragon Glory 1 for the green and Earth Glaze 1 for the brown. (They weren't quite right but that, too, was just like my childhood memory of Airfix – I never had enough pocket money to buy all the colours that might crop up so I just chose a green and a brown that were roughly right.) Then, just like I did as a kid, we carefully marked out the camouflage scheme with a narrow line of green paint, and when all 26 children started filling it in with wide brushes the whole thing came to life very quickly.

The crowning glory was the decals. We didn't need a giant saucer of water to soak them in because these were actually stickers rather than transfers. We'd chosen BTK, the erroneous lettering on the very first Airfix Spitfire, and we spent ages trying to decide where to place the letters and the roundel. Eventually, we decided it wasn't crucial because (as with the camouflage pattern) there was no standard placement – Spitfires would be delivered to the airfield with camouflage only and the numbers and roundels would be added at the airfield, which meant that each different squadron had

RIGHT: Camouflage and decal schemes for the Airfix Spitfire. There was no standard scheme for wartime camouflage or lettering so each squadron had its own idiosyncracies.

BELOW: Various RAF roundels for the 1:1 Spitfire.

BOTTOM: Once a dad, always a dad: James May Snr assists two of the Thomas Telford students with the correct application of the decals.

Spitfire parade

Some Spitfire colour schemes for the new Airfix model by **Peter G. Cooksley**

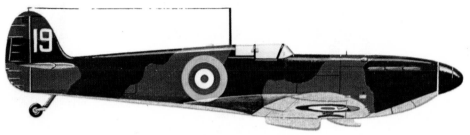

Mk I No 19 Sqdn. Duxford, August 1938

K9794. B Flt Scheme B. Upper roundels, type A1. Small serial numbers under wings. Wooden a/s. Also K9797. A Flt (red numeral) Scheme A.

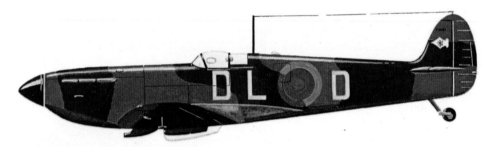

Mk I No 54 Sqdn. Hornchurch, May 1939

K9901, Scheme B. Upper roundels, type B. Black/white lower surfaces; colours divided down c/l. D/H a/s. Bulged hood. Sqdn badge on fin. Serial number repeated in reduced size on fin. Rim of former A1 roundel on fuselage overpainted.

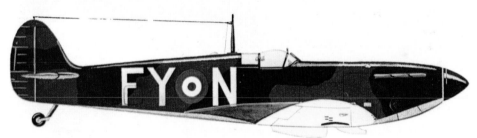

Mk I No 611 (West Lancashire) Sqdn. Digby, Feb 1940

L1036, Scheme A. Upper roundels, type B. 3 ft diameter. Under wings only, black/white. Also 'D', K9999 on fin (Scheme B). Under colours divided down c/l. Untapered radio mast. Port FY aft of roundel on both aircraft.

Mk I No 19 Sqdn. Duxford, July 1940

X4330, Scheme A. Upper roundels, type B. Lower, 3 ft diameter near tips. Also 'I' (with serifs) X4474 (Scheme A). Both a/c: Stbd QV forward of roundel and apparently VHF radio.

its own variation in the size, colour and placing of its code numbers and roundels. One inaccuracy which we faithfully copied from the Airfix decals is the bright RAF red at the centre of the roundel – the red that was used for wartime roundels was painted with red oxide, which is much duller. However, we were not making a wartime replica, we were making a scaled-up Airfix model, and that inaccuracy was one of the things that made the finished article look like a model rather than an attempt at the real thing.

And so, finally, we were ready to reveal our model to the world – if the undercarriage survived the journey through the hangar doors and into the daylight. We didn't have any scaled-up cotton strong enough to hang it from the ceiling so, instead, the 26 children lined up with two ropes ready to haul it out of the hangar as the doors were opened. We fired up the smoke machine and I went outside to introduce the children and our model to the assembled gathering of veteran Spitfire pilots, former Spitfire fitters and engineers, Airfix artists, designers and historians, an Air Commodore, an RAF band and an RAF guard of honour. Of course, it immediately started raining but that didn't dampen the sense of occasion.

> Ladies and gentlemen, thank you very much for coming to what one or two of you will still no doubt think of as No. 9 Maintenance Unit, RAF Cosford. We're here to witness the unveiling of the largest kit ever produced by the Airfix method… It has been built, as an Airfix model should be built, in a flurry of enthusiasm by young people. They are about to pull it out for you, and it's presented to you as a tribute to Airfix, to the joy that anybody has ever felt on holding a small Spitfire in the palm of their hand, to all the people who built, maintained and flew Spitfires and, most of all, to the Spitfire itself.

The band struck up, the hangar doors rolled open, and out of the smoke emerged my team of modelmakers hauling on their ropes. As the nose-cone emerged from the hangar the crowd broke into applause. Then the engine cowling and the leading edge of the wings emerged. Then the wheels lodged in the door runners and the whole thing ground to a halt. The children pulled harder and the undercarriage flexed. Was it going to collapse? Someone stepped forward to tell the children to stop pulling but before the instruction could be given the solid resin wheels bounced over the door runners and the model emerged into the afternoon in all its glory, the rain giving the wings and fuselage a dramatic sleek sheen.

Mission accomplished. There it stood, the world's first 1:1 scale Spitfire kit, and the world's biggest construction kit to be made on the Airfix principle. It looked superb. It was exactly as I'd hoped it would be. It was a childhood dream come true.

But it still couldn't quite match up to the realisation of my other childhood dream – actually flying the real thing.

I flew a Supermarine Spitfire Mk IX. It was a Spitfire. *I flew it.* Have I said that?

BELOW: There it stood, the world's first 1:1 scale Spitfire kit … a childhood dream come true. By this time we had tried to drag the Spitfire back into the hangar and the undercarriage had started to collapse, hence the trestles supporting the wings.

DESTRUCTIVE TENDENCIES

Having made *Toy Stories* I now accept that Airfix models should be the shonky products of a burst of enthusiasm and impatience, not museum pieces to sit on a shelf and gather the dust of history. Indeed, when I was a lad it was accepted practice to destroy old Airfix models once finished, and even Airfix acknowledged that this went on in some of their own research. Here are some memories from my own misspent youth – Health & Safety says don't try these at home.

Gunpowder was emptied into the *Bismarck*'s hull before the deck was cemented in place. The ship was then floated in a pond, and the superstructure set alight. The plastic tended to burn slowly, producing an authentic pall of sooty smoke, and once the flames reached the gunpowder the *Bismarck* exploded with a satisfying 'whoof'. There was a real danger of parts hitting you in the eye, and we quickly learnt that you should never go back to a *Bismarck* that hasn't gone off.

Petrol-soaked balls of cotton wool were pushed into the wheel wells of a Mitsubishi Zero and ignited. The plane was then (quickly) thrown from a bedroom window with accompanying shouts of 'Aieeee!'. Alternatively, a model was suspended from the washing line with nylon thread, and shot down with an air rifle from a sniper position behind the rockery. Ammunition was key: soft lead pellets were used to shatter a wing or the fuselage, while hard-tipped pellets were ideal for picking off a bomber's engines or gun turrets.

A plywood ramp was set up in the garage, running from a workbench to the floor. The cockpit and engine bay of an Alfa Romeo or Blower Bentley was stuffed with turps-soaked tissue paper. At the end of the ramp, a small puddle of meths was poured onto the floor and ignited, burning with an invisible flame. The car was launched down the ramp; on reaching the end it would mysteriously explode. It was essential to ensure Dad's car wasn't in the garage when carrying this out. Actually, in hindsight this was incredibly dangerous, but great fun at the time.

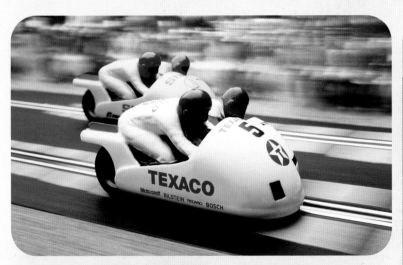

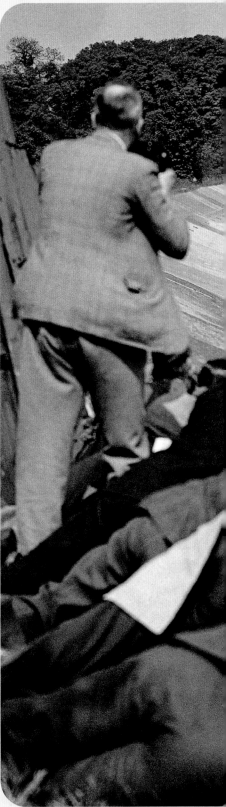

SCALEXTRIC

RACING AROUND THE WORLD'S LONGEST SLOT-RACING TRACK

WHY SCALEXTRIC?

When I was growing up my Scalextric set was somewhat eclipsed by my train set. Scalextric struck me as being slightly destructive because you just crash all the time, whereas train sets were a bit more intellectual. You can do complicated things with a railway layout, involving sidings and goods yards and shunting, and you have to think way ahead to work out how to get your wagons in the right order. By comparison, you don't have to think that far ahead in Scalextric – unless you're recreating the 2.75 miles of the Brooklands circuit, in which case you have to plan months ahead.

But as a child I didn't have enough track to recreate Brooklands, and consequently I didn't play with Scalextric as much as my trains. But that was because I hadn't yet discovered the Science of Scalextric, which I now think should be on the National Curriculum as a means of teaching kids the Newtonian Laws of Motion.

When I was about six my dad bought me the now very collectible James Bond set. I've still got some of the track but the cars wore out after far too many crashes and encounters with the baddies. I was too young for it really, and for me Scalextric didn't really come into its own until 1992 when I was fired from my job as a journalist on *Autocar* magazine. My erstwhile colleagues all chipped in to buy me a leaving present, and because it was a car magazine they bought me a Scalextric set. When I started playing with it I realised that there was actually a lot of physics involved and that Scalextric can be every bit as engaging as a train set. So I wrote a couple of articles about it and signed off by saying that if people wanted to buy me presents I'd much prefer a Scalextric car or a pork pie to champagne; since when my Scalextric collection has grown to about 30 cars and I've eaten a lot of pork pies.

> "Scalextric was the nearest thing you could get to being a racing driver"

I now have an annual Christmas Scalextric tournament with a group of my friends but I still think that it doesn't really work, in the sense that it's very difficult to have a proper race because you keep crashing. I've always maintained that there is really only a very tenuous relationship between slot-car racing and real motor racing, because the trick with slot racing is simply to drive around the track at a speed where you can finish and wait for the other bloke to crash, because he's excited about how fast he can overtake you. And once he's crashed, then you're away, because in his attempts to catch up he'll just keep crashing and then you'll win. Which is where the physics comes in.

In order to improve the situation I redesigned my Scalextric set-up by putting a train-set controller in line with the Scalextric hand throttle, so that I could reduce the power to the track. Then I carefully put black insulating tape over the rear wheels of the cars – precision-fitted with a scalpel so that I had a very thin tyre over the existing tyre, but one which was quite slippery. And that way the cars hardly ever came off the track, because the reduced power and the slick tyres meant there wasn't enough power and grip to go fast enough to crash. But if you did use too much power on the corners they skidded and slid sideways, which cost you a lot of time, whereas if you were very deft and gentle with it you went around a bit quicker, so it then became about the skill on the throttle. And despite the fact that the cars wouldn't go as fast it was much more like real racing – it became a true game of skill not interrupted by the crashes and having to walk across the room to put the car back on the track, which totally corrupts the race as far as I'm concerned.

For that reason my favourite Scalextric car is an old yellow Mini Cooper from the 1970s. The reason I like it is that the tyres behave as if they're already covered in insulating tape, because when the cars get very old the rubber deteriorates and the tyres become much harder and very slippery. When you drive the Mini it slides and skids and wheelspins, so you have to be really really gentle with the throttle to get it to accelerate off the line. Obviously you can't feel the grip like you can in a real car, but you have to carefully judge this one, squeezing it to get it going and then accelerating very gently to the bend, backing off as you go round and then squeezing it a bit more – otherwise it slides sideways and you really lose speed and grip. Definitely one for experts only. If they made Scalextric cars with 30-year-old tyres I'd be in my element, and Scalextric would require more of the skills of real racing.

When it first came out Scalextric was the nearest thing you could get to being a racing driver at home (on the carpet or on your dining table), but now that there are such realistic computer driving simulations Scalextric fulfils a different role. It suffers in the face of video games because they're fantastically sophisticated, and you appear to be actually sitting in the car, but what I like about Scalextric is that it's not pretending to be real cars and real driving. It has become a family game in a very tangible way. It's become an electrified board game, with playing pieces that you take round the track just like going round the board in Monopoly – except that you control pieces remotely and you make your moves much more quickly than when you have to throw a die.

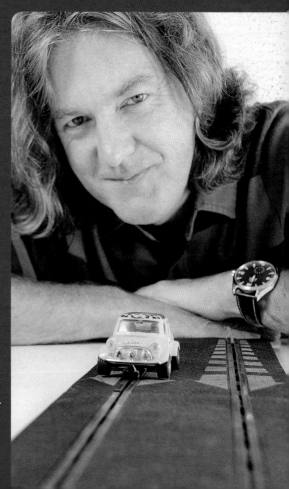

The other important thing about Scalextric over computer games is that it's a sociable activity. I concede that you can test your cars on your own and measure their maximum speed and try and beat your own lap time but that soon loses its appeal. It's really about the company. That's why you get Scalextric clubs whereas, as far as I know, you don't get PlayStation clubs. Yes, people play computer games competitively online but you never get together in an old Scout hut like Scalextric people do. But the best way to play Scalextric – the only way I do it these days, when it comes out once a year at Christmas – is to have a handful of mates round, draw up a leader board and then everyone race each other. It's like darts – it's an excuse for getting together and drinking. In fact, I don't know why they don't have Scalextric in pubs. Now there's an idea that would revive our moribund licensing industry – pub Scalextric. I can see it now – the Theakston's delivery truck (catalogue number C997) bombing down the Lounge Bar Straight and lapping the Gnatspiss Lager truck (C001) as it negotiates the Leap of Death over the bar flap.

SCALEX GOES ELECTRIC

No one who knows the story behind the birth of Scalextric would ever fall into the common error of calling it Scalectrix. And that is because Scalextric was a development of an earlier range of clockwork model cars called Scalex. It was therefore a natural progression to call the electric version Scalextric, a name that is now famous around the globe, despite its frequent mispronunciation.

Little is known about the early life of Bertram 'Fred' Francis, the man who started it all. Born in London in October 1919, he left school at the age of 14 and subsequently developed an enthusiasm and aptitude for both engineering and business. In 1939, at the age of 20, he set up a tool-making workshop which was kept busy throughout World War II. When hostilities ended he decided to channel his business resources and machinery into fulfilling a childhood ambition – he wanted to be a toymaker. And so he founded Minimodels Ltd in 1947 and, from his workshop in Mill Hill, north-west London, began making

TOP: Minimodels Clockwork Shunting Train. Of limited play value.

ABOVE AND BELOW: Minimodels Petrol Tanker and Articulated Truck. The gear and mechanism release levers protrude from the cab roof and the radiator grille.

sophisticated mechanical tinplate toys and models. These included a toy typewriter, replica speed record cars, a clockwork petrol tanker and an articulated lorry, both with forward and reverse gears, a clockwork shunter locomotive and two ranges of clockwork cars: Scalex and Startex.

The first Scalex model, introduced in 1952, was a 1:32 scale Jaguar XK120 powered by a groundbreaking keyless clockwork motor that Francis patented the same year. Instead of being wound by a key, like other contemporary clockwork motors, the Scalex motor had a fifth wheel built into the base of the car just behind and inboard of the driver's side front wheel. The motor was wound by pressing the car down onto a hard surface to engage the winding wheel and then pulling the car backwards, after which it would surge forwards under its own power for a distance of about ten feet. There is no record of whether or not it was capable of reaching a scale speed of 120 mph, after which the original XK120 was named.

Demand for the Scalex Jaguar and other Minimodels toys was so great that in 1954 Francis moved his business to a larger factory in Havant, Hampshire, which enabled him not only to mass produce toys but also to indulge his passion for sailing. For much of the time he lived aboard his 46-foot motor yacht *Yvalda* in Chichester harbour, close to Havant, so that he wouldn't have to commute from London to the factory. He was also a keen pilot, and owned his own Piper Cherokee light aircraft. Sailing and flying were expensive hobbies then, as now, but that wasn't a problem for Francis, whose business was booming – he extended the Scalex range to seven cars, and at the peak of production the factory was turning out 7,000 models a week. The Scalex cars were all accurate scale replicas of sports cars of the day, with two Grand Prix cars (a Ferrari 375 and a Maserati 250F) at 1:28 scale and five sports and saloon cars at 1:32 scale – the scale at which the core Scalextric range has been modelled ever since.

Francis was a restless inventor. Once something had proved successful he moved on to the next thing, so instead of expanding the Scalex range yet further he introduced a new range of three Startex models. These had similar motors but instead of being wound by the fifth wheel they were wound by pulling a string. On

ABOVE: The first Scalex model: a 1:32 scale Jaguar XK120, with complete instructions on the box: 'Push down – pull back – off she goes!'

BELOW: Fred Francis (foreground) cuts the first sod at the site of his new factory in Havant, Hampshire, in 1954.

the Startex Jaguar and Austin Healey this was attached to the exhaust, and on the Startex Sunbeam Alpine it was attached to the steering wheel, which made for a bizarre play experience, as the cars powered forward trailing their exhaust or steering wheel behind. In fact, the Scalex and Startex ranges seem to have been invented in the wrong order: an invisible fifth wheel hidden beneath the car is a far more elegant and subtle way of winding a motor than a string, which is sucked back in as the car moves forward. Had Scalex been invented second it would no doubt have been seen as a vast improvement on Startex.

According to most accounts, sales of clockwork cars declined gradually in the mid-1950s, but, according to Diana Francis's obituary of her husband, demand collapsed suddenly in early 1956, threatening the future of Minimodels. Either way a new innovation was clearly required, and Francis found the inspiration he needed at the London Toy Fair. There, according to Diana Francis, 'Fred saw a display featuring battery-powered cars running around a track, but without user control. He saw at once that this lacked any real play value – which his Scalex cars could add.'

Francis immediately adapted the Scalex Maserati 250F for an electric motor and created a two-lane track with metal slots, which meant that models could be independently controlled – if 'control' is the right word. Such control as existed was primitive by today's standards – the power was either on or off – but the result, when Francis launched it at the Harrogate Toy Fair in January 1957, was a phenomenon. Scalextric was born.

TOP: Startex model of the Sunbeam Alpine, and the winding mechanism attached to the steering wheel. **ABOVE:** The Aston Martin DB2 in production at the Scalex factory in Havant. **BELOW:** The first ever Scalextric cars: two versions of the Maserati 250F – adapted from the Scalex model to carry an electric motor – take to the grid on original Scalextric track. The earliest sets had no hand controls, just a simple on-off switch on the terminal box.

From tinplate to plastic

When adapting Scalex cars for Scalextric, Francis used a variation on an earlier theme – the guide and pick-up for the electric current were incorporated in a revolving fifth wheel known as a gimbal, now at the centre of the underpan behind the front axle. The first Scalextric set contained two Maserati 250Fs to race against each other; these were followed in spring 1958 by an electric version of the Scalex Ferrari Type 375, and later still by the Austin Healey 100/6. All of these tinplate Scalextric cars had removable rubber drivers, which came in two sizes; one for the 1:28 scale cars and one for the 1:32 scale. The two-lane slotted track was made of hard rubber and, although it was superseded in 1963 by plastic, it is still compatible with modern track more than 50 years later. All that is needed is a converter straight to connect one system to the other.

Francis had devised a revolutionary model racing system, but it wasn't perfect. The gimbal pick-up was efficient but it provided no friction to slow the cars down once the power was released, which made it difficult to corner, and if cars cornered too fast the gimbal often jumped out of the slot. It was soon replaced with a deeper gimbal (and later still by a pin guide and then a blade) but the problem of batteries running out remained a frustration for Scalextric fans until transformers were introduced in the early 1960s.

However, all the ingredients of modern Scalextric were in place, and Fred Francis had successfully laid the foundations for what would become 'the world's favourite model racing system'. But again, either bored or exhausted by his success, he decided to move on. In November 1958 he sold his rapidly expanding business to Lines Bros, the owners of Tri-ang. Leaving Scalextric to achieve world dominance under various owners, Francis followed up his passion for sailing with an alternative career in marine engineering. He put his inventive talents to use designing and manufacturing furling gear, winches and windlasses, and Francis Winches gained such repute that they were adopted by the RNLI and are still in use today. In 1985 he was diagnosed with cancer and given a year to live. With typical fortitude he proved the doctors wrong, battling the cancer for 13 years before he died on 6 January 1998.

ABOVE: The second Scalextric car: the Scalex Ferrari Type 375 adapted for an electric motor, with the gimbal pick-up visible on the underpan.

BELOW: Original patent drawings for the Scalextric track system and the proposed internal arrangement of Scalextric cars, showing the gimbal pick-up and motor.

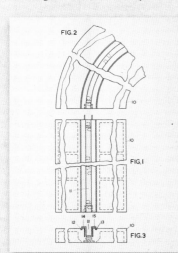

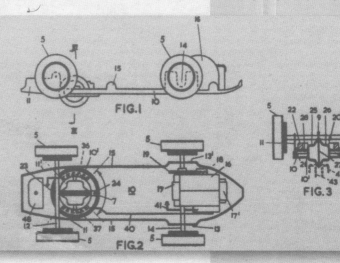

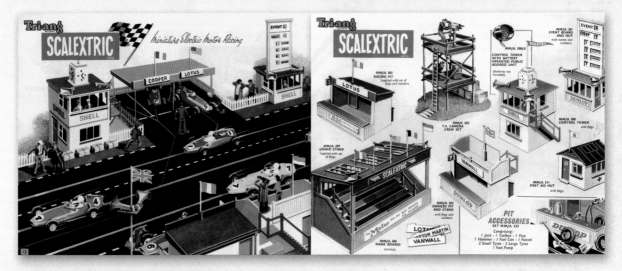

Meanwhile, Lines Bros had taken Scalextric from strength to strength. Soon after acquiring Minimodels, Lines Bros began introducing trackside accessories. This was vital to the early success of Scalextric because in those days slot-racing was as much about modelling as racing. Scalextric's Promotions Manager Adrian Norman explains: 'Nowadays it's more about racing and there are fewer accessories, but back in the 50s and 60s accessories filled out the range handsomely with novel grandstands, pit buildings, control towers, a first-aid post, timekeeper's hut, entrance building and turnstiles. You could make up quite a realistic, detailed circuit. It was much more of a modelling hobby, mirroring what was happening with model railways at that time.'

But that was about to start changing. Early in 1960 Lines Bros introduced a new generation of much faster, plastic-bodied cars – the true precursors of today's Scalextric cars – and a new variable speed thumb-operated controller, which made for much more realistic racing. These two innovations marked the start of Scalextric's transition from being primarily a modelling hobby to a racing one.

The first plastic model to be introduced was the Lotus 16, catalogue number C54, soon followed by the Vanwall (C55), Lister Jaguar (C56) and Aston Martin DBR1 (C57). The latter three were chosen for their recent successes on the track, the Aston Martin having won Le Mans the previous year, the Vanwall the Formula One Constructors' Title in 1958 and the Lister Jaguar the British Empire Trophy in 1957. The Lotus 16, dubbed the 'mini-Vanwall', was chosen because it was the new kid on the block, and seemed destined for great things when it entered Formula One in 1958. The real Lotus 16 never realised its early promise but the Scalextric version proved very popular and remained in production for six years. The drivers of these cars had even less chance of gripping the steering wheel than manually challenged drivers of the original tinplate cars, because the new drivers didn't have hands at all – merely a head and shoulders plonked on a flat base in the cockpit. This situation was rectified very quickly: more realistic drivers appeared soon afterwards with, at long last, their hands on the wheel.

ABOVE: In 1958 Fred Francis sold Scalextric to Tri-ang, which almost immediately began introducing trackside accessories as seen in this early Tri-ang catalogue.

BELOW: 'Competition Class Cars' from the 1961 Scalextric catalogue. Fortunately the competitions in question were not spelling competitions, which would have left the 'Porche' at a distinct disadvantage.

FAMOUS CIRCUITS

Silverstone

Silverstone is the fastest and largest of all the British aerodrome circuits. As a disused air field it was taken over after the war by the Royal Automobile Club, who held the first post war R.A.C. Grand Prix there in 1948. It has been completely re-surfaced.

ENGLAND

SILVERSTONE

SCX.1470B

2 LANE

8 Standard Curve	PT/51	2 Straight "A"	PT/57
1 Inner Curve "G"	PT/52	5 Straight "C"	PT/59
4 Outer Curve	PT/53	20 Straight "D"	PT/60
4 Half Standard Curve	PT/54	1 Starting Line	PT/63

14' 6" x 9' 9"   4·42m. x 2·97m. approx.

LANE LENGTH 37' 6"   11.47m. approx.

It has no slow corners and spectators and drivers can enjoy the thrills provided by a var... of really fast corners. The lap distance is about 3 miles, and being situated off the Towcester-Brackley Road (A.43) it is equally accessible from London and the Midlands via the A.5 road.

LEFT: This diagram shows the Scalextric track pieces required to make an early Silverstone circuit (circa 1966), featuring original Woodcote Corner and Becketts Corner layouts. A modern equivalent would need considerably more track to incorporate the many alterations that have been made at Silverstone over the years.

BELOW: Formula One's Lewis Hamilton tries his hand at Scalextric Digital on the Abbey-Santander Silverstone-styled circuit prior to winning the 2008 British Grand Prix.

How to achieve success in track building

There are only 12 basic sections in the Scalextric track system, yet the variety of circuits that can be made is effectively infinite. Problems usually centre around persuading the two ends of the circuit to join up under the sideboard.

It will join up, somehow, and usually by the judicious insertion of one of the short straights or curves somewhere further back. These are the pieces every set must have, but which most people overlook.

There are now virtual circuit design tools available on the internet, but they are not really necessary. Simply envisage the track in your mind, taking furniture and obstructions into account, and then start laying, aiming always to arrive back where you began with the start/finish straight.

The two ends will not quite line up. Now stand back and it should be clear where the odd short piece is needed. It will work. It is a Euclidian absolute.

Short sections worth having:
C8236 Short straight
C8200 Quarter straight
C8202 Radius 1 curve
C8278 Quarter curve
C8201 Radius 1 hairpin

With the advent of plastic cars and variable speed controllers Scalextric had come of age. Although it has been refined, there were no fundamental changes to the system until the arrival of Sport Digital in 2004, which is testament to how well-thought-out was the original concept. Computer-aided design and improved injection-moulding techniques have led to a greater level of finish and more intricate detail in the models but today's models still run on the original track, and vice versa. In fact, the history of Scalextric is not a tale of massive breakthroughs and innovative leaps: it is a catalogue of fascinating incremental improvements, inventive additional features and the occasional bizarre tangential development, which means that Scalextric in the 21st century remains very much the embodiment of Fred Francis's original idea.

ABOVE: Racing legend Stirling Moss playing with an early Scalextric set in 1958. But possibly not for long.

Racing for pole position: the 1960s

In the race to stay ahead of the competition, Scalextric has always relied on continuous improvements in the detail of its models and on being first with new innovations. This was helped in 1961 by a move to a larger factory in another part of Havant, which facilitated improvements in the production process. These improvements are visible in the two elaborately detailed vintage racing cars that appeared the following year: a 1929 Bentley 4.5 and a 1933 Alfa Romeo 8C. With these superb models Scalextric enthusiasts could relive the glory of Le Mans from the mid-20s to the mid-30s, which the Bentley won five times (in 1924 and 1927–30 inclusive) and the Alfa four times (1931–34 inclusive).

The year 1961 also saw the introduction of the first series of Scalextric cars to have working head- and tail-lights, although the added realism was slightly marred by the fact that, unlike real cars, the brightness of the lights varied according to how much throttle the car was given. At the same time two types of lighting accessories were introduced: one set that could be fitted inside the pit buildings, and a set of overhead floodlights on poles.

The first Scalextric model to have working lights was the Lister Jaguar (originally C56, the lit version being given the number E1), followed by two Aston Martins, a Ferrari 250GT and lastly, in 1964, the collectors' dream – the very rare Marshal's Car (E5). The Marshal's Car (an Aston Martin DB4 GT) not only had working head- and tail-lights but also a lighted dome on the roof, and is particularly valuable to collectors if it still has the two white flags that slot into the front and rear bumpers. For some reason, headlights were then abandoned until a second series of lighted cars appeared in 1980, starting with the Ford Escort Mexico (C118) and the Porsche 935 Turbo (C119), which initially had headlights only. Later models in the series had head- and tail-lights, and some had brake lights, which came on when the throttle on the hand-control was released. The Police Rover 3500, released in

BELOW: The Police Patrol Rover 3500 from 1981, complete with working blues 'n' twos.

C.362 Police Car. Length 5¼" 133 mm.
Roof light cluster illuminates when running.

1981, had full blues 'n' twos – a working siren and flashing blue roof lights.

The core element of Scalextric always has been and always will be 1:32 scale racing cars, but Scalextric has never been shy of trying out variations on the theme. The 1962 Typhoon motorcycle and sidecar combination was the first spin-off – literally as well as metaphorically, given that these intriguing models were so light that when cornering they were prone to either tip over or spin through 180° and head off at high speed in the wrong direction. The Typhoon came in red, green, blue and yellow, and early models had a skid instead of a front wheel. In 1963 it was joined by the 'left-hand drive' Hurricane, which had the sidecar on the right rather than on the left. The Hurricane also had a front wheel, a feature that was soon incorporated in the Typhoon in place of the skid. Both models remained in production for eight years before being discontinued in 1970. However, bikes have periodically reappeared in the Scalextric range, with updated versions of the motorcycle combination introduced in 1980, 1990 and 1995, and a British Superbike Championship set in 2005.

Another departure from the core theme was 1:24 scale Go-Karts, which were introduced in 1963. This reflected the increasing popularity of real karting, but while the real thing has remained popular the Scalextric version has not. Like the motorcycle combination, the Karts were too light to give the same performance or racing excitement as the cars, and they only remained in production for five years.

Meanwhile, in the more familiar Scalextric territory of motor racing, new model cars were introduced thick and fast throughout the 1960s, with the rate of new releases rising from four a year for the first three years of the decade to an average of 14 a year from 1966 to 1969. Of all the models introduced during the 1960s two stood out at the time and still remain the most sought after by collectors. These are the Bugatti Type 59 (C70 and C95) and the Auto Union C Type (C71 and C96), which are extremely rare – particularly the Bugatti – because so few were originally made. This, explains Adrian Norman, is because they were made to order rather than being mass-produced: 'They appeared in the catalogue and you could order them from your toyshop but the shop would then have to place a special order with the factory. They were handmade because they were too expensive and too complicated to be made in bulk. And they're even more expensive today – you can pay up to £9,000 for the C70 Bugatti!'

Both of these remarkable models were introduced in 1963 as an extension to the range of vintage racing cars, but by then interest in vintage models was in decline, which is another reason why so few were made. They remained in the catalogue until 1965, when they were replaced by 'race tuned' versions (with a blade rather than a pin guide to slot into the track), which were numbered C95 and C96 and remained in the catalogues until 1968.

A SELECTION FROM THE SCALEXTRIC RANGE OF RACING MODELS
(1/30 & 1/32)

C/67 LOTUS

C/72 B.R.M.

C/69 FERRARI G.T.

C/74 AUSTIN HEALEY

C/70 BUGATTI

B/I TYPHOON

K/I GO-KART

E/5 MARSHAL'S CAR

ABOVE: The Scalextric range in the 1964 Gamages catalogue, including two of the collectors' favourites: the E/5 Marshal's Car and the extremely rare C70 Bugatti.

The real Type 59 was the last of Ettore Bugatti's Grand Prix cars tasting success in the Belgian and Algerian Grands Prix of 1934 and setting a lap record of 140 mph for cars of its class at Brooklands. The real Auto Union was from the same era, designed by Ferdinand Porsche and built with state funding from Hitler, who was determined to show off German engineering to the world as part of his propaganda machine. The Auto Union A, B and C Types had several Grand Prix successes from 1934 to 1937 with the C Type being the most successful. The Auto Union was also the more popular Scalextric model, which is why the Bugatti is now considerably rarer and more valuable.

The 1960s were the heyday of slot-car racing, and the decade ended on a high for Scalextric, with a massive range on offer including more than 30 cars, nearly as many types of track section and no less than 52 accessories. The 1970s, though, proved to be a different story.

From the Swinging 60s to the Sorry 70s

The 1970s began with two unsuccessful innovations, and with hindsight these can be viewed as a sign of things to come. In 1970, despite the earlier lukewarm reception for motorbikes and Go-Karts, Scalextric tried another variation on the core theme: horse racing. The Jump Jockey Electric Steeplechasing Set featured a double-decker track, with the horses galloping along on poles, which protruded through the upper, green track, propelled by a four-wheeled buggy that ran on the lower track – weird and not very wonderful. The idea was revisited in the 1990s with four horse-racing sets: Ascot, Newmarket, the Derby and Australia's Gold Coast Cup. The horses were slightly more plausible than the Jump Jockey horses, being mounted on a four-wheeled chassis that would run on standard track, but these sets proved little more popular than the 1970s version.

The lesson was that Scalextric is really about motor racing. But even in that area not all innovations succeeded: for example, 'You Steer'. The concept was good but the reality was not: a steering wheel on the side of the hand control reversed the polarity of the motor, shifting a lever under the car, which made it slide up to 2 cm either side of the slot. The idea was to steer round an array of obstacles that were available as accessories or as part of the You Steer sets. However, controlling the system was difficult and the complication of steering round obstacles did little to add to the excitement of racing. Production of You Steer ended after just two years.

The cost of introducing Jump Jockey and You Steer, both in 1970, cannot have helped the finances of Lines Bros, the parent company. Profits had been falling since 1966, and in 1970 these turned to losses. Like the other companies in the group, Minimodels was instructed to make savings but such savings as were made were not enough to save the group, and in 1971 Lines Bros went into liquidation.

ABOVE: A 'pistol-grip' variable hand throttle, first introduced in 1968.

BELOW: Scalextric flirted unsuccessfully with slot-horse-racing in 1970. Despite the lack of success the idea was revisited in the 1990s with four horse-racing sets. These included the Gold Coast Cup set, which featured horses pulling two-wheeled 'Sulkies', as seen here.

The following year Minimodels – along with several other Lines Bros companies including Rovex-Tri-ang Ltd, makers of Tri-ang Hornby – was sold to Dunbee-Combex-Marx. This change of ownership subsequently saw production of Scalextric move to its current home in Margate, Kent, which was at that time the home of Tri-ang Hornby.

Under Dunbee-Combex-Marx (DCM) Scalextric proceeded with more caution, rationalising the range of accessories and producing a mere 46 new models in the entire decade – a far cry from the heady days of 14 new models a year at the end of the 1960s. Not only that but many of the models were very basic and relatively sparse on detail. However, this was perhaps not surprising given the economic climate of the 1970s, with an oil crisis, a miners' strike, a three-day week, massive inflation and frequent power cuts.

However, there was some good news – by the late 1970s the lack of moulded detail in models was offset by the introduction of a new printing process, known as tampo printing, which vastly improved the level of decorative detail. Liveries could now be printed in full, clear detail directly onto the shell of the cars, obviating the need for stickers or transfers with all their attendant problems of non-alignment, non-adhesion, wear and tear and the flakiness that came with age.

Among the first models to benefit from the new tampo printing process was the March 2-4-0 (C129), which was first introduced in 1978 and has proved to be one of Scalextric's most popular models, despite the fact that the real thing never saw F1 action. The logic behind Formula One cars having six wheels was that more rubber on the track means more traction transferred from the engine to the tarmac. But bigger wheels create more aerodynamic drag; therefore a greater number of smaller wheels should in theory be advantageous. Tyrrell therefore developed a six-wheeler with two standard rear and four small front wheels, while the Oxfordshire firm of March Engineering developed one with four small driven rear wheels. The Tyrrell saw some F1 success in 1976 but the March never saw action; on testing the handling proved poor and March did not have the resources to develop the car to race standard.

In the world of Scalextric, a Spanish import of the Tyrrell Ford (C48) was advertised in the 1973 catalogue but never

released. However, Scalextric fans eventually had the chance to try six-wheel racing when the March 2-4-0 was released in 1978. And the story has a happy ending for March. According to the Scalextric 50th anniversary book, March's royalties on sales of the Scalextric model exceeded the cost of building the 2-4-0 in the first place.

Notwithstanding the success of the March and other models, the 1970s had taken their toll on DCM. In 1980, despite the continuing popularity of Scalextric and Tri-ang Hornby (now known as Hornby Railways) history repeated itself – DCM went into liquidation and Scalextric was once again looking for a new owner. This time Scalextric was led into the future, along with Hornby Railways, by an independent company newly formed by a management buyout – Hornby Hobbies Ltd.

Back on track: from the 1980s into the 21st century

Adrian Norman is in no doubt that the 1980s represented a new beginning for Scalextric, not only on the business front but also in terms of modelling:

The level of detail in the original Scalextric model cars and accessories was superb by the standards of the time because there was money to be spent on them. In the 60s the big hobbies that people would spend their money on were slot-racing or model railways. In the 70s the cars began to get a bit basic. They weren't as detailed because things were in decline and the first electronic games were coming in. But in the 80s we started getting more detail back into the cars. And at the same time we started developing our own electronic control and accessories.

BELOW: The 1991 World Championship Set brought four-lane racing to your living room, with two Williams Hondas and two Lotuses (a Lotus Honda Turbo and a Lotus Renault 98T) to race independently or as teams.

BOTTOM: The McLaren Mercedes MP4/10 (left) and the Williams Renault FW 15C (right) battle it out in the 1996 catalogue.

These accessories included a trio of electronic systems designed to meet the competition from the fledgling computer games market head on: Sound Track, Think Tank and Fuel Tank. Sound Track, as the name suggests, provided a soundtrack for the race: tyre squeals, gear changes, engine noise, the works. Fuel Tank would calculate how fast each car was using up fuel depending on how it was being driven, taking into account speed and rate of acceleration, and would cut power to the car if it ran out of fuel; this introduced a tactical element to racing in addition to raw speed. Both of these accessories were in fact updates of 1960s ideas: 20 years earlier sound effects were available on a 45 rpm vinyl EP, and there was a 'Fuel Load Gauge', which had the same effect as the 1980s Fuel Tank. The difference was that the 1980s versions were electronic and had modern-looking (for the time) housings that made the side of the track look like the bridge of the Starship *Enterprise*.

The third element of the electronic triumvirate was Think Tank, an electronic timer, which could be programmed to give digital readouts of average overall speed, average lap time and fastest lap time. This, too, was a computerised version of an old idea: the 1970s 'Speed Computer', which was not a computer at all but a cardboard disc with dials for time and distance that could be aligned to show average speed.

Meanwhile, the rate of new releases was creeping back up, with an average of more than eight new models a year for the decade; a figure that looked a lot higher when colour and livery variations were taken into account. In addition to the usual mix of track and rally cars, the 1980s saw the introduction of Superstox in 1981 and a range of trucks from 1982 onwards. Superstox took Scalextric into the world of stock-car racing, with swivelling guide blades, which had the cars sliding or spinning right round on the corners, and removable body panels designed to fall off if the car was crashed or

ABOVE: The Roadtrain Low-Loader, first released in 1982, and the T45 Team Roadtrain (1985) as featured in the 1985 catalogue.

BELOW: A range of accessories was available for Scalextric layouts in the 1980s, including grandstands, a control tower, pit crew figures and the famous Dunlop bridge.

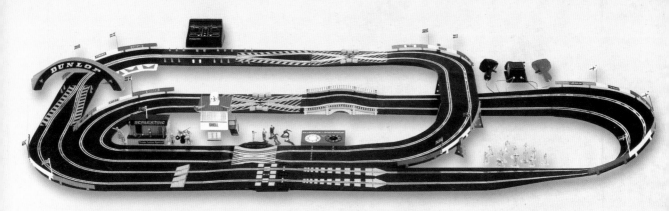

rammed. Trucking first reached the Scalextric track in the form of an articulated lowloader and several variations on the British Leyland Road Train liveried as race transporters. In 1984 Scalextric went on to introduce four- and six-wheel racing rigs based on the tractor unit of the Road Train.

Over the years, there have been more than a dozen different Scalextric motors. The original was specially designed by Fred Francis to fit the modified Scalex cars, and when Tri-ang introduced plastic cars they were powered by a Tri-ang Railways motor. Since then improvements in design have meant that motors have become ever smaller and lighter, which was good from a design point of view but bad from a performance point of view; the more lightweight cars were becoming, the harder it was to keep them on the track. This problem was solved in 1988 by the introduction of Magnatraction. As the name suggests, this innovation involved a magnet, which was located in the underpan and helped to keep the car on the track – unless you cornered too fast, sliding the car so that the magnet was no longer over the metal slot.

By now Scalextric fans were becoming accustomed to more and more intricate detail in their models but that was becoming increasingly expensive to achieve in Britain. In the mid-1990s Hornby Hobbies made the decision to move production to China, where cheaper manufacturing costs meant that far more detailed models could be produced for a fraction of the cost of manufacturing them at home. This meant that more resources could be spent on development and design back in Britain, resulting in another quantum leap in the detail of the end product. The last Scalextric cars and Hornby trains rolled off the Margate production lines in 1999, after which the machines fell silent and the factory floor became a distribution centre for products arriving from the Far East.

But Margate was still the headquarters of Scalextric, and it was here that the ideas were generated and the design work carried out to maintain Scalextric's position as 'the world's favourite model racing system'. In 2004 came the first truly fundamental change since the on-off control was replaced by a variable-power controller, and it was a change that would no doubt have been embraced by Fred Francis, had the technology been

ABOVE: This large layout shows the electronic Sound Track and Fuel Tank systems released in 1986.

BELOW: A superbly detailed Aston Martin DBR9 in famous Gulf Oil livery, as it appeared at the 2008 24 Hours of Le Mans race, which was the 40th anniversary of the legendary Gulf GT40 win. Car 007, with Heinz-Harald Frentzen, Andrea Piccini and Karl Wendlinger behind the wheel, finished fourth in the GT1 class.

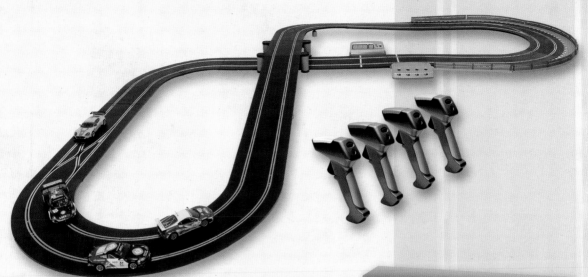

ABOVE: Scalextric sport track with digital control, which made it possible (at last!) to run more than one car on a single lane. Leading is a Ferrari F430, followed by a Porsche 911 GT3, a Maserati MC12 and an Aston Martin DBR9.

RIGHT: Scalextric regularly release new models of classic cars, like this limited edition pair of Alan Mann racing saloons. The set consists of a 1965 Ford Lotus Cortina and a 1968 BTCC Ford Escort.

available to him. Sport Digital meant that for the first time it was possible to run more than one car on each lane. In fact, it was now possible to run up to six cars on a two-lane track, each with independent control, even if they all ended up on the same lane. To add to the excitement, a lane-change button was added to the hand control, enabling racers to change lane for overtaking or blocking, or to divert to the pits.

The way it worked was that instead of the hand control varying the amount of power being delivered to the slot in the track, as it had traditionally always done, it now sent digital signals to a chip in the car. Each car's chip would respond only to the relevant hand controller, which meant that the track could be continuously fed with 15 volts; the signal from the hand control simply told the car how much of that 15 volts to take. Lane change was by a button on the hand control, which told the car to switch lanes at the next crossover point – the skill lay in predicting whether or not your opponents were going to change lanes as well. With that level of control, Scalextric had truly become slot-racing for the 21st century.

Fred Francis would be proud at how much and yet how little Scalextric has changed since he sold Minimodels in 1958. Sport Digital may be a fundamental change to the way the cars are controlled but the system as a whole is still essentially the same – though vastly more refined – as the one he invented. More than 50 years on, Scalextric models are still being designed and engineered to the highest standards of the time; the latest technology is still being used to add ever more realism to the racing experience; and all around the world people are still mispronouncing the name as Scalectrix.

REBUILDING BROOKLANDS

'Ladies and gentlemen, for one final time these ancient crumbling banks, these hallowed straights, these venerable trees will resonate to the bellow of raw competition and the howl of the excited crowd…'

So I boomed, in my best Churchillian rhetoric, to the assembled enthusiasts at the site of the legendary Brooklands Racing Circuit in Weybridge, Surrey.

I was here to accomplish two challenges: to recreate Brooklands, the world's first purpose-built motor racing circuit, in Scalextric, and by so doing to set a new Guinness World Record for the longest slot-car track ever raced. The real Brooklands track had seen its last puff of exhaust on 7 August 1939 and here we were, almost exactly 70 years later, attempting to reconstruct the 2.75 mile circuit with more than 14,500 short sections of plastic track, two 1:32 scale cars, 200 hand controllers and 100 12-volt batteries. The crowd of nearly 400 volunteers and Scalextric 'professionals' (the dedicated cognoscenti of the slot-racing world) had gathered to race the cars and to help lay the track. I was doing my best to inspire them.

For 70 years people have come to Brooklands to lovingly run their fingers through the dust of motor sport history – it's that magical. And if Brooklands is the spiritual home of British motor sport, Scalextric is the origin of childhood fantasies of Grand Prix glory. What child hasn't dreamt of taking the chequered flag as they power their car along the straight and round the final bend before crashing into the dining-table leg? There is a romance about both ideas and here we were attempting to capture that spirit of youthful adventure and misty-eyed dreams.

However, since 1939, the war effort and the local council had done their best to dash those dreams by installing a number of obstacles on the original racing circuit. In order to reconstruct Brooklands, therefore, we must somehow negotiate a business park, a pond, a river bridge, a 14-foot-high fence, a tunnel (enhanced by a rather pungent dead fox), a housing estate, a supermarket car park and two road crossings – to name but a few of the challenges facing us that never faced the Brooklands drivers of yore *or* the existing record holders for the world's longest slot-racing track.

ABOVE: Me addressing the assembled crowd of volunteers, inspiring them in my best Churchillian rhetoric.

ABOVE: Drivers running towards their cars for the start of the Brooklands Six Hours Race on 29 June 1929. **RIGHT:** Nearly 400 volunteers and Scalextric 'professionals' turned up to watch me volunteer, though for what exactly was never made clear.

BROOKLANDS MUSEUM

SLOT RACING EVENT & JAMES MAY VOLUNTEERS

P →

The way our record-breaking attempt had been conceived was that we would recreate the circuit and then stage a race between Scalextric Professionals and raw local recruits from the Brooklands neighbourhood, including the people through whose back gardens the track would run – henceforth known as the Locals and the Pros.

But the logistics of setting up the track was to cast a huge and potentially show-stopping shadow over the race itself. The Spirit of Competition would have to wait until the obstacles had been overcome by the Spirit of Improvisation and Dodgy Engineering.

Simeon the Resourceful

Take for instance the pond – or 'the Pond', as it should be known in due deference to its treacherous possibilities.

The day before the race, on a windy Saturday morning, I pitch up to see if I can lend a hand. The Pond is a sight to trouble any dedicated motor-racing fan: 60 metres of murky ornamental pondwater where once concrete track had provided surer passage. Artificially planted with reeds and populated by rather large carp, it stands three-quarters of the way round the original Brooklands circuit. Luckily Sim Oakley, our resourceful project manager, has an ingenious solution to the problem of getting the cars across the water – an improvised bridge of plywood supported by standard pipe insulation tubes. It's a triumph of mind over matter and, more importantly, mind over budget.

In order to get the Scalextric track onto the bridge, though, it becomes clear that someone will have to get into the Pond. And that's when I hear the dreaded words, 'James, see that dry suit over there?'

Ten minutes later I'm up to my neck in frankly fetid water with carp swimming round me menacingly. A metal pole, with which I'm gingerly testing the depth of the Pond, is my only means of defence. This is a rare occasion when I would have been grateful for an intervention from our good friend the Health and Safety officer.

To make matters worse, the bridge keeps drifting away from me in the strong breeze, which could easily blow a small plastic car off the track – and the test-run reveals a potentially record-foiling hazard: Scalextric cars do not float.

The rules of the competition, as stipulated by those fine fellows at Guinness World Records, dictate that the same car must complete the entire circuit – a lost, smashed or drowned car means starting again from the beginning with a

replacement. In other words, if you come off at the Pond, go to jail, do not pass 'Go', do not collect £200. Actually, it's worse than that. You *do* return to 'Go', but 'Go' is about two miles away. Now that makes my childhood memories of Scalextric look positively rosy – even the constant bane of retrieving a car from the other side of the living room seems as nothing compared with a two-mile hike back to the starting grid.

And not only that but *both* cars have to complete the circuit for the record to stand, so we didn't even have the option of letting the first one drown in the hope that the second would make it.

My brief to the Locals (who naturally I want to win) will be simple: go easy on the bridge over the Pond, particularly if race day is as windy as today. I may not pass that nugget on to the Pros, who are already showing, to my mind, a reckless self-confidence – they blithely predict a race time of around 20 minutes with few crashes.

If the Pond taxed my swimming skills, Dead Fox Tunnel challenged my olfactory defences. Festering in a corner, the ex-fox added what can best be described as a new dimension to slot-car racing. Scalextric has never offered a 'smell-o-rama' set, and based on this experience I recommend they never do.

Leaving Dead Fox Tunnel as quickly as possible we move on to the business park. Here, blocking our path, stands a 25-foot staircase in the offices of a popular toothpaste and shampoo-manufacturing conglomerate. Scalextric doesn't really like going up stairs: the track isn't that happy about it and the cars are even less keen. But Sim has been working on this problem for a while and has created a mini architectural masterpiece: a metal frame on which curved pieces of track can be fitted in a continuous upward spiral – henceforth to be known as the Spiral Ascent of Doom.

LEFT: The Pond, which the cars had to cross on an ingenious floating bridge, turned out to be 60 metres of murky water planted with reeds and inhabited by large carp.

ABOVE: The Dead Fox Tunnel confirmed why Scalextric never offered a 'smell-o-rama' set.

RIGHT: The Spiral Ascent of Doom: a 25-foot architectural masterpiece.

Each turn up the 25 tight 'levels' could lead to a spin-off every bit as lethal as a plunge into the Pond – the floor at shampoo HQ could be fatal to a plastic car dropping from a height. The gang is testing the track as I arrive and, for the first and only time over the whole weekend, I get to play Scalextric. Sim's ingenuity in creating the Spiral Ascent of Doom is matched only by the Locals' solution to the car write-off problem: the handily placed staff canteen provides tablecloths for anxious volunteers to catch any Kamikaze cars. Again, I won't be passing that tip on to the Pros.

The next obstacle is the 14-foot-high fence surrounding a car-repair yard. The ever-resourceful Sim has come to the rescue again, this time with a pleasing arch that straddles the fence with metal ramp sections leading up to and down from the arch. Assembling this is proper construction of the type I can't resist, so I spend a happy hour bolting together sections of the ramps and the arch, and helping knock up a support for the track as it comes down from the dizzy heights. When it comes to race time, negotiating the Fence of Fear will be like driving a real car down the world's highest rollercoaster with no possible means of survival should you leave the track – oh, and no one to pick you out of the giant stinging nettles either. To scale these are Redwood-sized nettles with barbs the size of boathooks.

Finally, in a pleasingly record-breaking way, we construct what must be the longest Scalextric bridge ever, to take us over the river. Time to leave the circuit and pray that on race day itself the wind will have abated and we get good racing conditions for this world record attempt.

BOTH PAGES: Over the 70 years since racing finished at Brooklands, a number of new and seemingly insurmountable obstacles have presented themselves to anyone attempting a whole lap. But Scalextric will always overcome. Or possibly go around.

King, Campbell and Cobb

Should we succeed, it won't be the first world record associated with Brooklands by a long chalk. In fact, Brooklands entered the record books as soon as it was completed in 1907, being the world's first purpose-built motor racing circuit.

It was built by local landowner Hugh Locke King, who gave over 330 acres of his country estate for what was initially intended to be a simple road circuit. However, the track designers convinced him that for cars to achieve the highest possible speeds the track would require two enormous banked sections nearly 30 feet high, parts of which survive to this day. You can now walk down a smart street of modern Weybridge houses, push through the undergrowth at the edge of the development, and there in front of you is that glorious sweep of concrete. It is crumbling, overgrown and fabulously haunted – if you listen carefully enough you can hear the ghostly echo of record-breaking cars tearing round it. Standing on the banking itself is like being Gregory Peck when he revisits the abandoned airfield at the beginning of *Twelve O'Clock High*. The Brooklands banking is magnificent in its glorious decay.

King's original concrete track was completed in just nine months, and the first of many world records to be set at Brooklands was achieved even before the first race. In June 1907, just a few days after the ceremonial opening of the circuit, Selwyn Francis Edge used Brooklands to set a 24-hour endurance speed record, which stood for 17 years: in 24 hours of solo driving, Edge covered 1,581 miles at an average speed of nearly 66 mph. The first race to be held at Brooklands came less than a month later, on 6 July 1907, and was dubbed 'Motor Ascot'. Indeed, in the absence of any motor racing precedent – this was, after all, the world's first motor racing circuit – race procedure echoed that of horse racing, with cars assembling before the race in a field known as the paddock, and drivers wearing jockeys' silks, so that the crowd could tell who was who.

Two years after that, on 8 November 1909, came the first of three Brooklands land speed records when Frenchman Victor Hémery took a German Blitzen Benz to 125.95 mph on the famous banked curves. On 24 June 1914 Englishman Major L.G. Hornsted reached 128.16 mph in another Blitzen Benz, but because this was the first time the speed record was measured over a two-way run his official speed (the average of both runs) was 124.10 mph – therefore, bizarrely, the new official land speed record was actually slower than the previous one. Motor sport at Brooklands was suspended for the duration of World War I and didn't return until 1920 but it wasn't long before the circuit was back in the record books. On 17 May 1922 Kenelm Lee Guinness (founder of the KLG spark plug company) drove a single-seater Sunbeam at a two-way average speed of 135.75 mph to claim the first land speed record to be achieved with an aero engine and the last to be set at Brooklands.

RIGHT: Brooklands, 8 May 1930: a 4.5 Litre Supercharged 'Blower' Bentley in practice for the Double 12 Hour Race.

INSET: The old banking is made ready for a reprise of racing glory.

John Cobb speed record

In 1947 Brooklands racing legend John Cobb broke the World Land Speed Record in the 'Railton Mobil Special'. This unique streamlined car was powered by two supercharged W12-block Napier Lion aircraft engines and had been custom-built at Brooklands by Thomson & Taylor. Cobb averaged 394 mph – an incredible feat that captured the public imagination. Making the most of this surge of interest, Fred Francis, the inventor of Scalextric, produced a clockwork replica of the famous car. So there was a remarkable Scalextric link to Brooklands (and a world record too) 62 years before *James May's Toy Stories*...

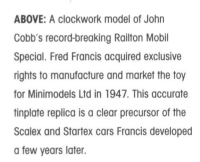

It may have been Brooklands' last land-speed record but more history was made on 7 August 1926 when Brooklands was the venue for the first ever British Grand Prix. The 110-lap race was won by Frenchmen Robert Sénéchal and Louis Wagner, who completed the distance in their Delage 155B in four hours 56 seconds, at an average speed of 71.61 mph. A second GP was held at Brooklands the following year but the British GP was then discontinued until 1948, when it was revived at Silverstone – by which time racing at Brooklands was no more than a distant memory.

In the meantime, Brooklands' connection with the land-speed record continued in the form of Thomson & Taylor's workshop, where several land-speed record-breaking cars were built. These included the first car to travel at more than 300 mph (Malcolm Campbell's 'Bluebird' in 1935) and the first to travel at more than 400 mph (John Cobb's 'Railton' in 1947). Campbell and Cobb were both legends on the Brooklands circuit itself, and Cobb still holds the lap record for the Brooklands Outer Circuit, the most prestigious record at the track. This he achieved in 1935 in his Napier Railton, with a top speed of 143.44 mph.

Cobb's record remained unbroken when the Brooklands Automobile Racing Club had held its last ever meeting at the famous circuit on 7 August 1939 – not that anyone knew it would be the last. A few weeks later the circuit was requisitioned for the duration of World War II, and when peace returned motor sport fans waited for racing to return to Brooklands as it had done after World War I. But they waited in vain. For various reasons, practical, political and commercial, the track was sold and parts of it redeveloped. It seemed that racing would never return to Brooklands.

Until now.

ABOVE: A clockwork model of John Cobb's record-breaking Railton Mobil Special. Fred Francis acquired exclusive rights to manufacture and market the toy for Minimodels Ltd in 1947. This accurate tinplate replica is a clear precursor of the Scalex and Startex cars Francis developed a few years later.

How to win at Scalextric

The basic flaw with Scalextric is that it is virtually impossible to avoid constantly crashing. It follows from that, though, that the secret to winning at Scalextric is simply *not* crashing.

Before the big race, drive the circuit and determine the speed at which your car will just make it around the tightest bend on the course. Then stick to that speed for the whole race. The other bloke will be able to overtake you at a terrific lick on the straight bits, but in his excitement will crash on the corner. He is now behind, and attempts to catch up will simply result in more crashes. You will win, it is a mathematical certainty.

Pimp your car

It's poor form, but there are simple ways to improve the performance of a Scalextric car, as employed by serious club racers and the sort of people who say 'my car's handling really well', which is an idiotic contention if you're not actually in it.

1 Fit a more powerful motor
These are available off the shelf, and simply have increased armature windings. Some experts even claim to be able to do this themselves.

2 Improve the tyres
This can be done by rolling them gently along the sticky side of parcel tape. Be aware that stickiness wears off through the race, as with real tyres. New tyres are covered with a slippery mould-release agent, and should be 'scrubbed in' over a few laps.

3 Fit more powerful magnets under the car
This will give higher cornering speeds, but will reduce outright speed on the straights. Decide magnet strategy in the light of circuit shape.

4 Lubricate all bearings
This will make more difference than you might imagine. Motor bearings, especially, benefit from a tiny drop of light oil. This can increase maximum revs by a few hundred.

Assessing the risks

Race day, 17 August 2009. Dawn promises ideal British racing conditions: gunmetal grey skies with no trace of the bothersome breeze of yesterday. All we have to do now is get the track laid and get the cars on the grid.

I go to check on track-laying progress at Staniland Drive – a section of the circuit populated now by 1990s houses – where the Locals are pitching in. The original Brooklands circuit would have bisected these people's front gardens, which is why the iconic black Scalextric track now does exactly that, stretching in a straight run across the well-kept lawns, propped up where necessary by books, brooms and bowls. It's a sight to lift the spirits: men, women and children of all ages slotting together track as if this were just as much a part of the normal Sunday routine as washing the car or mowing the lawn or sitting down to a roast.

But then we hit a classic Scalextric problem – joining together two long sections of track with a corner. Scalextric track isn't the most pliable material, and massive geometric headaches are commonplace while constructing your bedroom racing circuit. That problem is amplified over nearly three miles of track, which means the corner challenge occurs more than just the once by the bedroom door. Patience and ingenuity are the only answers. And maybe just the tiniest excess of force. After helping with that for a while I assist with one of the final tasks – feeding track through a tunnel constructed by Sim to

ABOVE: Typical Brooklands residents relaxing in the front garden, just a few feet from the historic Scalextric track of 2009.

navigate dense undergrowth – and then head back to Brooklands HQ to absorb the pre-race atmosphere.

The tension is starting to show as the teams line up on either side of the tracks. I feel I need moral support for this nerve-wracking event, especially after I spy a dapper fellow from Guinness World Records lurking with a clipboard. Luckily my old friend and former *Top Gear* presenter Tiff Needell – a proper TV presenter who doesn't dress like a tramp – is on hand. Tiff is going to be our roving reporter, and before we go trackside I discuss the upcoming contest with him. He tells me that his love of motor sport was born at Brooklands – his father watched the last race here in 1939, and as a boy Tiff used to creep over the barriers and race down the banking before getting chased off by the security guards. Later in his life he tested cars here and he's now a trustee of the Brooklands Museum, in which capacity he's involved in a project to restore the finishing straight to its former glory.

We discuss potential hazards facing the track; the cars, the milling crowds and the army of volunteers who have come together to make this a very special day. For health and safety purposes an event like this needs a Risk Assessment (RA), which details the potential hazards involved in putting together a toy that is widely sold for household use. Admittedly, the track is longer than average and the crowd is larger than will fit in the average bedroom but a glance at the RA would have anyone who actually bothered to read it running a mile – it turns out that the risks are absolutely terrifying.

This gargantuan document – a total waste of hundreds of hours of innocent

CAUTION

PLEASE DO NOT
CLIMB ON THE BANKIN
AS IT IS STEEP & SLIPPE
THE MUSEUM ACCEPTS
RESPONSIBILITY
FOR ANY INJURY

UNAUTHORISED DRIVIN
ON THE BANKING IS
STRICTLY FORBIDDEN

lives – points out that the track is itself a 'trip hazard' because it's black and therefore difficult to see. The solution? You must be 'very careful' not to fall over it. Or fall off the bridge, or fall in the Pond, or fall down the stairs in the headquarters of the popular toothpaste and shampoo-manufacturing conglomerate; you must be 'very careful' not to roll down the banking, or get stung by nettles, or impale yourself on the protective fence next to the retailer of domestic goods. The list is endless, and the precautions always the same – you must be 'very careful' not to fall over, or off, or in, or down.

Tiff wonders if the cars themselves may prove a hazard – might there be a danger of stubbing a toe during the reporting process? If so, we already know the solution – be 'very careful' not to stub a toe during the reporting process.

On the straights, the cars will in fact be travelling at up to 400 mph, and you don't have to be an H&S officer to see that such speeds engender certain risks. But that is scale speed. Actual speed will be more like 12 or 13 mph, so I can't see it – I am totally confident that nobody's health or safety will be endangered by the two Scalextric cars. But nonetheless, the RA highlights the risk of physical injury whilst addressing 'Scalextric car concerns'.

Scalextric car concerns! That is just the kind of vague, incomprehensible, pointless phrase which shows that this oversized dossier of cobblers has been compiled by people who see health and safety as a job opportunity, rather than a genuine means of protecting people. All it needs is an acronym and the circle of fatuity will be complete. A prick on the finger from the copper braiding will result in at least a dozen forms to fill out in duplicate. First question: how were your horrific pricking injuries sustained? Answer: SCC.

Anyway, enough of these pointless distractions – we have to finish before dark because the track is not lit, and the cars' tiny scale headlights will not be sufficient for the cameras to film anything.

But seeing as the Pros are convinced that the complete, world-record-breaking circuit should take about 20 minutes, that won't be a problem, will it?

OPPOSITE, TOP: Me with Tiff Needell, a proper presenter who doesn't dress like a tramp.

OPPOSITE, MIDDLE: Health & Safety at work again.

OPPOSITE, BOTTOM: Ready for the off.

BELOW: Our 'RAF Bomber Command' board for charting the cars' progress.

The best race I never saw

By 15:30, as if in personal tribute to our historic race, the sun is beating down as in halcyon summer days, pre-climate change. Ironically, this is a worse problem than our usual grey summer's drizzle, because it causes the track to buckle in several places. The heat is also causing the batteries to malfunction and several need replacing.

We're running late.

An expectant crowd has gathered, both trackside and on the bridge overlooking the start/finish.

By 16:30, the scheduled start of the race, there are still problems with the sunbaked track at Section 8. Final adjustments are being made to the cars by both teams. The tension and excitement is palpable.

Finally, at 17:05, with the shadows lengthening on the legendary banking behind us, all power and track difficulties have been overcome and we are set to go. But once the cars are off the grid I won't see the rest of this epic battle for a place in history. I will remain at mission control and the progress of the race will be relayed to me via my earpiece from Tiff's roving commentary. I will report the positions of the cars to my glamorous assistant Helen who, armed with a 99-pence croupier's stick, will manoeuvre two models of the model cars around a map of the track laid out on our RAF Bomber Command progress board.

The two cars sit proud, side by side on the track. The Locals will be powering a maroon Aston Martin DB9, while the Pros have commandeered a silver Mercedes McLaren SLR. It's the first motor race around the complete Brooklands circuit for 70 years, one week and two days! The crowd enthusiastically counts down from ten and I flag the cars off at 17:06 – a mere 36 minutes after the scheduled start.

Drama from the beginning: the Mercedes takes an early lead by what, to scale, is probably about a quarter of a mile. But then, for no apparent reason, it has a dreadful spin on the straight – perhaps just squeezing the

TOP LEFT: The race landmarks were mapped out with military precision on our progress board. **TOP RIGHT:** Me waving the starter flag. **ABOVE:** My glamorous assistant Helen charted the position of the cars with a 99-pence croupier's stick.

wrong throttle – and the Locals' Aston Martin is now way ahead and racing to the river bridge. The contest is not rigged in any way, but Tiff is enjoying the success of the Locals' car immensely. It is, of course, early days yet – there are still many treacherous obstacles to overcome before the race will be won and lost, or a world record can be set.

The Mercedes makes a good recovery and closes in on the Aston Martin. Both of them clear the river bridge without falling in and enter the railway straight, which leads up to the Fence of Fear in Section 5.

I keep losing radio contact with Tiff, which means I have no idea what is going on, except that one of the cars is maroon and one is silver.

At last, communications are re-established. The cars are still on the railway straight – a relatively easy section, though it did claim a few victims in the 1920s. The Aston is still in the lead but the Pros' Mercedes is closing fast as they approach the Fence of Fear, dividing the car repair centre from the Never Knowingly Undersold retailer of domestic goods.

Meanwhile, the residents of Staniland Avenue have apparently become impatient, lighting several barbecues and opening a wide range of alcoholic beverages. This may affect the performance of the Aston Martin just before the treacherous Pond.

By 18:00, 54 minutes after the start of the race, the Merc has overtaken the Aston. They approach the first road crossing and have to wait for the traffic to be stopped temporarily, so that an extra bit of track can be slotted in, the road crossed, and the track lifted to allow the flow of traffic to recommence.

Unfortunately, the Aston Martin chooses this moment to stall again – halfway across the road.

If it doesn't get across before the traffic starts it will be crushed and the Locals team will have to start all over again. I'm now getting updates from the enthusiastic crew of St John Ambulance attendants. There are so many of them that Brooklands today would be a very good place to have a baby or a heart attack, if indeed there is such a thing as a good place to do these things.

By 18:09 the road crossing is completed and the cars are on the move again, past the retailer of high quality, but very expensive, sandwiches and on to the retailer that stays open late and will eventually have a store in every back garden.

TOP: A giant Tiff Needell at the evocatively named high bridge over the fence at the edge of the car repair centre.

ABOVE: Tiff in roving commentator mode.

BELOW: Due to our strict adherence to the Risk Assessment report, no lives were lost in the crossing of 'the Pond'.

18:15 – the Pros' Mercedes spins off again and I have an orange Opal Fruit. Tiff heads off to Staniland Drive for a Pimm's and a sausage.

18:29 – Tiff has secured a Pimm's. I ask him if he can very carefully balance one on the back of a car and send it on to the finishing line. This is thirsty work.

18:31 – both cars are over the second road crossing and are neck and neck in Section 9. The Merc pulls ahead temporarily but as they head towards Staniland Drive, and the barbecues, the Aston Martin takes a 200-yard lead – community spirit, or some kind of spirit, pulling it ahead.

The silver Merc regains the lead in Section 10, but then the Aston Martin takes it back through the manicured lawns of Staniland Drive. This is exciting, if rather slow, stuff.

By 18:49 the Aston Martin is three-quarters of the way through the course but still facing some terrifying obstacles, including Dead Fox Tunnel and the Pond. Not to mention the Spiral Ascent of Doom. The Aston is way ahead now. The whereabouts of the Merc is a mystery – maybe it has been sabotaged by over-exuberant locals?

18:51 – disaster strikes for the Aston Martin! Halfway across the Pond it stops. We lose contact with Tiff and have no idea if the Merc has even completed the Staniland Drive barbecue and cocktail party.

18:54 – we're back on track. The Locals' Aston has miraculously cleared the Pond and climbed the Spiral Ascent of Doom with ease – after many disastrous trial runs earlier in the day.

18:58 – the Merc is now back in pursuit but too far behind to catch up, and the Aston Martin crosses the finishing line a full ten minutes before its expertly driven rival arrives to complete the world record attempt at 19:08 – two hours and two minutes after the start.

The Aston has lost a wing mirror, and the silver Mercedes has been dragging some of the undergrowth along with it. There's no doubt about it – Brooklands in Scalextric is a tough circuit.

OPPOSITE: It's not the first record to be set at Brooklands, but no one was expecting another one this late in the day.

BELOW: Victory for the Brooklands Community Racing Team's Aston Martin, closely followed home by the Scalextric Nerds' McLaren-Mercedes. Epic wheel-to-wheel stuff and no mistake.

Everyone's a winner

With the taste of victory thick in the air I speak to three members of the Locals' team – Ciara Farrell, 18, Sarah Tortolani, 17, and Stacie Foster, 17. Ciara reveals that she only passed her driving test two weeks ago, so to break a world record a fortnight later is quite an impressive effort.

I'm also joined by Diana Francis, the widow of Scalextric inventor Fred Francis. She is delighted, and assures me that Fred would have been very proud to see Scalextric still going strong, and that he would have loved to have been here. Brooklands is full of ghosts and spirits – on a quiet afternoon the glorious sweep of the concrete banking still resonates with the curling echo of John Cobb's Napier-Railton – so I tell Diana there's a good chance that Fred is here, along with Cobb and Campbell and the other Brooklands legends. Although Cobb might be slightly peeved that we'd beaten his track record. When it was on song, the old Aston belted along achieving a scale speed of well over 400 mph, beating Cobb's Outer Circuit Record of 143.44 mph by at least 256.56 mph.

Meanwhile, Tiff has made it back to the finishing line in one piece, and we reflect on the afternoon's epic events. He points out that I had a somewhat easier couple of hours than him. While I was standing at Bomber Command, charting the progress of the cars, he was running around, chasing cars down bankings, fixing the track, and rescuing small boys from ponds.

Ah yes, the Pond.

Apparently, ignoring all Health & Safety procedures, Tiff 'persuaded' a young boy to jump into a small dinghy to give the stranded Aston Martin a push. Luckily, the ripples from the boat were enough of a jog and the car sped off before the young man could fall into the water and drown.

And then comes the really good news.

The independent adjudicators have determined that the actual length of the track, by the time we'd added to it in order to get round rose bushes and manhole covers and the like, was actually 2.95 miles – some 350 yards longer than we had planned and totally smashing the previous record of 1.59 miles set in Berlin on 5 October 2007.

And so, with the sun all but disappeared over the museum behind us, Matt Boulton from Guinness World Records presents me with the certificate, acknowledging that on 17 August 2009, 52 years after Scalextric was launched and 102 years after Brooklands first opened, we have, indeed, brought these venerable institutions together to celebrate two remarkable historic achievements and to create a third historic achievement of our own.

LEGO

THE WORLD'S FIRST FULL-SIZE LEGO HOUSE

WHY LEGO?

Theoretically, the possibilities of Lego are endless, but inevitably those possibilities are limited by how many pieces you have – and as a kid I never had enough. As Walt Disney might have said, children have limitless imagination but a limited amount of Lego, and you can never quite build what your imagination can conceive.

I played with Lego endlessly as a kid and I've played with it a lot since. The arrival of a younger sister prolonged my childhood Lego experience, and fairly recently my girlfriend bought me a big tub of Lego because she'd heard that it's very therapeutic and she thought I was becoming a grumpy old man. I keep it on my desk and if I get bored or frustrated with my work I get out the Lego and make something. Then I take it to bits and put it away again and I'm happy. Or, at least, I was happy when I first started doing it. Then I realised that I still didn't have enough of it.

But now I can have as much of it as I like, so I decided to build a full-size house and find out whether a children's construction toy could be used as a full scale construction material. Designing a house out of Lego bricks is one thing – that's a fairly appropriate use of bricks. But designing Lego furniture and fittings is something else. One thing in my favour is that Lego has created its own design language, which means that angular furniture with studs sticking out doesn't look out of place; it's part of the *oeuvre*. Lego is now so ubiquitous and so familiar that the idea of building something that is meant to be smoothly curved but is actually covered in corners has assumed a currency of its own; Lego has become a design language in its own right, similar to the bit-mapping of pictures.

I asked Jørgen Vig Knudstorp, CEO of Lego, whether a Lego language really exists and he told me:

> There's a strange numeric logic which means that certain things can happen in Lego and other things definitely can't happen. There's no right or wrong way of doing anything with Lego but once you master the system you can express anything in it. So it teaches children a certain way of thinking. If children can use their right and their left brain at the same time, think systematically and think creatively, we've taught them something infinitely valuable about how to build their own future.

If I had seen that printed on the side of a box of Lego I'd have dismissed it as sales puff, but Jørgen clearly meant it. And I think it's true of Lego in its pure form. But I also think that Lego lost its purity when it started introducing specialised parts so that each model could be built more quickly. That corrupted the system, and reduced Lego from a means of thinking that was very philosophical and intellectual to just being a toy that you put together. Jørgen agreed: 'Lego lost the courage of its own convictions… Lego is not about instant gratification. It's about mastering something and getting better

"the possibilities of Lego are endless"

and better at it.' But the interesting thing is that in the 1950s and 60s the original Lego *was* almost instant gratification. If you weren't making Lego you'd be making a glider out of balsawood or making an Airfix model or a Meccano crane, and those things took days and days – whereas by comparison Lego was very fast: you picked it up and you pressed it together and you were already on your way. You didn't have to wait for the glue to dry, you didn't have to cut things out, and if you made a mistake you just took it apart and did it again.

But now of course it's Lego that takes time and effort compared with switching on a computer game. I find it very encouraging that what enabled Lego to compete with computer games was not to follow the route of over-simplification and instant gratification but to go the other way: 'To go back to your roots,' as Jørgen put it. 'You have to go back to your values and stay extremely true to what you are about.' And Lego did that by removing most of the specialised parts and returning to a system based on the core elements of bricks and plates.

And those bricks and plates are fast accumulating all around us. The Lego factory in Billund produces about 36,000 elements every minute of every day, and that is a lot of elements. They don't decay and they rarely break, which means that most of the 440 billion bricks that have been made since 1949 are still with us, outnumbering the human inhabitants of the planet by about 62 to one. Standing in the factory and watching them steadily flowing off the production line is very exciting but, just like a kid in a sweet factory, after a while I began to feel overwhelmed and slightly nauseated by it. The factory churns out Lego 24 hours a day and I couldn't help wondering what would happen if they forgot how to stop the machines – how long before the world would be drowning in Lego?

Mind you, as endings go, it would be less traumatic than global warming or asteroid strikes or flu pandemics. And it would certainly be more colourful.

THE LEGO UNIVERSE

Compared to our own, the Lego universe began quietly. There was no Big Bang. Instead there was a decade of intense research and development before Lego time began at the moment the rest of us know as 1:58 p.m. on 28 January 1958. At that precise moment the Danish patent office accepted Godtfred Kirk Christiansen's application for a patent to protect the 'clutch mechanism' that distinguishes Lego bricks from all others (that is, the tubes in the bottom of the bricks). The invention of the tubes marked the start of a phenomenon that saw Lego evolve from a simple toy into a complete building system with its own design language – a phenomenon that now sells to adults and children alike in 130 countries and which in 2000 was named Toy of the Century by the British Association of Toy Retailers. The prototype bricks that Godtfred Kirk Christiansen (GKC) created to support his patent have since propagated to the point where there are roughly 62 Lego bricks for every person on earth.

The secret behind the success of Lego is multi-faceted. Lego is simplicity itself – the impulse to join two bricks together or break them apart is intuitive, and requires no instruction – and yet at the same time it is highly complex: there are more than 900 million ways to connect just six eight-stud bricks of equal colour. Each element is based on a single design principle and yet the creative possibilities are infinite: like pixels in a visual image or words in a language, there are countless ways in which to put together the basic building blocks. And that means that Lego can be all things to all people, appealing to anyone of any age and any ability.

Each brick is a remarkable feat of engineering, manufactured to microscopic accuracy so that the bricks bind securely enough to be shaken without coming apart and yet can be separated so easily that a two-year-old can dismantle them with a push of the thumb. And Lego is a marketeer's dream, improving on even the famous Gillette principle. In the 1890s William Painter (inventor of the crimped metal bottle stopper known as a crown cork) advised his salesman King Camp Gillette, 'Invent something that will be used once and then thrown away. Then the

BELOW: To reach the moon would require a stack of approximately 40,000,000,000 Lego bricks. Go on, try it.

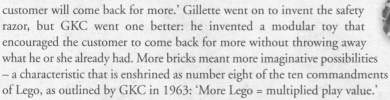

customer will come back for more.' Gillette went on to invent the safety razor, but GKC went one better: he invented a modular toy that encouraged the customer to come back for more without throwing away what he or she already had. More bricks meant more imaginative possibilities – a characteristic that is enshrined as number eight of the ten commandments of Lego, as outlined by GKC in 1963: 'More Lego = multiplied play value.'

In short, Lego is a concept of genius and an engineering marvel.

But it didn't all start with the 1958 patent. Just as there was quantum singularity prior to the Big Bang, so there was R&D prior to the Primordial Patent. The story of Lego really begins in 1932, when Ole Kirk Christiansen's carpentry business in Billund, Denmark, collapsed as a result of the Great Depression. Carpentry was all he knew but people could no longer afford expensive furniture or new wooden houses so Ole Kirk Christiansen (OKC) began making stepladders and ironing boards, and in his free time he made wooden toys including yo-yos, cars and pull-along ducks. Toy-making proved more recession-proof than household goods, and OKC decided that toys were where his future lay. In 1934 he confirmed this decision by naming his new business Lego, from the Danish words *leg godt*, meaning 'play well'. Only later did he learn that 'lego' can also be construed in Latin to mean 'I put together'.

World War II brought an end to the global depression and it heralded great changes in manufacturing. The war effort saw dramatic improvements in the production and use of plastics, and when peace came many industries saw plastic as the material of the future. OKC had the vision to embrace plastic, despite the reservations of his four sons, who were all by then working in the company. In 1947 Lego became the first Danish toy manufacturer to buy an injection-moulding machine, and OKC's instincts were soon proved right: by 1951 sales of plastic toys had reached 50 per cent of the company's total and the proportion of wooden toys was continuing to shrink.

In 1949, two years after purchasing the injection-moulding machine, OKC began manufacturing plastic building bricks based on a design patented by Englishman Hilary Harry Fisher Page five years earlier. These bricks, which Lego modified and marketed as Automatic Binding Bricks,

ABOVE: In 1932 Ole Kirk Christiansen was forced to shift the focus of his carpentry business from furniture and household goods to wooden toys such as this pull-along duck, which was a bestseller. In 1934 he changed the name of his business to Lego, from the Danish *leg godt*, meaning 'play well'. The new name, which would one day be world famous, can be seen emblazoned on the cockerel.

were approximately the same size as the modern Lego brick and had the characteristic studs on the top but nothing inside for the studs to bind on. The studs made these bricks more stable than traditional wooden building blocks but they lacked the defining characteristic of the modern Lego brick. Nonetheless they proved popular, particularly after the name was changed in 1953 to the snappier Lego *Mursten* (Lego Brick).

OKC's son Godtfred Kirk Christiansen (GKC) took over the company in 1950 with two goals in mind: developing a mechanism to make Automatic Binding Bricks even more stable, and rationalising Lego's product range. About four years later the manager of one of Denmark's most famous toyshops complained to GKC that most manufacturers' toys were too similar to other manufacturers' products, and that none of them had a basic unifying theme. This was the inspiration GKC needed. He realised that the modular Lego Brick could be the basis of an expandable unified range of toys, and in 1955 he launched the Lego System of Play, which comprised 28 building sets and eight vehicles, all based on the Lego brick.

The remaining problem was to make the brick more stable. GKC and his development team worked on a number of systems based on structures within the body of each brick which would grip the studs of any other brick. The team tried more than a dozen different methods, the best of which proved to be the tubular system which is so familiar today, and at last GKC was ready to file his patent. Shrewdly, the patent protected all of the different methods the team had developed to prevent competitors from devising an alternative method that would circumvent Lego's patent.

Perfecting the clutch mechanism was the breakthrough that enabled the Lego universe to expand beyond anything that OKC could have imagined. If a divine message were required to confirm that the future lay in plastic bricks, it came two years later in the form of a fire that destroyed the company's carpentry workshops. By then production of wooden toys had sunk so low that Lego decided it was not worth the expense of rebuilding the workshops, and the manufacture of wooden toys ceased there and then.

ABOVE: Lego began producing Automatic Binding Bricks in 1949 but they lacked the defining feature of today's Lego bricks – as seen above, there were no tubes in the underside of the bricks, therefore no clutch. The bricks are lying on a copy of GKC's 'ten commandments of Lego'. The first commandment is 'unlimited play possibilities'; the second, 'for boys, for girls', and the third 'enthusiasm to all ages'.

BELOW: In 1953 Automatic Binding Bricks were rebranded as Lego *Mursten*, making the previous packaging look decidedly outdated.

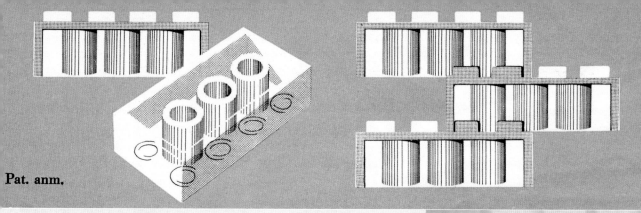

Pat. anm.

Populating the universe

The combination of the Lego System of Play and the tubular clutch mechanism was the key to success, but that success did not follow automatically. It required continuous innovation, and for nearly three more decades GKC provided the impetus behind that innovation, steering Lego to three coveted Toy of the Year Awards – for the Lego Family Set in 1974, the Lego Basic Set in 1975 and Lego Space in 1979 – before handing over to his son Kjeld Kirk Kristiansen (KKK), who confused the rest of the known universe by changing the spelling of the family name.

One of the foundations of Lego's lasting popularity has been its themed sets, the first of which was the Town Plan in 1955. This was launched as part of the Lego System of Play, in collaboration with the Danish Road Safety Council, so that children could build their own town in Lego bricks and, at the same time, learn how to behave safely in traffic. Both the educational and the play aspect of Town Plan proved remarkably durable. Lego has been used in education (and therapy) ever since, and the town theme has been perennially popular – Lego City remains the company's bestselling themed product more than 50 years later. This, research has shown, is because most children like to build versions of what they see in the world around them, a fact that has seen Lego town and city sets consistently outsell space and fantasy sets.

The 1960s saw the introduction of Lego wheels and tyres in 1962, Lego railways in 1966 (which evolved into a complete range), and Lego Duplo, for younger children, in 1969. The name Duplo is derived from the fact that every element in the system is twice as wide, twice as high and twice as long as a standard Lego element, making it ideal for smaller hands. And in 1968 the Legoland theme park opened in Billund, welcoming 625,000 visitors in its first year. It has long been Denmark's most popular theme park outside Copenhagen, and now comprises some 50 million bricks.

The 1970s were no less innovative, and in addition to the three Toy of the Year Awards GKC came up with two hugely significant innovations, which didn't catch the eye of the Toy Retailers' Association: Lego Technic in 1977 and Minifigures in 1978.

Having extended the age range of the Lego market downwards with Duplo, Lego Technic extended it upwards, enabling older children (and adults) to build complex technical models with moving parts such as working rack and pinion steering mechanisms for vehicles. As the name suggests, Technic elements have a technical function, and they include gears,

TOP: Patent drawings showing the Lego tubular clutch mechanism. **ABOVE:** Kjeld Kirk Kristiansen (sic) and his sister, the grandchildren of the inventor, appear in a 1950s advert for Lego. **BELOW:** Lego produces some 306 million tyres per year, making it the world's biggest tyre manufacturer.

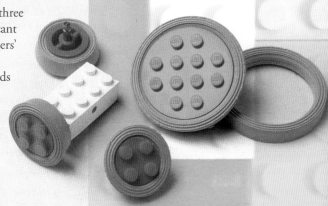

axles, cogs, levers, differentials and universal joints, as well as standard-sized bricks and beams containing holes that accept Technics pins and axles. The key to its success is that it is a system within a system, and all Technic elements are compatible with standard Lego elements.

In 1978 Lego introduced Minifigures (aka minifigs), one of their most important inventions after the brick. From the outset there had been something missing from Lego towns and villages – people. The success of the award-winning Family Set in 1974, which included the first Lego figures, prompted Lego to develop a set of figures that would be as universal as the original brick. The result was Minifigs: small Lego people in three pieces. Once assembled, the arms and legs can be posed, the hands grip and the head can be moved from side to side. Suddenly the imaginative possibilities of Lego had increased enormously. Cities, vehicles, ships and spacecrafts could all now be populated with scale Lego citizens – albeit to begin with they all had exactly the same bright yellow complexion and the same fixed smile. Just as with the brick, precision moulding is crucial to the success of Minifigures. The stud on the top of the head and the tubes under the feet are exactly the same size as those on the bricks, making them compatible with every other Lego element. And the hands have the same degree of clutch power as the stud-and-tube mechanism, so that a Minifigure can hold all Lego elements that are tubular in shape, from flagpoles to swords and pistols.

At first just seven male Minifigures were released as accessories for Lego Town, Space and Castle, closely followed later the same year by the first female Minifigure, a hospital nurse. For more than a decade Minifigures all had the

same neutral facial expression but in 1989, with the launch of Lego Pirates, they were available with one of two expressions: smiling or frowning, enabling them to be good or bad characters. Similarly, for a quarter of a century they all had the same primary yellow skin tone, until 2003 when Lego Basketball introduced more authentic dark and light skin tones. Minifigures also provided an ideal opportunity for producing licensed figures, starting with Star Wars in 1999 and later including Harry Potter, Indiana Jones, Bob the Builder and others.

Despite their restricted anatomy minifigs continue to propagate, and in the 30-plus years since their introduction more than four billion have been produced, making them the world's largest ethnic group.

As GKC handed over to KKK in 1979 everything was looking rosy in the Lego universe. Sales were high, and a survey in 1980 showed that ownership of Lego bricks extended to fully 70 per cent of all western European families with children under the age of 14. KKK had taken control of a thriving universe. But there was a cosmic storm brewing, and the new CEO was destined to lead the Lego Group through difficult times.

The third generation

Under KKK's leadership Lego continued to grow throughout the 1980s, and in 1990 became one of the world's ten largest toy manufacturers (it is currently the fifth largest). As the 1990s progressed the Lego Group diversified into films, computer games, clothing, own-brand stores and extending its theme parks to include Legoland Windsor in 1996, Legoland California in 1999, and Legoland Deutschland in 2002. But maintaining this level of expansion came at a price. Diversification into too many areas was draining resources and confusing consumers. Lego had lost sight of its core values, and was starting to lose money. Lego Communication Manager Jan Christensen explains:

One of the published theories of brand expansion is that you can only introduce a single new product line every five years, to give people time

OPPOSITE ABOVE: Copenhagen harbour, Legoland style.

OPPOSITE BELOW: Duplo: bigger bricks for smaller hands, weirdly.

ABOVE AND BELOW: Minifigures, first introduced in 1978, have propagated to become the world's largest ethnic group.

to adjust to the fact that this is what your brand is about. By the late 90s people were joking that the Lego Group executives had read that book upside down and started introducing five new lines in a single year! Of course, it wasn't actually that many but it was enough for the public to lose sight of what Lego was about.

The result was mounting losses, despite the success of innovations such as Lego Mindstorms in 1998 and a fourth Toy of the Year Award in 2001 for Bionicle – a combination of physical products and an online fantasy universe, with Bionicle construction kits enabling children to make action figures inspired by the evolving online fantasy storyline. In 2004 KKK had the mettle to step down as CEO and appoint Jørgen Vig Knudstorp, who has turned the company round. Knudstorp says that in addition to expanding too fast in too many directions, Lego also fell into the trap of 'dumbing down' many of its products in an attempt to provide instant gratification to compete with the computer games sector. The company had begun producing sets with bigger parts that were unique to that set, and that was not the Lego way:

Lego lost the courage of its own convictions. It was as if we were saying to children who don't like to build things, 'Look it's not that hard. We'll make bigger pieces for you so you'll be finished much faster and you can get on with playing with your helicopter.' That put off the people who love the construction side of it, and at the same time it didn't capture those who don't like building things, because they would still say, 'If I

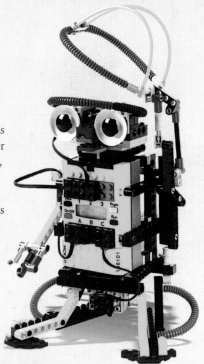

ABOVE: Lego Mindstorms is a system that combines programmable bricks, motors, sensors and Lego Technics elements. Mindstorms enables Lego enthusiasts to build programmable robots and other interactive systems.

BELOW: Three generations of the Lego dynasty: Ole Kirk Christiansen (top), Godtfred Kirk Christiansen (middle) and Kjeld Kirk Kristiansen (bottom), who changed the spelling of the family name.

want a helicopter I'll go and buy one; I don't need one that's semi-constructible.' That betrayed the whole idea that Lego is about hard fun. It's about challenges, just the same as reading a great book and losing yourself in it; it's not about instant gratification. It's about mastering something and getting better and better at it. That is what Lego is about but we lost faith in ourself. We lost our own character.

The other problem with making more and more elements that could only be used in one set was a practical one: it vastly increased the complexity of the production process, and that was costing Lego a lot of money. At their optimum the moulding machines run 24 hours a day, but to produce a specialised element meant stopping the machine, purging the plastic from the tubes, lifting out the mould with a crane, putting in a new mould by crane and running through the new coloured plastic, which could take several hours of valuable production time. By 2004 Lego was producing as many as 14,000 separate elements, many of them unique to only one set. One of Knudstorp's first reforms (along with selling off the theme parks, axing a number of product lines and making inevitable redundancies) was to rationalise the number of elements being produced. 'We've come back to the real deal. Modular parts that are part of a system. We're now back to about 7,500 elements.'

As for the future, Knudstorp intends to diversify again, but more slowly this time and founded in the core values of the system of play. In fact, it is already happening. The Lego Group is meeting the computer games challenge head on with its own computer games and its MMOG (massively multiplayer online game), Lego Universe, but this time the focus is clearly centred on Lego and what it stands for; the underlying principle will be to adapt the medium to Lego rather than adapting Lego to the medium. For instance, in 2009 Lego made its first steps into the tough market of board games, but on its own terms: you build your own board, and once you've played the game and seen how it works you adapt the structure of the game by rebuilding the board.

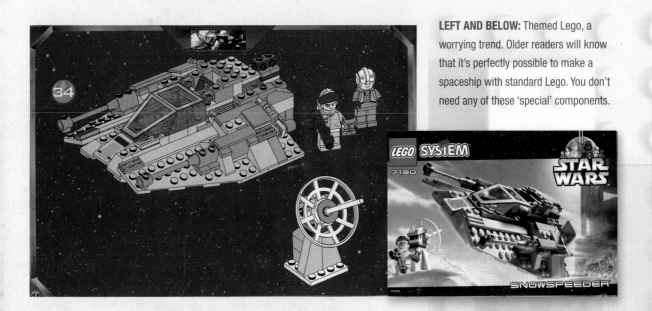

LEFT AND BELOW: Themed Lego, a worrying trend. Older readers will know that it's perfectly possible to make a spaceship with standard Lego. You don't need any of these 'special' components.

Making Lego

Approximately 19 billion Lego elements are made every year at the factory in Billund, which is about two million an hour, 36,000 a minute, or 600 every second of every day. These astronomical figures conjure up an image of the factory as a frantically busy place full of noisy, frenetic activity, but, in fact, it is calm, sedate, and surprisingly quiet. Robots move silently over spotless floors collecting plastic cartons of newly made Lego from the automated moulding machines, while human workers glide effortlessly round the premises on futuristic tricycle scooters. Every so often the hush is broken by a sound like the tinkling of hundreds of rainsticks, as millions of granules of plastic are sucked through a network of pipes from the storage silos to the moulding machines. Adding to the sense that Willy Wonka is overseeing the whole operation, each pipe is painted in the primary colour of the granules it contains, creating a rainbow of coloured tubes.

The Billund factory has 841 computer-controlled injection-moulding machines operating 24 hours a day, producing Lego elements to a tolerance of just two-thousandths of a millimetre, which is far less than the width of a human hair. There are also a further 337 machines at factories in Hungary and Mexico, which brings the total number of machines in operation to 1,120 worldwide with more coming on stream by 2010. The moulding tools in all of them are made with such precision that their success rate for achieving this microscopic level of accuracy is 99.9982 per cent – in other words, just 18 elements in every million fail to meet the Lego quality standard.

The reason for such exacting standards is that getting the binding of the

BELOW: Every few seconds scores of injection-moulding machines disgorge hundreds of newly made Lego elements in a huge variety of colours. Here 16 elements are pushed out of the mould (left) onto a conveyor belt (right) which carries them to a plastic container. When the container is full a robot replaces it with an empty one.

bricks right is absolutely vital to the success of Lego. The current CEO, Jørgen Vig Knudstorp, explains:

Any one of the 19 billion elements we make each year must bind with any other element that has been made since 1958. When bricks come out of the machines the clutch power is actually too hard. It is only after they have been stored for a couple of weeks that the clutch becomes perfect. If you put Lego bricks together for a long period, let's say ten years, the clutch wanes because they have been tight for such a long time. Then you take them apart and let them rest for a couple of weeks and the clutch is perfect again.

The first Lego bricks were made from cellulose acetate but since 1962 they have been made from acrylonitrile-butadeine-styrene copolymer, or ABS, which is a very robust, hardwearing thermo-plastic. ('Thermo-plastic' means a plastic that is pliable when heated but rigid when cool. Other Lego elements such as trees or ladders or chains are made of softer thermo-plastics, including polystyrene.) The ABS is delivered to the factory in the form of granules, and Billund uses approximately 60 tonnes of granulate per day. This is stored in silos outside the factory, from which the granulate is sucked through the rainbow network of pipes to the machine room and mixed to create one of the 60 colours in the current Lego palette.

BELOW: By pushing the wrong button on the control panel, I accidently made 1,000 million blue eighters and completely buried a whole Danish city under a stream of Lego lava.

The moulding machines heat the granulate to anywhere between 230 and 290° C, at which temperature the granules melt and congeal into a sticky mass with a texture similar to bread dough. This viscous mass is then injected into the moulds at a pressure of between 25 and 150 tonnes, depending on what type of element is being produced. It takes just seven seconds for the molten plastic to cool, the two halves of the mould to be separated, the finished elements to be ejected into a carton and the entire cycle to begin again. Each injection produces several elements (depending on what is being produced) so the cartons fill rapidly before being collected by robot and placed on a conveyor to be sent for checking and packing.

Thanks to the level of automation, two human employees can now oversee 64 computer-controlled machines. It is a far cry from the days when the moulds were hand operated and, according to one Lego employee, 'One man would be on each mould, pulling the lever to close it and then taking two puffs on a cigar, which would be the right time interval to release it again.'

Apart from the automation and the change from acetate to ABS, the process has changed very little since 1958, and many of the basic elements are made to exactly the same design. However, variety and innovation are to be found in the number and range of specialised elements, which changes year on year – Lego currently produces more than 7,000 different elements, comprising approximately 3,000 shapes in a variety of different colours.

LOCATION, LOCATION, LOCATION

One of the world's most widely recognised design icons is the famous ribbed bottle containing a well-known brand of cola. The design brief for the bottle was that it must be instantly recognisable, even in the dark (by touch) or if it was broken. That brief was admirably fulfilled, as anyone will testify who has ever found a sand-smoothed fragment of cola bottle on the beach or drunk cola in the dark.

But Lego has gone further.

Not only are Lego bricks instantly recognisable in the dark (particularly if you tread on one in your bare feet) and even if only a fraction of the brick is visible. But they are also instantly recognisable, even if you can't see them *or* feel them, by their sound: by that unique brittle clicking cascade as someone scrabbles around in the box or tips them onto the table.

That sound is the music of the spheres of the pointy-cornered universe that is Lego, where imperfection will not be tolerated and where defective elements are melted down and remade in the perfect image of the primordial brick. The mystery of the cosmos lies in Lego; in the way it is based around one very simple idea but done in such a way that it is infinitely variable. Lego, in its simple complexity – its complex simplicity – is a self-fulfilling plastic prophecy: yin and yang and alpha and omega all rolled into one.

The world's religions have given us a great many figurative icons – the Holy Grail, the Sword and Cloak of Mohammed and the Ark of the Covenant, to name but a few. But if I were to found a new religion I would base it on the original red eighter (eight-stud) Lego brick. Why? Because Lego obeys rules. It obeys the rules of the straight and the square and the cube, and the base system of numbers; it offers the ultimate in self-expression and creativity but couched within a reassuring framework of immutable Lego law; it is a universal force for good in the world because it is universally adored and everyone loves the sensation of clipping it together. And if you take just six eighters of the same colour, the number of ways you can combine them runs into the hundreds of millions. So you can make something the size of a temple, any shape you want, and yet all the pips will always point to heaven. So my Lego house would be not only an experiment in engineering, not only a country retreat in which I

BELOW: Lego – the full-size building material of the future, possibly.

would live for a few days and invite my friends to party; it would also be a temple, celebrating and affirming the very existence of Lego itself.

If, of course, it was even possible to build a life-size house out of Lego.

It's something I've wanted to do since I was a child. I would often fantasise, as I'm sure most kids do, about what I could do if I had an infinitely big box of Lego. How far could I keep going, how big could I build?

It sounds simple. You just clip the bricks together and away you go. But no one has ever done it before – no one has ever built a self-supporting Lego structure that you can actually go inside. So there were lots of questions that would have to be answered before I could build a two-storey Lego house that would not only stand up, but would be one in which I could sit on a Lego chair to eat at my Lego table, walk up my Lego stairs to shower in my Lego shower, and brush my teeth at my Lego basin before going to bed in my Lego bed.

Would I be able to relax and go to sleep? Or would I find myself lying awake all night worrying that the whole thing was going to collapse, and that I'd wake up – or not – buried in Lego?

The architect said he was confident it would work, telling me: 'You should wake up at the same height you go to sleep.'

I couldn't help noticing that he used the word 'should', not 'will'…

The Lego vernacular

Among the first questions to be answered were: where should I build my house, and what style should I build it in.

My first idea was to build it in a vacant plot on an ordinary urban street but it soon became apparent that I was going to have all sorts of problems with security and with planning permission: no local authority would give me permission, even when I promised them it would be brick-built.

Then it occurred to me that I've never lived in the country, because I don't really understand the countryside, so I decided to give it a try: my Lego house could be my country retreat. Denbies Wine Estate in Surrey was quite happy to have me, and I'm quite interested in drinking wine, so it seemed like the perfect solution from my point of view. But maybe not from Denbies' point of view. They'll be finding Lego bricks among the vines for years to come, and I can't help wondering whether that will affect the *terroir* – it might give the wine a rather angular quality.

Anyway, I invited Barnaby Gunning, my chosen architect, to come and view the site. He was slightly concerned about the sloping ground but that's an inevitable part of building in a vineyard – vines like a slope. So we decided that the house should look as if it had grown out of the slope; as if it had emerged out of the earth and the slope had fallen away below it.

'As if we've peeled back the grass to reveal the Lego beneath?' asked Barnaby.

'Yes,' I agreed, warming to the theme. 'As if the world is a great big ball of Lego and the house is a bit that's just poked through the surface.' But that didn't help us decide what it should look like. I didn't want to make a Lego

house like a scaled-up kit; I didn't want it to be a Lego representation of some tiresome Georgian pile. I wanted something very modern; something specifically designed to be made from Lego rather than something designed as a house that we then happen to make from Lego. If we were to design a house that played to the strengths of Lego and avoided its weaknesses we would get a specific type of house – an inherently Lego house, in the way that the design of concrete houses, brick houses and wooden houses all reflect the properties of the materials they are made from.

In other words, I didn't want a house made of Lego, I wanted a Lego house, which is subtly different.

Barnaby christened our revolutionary, and as-yet-unresolved, architectural style the Lego vernacular. He imagined a body of architecture growing to include modular Lego houses that could be stacked together to make Lego apartment blocks. That reminded me of a friend of mine who, as a child, had a Lego kit of a house. Sometimes she would use the bricks as intended, to build the house, but sometimes she would treat each brick like a separate house and spread them out to make a city of miniature houses. Both hers and Barnaby's ideas played on the incontrovertible logic of Lego, Barnaby expanding the logic outwards, imagining a complete house as a component of something larger, and my friend contracting it inwards, using the components of her house as complete units in themselves.

These two concepts gave me an idea for the design of the house: it should be based on the proportions of the eighter brick, which was the foundation stone of the entire Lego universe. Perhaps the interior could even have three supporting columns, like the tubes within the brick. It was an elegant idea, and if it turned out that the answer to the Lego house lay in the Lego brick itself that would be highly satisfying and would give unstoppable momentum to my idea that a new religion should be based around Lego. It would be Revelation in a plastic brick. It would be the Truth. It would be what humankind has been searching for.

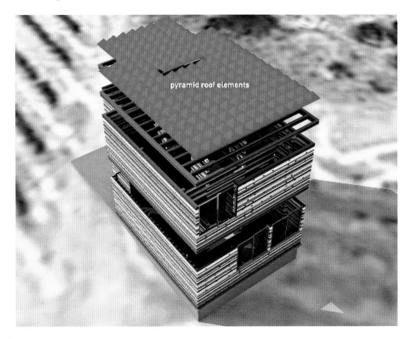

Pick 'n' Mix

As a child I always liked the feeling of dipping my hand in a box of Lego and stirring it about. When I saw the massive tubs of brand-new bricks at the factory I was tempted to shove my arm in up to the shoulder or put my entire head in there as the next best thing to being able to totally immerse myself in it. And I loved the Pick 'n' Mix brick boxes in the Legoland shop. But this was beyond my wildest dreams. I was standing in the doorway of a steel shipping container looking at 500,000 Lego elements. And there were five more containers next to this one. I now had three *million* Lego elements in 60 different colours to play with – enough to fill a swimming pool, let alone dip my head into.

Working out how many elements of each type and colour to order was tricky given that the house still only existed as a rough sketch, so I had simply made an educated guess at the minimum I would require and ordered that. As the design was refined I would order more. You can't buy more than about three million in one go anyway because nobody stocks that amount; not even the factory. In fact, when I tried to order another 500,000 from the factory a few weeks later they didn't have enough so in the end the house was made up of 3.3 million elements.

The next question was: how long would it take to put three million elements together?

Professional contractors can make estimates based on their existing knowledge of how long it takes a brickie to build a wall, or a cement mixer to pour cement. But no one had ever built Lego on this scale before, so there was no official measure or quantification of how long it takes to build life-size walls out of Lego – and I needed to know that in order to work out how long it would take to build a house. So I got three pairs of volunteers and gave them all two hours to build a wall with a window in it.

The end result was three very interesting-looking walls of varying degrees of flimsiness. But the frightening thing was just how much slower it was than I'd imagined; so slow, in fact, that I was starting to worry about whether we'd ever be able to build a house. All three teams had managed to build a passable wall but none of them was more than three feet square – and that was nothing compared to the size of a house.

We were going to need either hundreds and hundreds of days or hundreds and hundreds of people – or both. Even if 1,000 people put together 1,000 bricks each we would still only be a third of the way there. It was clear that the only way we were going to get the house built would be to design a modular building block and to get a very large team of people making these blocks on a production line off site. The blocks could then be ferried up to the site and the actual house should go together relatively quickly using those prefabricated components.

So Barnaby designed a standard modular component and I put out an appeal to the great British public.

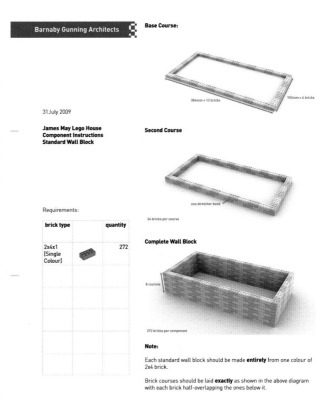

Barnaby Gunning Architects

31 July 2009

James May Lego House Component Instructions Standard Wall Block

Requirements:

brick type		quantity
2x4x1 [Single Colour]		272

Base Course:

384mm = 12 bricks   192mm = 6 bricks

Second Course

use stretcher bond

34 bricks per course

Complete Wall Block

8 courses

272 bricks per component

Note:

Each standard wall block should be made **entirely** from one colour of 2x4 brick.

Brick courses should be laid **exactly** as shown in the above diagram with each brick half-overlapping the ones below it.

ABOVE: Barnaby's technical drawing for the standard modular component to be made by the Great British Public.

OPPOSITE: Barnaby's model for the house, layer by layer.

Octuplo

Right, listen up workforce! You are effectively in the Victorian workhouse doing a repetitive job for no money and possibly a bowl of gruel. What you're doing is making the building blocks for the house out of the Lego bricks. I know it looks quite simple from the diagram – it's 272 Lego bricks in eight courses overlapped in a stretcher bond – but it's very important that you do it correctly, because one faulty block will ruin the structural integrity of the entire house. Right, we need tens of thousands of these blocks, all made up of Lego bricks of the same colour. That's it. Carry on!

The response from the public had been phenomenal. There were so many inquiries that we had to put out a second appeal for people to stay away because we weren't going to have room for them all. Despite that, more than 2,000 people turned up at Denbies from as far afield as Birmingham, and queued from 5:30 a.m. to help build the Lego breeze blocks from which the house would be constructed. Unfortunately, we only had room for 1,100 volunteers but they worked like Trojans and built about 4,000 breeze blocks in various colours.

At last, construction of the Lego house had begun and it seemed as if it could actually become a reality.

In the meantime, the design had evolved considerably, but it was still based on the idea of the house being a giant version of a standard eighter. Barnaby explained how he had developed the concept: 'One of the things I immediately noticed about the Lego brick is it has this strange mathematical logic where the dimensions of the brick scale up in multiples of two.'

This I already knew: Duplo bricks are double the length, height and width of a standard Lego brick, hence the name Duplo. But they are actually eight times as big as a standard brick because 2 x 2 x 2 = 8.

'On the same principle,' Barnaby continued, 'if you multiply each of the dimensions by 256, which is two times itself eight times, you get a shape which is about two metres in height from floor to floor. That's not a bad size for a house: slightly smaller than usual but quite nice. The fact that it's scaled up from a standard brick means that I can show you a very simple 1:256 scale model of the exterior of the house.'

And with that he clipped two eighters on top of each other and handed them to me: 'Here's your model.'

It was genius.

Not only was I going to be living in a Lego house, I was going to be living in two stacked eighters scaled up by two to the power of eight. You can keep your seventh heaven: here was paradise in eights. I would call it Octuplo, even though each storey of the house would actually be 256 x 256 x 256 = 16.8 million times the size of a standard brick. It meant, as I had expected all along, that the shape of the building was going to be very plain and austere – very brick-like, in fact – but that plainness was more than made up for by the design details and the colour scheme.

My first instinct had been that the colours should be quite random, because the random and chaotic nature of the mixing of Lego bricks is part of what Lego is about. But having seen Barnaby's visualisations I decided that I liked the idea of his more formal scheme – stripes of colour in the courses of the blockwork, or panels of colour à la Piet Mondrian. In the end, we settled on a mixture: stripes of colour for the exterior walls, bold blocks of red for two of the interior supporting walls and a random assortment for the third. But the randomness of that third interior wall had to be enlarged to suit the size of the house; if individual Lego bricks had been arranged randomly it would have made no visual sense at all. So each modular block was a single colour but those blocks were arranged randomly, thus scaling up the randomness so that the rhythm of randomness was as it should be.

BOTH PAGES: More than 2,000 people queued up to help build the house, and by the end of the day we had more than 4,000 blocks in various colours. Some of the blocks even contained 'micro windows', which would let a dappled light into the finished house.

Bricking it

So: we had a design, we had several thousand modular blocks, and we had a team of people in the winery making furniture, fittings and specialist parts. The components would be ferried up the hill and assembled on site – it would be just like making a Lego kit, except that the bricks would be bigger. And in theory it would be much quicker than building with bricks and mortar because we wouldn't have to mix cement, slap it on, and align each course of bricks using string and a spirit level. Lego is automatically level, and the integrity of Lego is such that once you've established the footprint you know it will go together – it has to, it's an immutable law of Lego. There's no way you can get half way up and then find that the Lego doesn't fit any more because any Lego brick fits with any other Lego brick. Which was quite reassuring, because it meant that nothing could go wrong.

Except that something did go wrong.

When it came to signing off the engineer's drawings we discovered that no one would insure the building because there was no existing data on Lego as a building material, which meant that no one could confirm that it was safe. We had thoroughly tested our components with bags of gravel that cumulatively weighed far more than I do, so we knew that our structure would work, but that was not enough. With a conventional building you can do structural calculations using an accumulation of knowledge about your materials, but no one had ever used Lego as a building material so that accumulated knowledge was not available. Which meant there was no way of doing the calculations. The drawings couldn't be signed off without insurance, and the insurers insisted on the building having a wooden frame, because there is an accumulation of knowledge about the strength of wood. But that completely defeated our object of using Lego as a building material.

I was devastated. It looked as if we would have to start the entire design again from scratch but then Barnaby came up with an ingenious solution: stick to our basic design but build it around the wooden frame without touching it, so that the frame would be there as a safety net if any of the Lego structure failed. The Lego structure itself would still be largely self-supporting. So that's what we did. The frame was erected and the Lego blocks were slotted over the wooden uprights, which stood like a skeleton within the cavities of the Lego brickwork. The only real structural concession was that the upper floor was supported by wooden joists instead of Lego ones, but otherwise the house remained true to itself – and at least *we* knew that Lego joists would have done the same job even if the insurers refused to take our word for it.

So it was still a Lego house, and when I was inside it I would still be walking on Lego, sitting on Lego, leaning on Lego and lying on Lego. And relieving myself on Lego, if my Lego lavatory was progressing according to plan. It would certainly put a new spin on the phrase 'bricking it'.

OPPOSITE: Lego is a force for good, bringing communities together in peace, etc.
ABOVE RIGHT: I was delighted with the public build day, the results of which were piling up all around me...
BELOW RIGHT: ... but very disappointed when the insurers insisted that for health and safety reasons the house had to have a wooden skeleton. We ended up building the walls around the skeleton without touching it.

Housewarming

They say that moving into a new house is one of the most stressful days of a person's life, but as I walked through the rows of Chardonnay on a glorious September morning I was really looking forward to it. The cursed wooden frame had caused all sorts of problems and delays but at last the house was finished and I was about to see the answer to the question I had asked myself as a six-year-old boy; a question I'm sure millions of other boys and girls have asked themselves as well: if you had enough Lego bricks, could you build a real Lego house?

The answer, as I rounded the last corner and looked up the hill, was clear: 'Yes you can.'

The house looked absolutely stupendous with its bold stripes and multi-faceted roof catching the morning light; with its vibrant primary plastic colours perfectly offsetting the natural green of the vines. And the view from the outside was nothing compared to the cornucopia of Lego treats that lay inside. True to homeowning tradition, the Lego key was hidden under the Lego flowerpot next to the Lego doormat. I inserted the key in the lock, slid it to the side, opened the Lego door (hung on Lego Technics hinges) and stepped over the threshold. It was like entering another dimension. This was my childhood fantasy come true. I was overwhelmed by Lego; this wasn't like stepping into a massive house made out of Lego, it was like being shrunk and stepping into a tiny Lego-scale house. Everything was Lego. Walls, floor, chairs, tables, newspaper. Cat. Light fittings. A kitchen with Lego toaster, Lego washing machine, Lego cutlery and utensils, even a Lego salad and an open bar of Lego chocolate.

Upstairs the imagination and wit of the people who had made these things continued to overflow everywhere I looked. The volunteers who had come up with all the ideas for Lego clutter, the Lego trappings of everyday Lego life, had excelled themselves. The fact that upstairs existed at all was amazing enough – I had originally thought we might manage a bungalow or a beach hut – but the details took it to another level. The Lego bed was made with Lego sheets and Lego pillows, and there was even a pair of Lego slippers. Next to the Lego basin in the Lego bathroom was a Lego razor, Lego toothbrush and flattened Lego tube of toothpaste; there was a working Lego shower and next to that the *pièce de résistance* – a stunningly engineered Lego lavatory, complete with flushing mechanism and ball-cock, all painstakingly made from Lego.

In short, it was a triumph. Barnaby's achievement in creating the structure was matched only by that of interior designer Christina Fallah and her team of volunteers in creating the furniture, fittings and lighting. When I looked in the Lego mirror I expected to see the face of a six-year-old boy looking back at me. I was living a childhood dream.

OPPOSITE: The house takes shape. Pressing all the pieces together was wearing on the fingers, so as the walls rose higher we started using rubber mallets.

TOP: When I arrived on the final day the Lego key was under the Lego plant pot by the Lego 'Welcome' doormat.

ABOVE: Someone anonymously donated a Lego cat to the Lego house. He was later stolen, and I hadn't had him chipped.

The reality of being in the house was better than I had ever imagined it could be, by a factor of ten. And it was about to get even better, as the guests started arriving for the housewarming. Gerald Scarfe arrived with a caricature of me – done in Lego of course – to hang on the wall; Jane Asher arrived in time to convince me that I was not going to be able to prepare food for 20 guests in a kitchen with no cooker (although we did manage to make cheese sandwiches with the Lego utensils) and then Oz Clarke arrived bearing the all-important wine, which I insisted we decant into a Lego bottle.

'What is that?' demanded Oz.

'It's a Lego Margaux bottle. We have to pour the wine out of a Lego bottle.'

'It looks like a pre-Second World War Cologne bottle. It's leaking! Oh James… James, this is good wine. This is New Zealand's most famous Pinot Noir and it's leaking everywhere! This is pathetic. What made you think you could make a wine bottle out of Lego?'

'I thought it would last long enough. Here, pour it into these.'

'What are those? They look like bird baths.'

OPPOSITE: Dining area, bathroom, stairs, and the view from the Minstrel's Gallery.
TOP: Goblets of wine for the party guests.
ABOVE: Gerald Scarfe's ten-second sketch, and the resulting Lego cartoon.

Christina's top tips

The design for the whole kitchen was based on 'words and colour', so the accessories had words on them rather than brand names – 'Ice' for the fridge, 'Jug' for pouring liquids and 'Chop' for the chopping board. The key to anything in Lego is to work in 3D, try things out and experiment as you go along. There is no such thing as the right or wrong way to make something in Lego.

Building the jug: Use 2 x 4 white studs as a frame (as with the main bricks for the house, see page 223), so that the perimeter surface is smooth; this is known in the business as 'studs not on top', aka SNOT. When halfway up simply set out the letters in black so that they stand out from afar.

'They're goblets. Pour it in, go on – I've waterproofed them.'

'James, you are destroying an outstandingly good bottle of wine. You are a lout … Good God that is excellent. I thought it was going to be completely ruined with your wretched plastic bottle and goblets but it's delicious. Do you get raspberry and a hint of beetroot?'

'No,' I said. 'I get cling film, which is what I waterproofed the goblets with.'

None of the other guests seemed to be worried about drinking from Lego goblets or eating their Lego-shaped canapés from Lego plates. In fact, the Lego crockery lent itself perfectly to party behaviour, because if anyone wanted to put down their plate or goblet all they had to do was fix it to the windowsill or the wall or the furniture. And if anyone dropped a goblet all they had to do was clip it back together, refill it and carry on drinking. Perfect.

My guests included Jane McAdam Freud, who had helped me unleash my creativity on the Plasticine garden, Tiff Needell, my roving reporter on the historic Scalextric race, several of the Liverpool University students who had helped build the Meccano bridge, and Oz, who had shared the disappointment of the model railway. All of them were magnanimous enough to be impressed with my Lego house but no one was more impressed than me, as I made clear in a heartfelt speech thanking all the people – nearly 2,000 in all – who had come together to make the house a reality.

Well, good evening everyone, thank you very much for coming, and welcome to my new house. Thanks especially to those of you here who helped to build it. I know it wasn't easy and there were a few tense moments and some tears along the way but I'm chuffed to bits with it. This Lego house stands as a monument to a childhood ambition shared with lots of people, and to the versatility of Lego, and to the way people come together and work for nothing on something if they think it's a great idea and it enthuses them. And Lego has that effect on people. Everybody loves the sensation of putting it together pulling it apart, and all your other cares and concerns fall away with the simple pleasure of sticking bits of plastic together and making something. And if you get enough people doing that you end up with a house to live in. It's the best house I've ever had, frankly. It's absolutely fantastic. We've possibly lost sight of the simple joy of playing with things. Maybe we should rediscover it; I think it might be good for us.

TOP LEFT: A selection of Lego housewarming gifts. **LEFT:** Christina Fallah, who designed so many wonderful things for my house. Here she is arriving at the party with her gift of a teapot. **TOP RIGHT:** Oz Clarke, me, Jane McAdam Freud and Tiff Needell toast the house with our Lego goblets. **RIGHT:** The lovely Jane Asher, Lego chocs in hand, admires my brickwork.

And so to bed...

At last everyone left – even Oz, despite his protestations that he wanted a lock-in and expected to stay the night. I discovered that certain other home-owning traditions were still alive and well in the Lego universe, like deciding to leave the washing up till the following morning and discovering that one of your guests has left an extra housewarming present in your lavatory – having made my weary way up the stairs to go to bed I discovered a single brown eighter floating in the pan. Luckily Kevin Cooper's ingenious Lego flush mechanism worked perfectly and swept the offending brick out of sight.

And now came the real measure of any new house – how soundly would I sleep? The bed was hard, but not unpleasant (an opinion I would revise by morning) but the Lego sheets proved to be purely ornamental – I was going to need a real blanket made out of real fabric. So I curled up under my luxurious red blanket and filmed the final scene: 'Well viewers, it's been absolutely fantastic. I hope you've enjoyed the Lego house as much as I have but, the fact is, all I've done so far is mince around drinking some wine and eating some sandwiches. Now I'm putting it to the acid test. I'm about to become the first person in history to spend the night in his own Lego house. Here goes... Goodnight everyone.'

And I turned off the lights.

Then I turned them on again, said goodbye to the film crew, and did it again for real.

Now I really was about to become the first person in history to spend the night in a Lego house. The generator was turned off and silence descended on the vineyard.

Despite Barnaby's reticence all those months earlier, I was confident that I would wake up at the same height I went to sleep. I expected that my dreams would be angular and primary coloured. As I drifted towards sleep I still couldn't shake off the sensation that I had passed through some hole in the space–time continuum and that I might now be forever in a land of Lego; that when I woke up the following morning the sun would be made of Lego, and the clouds.

And so I fell asleep with the thought that if it was ever overcast in my Lego world I would be able to dismantle the clouds and remake them as a battleship, or a tank, or a piano, or a Citroën 2CV like the one my mother used to drive. Lego has no permanence, but it will surely go on for ever.

RIGHT: Feeling weary but happy I bade goodbye to my guests and made my way to bed. The pillows were hard, the mattress was hard, the sheets didn't work and the slippers made me look as if I had elephantitis of the feet but it was still a historic moment. I was about to become the first person ever to sleep in a Lego house.

OPPOSITE: The house looked splendid in the floodlights... until the crew went home and turned off the generator.

MMIX

REFERENCE
ANORAKS' CORNER

101 USES FOR 'Plasticine'®

MADE ONLY BY HARBUTT'S PLASTICINE LTD

Plasticine has many other uses than that of Modelling. It is impossible to give anything like a complete list because those who have Plasticine are continually finding fresh uses for it. Plasticine being an "Ever Permanent Pliable Material". "Clean and Non-toxic, Harmless and Innocuous", it is only natural that there are many uses for it.

It is used extensively in many factories and industries for experimental work and other purposes.

We may state that we were invited to visit the National Physical Laboratory at Teddington to observe the uses to which Plasticine had been put.

Plasticine can be regarded as of real practical use to industries in technical development. You may have some difficulty or problem that Plasticine may be the means of solving, so bear this in mind or better still obtain a supply at once.

Many of the 101 Uses given to help you may be only of a temporary nature but having Plasticine ready to hand it may be invaluable in an emergency.

Most of the 101 Uses we have tried ourselves and found sound and practical.

Harbutt's started producing 'Uses for Plasticine' leaflets in 1908. By the time that this undated leaflet (priced at 2 pence) was printed, the number of uses was far in excess of 101.

A FEW HINTS

Be sure to apply Plasticine to a dry surface, it will not stick to anything wet. The best way of removing Plasticine is to rub with a large lump of it. A touch of Petrol from a cigarette lighter fuel tin will remove traces of it from fabrics or the hands.

It can be painted with shellac, varnish and oil colours, which forms a protective skin.

In fixing a piece to a surface, better adhesion is obtained by first smearing a thin layer thereon before attaching the larger piece, which should be well worked on. If surface is porous it should be shellac varnished to prevent absorption.

Avoid dust and dirt being worked into Plasticine.

Slightly warming will make Plasticine more easily workable or working in petroleum jelly will render softer.

ADVERTISING AGENTS

For producing effective illustrations, lettering, etc., by photograph from original models.

ARCHITECTS

Scale models of houses, public buildings, etc.

The model of Charing Cross Bridge and approaches, exhibited by Sir Reginald Blomfield, R.A. was made in Plasticine.

ARTISTS

Artists and painters can carry two wet oil paintings by placing a small piece of Plasticine at each corner and tying together with string.

An emergency water pot when sketching – *can be stuck on edge of canvas or drawing board.*

DOCTORS, DENTISTS AND MEDICAL

Demonstrating many features of difficult operative surgery.

Occupational therapy, rheumatism, working with Plasticine eases joints and stiffness in fingers and hands, patients should manipulate Plasticine by copying demonstrator.

Plasticine is also of great benefit to convalescent, mentally deficient and blind children, to keep them occupied.

Operative surgery in the absence of a Cadaver can be taught better from a Plasticine Model than from a cast.

Ear Plugs. Plasticine has been used in the Navy and Army during heavy gun fire, *and also in Boiler Maker Shops.*

For Dentists to display artificial teeth, a board coated with Plasticine enables them to be removed or replaced with ease and they are not likely to fall off or get out of place.

ELECTRICAL WORK

For filling joint boxes and keeping cable glands watertight. Fulfils Admiralty requirements.

Non-conducting bed for electric wires.

Temporary fixing of electric wires.

Locating different circuits – ends of conductors may be located by nipping a small piece of Plasticine on each end; one, two, or more pieces on individual wires and coloured Plasticine will increase the range.

ENGINEERING AND WORKSHOP

Model making, experiments, alterations, and an aid to designing jigs and tools.

In Inventing. Actual results may often be determined and foreseen by making a model in Plasticine where practicable.

In sheet metal work for the development of surfaces.

To take squeeze moulds of carving and any relief work.

To find any point of contact on hinged or other articles.

Holding a scriber or pointer in any desired position.

Awkward shaped parts or objects can be held firmly in position on face plate while being checked and measured.

To ensure a large drill is in correct position for drilling a hole – fix pin or small drill with Plasticine to the centre and end of drill, on rotating will show any error in setting over centre pop.

A wall or weir of Plasticine round small object, will stand up long enough to allow a lead casting to be made.

Determining gap or clearance between two surfaces that cannot be readily measured, a pellet of Plasticine is squeezed between the two and afterwards measured, moisture will prevent sticking.

Fixing a metal thread screw in an awkward position. Place pellet of Plasticine on head of screw, insert screwdriver in slot securing Plasticine well to screwdriver and screw, screw can be guided to the hole and will not fall.

Balancing a wheel, crankshaft, propeller or revolving object, a piece of Plasticine is stuck at one portion until the wheel is in equilibrium, metal is removed at opposite side, the amount of which should be weighed to balance the Plasticine.

To illustrate, particularly to the uninitiated, a section, by cutting a model of Plasticine at desired points – also applicable to Geographical and Architectural models. (Cut with a fine wire or razor blade.)

Die Sinkers and Tool Makers – to test the progress of the work.

Pattern making – to form a radius where two adjacent surfaces meet, a thin roll of Plasticine smeared along by the finger afterwards shellacked or painted.

Oil Bath. It is sometimes necessary to let oil soak into a tight, rusted or seized bearing which may be also in an awkward position. A bath or wall of Plasticine is built round the bearing and filled with oil.

Forging. Determining amount of metal to be allowed for in forging work. In many cases an actual "forging" can be made beforehand with Plasticine – which behaves to a certain extent as plastic red hot iron would.

Holding Micrometer Gauges safe on a work bench. The slightest touch when a micrometer is placed on the bench may upset the reading – have a lump of Plasticine on the bench and this will hold the arm of the micrometer.

To Hold Two Objects in exact position while being soldered together.

Heat, of course, should not be allowed to reach the Plasticine to any extent.

A Collar or Band around a twist drill will determine the depth it is intended to drill.

Fill socket screws with Plasticine to prevent filling with paint or enamel. The hard skin can be broken at any time and key inserted.

GARDENING

Grafting fruit trees, shrubs, etc.

Protecting cut branches of trees, and for wounds on trees.

Training small creepers and shoots on walls.

"Train a creeper in the way it should grow."

Plasticine straps here and there will last long enough in the open for the plant to get a good hold of the wall or fence.

Glazing greenhouses, frames, etc.

HOME USES

Should an accident occur, and you have a broken plate or vase, just keep the bits in place with Plasticine, *till you can get the edges to stick together*.

Leaky Buckets, Pots and Pans are instantly rendered fit for use by a small pellet – *be sure to apply dry*.

Indeed it has been found that water may be boiled in a kettle so mended.

To prevent a window or door rattling in windy weather.

Stopping a draught crack in door or window.

Emergency corks for bottles.

Temporary positioning of Electric Wires or Flex.

To dull the tick of a clock, alarm or telephone bell, or any other type of bell.

Leaky farm boots, worked in round welt (dry boots first).

Stop mouse hole.

For large holes roll Plasticine round a wad of paper first; mice will not touch Plasticine.

To balance small scales. (Not for Trade purposes.)

Temporary repair only of leaking gas pipes.

Leaking water pipes not subject to pressure, apply a pad of Plasticine when pipe is quite dry and bind round with tape.

An emergency repair to spectacle frames, lenses can also be held in position.

For making cases, or tins, etc., airtight.

For keeping small objects safe on glass shelves *(As used in the British Museum.)*

To fix Christmas decorations and evergreens.

To hold decorations on a Christmas Tree.

To hold small piece of glass over a hole in a window pane.

For holding fractured window panes together.

For leaks in lead casement windows.

To fill cracks in a draughty and uneven floor.
Can be stained or painted afterwards.

Temporary repairs to leaks in roof – *In slate tiles repairs may be made without disturbing tiles.*

As a wash basin or bath plug.

As a spout – fixed on a bucket or other vessel when pouring out liquid.

As a pin cushion also needles and drawing pins.

When having broken glass, numerous fine splinters remain on the floor or other place – these cannot always be removed entirely with a brush – a piece of Plasticine dabbed all over the locality will

effectually pick up and retain same – *Plasticine should then be burnt.*

Stopping mats from slipping.

LANDSCAPE GARDENING, FOUNTAINS, WATERFALLS, STREAMS, ETC.

Many public and private Golf Courses are first laid out with the aid of Plasticine in natural colours.

Owners of large estates often have a small scale model of their own grounds.

LUTING

For bottles with volatile contents, and to keep samples sealed and water tight. Also as a temporary cover for glasses containing liquids that are liable to oxidise or evaporate (*ascertain Plasticine is not affected by the liquid*).

MOTORING

Plasticine should always be included in "Spares" outfit.

To pick small nuts, etc., out of awkward places – *place a lump on the end of a stick*.

Temporary repair to leaky petrol pipe, tank, water joint or radiator.

Filling cracks and holes to prevent fumes entering car.

Holds inspection lamp in any position while doing repairs on road.

Testing ignition, H.T. cables end is securely held close to "earth" or cylinder head, while engine is turned and condition of spark observed. Spark plugs tested same way.

Fixing tools in a bed of Plasticine – cover bed with cheese cloth before pressing each tool into its permanent place.

NATURALISTS

Insects can be preserved by placing between two pieces of glass or celluloid separated by Plasticine – an antiseptic can be introduced.

Taking impression of leaves, etc.

For collecting and preserving butterflies, insects and specimens.

Approved by Entomological Department, Royal College of Science, London.

For Microscope Work

If you have a particularly lively insect that you wish to examine under the microscope, catch him on the end of a stick of Plasticine.

He will stay in the one spot till you tire of looking at him.

OFFICE AND BUSINESS

Removing dirt or fluff from typewriter letters or keys.

A piece stuck to the window pane enables a show card or object to be hung from it.

Packing delicate and fragile objects for parcel post.

A useful pen or pencil holder on the side of a desk – not for nibs.

PHOTOGRAPHERS

Cracks in the dark-room door, one touch of Plasticine and the room is safe again.

To hold flowers in position, even when placed in a vase, it is indispensable; many a leaf will bend to its proper place if a little lump of Plasticine of sufficient weight is pressed on to the reverse side.

A strip of it placed round the edges of a plate will form a glass-bottom tray for emergency developing, when no proper dish is handy.

For steadying the camera, or a small background when placed on a table, it has no equal – *as Plasticine will not slip.*

To level a developing dish.

An emergency lens shade.
Flatten a piece out and press it around the lens.

PLASTER CASTING

Plasticine is of course ideal for casting in Plaster of Paris; impression from objects are rendered easy by building a wall of Plasticine round the object.

SCIENTIFIC INSTRUMENT MAKERS AND LABORATORY WORK

For adjusting lenses, holding indicators, etc.

In optical work to hold lenses when adjusting foci.

For keeping very small objects safely.

For holding test tubes containing liquids.

For holding retorts.

For directing and regulating flow of liquids.

Masking an electric lamp to exclude all light except at a given point (*lamp should be only used for a few moments otherwise heat could be dangerous*).

Screening of X-rays.

To remove iron filings or powder from a magnet or magnetised article.

TOYS, GAMES AND SPORTS

For mending broken toys.

For dart boards.

To steady fireworks when placed on a wall.

Used in conjunction with "Meccano" it has a score of uses.

As mortar in toy brick building.

To weight a fish line.

As stands for broken toys and other objects.

Weighing down model cars to hold track, and stabilizing model aeroplanes and boats.

A design with a pointed modelling tool on a flat piece of Plasticine – a sheet of paper pressed on to this and left for a few moments. It is then dusted over with a piece of cotton wool on which there is a little powder colour or blacklead. A number of copies may be made.

As a grip for Athletes to hold in the hand when running.

As a jump off marker strip for Athletes and Horses.

To test the correctness of swing in golf.
When a small ball of Plasticine is driven from the tee it adheres to the club head and indicates by its shape whether there has been a "pull" or "slice".

As a golf tee.

Ballasting and trimming model yachts.

MISCELLANEOUS

Aquariums

For fixing the sides of same.

Mending Leaks in Row Boats, Punts, etc.
This should be put on when wood is dry – an actual case of where a large hole had been made in a rowing boat was repaired with Plasticine and the occupants were able to continue their journey. Plasticine should protrude from both sides of the hole and flattened down as in the form of a rivet – the repair should only be considered as an emergency.

As an Adhesive
Plasticine should be smeared well on to both surfaces before joining together.

To Users of Safety Razors
For keeping the blades clean and safe, and preserving the keenness of edge.

Get an empty tin, cigarette or tobacco box, place an even layer of Plasticine over the bottom, half an inch thick. The razor blades can be just pushed into this after use. The edge will be kept free from rust, and the blade will stay in its proper order, and can be picked out without disturbing the others or cutting the fingers.

An Emergency Weight
Very useful for replacing a missing weight – ¼ oz. missing – Weigh ½ oz. of Plasticine, divide into approximate two pieces with small piece retained in hand, proceed to distribute this in small pieces until the scales balance. Plasticine can also be used to neutralise objects on the scales that it is not desired to weigh. Use Plasticine also for a correction in error of scales.

Holding Candles
As a base to hold a candle. This may appear of small importance – but wait until you are camping out or working in the dark – Plasticine will hold candles to an upright post or other object.

Always smear Plasticine well to the article it has to be attached to.

Retrieving Objects

Having dropped a coin or object down a grating, how are we to get it up? Get a stick and put a lump of Plasticine on the end and there you are.

If at a considerable depth, a weight with Plasticine on the bottom of same attached to a string may often be manoeuvred to effect the recovery – even if the object cannot be seen (such as between a partition), it may be recovered in the same way.

Setting stones and gems in position when designing jewellery.

In Repousse work instead of wood and pitch blocks.

In Block printing instead of lino or wood.

In projection and solid geometry. To show models in sections.

For studying Geology, showing various strata in different colours.

To make contour models in physical Geography.

To steady mechanical models *when working on a smooth surface*.

Pianists find modelling with Plasticine makes the fingers stronger and more supple.

Emergency water cup when hiking or scouting, or an egg holder.

To prevent vibration in Wireless Sets and microphonic noises.

Bed for hooks of flies for fishing, keeps hooks from rusting.

As a liquid gauge, fix piece of Plasticine in bottom of a jug or beaker to obtain a predetermined amount of liquid.

A spout or lip affixed to any vessel for pouring liquid.

Masking. (1) in Plating. (2) Cellulose Spraying – portions of object are coated with Plasticine which does not injure polished surfaces.

Engraving, controlling acid on copper plates.

Acid can be confined to any part of a surface by building a wall or weir to contain it. Plasticine is affected by acid, but can be protected by coating surface with vaseline petroleum jelly.

Increasing pendulum weights.

An emergency funnel – *spout can be bent to any angle*.

A beekeeper says there is nothing like a lump of Plasticine for wedging a frame and keeping it from slipping when a hive is being transported in a vehicle.

Holding a piece of wood in position while nailing it.

PLASTICINE HAS BEEN USED FOR:

Determining capacity of compression space of I.C. engines.

Motor car bodies and streamlining aeroplane models in wind tunnels.

Holding gun cotton or explosives and fuses in position in demolition work and for training with plastic explosives.

To show entry and exits of bullet wounds, by models of a portion of the body.

Models of scenes of accidents and crimes.

As a substitute for hot rolled steel in designing new plant.

1914-18 and Last War

The model for the Vimy Ridge attack was made in Plasticine.

The model of the Zeebrugge attack was made in Plasticine.

Used in connection with Gas Masks, Machine Guns, Armoured Cars, Aeroplanes, Hand Grenades, Gunnery, Training Schools, Trench Warfare, etc. Machine Gun Water Jackets when punctured, a piece of Plasticine bound round same enabled water to be retained. In early Hand Grenades, to avoid premature explosion, used as a luting to prevent sparks from the cap firing the charge before the burning of the fuse.

The Original model of the Cenotaph was made in Plasticine, and is placed in the Imperial War Museum.

A.R.P. – For rendering rooms gas proof, and many other uses.

THE MOST ECONOMICAL WAY OF BUYING PLASTICINE FOR 101 USES

1 lb. any colour or "Corona" outfit, contains *assorted colours*, and in Bulk.

Plastone – a self hardening modelling material.

Industrial Chalks and Crayons

INDUSTRIAL USES OF PLASTICINE DERIVATIVES AND COMPOUNDS

Harboseal – A sealant for electrical work to exclude moisture.

Standard Hard Plasticine with a wax base for design work.

Soft Plasticine with extra adhesive qualities.

Barplas – with barium for X-ray screening.

Other Types with acid resistance, magnetic and non-magnetic iron oxide filings.

We are always pleased to co-operate in evolving Plasticine compositions to suit clients special requirements.

Particulars of above compounds sent free on request

All Information is given in good faith but without acceptance of liability.

HARBUTT'S LTD., BATHAMPTON, BATH BA2 6TA

Above: Early packaging for Harbutt's coloured Plasticine.
Below: The current range of 24 colours.

Complete list of Meccano Parts (1977)
Komplete lijst van Meccano-onderdelen
Liste complète des pièces Meccano
Distinta delle componenti del Corredo Meccano
Vollständige Liste der Meccano-Teile
Fullständig förteckning över Meccanodelar
Lista completa de piezas de Meccano
Lista completa de peças do Meccano
Komplett liste over Meccanodeler

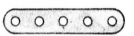

5   PERFORATED STRIPS   6

1	– 12½"; 32 cm	3	– 3½"; 9 cm
1a	– 9½"; 24 cm	4	– 3"; 7½ cm
1b	– 7½"; 19 cm	5	– 2½"; 6 cm
2	– 5½"; 14 cm	6	– 2"; 5 cm
2a	– 4½"; 11½ cm	6a	1½"; 38 mm

9c   ANGLE GIRDERS

7	– 24½"; 62 cm	9a	– 4½"; 11½ cm
7a	– 18½"; 47 cm	9b	– 3½"; 9 cm
8	– 12½"; 32 cm	9c	– 3"; 7½ cm
8a	– 9½"; 24 cm	9d	– 2½"; 6 cm
8b	– 7½"; 19 cm	9e	– 2"; 5 cm
9	– 5½"; 14 cm	9f	– 1½"; 38 mm

FISHPLATE
10

DOUBLE B
11 – ½" × ½"

SPOKED WHEEL
19a – 3"; 75 mm

PULLEYS
19b – 3"; 75 mm
20a – 2"; 5 cm

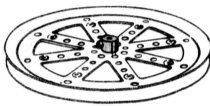

PULLEY
19c – 6"; 15 cm

22a   23 & 23b   23a
PULLEYS
22a – 1"; 25 mm   23a – ½"; 12 mm
23 plastic – ½"; 12 mm 23b metal – ½"; 12 mm

BUSH WHEEL
24 – 1⅜"; 34 mm

WHEEL DISC
24a – 1⅜"; 34 mm

BUSH WHEEL
24b – 1⅜"; 34 mm

W
24c

27f MULTI-PURPOSE
GEAR WHEEL

28
CONTRATE WHEEL
28 – 1½"; 38 mm
29 – ¾"; 19 mm

29
BEVEL GEAR
For use in pairs.
30 – ⅞"; 22 mm

30

BEVEL GEARS
can only be used together.
30a – ½"; 12 mm
30c – 1½"; 38 mm

GEAR WHEEL
31 -1" × ¼"
25mm × 6mm

32

BOLT
– ³⁄₁₆"; 5 mm
37b

NUT
38 – ⅜"; 10 mm
37c
38d – ¾"; 19 mm

WASHERS

NUT AND
37 BOLT

HANK OF CORD
40

PROPELLER BLADE
41

ECCANO®

DOUBLE BRACKET
– 1″ × ½″; 25 × 12 mm

12

ANGLE BRACKETS
12 – ½″ × ½″; 12 × 12 mm
12a – 1″ × 1″; 25 × 25 mm
12b – 1″ × ½″; 25 × 12 mm

**ANGLE BRACKET
(OBTUSE)**
12c – ½″ × ½″; 12 × 12 mm

AXLE RODS
13 – 11½″; 29 cm   16 – 3½″; 9 cm
13a – 8″; 20 cm   16a – 2½″; 6 cm
14 – 6½″; 16½ cm   16b – 3″; 7½ cm
14a – 5½″; 14 cm   17 – 2″; 5 cm
15 – 5″; 13 cm   18a – 1½″; 38 mm
15a – 4½″; 11½ cm   18b – 1″; 25 mm
15b – 4″; 10 cm

CRANK HANDLE
19h – 5″; 13 cm
19s – 3½″; 9 cm

FLANGED WHEELS
20 – 1⅛″; 28 mm   20b – ¾″; 19 mm

PULLEY
21 – 1½″; 38 mm

PULLEY
22 – 1″; 25 mm

PINIONS
25 – ¾″ × ¼″; 19 × 6 mm
25a – ¾″ × ½″; 19 × 12 mm
25b – ¾″ × ¾″; 19 × 19 mm
26 – ½″ × ¼″; 12 × 6 mm
26a – ½″ × ½″; 12 × 12 mm
26b – ½″ × ¾″; 12 × 19 mm
26c – 7⁄16″ × ¼″; 11 × 6 mm

27   **27d**

GEAR WHEELS
27 – 1¼″; 32 mm
27a – 1½″; 38 mm
27d – 1⅝″; 41 mm

GEAR WHEELS
27b – 3½″; 9 cm
27c – 2½″; 6 cm

27c

**SPANNER
34c**

**SPRING CLIP
35**

SCREWDRIVERS

36

36b

**DRIFT
36c**

**BOX SPANNER
34b**

**NG
m**

**BENT STRIP
STEPPED
44**

**DOUBLE BENT STRIP
45**

48a

DOUBLE ANGLE STRIPS
46 – 2½″ × 1″; 60 × 25 mm
47 – 2½″ × 1½″; 60 × 38 mm
47a – 3″ × 1½″; 75 × 38 mm
48 – 1½″ × ½″; 38 × 12 mm
48a – 2½″ × ½″; 60 × 12 mm
48b – 3½″ × ½″; 90 × 12 mm
48c – 4½″ × ½″; 115 × 12 mm
48d – 5½″ × ½″; 140 × 12 mm

**SLIDE PIECE
50**

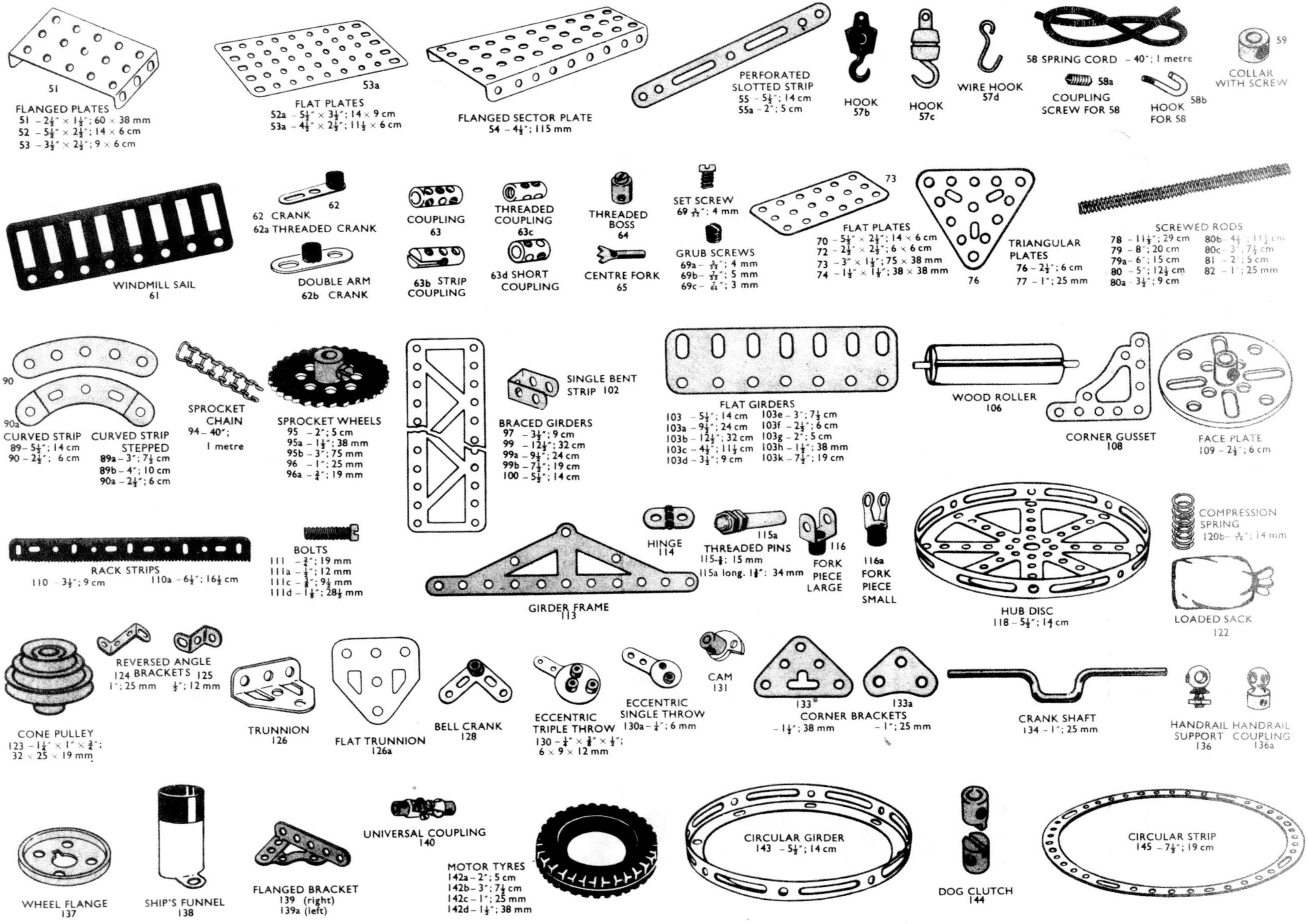

51
FLANGED PLATES
51 – 2½" × 1½"; 60 × 38 mm
52 – 5½" × 2½"; 14 × 6 cm
53 – 3½" × 2½"; 9 × 6 cm
53a
FLAT PLATES
52a – 5½" × 3½"; 14 × 9 cm
53a – 4½" × 2½"; 11½ × 6 cm
FLANGED SECTOR PLATE
54 – 4½"; 115 mm
PERFORATED SLOTTED STRIP
55 – 5½"; 14 cm
55a – 2"; 5 cm
HOOK
57b
HOOK
57c
WIRE HOOK
57d
58 SPRING CORD – 40"; 1 metre
58a
COUPLING SCREW FOR 58
58b
HOOK FOR 58
59
COLLAR WITH SCREW
WINDMILL SAIL
61
62
62 CRANK
62a THREADED CRANK
DOUBLE ARM CRANK
62b
COUPLING
63
THREADED COUPLING
63c
63b STRIP COUPLING
63d SHORT COUPLING
THREADED BOSS
64
CENTRE FORK
65
SET SCREW
69 5/32"; 4 mm
GRUB SCREWS
69a – 5/32"; 4 mm
69b – 7/32"; 5 mm
69c – 7/64"; 3 mm
73
FLAT PLATES
70 – 5½" × 2½"; 14 × 6 cm
72 – 2½" × 2½"; 6 × 6 cm
73 – 3" × 1½"; 75 × 38 mm
74 – 1½" × 1½"; 38 × 38 mm
76
TRIANGULAR PLATES
76 – 2½"; 6 cm
77 – 1"; 25 mm
SCREWED RODS
78 – 11½"; 29 cm
79 – 8"; 20 cm
79a – 6"; 15 cm
80 – 5"; 12½ cm
80a – 3½"; 9 cm
80b – 4½"; 11½ cm
80c – 3"; 7½ cm
81 – 2"; 5 cm
82 – 1"; 25 mm
90
90a
CURVED STRIP
89 – 5½"; 14 cm
90 – 2½"; 6 cm
CURVED STRIP STEPPED
89a – 3"; 7½ cm
89b – 4"; 10 cm
90a – 2½"; 6 cm
SPROCKET CHAIN
94 – 40"; 1 metre
SPROCKET WHEELS
95 – 2"; 5 cm
95a – 1½"; 38 mm
95b – 3"; 75 mm
96 – 1"; 25 mm
96a – ¾"; 19 mm
SINGLE BENT STRIP 102
BRACED GIRDERS
97 – 3½"; 9 cm
99 – 12½"; 32 cm
99a – 9½"; 24 cm
99b – 7½"; 19 cm
100 – 5½"; 14 cm
FLAT GIRDERS
103 – 5½"; 14 cm
103a – 9½"; 24 cm
103b – 12½"; 32 cm
103c – 4½"; 11½ cm
103d – 3½"; 9 cm
103e – 3"; 7½ cm
103f – 2½"; 6 cm
103g – 2"; 5 cm
103h – 1½"; 38 mm
103k – 7½"; 19 cm
WOOD ROLLER
106
CORNER GUSSET
108
FACE PLATE
109 – 2½"; 6 cm
RACK STRIPS
110 – 3½"; 9 cm
110a – 6½"; 16½ cm
BOLTS
111 – ¾"; 19 mm
111a – ½"; 12 mm
111c – ⅜"; 9½ mm
111d – 1⅛"; 28½ mm
GIRDER FRAME
113
HINGE
114
115a
THREADED PINS
115 – ⅝"; 15 mm
115a long. 1⅜": 34 mm
116
FORK PIECE LARGE
116a
FORK PIECE SMALL
HUB DISC
118 – 5½"; 14 cm
COMPRESSION SPRING
120b – 9/16"; 14 mm
LOADED SACK
122
CONE PULLEY
123 – 1½" × 1" × ¾";
32 × 25 × 19 mm
REVERSED ANGLE BRACKETS
124 – 1"; 25 mm
125 – ½"; 12 mm
TRUNNION
126
FLAT TRUNNION
126a
BELL CRANK
128
ECCENTRIC TRIPLE THROW
130 – ¼" × ⅜" × ½";
6 × 9 × 12 mm
ECCENTRIC SINGLE THROW
130a – ¼"; 6 mm
CAM
131
133
133a
CORNER BRACKETS
– 1½"; 38 mm
– 1"; 25 mm
CRANK SHAFT
134 – 1"; 25 mm
HANDRAIL SUPPORT
136
HANDRAIL COUPLING
136a
WHEEL FLANGE
137
SHIP'S FUNNEL
138
FLANGED BRACKET
139 (right)
139a (left)
UNIVERSAL COUPLING
140
MOTOR TYRES
142a – 2"; 5 cm
142b – 3"; 7½ cm
142c – 1"; 25 mm
142d – 1½"; 38 mm
CIRCULAR GIRDER
143 – 5½"; 14 cm
DOG CLUTCH
144
CIRCULAR STRIP
145 – 7½"; 19 cm

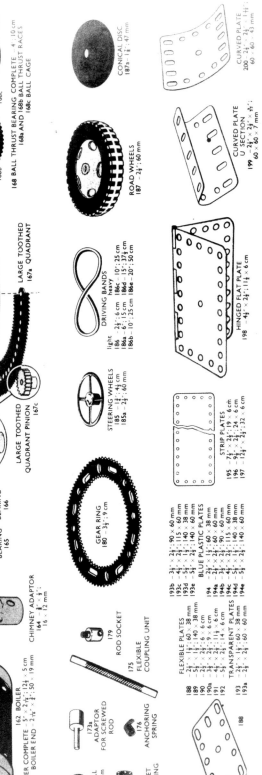

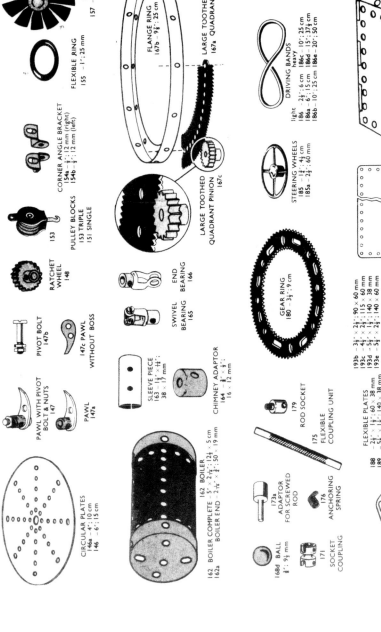

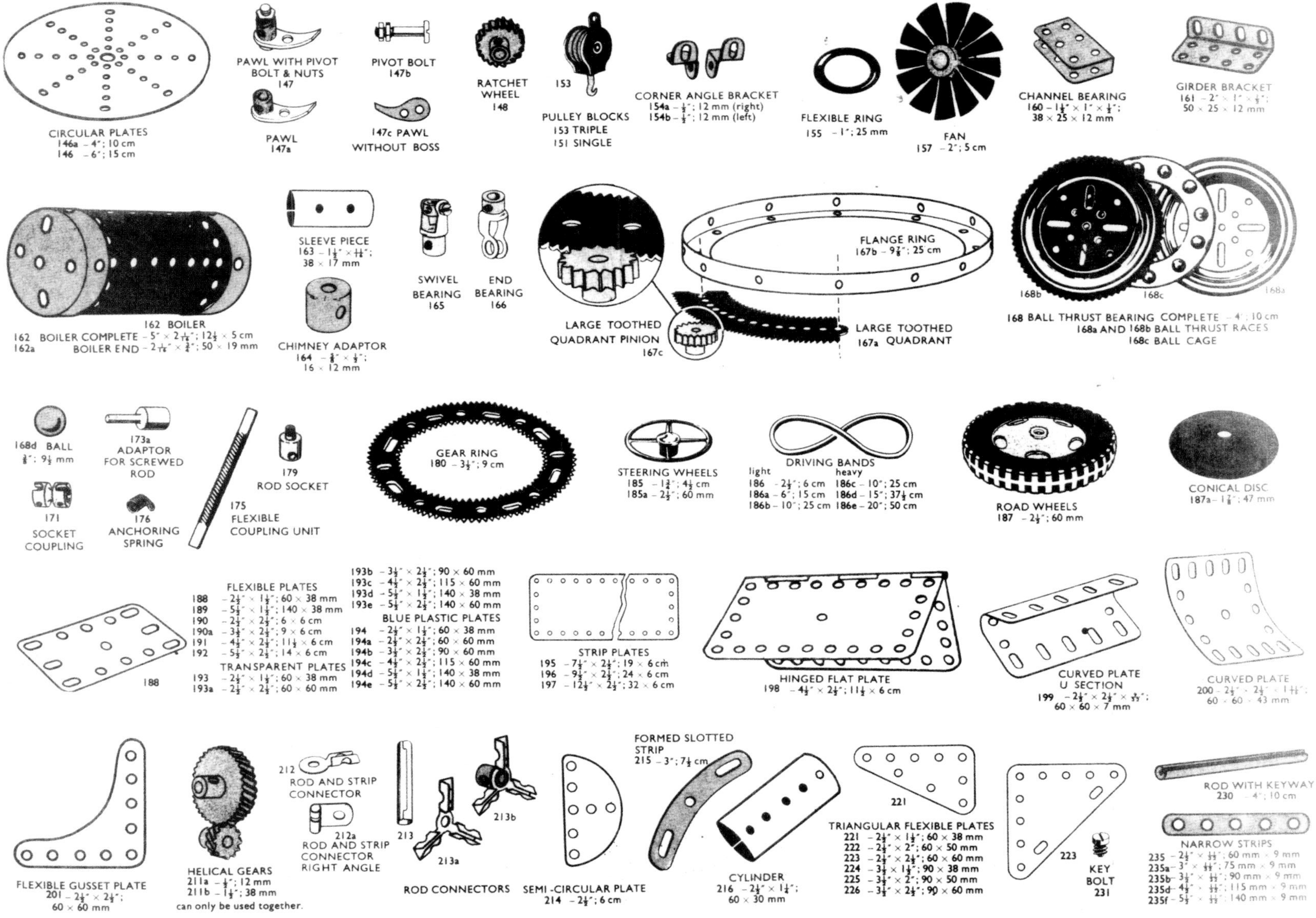

CIRCULAR PLATES
146a – 4"; 10 cm
146 – 6"; 15 cm
PAWL WITH PIVOT BOLT & NUTS
147
PAWL
147a
PIVOT BOLT
147b
147c PAWL WITHOUT BOSS
RATCHET WHEEL
148
153
PULLEY BLOCKS
153 TRIPLE
151 SINGLE
CORNER ANGLE BRACKET
154a – ½"; 12 mm (right)
154b – ½"; 12 mm (left)
FLEXIBLE RING
155 – 1"; 25 mm
FAN
157 – 2"; 5 cm
CHANNEL BEARING
160 – 1½" × 1" × ½";
38 × 25 × 12 mm
GIRDER BRACKET
161 – 2" × 1" × ½";
50 × 25 × 12 mm
162 BOILER
162 BOILER COMPLETE – 5" × 2 1/16"; 12½ × 5 cm
162a BOILER END – 2 1/16" × ¾"; 50 × 19 mm
SLEEVE PIECE
163 – 1½" × 11/16";
38 × 17 mm
CHIMNEY ADAPTOR
164 – ⅝" × ½";
16 × 12 mm
SWIVEL BEARING
165
END BEARING
166
LARGE TOOTHED QUADRANT PINION
167c
FLANGE RING
167b – 9⅞"; 25 cm
LARGE TOOTHED QUADRANT
167a
168b
168c
168a
168 BALL THRUST BEARING COMPLETE – 4"; 10 cm
168a AND 168b BALL THRUST RACES
168c BALL CAGE
168d BALL
⅜"; 9½ mm
173a
ADAPTOR FOR SCREWED ROD
171
SOCKET COUPLING
176
ANCHORING SPRING
175
FLEXIBLE COUPLING UNIT
179
ROD SOCKET
GEAR RING
180 – 3½"; 9 cm
STEERING WHEELS
185 – 1¾"; 4½ cm
185a – 2½"; 60 mm
DRIVING BANDS
light
186 – 2½"; 6 cm
186a – 6"; 15 cm
186b – 10"; 25 cm
heavy
186c – 10"; 25 cm
186d – 15"; 37½ cm
186e – 20"; 50 cm
ROAD WHEELS
187 – 2½"; 60 mm
CONICAL DISC
187a – 1⅞"; 47 mm
188
FLEXIBLE PLATES
188 – 2½" × 1½"; 60 × 38 mm
189 – 5½" × 1½"; 140 × 38 mm
190 – 2½" × 2½"; 6 × 6 cm
190a – 3½" × 2½"; 9 × 6 cm
191 – 4½" × 2½"; 11½ × 6 cm
192 – 5½" × 2½"; 14 × 6 cm
TRANSPARENT PLATES
193 – 2½" × 1½"; 60 × 38 mm
193a – 2½" × 2½"; 60 × 60 mm
193b – 3½" × 2½"; 90 × 60 mm
193c – 4½" × 2½"; 115 × 60 mm
193d – 5½" × 1½"; 140 × 38 mm
193e – 5½" × 2½"; 140 × 60 mm
BLUE PLASTIC PLATES
194 – 2½" × 1½"; 60 × 38 mm
194a – 2½" × 2½"; 60 × 60 mm
194b – 3½" × 2½"; 90 × 60 mm
194c – 4½" × 2½"; 115 × 60 mm
194d – 5½" × 1½"; 140 × 38 mm
194e – 5½" × 2½"; 140 × 60 mm
STRIP PLATES
195 – 7½" × 2½"; 19 × 6 cm
196 – 9½" × 2½"; 24 × 6 cm
197 – 12½" × 2½"; 32 × 6 cm
HINGED FLAT PLATE
198 – 4½" × 2½"; 11½ × 6 cm
CURVED PLATE U SECTION
199 – 2½" × 2½" × 9/32";
60 × 60 × 7 mm
CURVED PLATE
200 – 2½" × 2½" × 1 11/16";
60 × 60 × 43 mm
FLEXIBLE GUSSET PLATE
201 – 2½" × 2½";
60 × 60 mm
HELICAL GEARS
211a – ½"; 12 mm
211b – 1½"; 38 mm
can only be used together.
212
ROD AND STRIP CONNECTOR
212a
ROD AND STRIP CONNECTOR RIGHT ANGLE
213
213a
213b
ROD CONNECTORS
SEMI-CIRCULAR PLATE
214 – 2½"; 6 cm
FORMED SLOTTED STRIP
215 – 3"; 7½ cm
CYLINDER
216 – 2½" × 1¼";
60 × 30 mm
221
TRIANGULAR FLEXIBLE PLATES
221 – 2½" × 1½"; 60 × 38 mm
222 – 2½" × 2"; 60 × 50 mm
223 – 2½" × 2½"; 60 × 60 mm
224 – 3½ × 1½"; 90 × 38 mm
225 – 3½" × 2"; 90 × 50 mm
226 – 3½" × 2½"; 90 × 60 mm
223
KEY BOLT
231
ROD WITH KEYWAY
230 – 4"; 10 cm
NARROW STRIPS
235 – 2½" × 11/32"; 60 mm × 9 mm
235a – 3" × 11/32"; 75 mm × 9 mm
235b – 3½" × 11/32"; 90 mm × 9 mm
235d – 4½" × 11/32"; 115 mm × 9 mm
235f – 5½" × 11/32"; 140 mm × 9 mm

Complete UK catalogue of O and OO gauge locomotive types

This list is restricted to the date of introduction of each locomotive type, and does not include variations of power, control, livery, name or number.

1920
Hornby Gauge 0
Locomotive for tinprinted train set (later renamed No. 00 and later still M3 – first released as GNR/MR/LNWR *George V*)
Hornby tender locomotive 2710 (later renamed No. 1, first released in black, green, maroon & blue)

1921
Hornby Gauge 0
No. 2 tender locomotive 2711 (first released in maroon, green, black & blue)

1922
Hornby Gauge 0
Zulu tank locomotive (later renamed No. 1 tank locomotive – first released in black only)

1923
Hornby Gauge 0
Zulu tender locomotive (later renamed No. 0 locomotive – first released in black only)
Hornby tank locomotive (later renamed No. 2 tank locomotive – first released in red, green & black)

1925
Hornby Gauge 0
Hornby electric locomotive (Metropolitan locomotive)

1926
Hornby Gauge 0
M1 locomotive (first released in green only)
Riviera Blue Train locomotive

1927
Hornby Gauge 0
No. 3 tender locomotive (*Royal Scot, Flying Scotsman, Caerphilly Castle* and, in 1928, *Lord Nelson*)

1929
Hornby Gauge 0
No. 1 Special tender locomotive (first released in all four company liveries)

No. 1 Special tank locomotive (first released in all four company liveries)
No. 2 Special tank locomotive (first released in all four company liveries)
No. 2 Special tender locomotives: LMS Compound 1185 (maroon)
LNER Shire class *Yorkshire* (later issued as Hunt class 201 *Bramham Moor* – both first released in green)
GWR Churchward County Class *County of Bedford* (green)
SR Class L1 A759 (green)

1930
Hornby Gauge 0
M0 tender locomotive (later renamed No. 20 – first released in green & red)

1931
Hornby Gauge 0
M3 tank locomotive (first released in all four company liveries)

1932
Hornby Gauge 0
'Swiss type' electric locomotive (with dummy pantographs)
'Continental' electric locomotive (modified Metropolitan locomotive)

1936
Hornby Gauge 0
No. 0 *Silver Link* A4 class tender locomotive

1937
Hornby Gauge 0
No. 4 *Eton* Schools class tender locomotive (first released in SR green and, extremely rare, SR black mainly for export)
Princess Elizabeth Princess Royal class tender locomotive (LMS maroon)

1938
Hornby-Dublo
0-6-2 tank locomotive, based on Class N2 and first released as:
LNER Class N2 tank No. 2690 (black)

SR Class E5 tank No. 2594 (green)
GWR standard tank No. 6699 (green)
LMS Class 69 tank No. 6917 (black)
A4 class tender locomotive (first released as *Sir Nigel Gresley* in LNER blue)

1939
Hornby-Dublo
Duchess of Atholl Princess Coronation class tender locomotive appeared in catalogues but was not available until after the war

1939-1945
World War II

1947
Hornby Gauge 0
No. 101 tank locomotive (modified version of M3 tank, first released in all four company liveries – renamed No. 40 in 1954 when first released BR livery)

1948
Hornby Gauge 0
No. 501 tender locomotive (first released in all four company liveries – renamed No. 50 and No. 51 in 1954 when first released in BR black [50] and BR green [51])
Hornby-Dublo
Princess Coronation (Duchess) class tender locomotive (first

released as *Duchess of Atholl* in LMS maroon)

1950
Rovex
Princess Royal Class tender locomotive (first released as *Princess Elizabeth*)

1951
Tri-ang Railways
Class N2 tank locomotive

1953
Tri-ang Railways
Class 3F Jinty tank locomotive

1954
Hornby-Dublo
Class 4MT standard tank locomotive

1956
Hornby Gauge 0
No. 30 tender locomotive
Tri-ang Railways
Class 3MT standard tank locomotive
Class 08 diesel shunter
Class S saddle tank locomotive

1957
Hornby-Dublo
Castle class tender locomotive (first released as *Bristol Castle* in BR green)
Tri-ang Railways
Class 4-SUB EMU
Dock Shunter/Switcher diesel shunter

1958
Hornby-Dublo
Class 8F tender locomotive
Type 1 (Class 20) Bo-Bo diesel
  locomotive

Tri-ang Railways
Class 101 DMU
Class 3F tender locomotive

1959
Hornby-Dublo
Class R1 tank locomotive

Tri-ang Railways
Steeple Cab 0-4-0 electric
  locomotive

1960
Tri-ang Railways
Class L1 tender locomotive
Britannia Class 7P6F tender
  locomotive (first released as
  Britannia)
Industrial 0-4-0 tank locomotive

1961
Hornby-Dublo
Rebuilt West Country Class
  tender locomotive (first released
  as *Barnstaple* in BR green)
Class 55 'Deltic' Co-Co diesel
  locomotive
0-6-0 Class 08 diesel shunter
Metro-Vic (Class 28) Co-Bo diesel
  locomotive

Tri-ang Railways
Class 3031 Dean Single tender
  locomotive
Class EM2 Co-Co electric
  locomotive
Battle of Britain/West Country
  Class tender locomotive (first
  released as *Winston Churchill*)

1962
Hornby-Dublo
Class 501 EMU/Electric
  Suburban Train

Tri-ang Railways
Class 31 A1A-A1A diesel
  locomotive
North British 0-4-0 diesel shunter

1963
Hornby-Dublo
0-4-0 tank locomotive of the
  starter sets

Tri-ang Railways
Class B12 tender locomotive
'Blue Pullman' DMU
Stephenson's *Rocket*
Caledonian Single tender
  locomotive

1964
Hornby-Dublo
0-4-0 diesel shunter of the starter
  sets
E3000/Type AL1/Class 81 electric
  pantograph locomotive
  (released as E3002)

1966
Tri-ang Hornby
Class 37/Type 3 Co-Co diesel
  locomotive
E3000/Type AL1/Class 81 electric
  pantograph locomotive
  (released as E3001)
Class 49XX Hall Class tender
  locomotive

1967
Tri-ang Hornby
Class 35 Hymek diesel hydraulic
  locomotive
Class M7 tank locomotive
Wrenn (using former Hornby-
  Dublo tools)
Castle class tender locomotive
Class 8F tender locomotive
Class 4MT tank locomotive

1968
Tri-ang Hornby
Class A1/A3 tender locomotive
  (first released as *Flying
  Scotsman*)

Wrenn (using former Hornby-
  Dublo tools)
Class R1 tank locomotive
Rebuilt West Country class tender
  locomotive

1969
Wrenn (using former Hornby-Dublo
tools)
Class A4 tender locomotive
Princess Coronation (Duchess)
  class tender locomotive
0-6-2 tank locomotive based on
  Class N2

1970
Tri-ang Hornby
Coronation class tender
  locomotive (under-scale model)

1971
Tri-ang Hornby
Class 9F tender locomotive (first
  released as *Evening Star*)
Class 57XX pannier tank
  locomotive

1973
Hornby Railways
Black Five class tender locomotive
Class 2P tender locomotive (over-
  scale model modified from the
  Tri-ang Railways L1; see 1960)

1974
Wrenn (using former Hornby-Dublo
tools)
0-6-0 Class 08 diesel shunter

1975
Hornby Railways
Class 47 Co-Co diesel locomotive
Class 2F 'Ivatt' tender locomotive

1976
Hornby Railways
Class J83 tank locomotive
Class N15 King Arthur Class
  tender locomotive
Class 08 diesel shunter (new body;
  see 1956)

1977
Hornby Railways
Princess Coronation (Duchess)
  class tender locomotive (first
  released as *Duchess of
  Sutherland*)
Class 25 Bo-Bo diesel locomotive
Wrenn (using former Hornby-Dublo
tools)
Bo-Bo diesel locomotive

1978
Hornby Railways
Class 101 Holden tank locomotive
Class 29 Bo-Bo diesel locomotive
King Class (Class 6000) tender
  locomotive (*King Edward I*)
Class 3F Jinty tank locomotive
  (new model; see 1952)
Class 43 'HST' Inter-City 125
  diesel locomotive

1979
Hornby Railways
Class A4 tender locomotive (first
  released as *Mallard*)
Class E2 tank locomotive
Class 52 'Western' diesel hydraulic
  locomotive
Patriot Class tender locomotive
  (first released as *Duke of
  Sutherland*)

1980
Hornby Railways
Class 0F Caledonian Pug tank
  locomotive
LMS Fowler Class 4P tank
  locomotive
Class B17/4 Footballer Class
  tender locomotive (first released
  as *Manchester United*)
Class 370 APT (the 'tilting train')
King Class (Class 6000) tender
  locomotive (re-tooled, first
  released as *King Henry VIII*;
  see 1978)

1981, 'The Year of the Locomotive'

Hornby Railways

Class 2721 pannier tank locomotive

Schools Class tender locomotive (first released as *Stowe*)

Class 4P Compound tender locomotive

Class D49/1 Shire/Hunt class tender locomotive (first released as *Cheshire*)

Class 38XX Churchward County Class tender locomotive (first released as *County of Bedford*)

Class J13/J52 saddle tank locomotive

Class 86/2 electric pantograph locomotive

Class A1/A3 tender locomotive (re-tooled, first released as *Flying Scotsman*; see 1968)

Britannia class tender locomotive partly re-tooled

1982

Hornby Railways

Class 110 DMU

Class 58 Co-Co diesel locomotive

1984

Hornby Railways

Princess Royal class tender locomotive (new model, first released as *The Princess Royal*; see 1950)

1986

Hornby Railways

Class 29XX Saint Class tender locomotive (first released as *Saint David*)

1987

Hornby Railways

Class 142 Pacer DMU

Black Five class tender locomotive (modified body; see 1973)

1988

Hornby Railways

Class 8F tender locomotive

Class 90 electric locomotive

Class 06 Barclay diesel shunter

1990

Hornby Railways

Class 91 electric locomotive

1991

Hornby Railways

Class 2800 tender locomotive

Class D tank locomotive

1995

Hornby Railways

Class 92 electric locomotive (first released as *Elgar*)

Class 373 'Eurostar' (Jouef H0 scale model)

1996

Hornby Railways

Class 373 'Eurostar' (Hornby Railways 00 scale model; see 1995)

1997

Hornby

Class 14XX tank locomotive

Castle Class tender locomotive (first released as *Winchester Castle*)

Class 1000 Hawksworth County Class tender locomotive (first released as *County of Somerset*)

Class 466 Networker DMU

1998

Hornby

L&Y Class 0F Pug tank locomotive

Class A1X Terrier tank locomotive

Class J94 Austerity saddle tank locomotive

Class 4F tender locomotive

Class 56 Co-Co diesel locomotive

Class 2301 Dean Goods tender locomotive

Class A1/A3 tender locomotive (modified tooling, first released as *Flying Scotsman*; see 1981 & 1968)

Class A4 tender locomotive (modified tooling; see 1979)

1999

Hornby

Class 2P tender locomotive (replaced 1973 version)

Class 155 Super Sprinter DMU

Class 61XX Prairie tank locomotive

Class 9F tender locomotive (modified tooling; see 1971)

2000

Hornby

Class N2 tank locomotive

Rebuilt Merchant Navy Class tender locomotive (first released as *Clan Line*)

Hornby Virtual Railway (HVR)

Britannia Class 7P6F tender locomotive (modified tooling, first released as *Clive of India*; see 1960)

2001

Hornby

Princess Coronation Class tender locomotive, streamlined version (totally new tooling, see 1977)

Battle of Britain/West Country class tender locomotive (totally new super-detailed tooling, first released as *Blackmoor Vale* and *92 Squadron*; see 1961)

Princess Royal class tender locomotive (totally new super-detailed tooling, first released as *Princess Arthur of Connaught*; see 1984 & 1950)

2002

Hornby

Princess Coronation (Duchess) class tender locomotive (totally new super-detailed tooling, first released as *Duchess of Rutland* and *Duchess of Buccleuch*; see 1977)

Black Five Class tender locomotive (totally new super-detailed tooling; see 1973 & 1987)

LMS Fowler Class 4P tank locomotive (totally new super-detailed tooling; see 1980)

Class 8F tender locomotive (totally new super-detailed tooling)

HVR-2

2003

Hornby

King Class (Class 6000) tender locomotive (re-tooled to super-detail standard; see 1980 & 1978)

Class Q1 tender locomotive

Class A4 tender locomotive (live steam version, first released as *Mallard*, see 1998 & 1979)

2004

Hornby

Class A4 tender locomotive (totally new super-detailed tooling; see 2003, 1998 & 1979)

Class 50 Co-Co diesel locomotive

2005

Hornby

Class 68XX Grange Class tender locomotive

Class A1 tender locomotive (totally new super-detailed tooling, first released as *Great Northern*)

Class A3 tender locomotive (totally new super-detailed tooling, first released as *Flying Scotsman* et al; see 1998, 1981 & 1968)

Class A3 tender locomotive (live steam version)

Class 08/09 diesel shunter

Class 31 A1A-A1A diesel locomotive (totally new super-detailed tooling; see 1962)

Class 31 A1A-A1A 'Skinhead' diesel locomotive

Class 60 Co-Co diesel locomotive

2006

Hornby

Class M7 tank locomotive (retooled to super-detail standard; see 1967)

Rebuilt Battle of Britain/West

Country Class tender locomotive (totally new super-detailed tooling, first released as *Plymouth*; see 2001 & 1961)

Britannia Class 7P6F tender locomotive (totally new super-detailed tooling; see 2000 & 1960)

Class 59 Co-Co diesel locomotive

Class 67 Co-Co diesel locomotive

Class 73 Bo-Bo diesel locomotive

Class 101 DMU (new model; see 1958)

Class 121 Railcar

Class 156 DMU

AEC railcar

2007
Hornby

LMS Stanier Class 4P tank locomotive

Rebuilt Patriot Class tender locomotive (see 1979)

Rebuilt Royal Scot Class tender locomotive

Class N15 King Arthur Class tender locomotive (totally new super-detailed tooling; see 1976)

Class 47 Co-Co diesel locomotive (former Lima model with new drive unit; see 1975)

Class 55 'Deltic' Co-Co diesel locomotive (former Lima model with new drive unit)

Class 56 Co-Co diesel locomotive (totally new tooling; see 1998)

Class 66 Co-Co diesel locomotive (former Lima model with new drive unit)

Class 390 'Pendolino' EMU

2008
Hornby

Class T9 'Greyhound' tender locomotive (first released in SR olive green and BRb black)

Schools Class tender locomotive (totally new super-detailed tooling first released as *Brighton*, *Wellington*, *Charterhouse* and *Blundells*; see 1981)

Class 75000 tender locomotive

Class A4 tender locomotive (new body for RailRoad range; see 2004, 2003, 1998 & 1979)

Class 20 Bo-Bo diesel locomotive (former Lima model with new drive unit)

Class 37/Type 3 Co-Co diesel locomotive (former Lima model with new drive unit; see 1966)

Class 43 'HST' Inter-City 125 diesel locomotive (totally new super-detailed tooling; see 1978)

Class 87 AC electric locomotive (former Lima model with new drive unit)

Class 153 Super Sprinter railcar

AEC Parcels railcar (former Lima model with new drive unit)

2009
Hornby

Clan Class tender locomotive (first released as *Clan Buchanan* and *Clan Macleod*)

Castle Class tender locomotive (totally new super-detailed tooling; see 1997)

BR Standard 4 loco (announced 2008, released 2009)

Useful websites

Official Hornby Collectors Club
  http://www.hornby.com/collectors-club

Official Hornby forum **http://www.hornby.com/forum**

Hornby Railway Collector's Association **http://www.hrca.net**

http://www.themodelrailwayclub.org

http://www.ukmodelshops.com/other/clubs.shtml

Complete catalogue of Airfix kit planes, trains, automobiles and ships by year

This list is restricted to new or converted/modified toolings only; note that kits of buildings, dioramas, accessories, figures and animals are not included in this catalogue.

1949
Ferguson Tractor (ready-assembled promotional item for Ferguson; not available to the public as a kit until several years later)

1952
Golden Hind

1953
Spitfire Mk I (BTK)

1954
Santa Maria
Shannon

1955
Cutty Sark
Southern Cross
1911 Rolls Royce
Spitfire Mk IX

1956
Gloster Gladiator Mk I
Bristol Fighter

Me Bf109
Hawker Hurricane IV RP
Golden Hind
HMS *Victory*
Westland Lysander
Westland S55
1911 Rolls Royce
1904 Darraq
1930 Bentley
1910 Model T Ford
1905 Rolls Royce

1957
SE 6B
Fokker DRI
Sopwith Camel
Albatross DV
JU-87B Stuka
DH Comet
DH Tiger Moth
RE8
Hawker Hart
Great Western
Santa Maria
Shannon
Cutty Sark
Mayflower

DH Mosquito FB VI
Walrus Mk II
1907 Lanchester

1958
MiG-15
P-51D Mustang
FW-190D
Douglas Skyhawk
Auster Antarctic
Grumman Gosling
Revenge
Bristol Beaufighter
P-38J Lightning
Saunders Roe SR53
DH Heron
Wellington B111
Avro Lancaster B1
Westland Whirlwind
Fairey Swordfish II

1959
Hawker Sea Hawk
Fiat G91
Mitsubishi Zero
Hawker Typhoon
Jet Provost

HMS *Cossack*
Me Bf110D
Bristol Belvedere
Dornier Do 217
Fairey Rotodyne
1926 Morris Cowley
Travelling crane
HMS *Victorious*
Bristol Superfreighter
Short Sunderland

1960
Spitfire Mk IX (2nd mould)
Me 262
BP Defiant
Hovercraft SR-NI
Hawker Hunter
Bristol Bloodhound
Esso Tank Wagon
Blackburn/H-S Buccaneer
HMS *Tiger*
Railbus
Douglas Dakota
HMS *Hood*
Fokker Friendship

1961
Vickers Vanguard
HMS *Daring*
HMS *Campbeltown*
Panther Tank
Sherman Tank
Churchill Tank
Sunbeam Rapier
Austin Healey Sprite Mk I
Renault Dauphine
Morris Minor
Mineral Wagon
Brake Van
Cattle Wagon
Cement Wagon
Sud Aviation Caravelle
HMS *Nelson*
HP Halifax
SS *Canberra*
DH Comet 4B

1962
Stalin 3 tank
Avro Anson
NA Harvard II
Scammel Tank Transporter
1904 Mercedes
Meat Van
Refrigerated Van
Heinkel He III H20
Hawker P 1127
RMS *Queen Elizabeth*
Omnibus B Type
Boeing B17G Flying Fortress

1963
Yak-9D
EE Lightning
F-104 Starfighter
E Type Jaguar
Ariel Arrow Motorcycle
Lockheed Hudson III
HMS *Devonshire*
Lowmac
Scammel Scarab
Boeing Sea Knight
HMS *Warspite*
B-24J Liberator
SS *France*
Endeavour
Royal Sovereign

1964
Folland Gnat
Grumman Wildcat
Curtiss Kitty Hawk
15 ton Diesel Crane
Aichi D3 A1 Val
HMS *Hotspur*
Tiger Tank
German Armoured Car
Mirage IIIC
Il-2 Sturmovik
Vought F-4U Corsair
Centurion Tank
Volkswagen Beetle
MG 1100
Junkers Ju-88
HMS *Suffolk*
Prestwin Silo Wagon
Vickers VC-10
Scharnhorst
Mauretania
Catalina PBY-5A
1914 Dennis Fire Engine
Revenge

1965
Me Bf109 G
Bell Airacobra
Roland CII
CAC Boomerang
DUKW
Vertol 107-11
BAC III
Mitsubishi Dinah
Fairey Firefly
Buffalo & Jeep
Grumman Avenger TBM 3
HP42 Heracles
Boeing 727
HMS *Ajax*
LCM3 & Sherman Tank
B25 Mitchell
Junkers Ju52/3M
HMS *Victory*

1966
F5 Freedom Fighter
Westland Scout
M3 Half Track Personnel
   Carrier
Arado Ar-96
Thunderbolt
Westland HAR Mk I
Triumph TR4A
MGB
H-S Trident
HMS *Ark Royal*
Concorde

Old Bill Type Bus
Short Stirling
B-29 Superfortress
Trevithick Locomotive

1967
Fiat G50
Fieseler Storch
Avro 504K
Spad VII
Hannover CLIII
WWI Tank (Mother)
Vought Kingfisher
Douglas Dauntless
MiG-21 C
Airco DH4
Free Enterprise II
Aston Martin DB5
Porsche Carrera 6
1902 De Dietrich
Triumph Herald
Black Widow
Savoia-Marchetti SM79
Boeing 314 Clipper
Heinkel He-177
1804 Steam Loco
Cutty Sark
Wallis Autogyro

1968
Hawker Demon (conversion)
T-34 tank
Grumman Hellcat

Beagle Bassett
Angel Interceptor
Douglas Skyraider
Bristol Blenheim
Grumman Helldiver
Henschel Hs-129
Mercedes 280SL
Model T Ford 1912
Honda CB450
HS 125 Dominie
Grumman Duck
Fairey Battle
Petlyakov Pe-2
HMS *Fearless*
Ferrari 250LM
Ford Trimotor
Ilyushin Il-28
HP Hampden
Tirpitz
Handley Page 0/400
Queen Elizabeth II
James Bond Toyota
Prince
F-IIIA Aardvark

1969
Cessna
Lee Grant tank
Bronco OV-10A
Focke Wulf Fw-189
Douglas Devastator TBD-1
RAF Emergency Set
Ford Escort

Alfa Romeo 1933
Sikorsky Sea King
HP Jetstream
Lunar Module
Boeing 737
Jaguar 420
Ford 3 litre GT
BSA C15
BMW R69
Orion Space Craft
Boeing 747
Lockheed Hercules
Apollo Saturn V
Discovery
Hawker Harrier
SR-N4 Hovercraft

1970
DH Chipmunk
Bristol Bulldog
HMS *Leander*
Gloster Meteor
Henschel Hs 123 A-I
Leopard Tank
BAC Jaguar
Blohm & Voss BV-141
RAF Refuelling Set
Ford Capri
HMS *Iron Duke*
Russian Vostok
BHC SRN4
Supermarine Spitfire Mk I

1971
Saab Draken
Rommel
HMS *Manxman*
Chieftain Tank
Panzer IV Tank
Crusader Tank
Bond Bug 700E
Saab Viggen
DHC Beaver
Maxi BMC
Porsche 917
Vauxhall Prince Henry 1911
N American Vigilante
F-4 Phantom
Graf Spee
Douglas Invader
Lockheed Tristar
Saturn IB
Me Bf109 (1/24th)
1930 4½ litre Bentley
    (1/12th)

1972
Britten Norman Islander
Super Mystere B2
Morris Marina
Dornier Do -17
Monty's Humber
Wasa
P-51D Mustang (1/24th)
HMS *Amazon*

1973
Cessna Bird Dog
Gazelle SA 341
HMS *Hood*
Bismarck
Puma SA 330
DC-9
RAF Recovery Set
Maserati Indy
Martin B-26 Marauder
HMS *Belfast*
Moskva
Saint Louis
Hurricane Mk I (1/24th)
Dakota Gunship
    (Conversion)
Vosper MTB
Matilda Tank
Hurricane Mk IIB

1974
Cherokee Arrow II
Sopwith Pup
HMS *Cossack*
Chi Ha Tank
Scorpion Light Tank
Shooting Star
BAC Strikemaster
P-51D Mustang
Spitfire Mk Vb
German Reconnaissance Set
Republic Thunderstreak
BAC Canberra
Prinz Eugen
Harrier GRI

1975
SA Bulldog
NA Sabre
Narvik Class Destroyer
HMS *Ark Royal*
Bugatti 35B
Short Skyvan
Panavia Tornado
A300B Airbus
Rommel's Halftrack
Crusader III Tank
German E Boat

1976
HMS *Suffolk*
Fouga Magister
Me Bf109E
HA 5 22 Westland
Britten Norman Defender
    (conversion)
Army Lynx Helicopter
MG Magnette 1933
FIII E (conversion)
F14-A Tomcat
Concorde (update)
Junkers Ju-87B Stuka (1/24th)

1977
Me-163 Komet
Prinz Eugen (1/600)
Sepecat Jaguar
Navy Lynx Helicopter
Douglas Skyray

Henschel HS-126
Lee Tank (1/32nd)
Grant Tank (1/32nd)
Golden Hind
FW-190 A8/F8

1978
Whirlwind Mk I
P-51B Mustang
Star Cruiser
US Army Cargo Truck
Space Shuttle
USS *Forrestal*

1979
FW 190D
Spitfire Mk IA
MBB 105 Helicopter
Auster AOP6 (conversion)
Ju-87 Stuka
Boeing Sea Knight
Hawker Hurricane
Opel Blitz & Pak 40
Spitfire Mk Vb (1/48th)
Me Bf109F (1/48th)
Hawker Hurricane (1/48th)
Dassault Mirage F1C
Fokker Troopship
  (conversion)
S-3A Viking
F-15 Eagle
RAF Rescue Launch
HMS *Bounty*
Norton Motorcycle

1980
Douglas DC10
FW 190 A5 (1/24th)
MiG 23 Flogger
Alpha Jet
Hawker Fury (1/48th)
McDonnell F2H Banshee
Ford Cortina
Ford Zodiac
Ford Capri
Starcruiser Interceptor
DH Mosquito (1/48th)
Lancaster BIII
Ford C900
Countach LP500s
BMW MI
BMW Motorcycle

1981
Sikorsky HH 53C
Focke Wulf FW 190A
Christie Fire Engine (1/12th)
Shelby Cobra (1/16th)

1982
F-18A Hornet
F-16A Falcon
Sikorsky CH 53G Helicopter
Ju87 Stuka (1/48th)
HMS *George V*
HMS *Repulse*
Ford Express
Wild Breed Mustang
SR71 Blackbird
Burnout Firebird
Squad Rod Nova
Dragster
Black Belt Firebird
Night Stalker
Ford Mark VI
Chevrolet Cavalier
Sidewinder
Rolling Thunder
Saddle Tramp
Ground Shaker
Swamp Rat Jeep
Freedom Rider
Mount'n'Goat Jeep
Class Act
Sabre Vette
McLaren Mk 8D
Dust Devil
Bad Company
Thunder's Truck
Duke's Digger
Boss Hogg's Hauler
Cooter's Cruiser
General Lee Charger
Cooter's Tow Truck
Millennium Falcon™
Snow Speeder™
AT-AT™
Star Destroyer™
Flying Saucer

1983
X-Wing Fighter™
Hunter FGA 9 (conversion)
VC10 Refuelling (conversion)
Avro Vulcan B2
Kaman SH2 Seasprite
F5-E Tiger

A10 Thunderbolt
F 105 Thunderchief
Grumman Prowler
OV-10D Bronco (conversion)
Sea Harrier (1/48th)
Porsche 935
Ford Escort
Supercharged Dragster
Indy Pace Car
1983 Corvette
Toyota Supra
Fall Guy Truck™
Fall Guy Camaro™

1984
Kamov Ka-25 Hormone
Boeing 727-200 (Iberia
  conversion)
Rockwell B-1B
Lockheed U2B/D
Tornado GR1 (conversion)
Tie Interceptor™
Hughes AH-64 Apache
A-Wing Fighter™
B-Wing Fighter™
Hercules Gunship
  (conversion)
Tornado F2
Mil Mi-24 Hind
Sikorsky Sea King
Westland Sea King
  (conversion)
HP 0/400
Knight Rider™
Martin B-57B (conversion)

1985
Tornado F2 ADV
Hardcastle & McCormick
  Pick-up™
Hardcastle & McCormick
  Coyote™
Streethawk Car™
Streethawk Bike™

1986
No new toolings

1987
No new toolings

AIRFIX - 144 SCALE
SATURN 1B

1988
BAe T45 Goshawk (tooled
  but not released)
Harrier GR-3 (1/48th)
Lightning F3 (conversion)

1989
Hawker-Siddeley Buccaneer
  S2B
Tornado F-3

1990
Short Tucano
Super Etendard
Mirage 2000
MiG Fulcrum two seater
Su 27A Flanker two seater
Hughes Apache (1/48th)

1991
Harrier GR5
Harrier GR7
Boeing AWACS E-3D Sentry
  (conversion)
Etendard (1/48th)
Ferrari 250 GTO (1/24th)
Triumph TR2 (1/24th)
Austin Healey Sprite (1/24th)

Jaguar XK-E (1/24th)
Jaguar E-Type (1/24th)
Mercedes 170 (1/24th)
Mercedes 500K (1/24th)
Alfa Romeo (1/24th)
Bugatti T50 (1/24th)

1992
YF-22 Lightning II
F-117A Stealth
Eurofighter EFA
Etendard IVP (1/48th)
Mirage 2000 (1/48th)
Tornado GR1A (1/48th)
MiG 17 (1/48th)
Scania Eurotruck (1/24th)
Refrigerated Trailer (1/24th)
Semi Trailer (1/24th)
Triumph TR-7 (1/24th)
Mercedes 300 SL (1/24th)
Bugatti EB 110 (1/24th)
Citroen 2CV (1/24th)
BMW M1 (1/24th)
3.5 CSL (1/24th)
Maserati Bora (1/24th)
CAC Boomerang
Maserati Merak (1/24th)
Ferrari Rainbow (1/24th)
Ferrari Dino (1/24th)
Daytona (1/24th)
Lotus Esprit (1/24th)
Lamborghini Jota (1/24th)
Lamborghini Countach
 (1/24th)
Lamborghini Countach
 LP500S (1/24th)
De Tomaso Pantera (1/24th)
Corvette (1/24th)
Renault Alpine (1/24th)
Porsche 928 S4 (1/24th)
Peugeot 905

1993
Avro Lancaster BIII Special
 'Dambuster' (conversion)
HMS *Amazon, Leander* and
 Devonshire (all conversions)
F-15E Strike Eagle
 (conversion)

1994
Gloster Javelin FAW 9/9R
Sepecat Jaguar GR1A (1/48th)
HS Buccaneer S2B (1/48th)

1995
HS Buccaneer S2, S2C, S2D,
 SMK50 (1/48th)
Tornado GR1B (1/48th
 conversion)
DH Mosquito NF XIX/J30
 (conversion)

1996
Supermarine Spitfire F22/24
 (1/48th)
Supermarine Seafire FR46/47
 (1/48th)

1997
No new toolings except for
Airfix Junior 'Battle Zone'

1998
'Ships in Bottles' (tools from
 MB): *Mayflower, Cutty
 Sark,* Charles Morgan
 Whaler
Gulf Porsche 917 (1/32nd)
Ferrari 250 LM (1/32nd)
Vampire FB5
English Electric Lightning F-
 2A/F6 (1/48th)
English Electric Lightning F-
 1/F-1A/F-2/F-3 (1/48th)

1999
Wallace & Gromit Aeroplane
Wallace & Gromit Motorbike
 & Sidecar
B-17 Flying Fortress

Corsair F4U-1A (1/48th)
FW 190A-8 (1/48th)
P51-D Mustang (1/48th)
MiG 23 (1/144th)
F-20 Tiger Shark (1/144th)
General Dynamics F-16XL
 (1/144th)
F-4E Phantom II (1/144th)
MiG 21 (1/144th)
Fiat G91 Frecce Tricolori
Boeing 747-400 (1/300th)
Boeing 777 (1/300th)
Boeing AWACS Sentry
Eurofighter Typhoon

2000
BAe Harrier GR3 /AV-
 8A/AV-8S (1/24th)
Saab Viggen (1/144th)
F-104 Starfighter (1/144th)
Supermarine Spitfire Mk
 VIIIc (1/48th)
Grumman F6F-3 Hellcat
 (1/48th)
Curtiss Kittyhawk Mk Ia
 (1/48th)

2001
Westland Navy Lynx HMA8
 (modification)
Lancaster BI Special
 (modification)
Supermarine Spitfire Mk Vb
 (1/24th modification)
Dornier Do 217 Mistel
CH-47 Chinook

Douglas DC3 Dakota
C130 Hercules
Toyota Rav 4 (1/24th)
MGB (1/24th)
Aston Martin DB5 (1/24th)
McLaren F1 (1/43rd)
Williams F1 (1/43rd)
Citroen Xsara T4 WRC
 (1/43rd)
Subaru Impreza (1/43rd)
Peugeot 206 WRC (1/43rd)
Citroen Xsara T4 WRC
 (1/24th)
Peugeot 206 WRC (1/24th)

2002
Spitfire Mk Vc/Seafire IIIc
 (1/48th modification)
BAe Sea Harrier FRS-1
 (1/24th modification)
Saab JA-37 Viggen (1/48th)
Sepecat Jaguar GR3 (1/48th)
Dassault Super Etendard
 (1/48th)
Ford Focus (1/43rd)
Mitsubishi WRC (1/43rd)
Mitsubishi WRC (1/24th)
Subaru Impreza WRC
 (1/24th)
Honda 500cc (1/24th)
Suzuki 500cc (1/24th)
Yamaha 500cc (1/24th)

2003
BAe Red Arrows Hawk
 (1/48th)

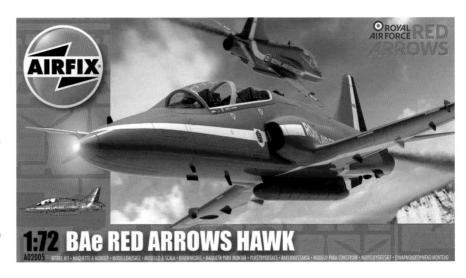

1:72 BAe RED ARROWS HAWK

1:72 SUPERMARINE SPITFIRE PRXIX

BAe Hawk 100 Series (1/48th)
DH Mosquito NF 30 (1/48th modification)
DH Mosquito B Mk XVI/PR XVI (1/48th modification)
NA F-86F Sabre
Subaru Ev2 Asphalt (1/43rd)
Ford Focus WRC (1/24th)
Peugeot 206 WRC Safari (1/24th)
Honda 4-stroke (1/24th)
Honda 500cc NSR500 (1/24th)
Yamaha 500cc Y2RM1 (1/24th)

2004
Panavia Tornado GR4/4A
Panavia Tornado F3/EF3 (1/48th)
Boeing AH-64D Apache Longbow
Bell AH-1T Sea Cobra
Challenger II Tank (1/35th)
Abrams M1A2 Tank (1/35th)
GMC DUKW (1/35th)
Sukhoi Su-27 Flanker B
Concorde
LCVP Landing Craft
Willys Jeep
GMC Truck

2005
BAC TSR-2
Supermarine Spitfire Mk IX/Mk XVIe (1/48th)
Supermarine Spitfire Mk Vc (modification)
NA P-51K Mustang (1/24th modification)
Sherman 'Crab' Tank (1/76th)
Churchill 'Crocodile' Tank (1/76th)

NA T-6G Texan
Saab S/J-29 Tunnan

2006
Wallace & Gromit Anti-Pesto Van (1/12th)
Britten Norman Islander (modification)
DH Drago Rapide
Lockheed Super Constellation
HMS *Hood* (1/400th)
HMS *King George V* (1/400th)
Scharnhorst & *Gneisenau* (1/400th)
Bismarck & *Tirpitz* (1/400th)

2007
HS Nimrod MR-2P
RNLI Severn Class Lifeboat
Dr Who 'Welcome Aboard'
Supermarine Spitfire Mk I (1/48th modification)

2008
BAe Red Arrows Hawk
Supermarine Spitfire Mk IXc
BAe Hawk 128/132
EE Canberra B(I)8
EE Canberra PR 9
EE Canberra B2/B20 (1/48th)
EE Canberra B(I)8 (1/48th)
EE Canberra PR 9 (1/48th)
BAC TSR-2 (1/48th)

Shaun the Sheep with Land Rover (1/48th)
Shaun the Sheep with Tractor (1/48th)
Fairey Fulmar Mk I/II
Hawker Sea Fury
Hawker Tempest V
Gloster Meteor F8
Boeing AH-64 Apache Longbow
Boeing Chinook
Horsa Glider
Vickers Wellington Mk IA/IC
Focke Wulf Mistel
HMS *Montgomery* (1/400th)
HNoMS *St Albans* (1/400th)
Gloster Gladiator (modification)
HS Buccaneer RAF & Navy (modification)
Westland Sea King HAS5 (modification)
Fokker F27 Friendship (modification)
Supermarine Spitfire Mk XVIe (modification)
Sherman 'Calliope' Tank
Matilda 'Hedgehog'
Churchill Bridge Layer
Airfix also released 12 former JB models of 1/76th scale military vehicles.

2009
De Havilland Mosquito NF II/FB VI (1/24th)
Yakovlev Yak 9D
Bell P-39Q Airacobra
Grumman Widgeon/Gosling
Hannover CL111
RE8
Albatross D.Va
Bristol Fighter F2B
Supermarine Walrus Mk II
Ilyushin Sturmovik

Spitfire PR XIX
Messerschmitt BF-109 G
Curtiss SB2C Helldiver
Vought F4U Corsair (FAA)
Blohm & Voss Bv141
Petlyakov Pe2
Focke Wulf FW189
HS Sea Vixen FAW2 (1/48th)
Sea Harrier FRS1 (new tool)
Sea Harrier FA2 (new tool)
Hawker Hurricane MkIIc (new tool)
MiG 15 (new tool)
HMS *Warspite* (1/600th)
HMS *Iron Duke* (1/600th)
HMS *Illustrious* (1/350th)
Titanic (1/700th)
Golden Hind (1/72nd)
WWI Male Tank
WWI Female Tank (modification)
DUKW
F-18 Hornet (1/144th new tool)
Hughes AH-64 Apache (1/144th new tool)
Vulcan XH558
BBMF Spitfire Mk Vb
Apollo Saturn V (modification)
Lunar Module
Airfix also released 20 'Starter Kits' of simplified aircraft and cars

Useful websites
Official Airfix Club **http://www.airfix.com/official-airfix-club-membership**
Airfix Clubs directory **http://www.airfix.com/clubs-directory**
Airfix Collectors' Club **http://pws.prserv.net/gbinet.dbjames/acc.htm**
Online community for collecting enthusiasts, with contributions from Airfix historian Arthur Ward: **http://collectingfriends.com/content**
International Plastic Modelling Society **http://www.ipms-uk.co.uk**

Scalex, Startex and Scalextric catalogue

Complete listing of all cars released as part of the standard ranges of Scalex, Startex and Scalextric. Livery appears in brackets after car make and model where relevant. Data supplied by Adrian Norman (http://www.slotcarportal.com).

Scalex

Aston Martin DB2
Austin Healey 100M
Jaguar 2.4 Saloon
Jaguar XK120
MG TF
Ferrari 375
Maserati 250F

Startex

Austin Healey 100/6
Jaguar 2.4 Saloon
Sunbeam Alpine

Scalextric tinplate cars:

1957

MM/C51 Maserati 250F
MM/C52 Ferrari 4.5L 375 F1 GP

1958

MM/C53 Austin Healey 100/4

Scalextric plastic cars:

1960

C0054 Lotus 16
C0055 Vanwall
C0056 Lister-Jaguar
C0057 Aston Martin DBR

1961

C0058 Cooper
C0059 BRM P25
C0060 Jaguar D Type
C0061 Porsche Spyder

1962

B0001 Motorbike/Sidecar Typhoon
C0062 Ferrari 156 Sharknose
C0063 Lotus 21
C0064 Bentley 4.5 Litre
C0065 Alfa Romeo 8C 2300

1963

B0002 Motorbike/Sidecar Hurricane
C0066 Cooper Formula Junior
C0067 Lotus Formula Junior
C0068 Aston Martin DB4 GT
C0069 Ferrari 250 GT
C0070 Bugatti Type 59
C0071 Auto Union C Type
E0001 Lister-Jaguar
E0002 Aston Martin DBR
E0003 Aston Martin DB4 GT
E0004 Ferrari 250 GT
E0005 Aston Martin DB4 GT (Marshal)
K0001 Go Kart

1964

C0072 BRM Formula Junior
C0073 Porsche Formula Junior (804)
C0074 Austin Healey 3000
C0075 Mercedes 190SL

1965

C0076 Mini Cooper

1966

C0077 Ford GT40
C0078 AC Cobra
C0079 Offenhauser
C0080 Offenhauser
C0081 Cooper Formula Junior
C0082 Lotus Formula Junior
C0083 Sunbeam Tiger
C0084 Triumph TR4A
C0085 BRM Formula Junior
C0086 Porsche Formula Junior (804)
C0087 Vanwall
C0088 Cooper
C0089 BRM P25
C0090 Ferrari 156 Sharknose
C0091 Jaguar D Type
C0092 Porsche Spyder
C0094 Mercedes 190SL
C0095 Bugatti Type 59
C0096 Auto Union C Type
Ck002 Porsche 904

1967

C0031 Seat 600
C0097 Aston Martin DB4 GT

1968

24C-100 Alfa Romeo GTZ
24C-101 Jaguar E Type
24C-500 Lotus Indianapolis T38
24C-501 Ferrari 158 V8 F1
24C-602 Alfa Romeo GTZ (ACE)
24C-603 Jaguar E Type (ACE)
C0001 Alpine Renault
C0002 Matra Jet
C0003 Javelin
C0005 Europa Vee
C0006 Panther
C0007 Mini Cooper
C0010 Javelin (Super)
C0011 Electra (Super)
C0032 Mercedes 250SL
C0033 Mercedes 250SL Sport
C0035 Ford GT40
C0099 Fiat 600

1969

C0004 Electra
C0008 Lotus Indianapolis
C0009 Ferrari 158 V8 F1

C0014 Matra MKII
C0015 Ford Mirage
C0016 Ferrari P4
C0017 Lamborghini Miura
C0018 Ford 3L GT
C0019 McLaren M4A (Scalextric Team Car)
C0036 Honda RA273
C0038 Cooper
C0039 Ferrari 156 Sharknose
C0040 Alfa Romeo 8C 2300
C0040 Chaparral 2G
C0042 Fiat Abarth 850TC

1970

C0020 Dart
C0021 Cougar Sports
C0045 Mini Cooper (MOVI)
YS103 Javelin
YS115 Ford Mirage
YS116 Ferrari P4
YS117 Lamborghini Miura
YS118 Ford 3L GT

1971

C0022 Porsche 917
C0023 Scalletti Arrow
C0024 McLaren M4A (Scalextric Team Car MKII)
C0034 Jaguar E Type
C0037 BRM H16

1972

C0026 March Ford 721
C0027 Lotus Turbine
C0029 Ferrari 312 B2
C0041 Ferrari 330 GT
C0043 McLaren M9A
C0044 Mercedes Wankel C111

1973

C0025 Ferrari 312 B2
C0028 Alpine Renault
C0046 Porsche 917K
C0047 Sigma Sigma
C0048 Tyrrell Ford 002
C0052 Ferrari B3

1974

C0007 Mini Cooper
C0012 Shadow
C0013 Electra (Tiger Special)
C0052 Ford Escort Mexico

1975

C0050 Lotus 72 (JPS)
C0051 BRM P160
C0053 Datsun 260Z

1976

C0120 Brabham BT44B (Martini)
C0121 Tyrrell Ford 007 (Elf)
C0122 Mini 1275 GT Clubman
C0123 Shadow (UOP)
C0124 Ferrari 312 T

1977

C0125 Porsche 911/935

1978

C0127 McLaren M23 (Marlboro)
C0128 BMW 3.0 CSL
C0129 March 240 (Rothmans)
C0130 Triumph TR7

1979

C0133 Wolf WR5
C0134 Renault RS-01 (Renault/Elf)
C0135 Tyrrell T008 (Elf)
C0136 Ferrari 312 T3

1980

C0103 BRM P160
C0104 Brabham BT44B (Martini)
C0105 Shadow (UOP)
C0106 Wolf WR5
C0107 Wolf WR5
C0108 McLaren M23 (Marlboro)
C0109 Ford Escort Mexico
C0110 Mini 1275 GT Clubman
C0112 Mini 1275 GT Clubman
C0113 Triumph TR7
C0114 Triumph TR7
C0115 Porsche 911/935
C0116 BMW 3.0 CSL
C0117 Ford Capri 3L
C0118 Ford Escort Mexico
C0119 Porsche 911/935
C0126 Lotus 77 (JPS)
C0131 March 240 (March)
C0281 Motorbike/Sidecar
C0282 Motorbike/Sidecar

1981

C0137 Ligier JS11
C0139 Brabham BT49 (Parmalat)
C0283 Rover 3500 (Triplex)
C0284 Rover 3500 (Police Car)
C0285 Superstox (Stickshifter)
C0286 Superstox (Fenderbender)
C0287 Ford Escort Mexico (Westwood Racing)
C0288 Porsche 911/935
C0289 Porsche 911/935

1982

C0280 Rover 3500 (PMG)
C0282 Motorbike/Sidecar
C0290 Mini 1275 GT Clubman (Mini-Ha-Ha)
C0291 Mini 1275 GT Clubman (Mad Hatter)
C0294 Triumph TR7
C0295 Porsche 911/935
C0296 BMW 3.0 CSL
C0300 Ford Capri 3L
C0301 Truck Roadtrain (Mobil/Saudia Leyland)
C0302 Truck Roadtrain (Low-Loader)
C0303 MG Metro (Datapost/Hepolite)
C0304 MG Metro (McCain)
C0305 Bentley 4.5 Litre
C0306 Alfa Romeo 8C 2300
C0311 Ford Capri 3L
C0315 Rover 3500 (Police Car)

1983

C0307 Ford Escort XR3i (Shell)
C0308 Ford Escort XR3i (Texaco)
C0309 Triumph TR7
C0310 MG Maestro
C0312 Superstox
C0313 Superstox
C0314 Ford Fiesta XR2i (Hisinsa)

1984

C0138 Williams FW07B (Saudia Leyland)
C0317 MG Metro (Turbo)
C0318 MG Metro (Turbo)
C0319 Truck Racing Rig (Rebel Rig)
C0320 Truck Racing Rig (Knight Raider)
C0321 Triumph TR7 (Spiderman)
C0322 Triumph TR7 (Spiderman)
C0323 MG Metro (Unipart)
C0324 MG Metro (Valvoline)
C0326 Ford Capri 3L (General Lee)
C0328 Datsun 4x4
C0329 Datsun 4x4
C0330 Rover 3500 (Golden Wonder)
C0331 MG Metro (Melitta)
C0332 MG Maestro
C0335 Truck Roadtrain (Parmalat)
C0336 Truck Racing Rig (Old Glory)
C0337 Truck Racing Rig (UFO)
C0340 Rover 3500 (Marshal)
C0341 Ford Escort XR3i
C0342 Ford Escort XR3i (Ford Escort Championship)

C0343 Datsun 4x4 (King Cab)
C0344 Datsun 4x4 (Falcon)
C0345 Ford Escort XR3i (Ford Escort Championship)
C0350 Williams FW07B (Casio F2)
C0351 Williams FW07B (G.P. International F3)
C0352 Brabham BT49 (Shell Oils F3)
C0353 Brabham BT49 (Sieger F3)
C0358 McLaren M23 (Track Flash)
C0359 McLaren M23 (Track Champ)

1985

C0146 MG Metro 6R4 (Navico)
C0327 Ford Escort XR3i
C0347 BMW M1
C0348 Audi Quattro (Shell Oils)
C0356 Ferrari 312 T (Track Ace)
C0357 Ferrari 312 T (Track Burner)
C0360 MG Metro 6R4 (Ternco)
C0362 Rover 3500 (Police Car)
C0363 Porsche 911/935
C0366 MG Metro (Duckhams)
C0370 Truck Roadtrain (T45)

1986

C0140 Ford Escort XR3i (Commodore)
C0141 Rover 3500
C0142 Rover 3500
C0143 BMW 3.0 CSL
C0144 Lancia L037 (Martini)
C0145 Lancia L037 (Pioneer)
C0147 Ferrari 312 T (Qudos)
C0148 Brabham BT44B (Kotzting)
C0149 MG Metro 6R4 (Computervision)
C0367 Datsun 4x4 (Highwayman)
C0368 Datsun 4x4 (Hawaiian Cruiser)
C0375 Ford Escort XR3i (Palmer Tube Mills)
C0376 Ford Escort XR3i (Mobil)
C0377 Ferrari 312 T3 (Tyler Autos)
C0378 Renault RS-01 (Graves Engineering)
C0379 Ford Capri 3L (Valvoline)
C0380 Datsun 260Z (Bison Computers)
C0390 Ford Escort XR3i (Mobil)
C0392 Ford Escort XR3i (Palmer Tube Mills)
C0837 Ford Escort XR3i (Mobil)
C0838 Ford Escort XR3i (Palmer Tube Mills)

1987

C0016 Lancia LC02 (Totip)
C0017 Peugeot 205 Turbo 16
C0018 Porsche 956 (Skoal)
C0019 Mercedes 190E 2.3-16
C0022 Porsche 956 (Mobil)
C0100 Pontiac Firebird (Knight Rider)
C0101 Datsun 260Z
C0102 Wolf WR5 (Team Talbot)
C0349 Audi Quattro (Audi)
C0373 Lotus Honda (Elf)
C0373 Lotus Renault 98T (De Longhi)
C0374 Williams FW11 Honda
C0383 Pontiac Firebird (Firebird)
C0384 Rover 3500 (Taurus)
C0385 Ferrari 312 T (Deserra Sports)
C0386 Ferrari 312 T (Stone Avionics)

C0387 Truck Racing Rig (RMS)
C0388 Truck Racing Rig (ATS)
C0389 Ford Escort XR3i (Ilford Photos)
C0390 Ford Escort XR3i (Bosch)
C0391 Ferrari GT0 (Cimarron)
C0394 Ford Escort XR3i (Ford/Shell)
C0395 Ford Escort XR3i (STP Sky Travel)

1988

C0214 MG Metro 6R4 (Total)
C0215 MG Metro 6R4 (Valvoline)
C0294 Pontiac Firebird (Redcote)
C0295 Pontiac Firebird (Bob Jane T Marts)
C0382 Jaguar XJR9 (Castrol)
C0403 Pontiac Firebird (Mask - Thunderhawk)
C0404 Pontiac Firebird (Venom - Manta)
C0425 Lotus Renault 98T (De Longhi)
C0426 Williams FW11 Honda (Canon)
C0427 Porsche 911/935
C0428 Porsche 911/935
C0429 Ford RS200 (Radiopaging)
C0432 Ford RS200 (Shell)
C0433 Ford Escort XR3i (Pirelli)
C0434 Lotus Honda Turbo (Camel)
C0436 Porsche 962C (Autoglass/Shell Gemini)
C0441 Ford Escort XR3i (Texaco)
C0446 Ford Escort XR3i (Supasnaps)

1989

C0020 McLaren F1 (Saima)
C0021 Ferrari F1
C0228 Ferrari 312 T (Qudos)
C0229 Brabham BT44B (Kotzting)
C0369 Williams FW11 Honda (Piquet)
C0401 Porsche 911/935 (Dunlop)
C0435 Porsche 911/935 (Shell)
C0437 Ferrari 312 T (Hi-Tech/Bilstein)
C0438 Brabham BT44B (Automech)
C0443 Jaguar XJR9
C0444 Porsche 962C (Rothmans)
C0449 Porsche 969
C0455 Ford Sierra Cosworth (Texaco)
C0456 Ford Sierra Cosworth (Firestone)
C0457 Ferrari F1-87
C0457 Ferrari F1-87

1990

C0238 Motorbike/Sidecar (Racing Red)
C0239 Motorbike/Sidecar (Yellow Flash)
C0250 Pontiac Firebird
C0255 Pontiac Firebird
C0307 Benetton B189
C0360 Lamborghini Diablo (Palau)
C0361 Lamborghini Diablo (Palau)
C0365 Ford Sierra Cosworth (Palmer Tube Mills)
C0458 Audi Quattro (Audi/BBS)
C0459 Datsun 260Z (Shell)
C0460 Ford Escort XR3i (STP)
C0461 Benetton B189
C0462 McLaren MP4/4
C0462 McLaren MP4/4
C0463 Porsche 962C (Shell)

C0464 BMW M3 (Michelin/BBS)
C0465 Batmobile
C0466 Porsche 911/935 (The Joker)
C0467 Tyrrell Ford 018 (Epson, Alesi)
C0468 Mercedes Sauber C9/88
C0469 Ford Sierra Cosworth (Shell)
C0472 Ferrari 312 T3 (Dunlop)
C0473 Renault RS-01 (Panasonic/Technics)
C0474 Ford Sierra Cosworth (Shell - Palmer Tube Mills)
C0475 Ford Sierra Cosworth (Mobil)

1991

C0123 Ford Sierra Cosworth (Janspeed)
C0124 Porsche 911/935 (Havoline)
C0125 Porsche 962C (Fina)
C0126 Ford Escort XR3i (Bardahl)
C0127 Lamborghini Diablo
C0128 Horse Horse & Jockey (Fairweather Lady)
C0129 Horse Horse & Jockey (Tim's Folly)
C0130 Skateboard Turtle & Skateboard (Leonardo)
C0131 Skateboard Turtle & Skateboard (Donatello)
C0132 Skateboard Turtle & Skateboard (Raphael)
C0134 Skateboard Turtle & Skateboard (Shredder)
C0232 Renault RS-01 (Pennzoil Indy)
C0233 Renault RS-01 (Toshiba Indy)
C0241 Horse Horse & Jockey
C0242 Horse Horse & Jockey
C0275 MG Maestro
C0276 MG Maestro
C0281 Triumph TR7 (Toys-R-Us)
C0282 Triumph TR7 (Toys-R-Us)
C0338 Skateboard Turtle & Skateboard (Michaelangelo)
C0339 Skateboard Turtle & Skateboard (Footsoldier)
C0405 BMW M1 (BMW)
C0406 BMW M3 (Mobil)
C0407 Porsche 911/935 (Porsche)
C0408 Ford Sierra Cosworth (Syntron-X)

C0409 BMW M3 (Demon Tweeks)
C0411 Lamborghini Diablo
C0413 Porsche 911/935 (Pirelli)
C0418 Jaguar XJR9 (Castrol)
C0419 Horse Horse & Sulky (Terry's Challenge)
C0420 Horse Horse & Sulky (Julie's Choice)
C0421 Volkswagen Turtle Partywagon (VW Camper)
C0422 Datsun 4x4 (Turtle Pick-Up Truck)
C0486 Porsche 962C (Kenwood)

1992

C0093 Tyrrell Ford 007
C0094 Ferrari 312 B2
C0095 Ford 3L GT
C0096 Ferrari P4
C0097 Vanwall
C0098 BRM P25
C0099 Mini Cooper
C0169 Ford Sierra Cosworth (Monroe)
C0175 Ford Sierra Cosworth (Cortez)
C0188 Porsche 962C (Take Fuji)
C0189 Mercedes Sauber C9/88
C0206 Mini Cooper
C0265 Motorbike/Sidecar (Texaco)
C0269 Motorbike/Sidecar (Shell)
C0272 Porsche 962C (Froma)
C0283 Lamborghini Diablo
C0287 Ford Fiesta XR2i (Fiesta)
C0296 Porsche 962C (962C-R Road Livery)
C0304 Porsche 962C (Froma)
C0309 Porsche 962C (Repsol)
C0310 Ferrari F40
C0319 Ferrari 643 F1
C0321 Ford Fiesta XR2i (Ford Motorsport)
C0323 Mini Cooper
C0333W MG Metro 6R4 (Navico)
C0334W MG Metro 6R4 (Esso)
C0335 Ford Fiesta XR2i (Fiesta)
C0398 Mini Cooper (Toys-R-Us Union Jack)
C0399 Mini Cooper (Toys-R-Us Union Jack)
C0423 Ford Sierra Cosworth (Fina)

1993

C0150 Mini Cooper

C0184 Ferrari 643 F1 (Minardi F92/1)
C0195 Ferrari F40
C0200 Ferrari 643 F1 (Indianapolis 'Pennzoil')
C0201 Ferrari 643 F1 (Indianapolis 'Texaco')
C0203 Ford Escort Cosworth (Team Ford)
C0204 Ford Escort Cosworth (Panasonic)
C0256 Porsche 962C (Repsol)
C0257 Jaguar XJ220
C0280 Ford Sierra Cosworth (Duckhams)
C0290 Jaguar XJ220
C0316 Ford Fiesta XR2i (Valvoline)
C0328W Mini Cooper
C0329W Mini Cooper
C0350 Ferrari 312 T3 (Gold Star)
C0351 Renault RS-01 (Exchange Services)
C0352 Renault RS-01 (Watt's Racing)

1994

C0137 Ford Sierra Cosworth (Police Car)
C0142 Benetton B193 (Ford 1993)
C0143 Williams FW15C Renault (Renault/Elf)
C0193 Ford Escort Cosworth (Beatties)
C0291 Ferrari F40
C0311 Ferrari 643 F1 (Indianapolis 'Texaco')
C0330 Porsche 911/935
C0356W Porsche 962C (Toshiba)
C0357W Mercedes Sauber C9/88 (AEG)
C0358W BMW 318I (Daily Express)
C0359W Ford Mondeo (Fordsport/ICS Rouse)
C0366W Porsche 911/935 (Hot Pursuit)
C0370 Ford Escort Cosworth (Pilot)
C0381W Ford Fiesta XR2i (Q8)
C0390W Ford Fiesta XR2i (Shell/Helix)
C0392/J MG Metro 6R4 (BP)
C0393 Mini Cooper (Motoworld)
C0402 Porsche 962C (Omron)

C0424 Ford Mondeo
  (Fordsport/ICS Radisich)
C0430 Tyrrell Ford 018
  (Omega/Securicor)
C0442 Brabham BT44B (Pirelli)
C0445 Mercedes Sauber C9/88
  (AEG)
C0447 Ferrari 643 F1 (Indianapolis
  'Pennzoil')
C0450 Ferrari F40 (Bridgestone)
C0451 Lamborghini Diablo
  (Diablo Racing)
C0452 Lamborghini Diablo
C0453 Brabham BT44B (Team
  Dodger)
C0462 BMW 318I (Westminster)
C0470 Ford Fiesta XR2i (Uniroyal)
C0471 Ford Escort Cosworth
  (Barry Squibb/Graydon Motors)
C0480 MG Metro 6R4 (Esso)
C0481 Mini Cooper (Monte Carlo)
C0483 Jaguar XJ220
C0485 Ferrari 643 F1 (Delarra
  'Lusfina')
C0488 Truck Racing Rig (Silkolene)
C0491 Truck Racing Rig (Bardahl)

1995
C0194 Team Indianapolis (Team
  Duracell)
C0196 Ford Mondeo (Dagenham
  Motors)
C0197 Alfa Romeo 155
C0213 Ford Mondeo
  (Fordsport/ICS)
C0226 Williams FW15C Renault
  (Renault/Elf)
C0227 Williams FW15C Renault
  (Renault/Elf)
C0230 Jaguar XJ220
C0237 Benetton B193 (Ford 1994)
C0241 Alfa Romeo 8C 2300
C0242 Bentley 4.5 Litre
C0251 BMW 318I (Esso/Ultron)
C0324 Ford Escort Cosworth
  (Shell/Helix)

C0340 Ford Mondeo (Dick
  Johnson/Shell)
C0394 Porsche 911/935 (Demon
  Tweeks)
C0403 Ford Escort Cosworth
  (Hendy)
C0410 Ferrari 643 F1
C0412 Ferrari F40 (Endurance
  'Maxell')
C0416 Ford Fiesta XR2i (Repsol)
C0417 Mini Cooper (Bardahl)
C0478 Mini Cooper (Mobil)
C0479 Ferrari 312 T (BP)
C0487 Brabham BT44B (Firehawk)
C0490 Ferrari 643 F1
C0492 Benetton B193 (Ford 1993)
C0496 Alfa Romeo 155
C0546 Benetton B193 (Ford 1994)
C0549W Benetton B193
  (Ford 1993)
C0550W Ferrari 643 F1
C0559 Porsche 962C (Syntron-X)
C0560 Porsche 962C (Texaco)
C0570 Ford Mondeo (Dagenham
  Motors)
C0579 Ford Mondeo (Dagenham
  Motors)
C0602W Jaguar XJR9 (Unipart)
C0603W Jaguar XJR9 (Jaguar
  Sport)
C0630 Team Indianapolis (Team
  Eurosport)
C0882 Motorbike/Sidecar Power
  Rangers Battle Bike
C0883 Motorbike/Sidecar Power
  Rangers Battle Bike
C0884 Motorbike/Sidecar Power
  Rangers Battle Bike
C0885 Motorbike/Sidecar Power
  Rangers Battle Bike

1996
C0288 Aston Martin DBR
C0289 Aston Martin DBR
C0522 Team Indianapolis (Team
  Rahal Hogan)

C0533 Williams FW15C Renault
  (Renault/Elf)
C0534 Team Indianapolis (Team
  Pennzoil)
C0535 Renault Laguna
C0536 Alfa Romeo 155 (Old Spice)
C0537 Truck Racing Rig (Texaco)
C0538 Truck Racing Rig
  (Energizer)
C0561 Rover 3500 (NSCC)
C0562 Rover 3500 (NSCC)
C0571 BMW 320I (Autosport)
C0572 Alfa Romeo 155 (Racing
  Martini Livery)
C0582 Lamborghini Diablo
  (Diablo Racing)
C0583 Benetton B193 (Renault)
C0584 Williams FW15C Renault
  (Renault/Elf)
C0585 McLaren MP4/10 Mercedes
C0587 BMW 320I (Benzina)
C0589 Ferrari F40 (Gulf)
C0590 Ferrari F40 (Kenwood)
C0591 Jaguar XJ220 (PC
  Automotive)
C0592 Ford Escort Cosworth
  (Cepsa)
C0601 Mercedes C Class (AMG
  'Sonax')
C0613 Team Low Nose (Navico)
C0616 Team Low Nose (Simpson)
C0631 Opel-Vauxhall Calibra
  (Team Joest Cliff)
C0632 Opel-Vauxhall Calibra
  (Team Joest)
C0676 Ford Escort Cosworth (Fina)
C0677 Ford Escort Cosworth
  (Pilot)
C0685 McLaren MP4/10 Mercedes
C0690 BMW 320I (Autosport)
C0692 Ford Mondeo (Team
  Valvoline)
C0693 Team Low Nose (Sally
  Ferries)
C0698 Team High Nose (Avon
  Tyres)

C0699 Mercedes C Class (AMG
  'Promarkt')
C0701 Opel-Vauxhall Calibra
  (Team Joest)
C0716 Ford Mondeo ('100+')
C0746 Ford Mondeo (Team
  Valvoline)
C0782 Brabham BT44B (Kwik-Fit)
C0783 Ferrari 312 T (Sparco)

1997
C0063 Ford Mondeo (Shell/Fai
  Dick Johnson)
C0136 Renault Laguna (1996
  Livery)
C0383 Ford Mondeo (Valvoline
  Steven Richards)
C0431 Ford Mondeo (Nokia/Phil
  Ward)
C0432 Ford Mondeo (Dick
  Johnson/Shell)
C0530 Ford Mondeo (Nokia/Phil
  Ward)
C0548 Ford Escort Cosworth
  (Repsol - Carlos Sainz)
C0596 Opel-Vauxhall Calibra (Old
  Spice)
C2000 Opel-Vauxhall Vectra
  (Promarkt)
C2001 Opel-Vauxhall Vectra
  (BTCC)
C2002 Audi A4 (BTCC)
C2003 Lamborghini Diablo
  (Phillipe Charriol)
C2004 McLaren MP4/10 Mercedes
C2005 Renault Laguna (1995
  Livery)
C2006 Opel-Vauxhall Vectra
  (Villamil)
C2007 Renault Megane (Diac)
C2008 Audi A4 (Adac)
C2010 Renault Megane (Red
  Renault)
C2011 Ferrari 643 F1
C2013 Jaguar XJ220 (Italia
  Cup ERG)

C2014 Ferrari 312 T (Team Recaro)
C2015 Brabham BT44B (Team
  Qxr Duckhams)
C2016 Team High Nose (Virgin
  Cola)
C2017 Alfa Romeo 155 (Contract
  Hire)
C2018 Team Low Nose (Team GQ)
C2019 Ferrari F40
C2020 Ford Thunderbird Nascar
  (Valvoline - Mark Martin)
C2027 Ford Escort Cosworth
  (Motosport (McRae))
C2028 Ford Escort Cosworth
  (Repsol - Carlos Sainz)
C2029 Renault Megane
C2030 Opel-Vauxhall Calibra (Old
  Spice)
C2031 Opel-Vauxhall Calibra
  (Promarkt)
C2032 Mercedes C Class (D2)
C2033 Mercedes C Class (Team
  Persson/Points)
C2034 Audi A4 (Repsol)
C2037W Opel-Vauxhall Calibra
  (Promarkt)
C2038W Mercedes C Class (D2)
C2041/W Porsche 911/935 (Gulf)
C2042/W Porsche 911/935 (Fina)
C2043 Ford Mondeo (Nokia/Phil
  Ward)
C2044 Ford Mondeo (Valvoline
  Steven Richards)
C2056 Opel-Vauxhall Vectra
  (BTCC)
C2057W Chevrolet Montecarlo
  (Nascar)
C2058W Ford Thunderbird Nascar

1998
C0532 Benetton B193 (Renault)
C2012/W Williams FW15C
  Renault (Renault/Elf)
C2021 Ford Thunderbird Nascar
  (Exide Batteries - Jeff Burton)

C2022 Chevrolet Montecarlo (Kodak Film - Sterling Marlin)
C2023 Chevrolet Montecarlo (Kellogg's - Terry Labonte)
C2026W Porsche 911 GT1 (Fontana)
C2035W Porsche 911 GT1 (Giesse)
C2036 Ferrari F40 (Igol)
C2039 Jaguar XJ220 (Italia Cup ERG)
C2040 Jaguar XJ220
C2045 Porsche 911 GT1
C2046 Ferrari 643 F1
C2059 Ford Capri 3L
C2060 Ford Capri 3L
C2061 Aston Martin DBR
C2062 Aston Martin DBR
C2063 Aston Martin DBR
C2064 Jaguar XJ220
C2065 Ford Mondeo (Valvoline Steven Richards)
C2069RP Lamborghini Diablo (Range Presentation)
C2070/W Truck Racing Rig (Demon Tweeks)
C2071/W Truck Racing Rig (Valvoline)
C2072W Mercedes C Class (Daim)
C2073W Opel-Vauxhall Calibra (Opel LNE)
C2074 Team High Nose (Texaco)
C2075 Team Low Nose (Kwik Fit)
C2076 Ford Escort Cosworth (BP)
C2078/W Renault Laguna
C2079/W Jordan F197 (Snake)
C2080 Jordan F197 (Snake)
C2083 Jaguar XJ220
C2084 Opel-Vauxhall Vectra (Masterfit)
C2085 Opel-Vauxhall Vectra (Times/Opel Motor Sport)
C2086 Audi A4 (Orix)
C2087 Audi A4 (Talkline/Autoplus)
C2088 Renault Megane (Cup Super)
C2089 Porsche 911 GT1 (Giesse)
C2090 Ford Mondeo (Shell)
C2091 BMW 320i (Teleshop)
C2092 Porsche 911 GT1 (Fontana)
C2093 Lamborghini Diablo (Teng Tools)
C2094 Renault Megane (Diac)
C2095W Team Low Nose (Bridgestone)
C2096W Team High Nose (Minolta)
C2097W Renault Megane (Diac)
C2102W Renault Megane
C2103/W Mini Cooper
C2104/W Mini Cooper
C2105W McLaren MP4/10 Mercedes (Mobil (West))
C2106W Benetton B193 (Renault Fed Ex 1998)
C2107W Audi A4 (No 1)
C2108W Ferrari 643 F1
C2114 Benetton B193 (Renault Fed Ex 1998)
C2115 Ferrari 643 F1
C2116 Opel-Vauxhall Vectra (Protec)
C2117 Audi A4
C2118 Subaru Impreza (Works)
C2119 Toyota Corolla
C2120 Opel-Vauxhall Vectra (Police Car (Kent))
C2121 BMW 320I (Police Car)
C2123 Chevrolet Montecarlo
C2124 McLaren MP4/10 Mercedes
C2137N Jaguar XJ220 (NSCC)

C2147 Ferrari F40 (Celtic)
C2148 Ferrari F40 (Rangers)
C2149 Ferrari F40 (Newcastle)
C2150 Ferrari F40 (Liverpool)
C2151 Ferrari F40 (Arsenal)
C2152 Ferrari F40 (Chelsea)
C2153 Ferrari F40 (Spurs)
C2161 Williams FW20
C2162 Williams FW20

1999
C2081 Mercedes CLK GT1 (D2 Privat)
C2082 Mercedes CLK GT1 (Westminster)
C2110W Opel-Vauxhall Calibra (Hutchinson Telecom)
C2111W Opel-Vauxhall Calibra (Old Spice)
C2112W Team Low Nose (Agip)
C2113 Team High Nose (Avon Tyres)
C2126 Jordan F197 (Hornet)
C2127 Jordan F197 (Hornet)
C2129 Subaru Impreza
C2130 Toyota Corolla
C2132W Subaru Impreza (Works)
C2133W Toyota Corolla
C2135 Chevrolet Montecarlo (Kodak - Bobby Hamilton)
C2136 Chevrolet Montecarlo (Kellogg's - Chicken Looks Right)
C2138 Porsche 911 GT1
C2139 Porsche 911 GT1
C2139 Porsche 911 GT1
C2140 Subaru Impreza
C2141 Ford Taurus Nascar (Exide Batteries - Jeff Burton)
C2142 Ford Taurus Nascar (Mcdonalds)
C2143 Ford Taurus Nascar (Mobil1)
C2146 Ford Taurus Nascar (Valvoline - Mark Martin)
C2154 Renault Megane
C2155 Renault Megane (Diac)
C2156 Team Low Nose (Bridgestone)
C2157 Team High Nose (Minolta)
C2158 Williams FW15C Renault (Renault/Elf)
C2159 Ferrari 643 F1
C2160 Toyota Corolla (Sainz & Moya)
C2163 Audi A4 (European-Engen)
C2165 Opel-Vauxhall Vectra (TNT)
C2166 Renault Laguna (Nescafe Blend 37)
C2167 Renault Laguna (D.C.Cook/Ultron)
C2168 BMW 320I (Castrol - Fabrizio De Simone)
C2169 BMW 320I (Johnny Ceccoto)
C2170 Ford Mondeo
C2171 Ford Escort Cosworth (Works)
C2174 Ford Escort Cosworth (Works)
C2177 Subaru Impreza (Stomil)
C2178 Toyota Corolla
C2185 Pontiac Grand Prix (Home Depot)
C2187 Benetton B193 (Playlife 1999)
C2190 Porsche 911 GT1 (IBM)

C2191 Porsche 911 GT1 (PlayStation)
C2192 Lamborghini Diablo (Valvoline)
C2193 Lamborghini Diablo (SV)
C2194 TVR Speed 12
C2195 TVR Speed 12
C2196 Opel-Vauxhall Vectra (Marshalls Car)
C2197 Opel-Vauxhall Vectra (Paramedic Car)
C2198 Opel-Vauxhall Vectra (Fire Car)
C2200 Lotus Seven (Classic)
C2201 Caterham Seven (Coldstream)
C2202 Porsche 911 GT1 (100+)
C2203 Subaru Impreza
C2204 McLaren MP4/10 Mercedes (Shake Down Car)
C2205 Toyota Corolla
C2206 TVR Speed 12 (Collector's Edition)
C2207 Ferrari F40
C2208 Ford Taurus Nascar (Rusty Wallace)
C2211 Caterham Seven
C2212 Caterham Seven
C2213 Williams FW15C Renault (Senna)
C2214 Williams FW15C Renault (Senna)
C2215 Audi A4 (Senna)
C2216 Audi A4 (Senna)
C2217 Ford Taurus Nascar (Exide 99)
C2219 Ford Taurus Nascar (Valvoline 99)
C2221 Subaru Impreza (Senna)
C2222 Subaru Impreza (Senna)
C2223 Lamborghini Diablo (Senna)

C2224 Lamborghini Diablo (Senna)
C2225 Ford Taurus Nascar (John Deere)
C2226W Pontiac Grand Prix (Interstate Batteries)
C2228RP Jaguar XJ220 (Range Presentation)
C2229 Porsche 911 GT1 (Paragon)
C2230 Lotus Seven (Classic)
C2231 Caterham Seven (Comma)
C2235W Subaru Impreza (Works)
C2236W Subaru Impreza (Works)
C2237 Ford Escort Cosworth
C2238 Ferrari F40
C2239 Opel-Vauxhall Vectra
C2240W Subaru Impreza (Works)
C2241W Toyota Corolla
C2243A Subaru Impreza (Barratts)
C2244 Mini Cooper (40th Anniversary)
C2245 TVR Speed 12 (40th Anniversary)
C2246 Subaru Impreza (Collector Centre)
C2247 TVR Speed 12 (Collector Centre)
C2248 TVR Speed 12
C2249 Mini Cooper (40th Anniversary)
C2302 TVR Speed 12 (SLN 5 Year Anniversary)
C2307 Caterham Seven
C2308 Caterham Seven

2000
C0494 Mini Cooper
C2118 Subaru Impreza (Motorists Centre)
C2131 Audi A4 (Euro Jever)
C2137jec Jaguar XJ220 (Jaguar Enthusiasts Club)

C2144 Opel-Vauxhall Vectra (Westminster STW)
C2145 Renault Laguna (Nescafe Blend 37)
C2172 Ford Mondeo (Rapid Fit)
C2173 Toyota Corolla (Works 1999)
C2175 Ford Focus (Iridium)
C2176/W Ford Focus (Works McRae)
C2179 Ford Focus (Carlos Sainz)
C2183 Toyota Corolla (V Rally)
C2184 Toyota Corolla (Privateer)
C2188 Porsche 911 GT1 (Team Champion)
C2189 TVR Speed 12 (Esso Ultron)
C2209 TVR Speed 12 (Demon Tweeks)
C2218 Ford Taurus Nascar (Macdonalds 99)
C2220W Jordan F197 (Hornet)
C2227 Pontiac Grand Prix (STP)
C2233 Volkswagen Beetle (Pirelli)
C2234 Volkswagen Beetle (Mobil 1)
C2253W Renault Laguna (Blend 37)
C2254 Mercedes CLK GT1
C2255 Subaru Impreza (Works 1999 Livery)
C2256 Subaru Impreza (Belgacom)
C2257/WA Subaru Impreza (Works 2000)
C2260/WA McLaren MP4/10 Mercedes (Mika)
C2261 McLaren MP4/10 Mercedes (David)
C2264WA Williams FW20 BMW F1 (BMW.WilliamsF1)
C2265WA Williams FW20 BMW F1 (BMW.WilliamsF1)
C2266 Benetton B193 (Marconi 2000)

C2269 Lotus Seven
C2270 Lotus Seven
C2271 Caterham Seven (Road Trim)
C2272 Caterham Seven (Road Trim)
C2273 Subaru Impreza (Police Car)
C2276 Volkswagen Beetle
C2277WA Benetton B193 (Playlife 1999)
C2279 Ford Taurus Nascar (Mobil 1 2000)
C2280/WAM Ford Taurus Nascar (De Walt 2000)
C2281 Ford Taurus Nascar (Exide 2000)
C2283 Ford Taurus Nascar (Valvoline 2000)
C2284 Pontiac Grand Prix (Lycos)
C2285WA Pontiac Grand Prix (Interstate Batteries)
C2286 Ford Taurus Nascar (Tide)
C2287WA Pontiac Grand Prix (Home Depot)
C2295W Ford Focus (Ford)
C2296W Toyota Corolla (Corolla)
C2299 Volkswagen Beetle (New Beetle Cup)
C2300 Volkswagen Beetle (New Beetle Cup)
C2301 Volkswagen Beetle
C2303 Opel-Vauxhall Vectra (Masterfit)
C2309 Opel-Vauxhall Vectra (BTCC Works 2000)
C2310 Opel-Vauxhall Vectra (Opel Line)
C2311 Ford Mondeo (Rapid Fit)
C2312 Toyota Corolla (Zucchetti)
C2313 Subaru Impreza (Norisbank)
C2314 Volkswagen Beetle (Cabriolet)
C2315 Volkswagen Beetle (Cabriolet)
C2316 TVR Speed 12 (Brussels Retro)
C2317 Porsche 911 GT1 (Range Presentation)
C2318 Team High Nose (Firestone)
C2319 Team Low Nose (Shell)
C2323 Jaguar XJ220 (Gamleys)
C2324 Jaguar XJ220 (Gamleys)
C2325N TVR Speed 12 (NSCC)
C2326 Ford Taurus Nascar
C2327 Pontiac Grand Prix
C2329WAA Opel-Vauxhall Vectra (Vectra)
C2330 Jaguar XJ220 (Hamleys)
C2331 Caterham Seven (Drive@ Silverstone)
C2332 Caterham Seven (Drive@ Donnington)
C2333 Caterham Seven (Drive@ Croft)

2001

C2258 Cadillac Northstar 4l (GM Racing)
C2259 Cadillac Northstar 4l (Dams)
C2267WBK BMW 320i (Index)
C2274/Wl Porsche 911 GT3R (Paragon)
C2275 Porsche 911 GT3R (Red Bull)
C2278 TVR Speed 12 (Scania)
C2297 Opel-Vauxhall Astra V8 DTM Coupe (Opel Service)
C2298 Opel-Vauxhall Astra V8 DTM Coupe (Sport Bild)

C2336 Volkswagen Beetle (Neubeck.Online)
C2337 Volkswagen Beetle (Optimax)
C2340 Cadillac Northstar 4l (Dams)
C2341A Subaru Impreza (Works)
C2342 Ford Focus (Works 2000)
C2343 Ford Focus (Laukkanen)
C2344 Caterham Seven (Peter Ritche Racing)
C2345 Caterham Seven (Team Taran)
C2346 Ford Taurus Nascar (Tide 2001)
C2347 Ford Taurus Nascar (Mcdonalds)
C2348 Ford Taurus Nascar (Mobil 1)
C2352 Mercedes CLK GT1 (Range Presentation)
C2354WA Porsche 911 GT3R (Hewlett-Packard)
C2355WA Porsche 911 GT3R (UPS)
C2356WA TVR Speed 12
C2357WA TVR Speed 12
C2358WA Opel-Vauxhall Astra V8 DTM Coupe (Opel Motorsport)
C2359WA Opel-Vauxhall Astra V8 DTM Coupe (Sport Bild)
C2362 Subaru Impreza (Works 2001)
C2363 TVR Speed 12
C2368 Porsche 911 GT3R
C2369 Porsche 911 GT3R
C2370 Ford Taurus Nascar (Pfizer 2001)
C2371/W Ford Taurus Nascar (Citgo 2001)
C2372 Ford Taurus Nascar (Dewalt 2001)
C2373/W Ford Taurus Nascar (Motorcraft 2001)
C2374 Ford Taurus Nascar (Rusty Wallace 2001)
C2375/W Pontiac Grand Prix (Valvoline 2001)
C2376/W Pontiac Grand Prix (Conseco 2001)
C2377W Pontiac Grand Prix (Home Depot 2001)
C2378W Pontiac Grand Prix (Interstate Batteries 2001)
C2379WA Subaru Impreza (Works)

C2380WA Ford Focus (RS)
C2381WA Ford Focus (RS)
C2382WA Renault Megane (Megane)
C2383WA Renault Megane (Megane)
C2386/W TVR Speed 12 (Hamleys 2001)
C2387 Subaru Impreza (Gamleys 2001)
C2388 Porsche 911 GT3R

2002

C2262A McLaren MP4/16 (Mika)
C2263/W McLaren MP4/16 (David)
C2268WL Porsche 911 GT3R (Tengtools)
C2334A Williams FW23 BMW (Ralf Schumacher)
C2335 Williams FW23 BMW (Juan Pablo Montoya)
C2338/W Porsche 911 GT3R (Seikel)
C2339/W Porsche 911 GT3R (White Lightning)
C2350 Cadillac Northstar 4l (Range Presentation)
C2360 Porsche 911 GT3R
C2361 Porsche 911 GT3R
C2364A Mitsubishi Lancer Evo 7
C2365 Mitsubishi Lancer Evo 7
C2366A MG Lola EX257 (MG Sport & Racing)
C2393 Ford Focus (Grist/McRae)
C2399A Chevrolet Camaro (Penske Sunoco)
C2400 Chevrolet Camaro (Penske Sunoco)
C2401A Ford Mustang (Boss 302 - Bud Moore)
C2402 Ford Mustang (Boss 302 - Bud Moore)
C2403A Ford GT40 (Gulf)
C2404 Ford GT40 (Gulf)
C2405W Ford Focus (KA Livery)
C2406W Ford Focus (KA Livery)
C2407 Pontiac Grand Prix (Valvoline)
C2408 Pontiac Grand Prix (M&Ms)
C2409 Opel-Vauxhall Astra V8 DTM Coupe (Sat1)
C2410 Opel-Vauxhall Astra V8 DTM Coupe (Oase)

C2411 Ford Focus (Works 2002)
C2412/W Subaru Impreza (Works 2002)
C2413 Chevrolet Camaro (Bob Jane)
C2414 Subaru Impreza (Privateer 2002)
C2415 McLaren MP4/16 (David)
C2416 McLaren MP4/16 (Kimi)
C2417 Williams FW23 BMW (HP)
C2418 Williams FW23 BMW (HP)
C2419 Ford Taurus Nascar (Tide 2002)
C2420 Ford Taurus Nascar (Alltel 2002)
C2421 Porsche 911 GT1 (GT1)
C2422 Porsche 911 GT1 (GT1)
C2426T Cadillac Northstar 4l (Model Car Racing (USA 2002))
C2427W Ford Focus (Focus Rally)
C2428W Ford Focus (Focus Rally)
C2429W Opel-Vauxhall Astra V8 DTM Coupe (Sport Bild)
C2430W Opel-Vauxhall Astra V8 DTM Coupe (Opel Motorsport)
C2431W Ford Taurus Nascar (Robo Racer)
C2432W Ford Taurus Nascar (Test Track)
C2435 Ford Taurus Nascar
C2436A Ford Mustang (Boss 302, 1969)
C2437 Ford Mustang (Boss 302, 1970)
C2438W Mercedes C Class
C2439W Mercedes C Class
C2440W Team High Nose (Xerox/Pioneer)
C2441W Team High Nose (Castrol/Rapid/Minolta)
C2444/W Pontiac Grand Prix (Home Depot)
C2445/W Pontiac Grand Prix (Interstate Batteries)
C2446W Holden Commodore (Castrol)
C2447W Ford Falcon (Pirtek)
C2448N TVR Speed 12
C2449 Porsche 911 GT1
C2450T Ford Mustang
C2451T Chevrolet Camaro
C2452 TVR Speed 12 (ASSRC)

C2455A Toyota TF102
C2456 Toyota TF102
C2457 TVR Speed 12 (Mobil 1)
C2458 TVR Speed 12 (Valvoline)
C2459/W Team High Nose (Supernova)
C2460/W Team High Nose (Petrobas)
C2461 Porsche 911 GT3R (Luc Alphand)
C2462 Porsche 911 GT3R (Switzerland)
C2463A Ford GT40 MKII (Shelby)
C2463AWD Ford GT40 MKII (Shelby)
C2464 Ford GT40 MKII (Shelby)
C2464AWD Ford GT40 MKII (Shelby)
C2465 Ford GT40 MKII (Holman)
C2465AWD Ford GT40 MKII (Holman)
C2466 Opel-Vauxhall Vectra (Jersey Police 50th Anniversary)
C2467 Opel-Vauxhall Vectra (Metropolitan Police)
C2468N TVR Speed 12 (NSCC)
C2469 Porsche 911 GT3R (Hamleys)
C2470 Porsche 911 GT3R (Modelzone)
C2471A Ford Focus (Gamleys 2002)
C2471B Ford Focus (Gamleys 2002)
C2472 Ford GT40 (Plain White)
C2473 Ford GT40 MKII (Plain White)

2003

C2349 Mitsubishi Lancer Evo 7
C2351 Ford Focus
C2367 MG Lola EX257 (Knighthawk Racing)
C2391A Mercedes CLK DTM (Vodaphone)
C2392A Mercedes CLK DTM (Works)
C2394 Dallara Indianapolis (Red Bull)
C2424 Ford GT40 MKII
C2442/W Dallara Indianapolis (Pennzoil)
C2443/W Dallara Indianapolis (Corteco)
C2453A TVR Tuscan (Dewalt)

C2454/W TVR Tuscan (Eclipse)
C2474 Opel-Vauxhall Astra V8 DTM Coupe (Phoenix)
C2475 Opel-Vauxhall Astra V8 DTM Coupe (TV Today)
C2476W Renault Megane
C2477W Renault Megane
C2480 Porsche 911 GT3R (Orbit Racing - Yankees)
C2481 Porsche 911 GT3R (De Walt)
C2482 MG Lola EX257 (Intersport Banana Joe)
C2483 MG Lola EX257 (Dyson Thetford)
C2484A BMW Mini Cooper (John Cooper Challenge)
C2485 BMW Mini Cooper (John Cooper Challenge)
C2488 Ford Focus (Police Car)
C2489 Ford Focus (Works 2003)
C2490 Caterham Seven (Gulf)
C2491 Subaru Impreza (Works 2003)
C2492 Subaru Impreza (Battery +)
C2494 Mitsubishi Lancer Evo 7 (Works 2003)
C2495 Mitsubishi Lancer Evo 7 (Facom)
C2496 Ford Focus (German)
C2498 Dallara Indianapolis (Kelly Racing - Delphi)
C2499 BMW Mini Cooper (Hamleys)
C2502A Chevrolet Corvette Stingray (L88 1972)
C2503 Chevrolet Corvette Stingray (L88 1972)
C2508 Chevrolet Camaro
C2509 Ford GT40 MKII (Le Mans 1966)
C2510 Ford Mustang (Range Presentation)

C2515 Dallara Indianapolis (Coca Cola)
C2516 Dallara Indianapolis (Mobil 1)
C2517 Dallara Indianapolis (Gulf)
C2518 Dallara Indianapolis (Pirelli)
C2519 Holden Commodore (Valvoline)
C2520 Ford Falcon (Shell)
C2524 Porsche 911 GT3R (The Entertainer)
C2525 Chevrolet Corvette Stingray
C2526W BMW Mini Cooper
C2527W BMW Mini Cooper
C2528W Opel-Vauxhall Astra V8 DTM Coupe (Vauxhall)
C2529A Ford GT40 (Goodwood 3 Pack)
C2531W Subaru Impreza (Petter Solberg)
C2532W TVR Tuscan (Mobil 1 - Harman Kardon)
C2533W TVR Tuscan (Texaco - Xavex)
C2534A Ford GT40 MKII (German Livery)
C2535W Porsche 911 GT1 (Chequered Flag.)
C2536W Porsche 911 GT1 (Chequered Flag.)
C2537W Porsche 911 GT3R (Luc Alphand)
C2538A BMW Mini Cooper S (Italian Job)
C2539A BMW Mini Cooper S (Italian Job)
C2540W BMW Mini Cooper (Italian Job)
C2541W BMW Mini Cooper (Hamleys)
C2542W BMW Mini Cooper (Hamleys)
C2545 Ford Mustang (Modelzone)
C2548 Dallara Indianapolis

C2397 Renault R23 F1 (Alonso)
C2398 Renault R23 F1 (Trulli)
C2478 Porsche Boxster
C2479 Porsche Boxster
C2486A Skoda Fabia (Works 2003)
C2487 Skoda Fabia (Works 2003)
C2506 Audi TT
C2507 Audi TT
C2522A Dodge Viper
C2523 Dodge Viper
C2549 Ford GT40 (Range Presentation)
C2550 Subaru Impreza (The Sun)
C2551A Maserati 250F (1957)
C2552A Vanwall (1961)
C2553A Ford Gran Torino (Starsky & Hutch)
C2554 McLaren MP4/16 (David 2004)
C2555 McLaren MP4/16 (Kimi 2004)
C2562 BMW Mini Cooper (England Flag)
C2563 BMW Mini Cooper (S4C)
C2563 BMW Mini Cooper (S4C)
C2564 BMW Mini Cooper S (XNRG)
C2565 BMW Mini Cooper S (Broad Oak)
C2566 Chevrolet Corvette Stingray (Open Top)
C2567 Mercedes Clk DTM (Express Service)
C2568 Mercedes Clk DTM (Service 24hr - Collectors Centre 2004)
C2569 Opel-Vauxhall Astra V8 DTM Coupe (Opc/Gmac)
C2570 Ford GT 2004
C2571 Dallara Indianapolis (Arcalex)
C2572 Dallara Indianapolis (7 Eleven)

C2573 Chevrolet Camaro (Street Car)
C2574 Ford Mustang (Street Car)
C2575 Chevrolet Corvette Stingray (Street Car)
C2576 Ford Mustang (1969)
C2578A Ford GT40
C2579 Porsche 911 GT3R (Freisinger)
C2580 Porsche 911 GT3R (Seikel)
C2580W Porsche 911 GT3R
C2581A Renault R24 F1 (Trulli)
C2582 Renault R24 F1 (Alonso)
C2583 Williams FW23 BMW F1 2004 (HP)
C2584 Williams FW23 BMW F1 2004 (HP)
C2585 Ford Taurus Nascar (Ascar - Territorial Army)
C2586 Ford Taurus Nascar (Ascar - USA/UK Flags)
C2587 Subaru Impreza (2004)
C2588 Mitsubishi Lancer Evo 7 (2004)
C2589 Caterham Seven (40th Anniversary)
C2590/W TVR Tuscan (CDL Racing/Synergy)
C2591 TVR Tuscan (JCB)
C2600W Dallara Indianapolis (Sport)
C2601W Dallara Indianapolis (Sport)
C2602W/WA Chevrolet Corvette Stingray
C2603A Multi-Pack Ford Torino & Chevrolet Corvette (Starsky & Hutch)
C2604 Ford Taurus Nascar
C2605 Chevrolet Montecarlo
C2606 Dallara Indianapolis
C2607W Subaru Impreza (Street Car)

C2612 Holden Commodore (Castrol)
C2613 Ford Falcon (Pirtek)
C2614 Ford Falcon (Caltex)
C2615 Ford Falcon (Cat)
C2616W Williams FW23 BMW F1 2003 (Montoya)
C2618 TVR Tuscan (Hamleys)
C2619 Subaru Impreza
C2622W Chevrolet Corvette Stingray
C2623W Dallara Indianapolis
C2624W Dallara Indianapolis
C2625W Holden Commodore (Racer V8)
C2626W Holden Commodore (Racer V8)
C2627 Dallara Indianapolis (Microchip)
C2629 Porsche 911 GT3R (Schmidbauer Modellauto)
C2631 BMW Mini Cooper S (Modelzone 2004)
C6000 Honda Repsol 2003 (Valentino Rossi)
C6001 Honda Camel Pramac 2003 (Max Biaggi)
C6003 Honda Telefonica Movistar 2003 (Sete Gibernau)
C6003WA Honda Telefonica Movistar 2003 (Sete Gibernau)
C6005 Yamaha Gauloises 2004 (Valentino Rossi)
C6006 Yamaha Fortuna 2004 (Carlos Checa)
C6008 Ducati Marlboro 2003 (Loris Capirossi)
C6009 Ducati Marlboro 2004 (Troy Bayliss)
C8157 Mercedes Clk DTM (Challenger)
C8159 Mercedes Clk DTM (Challenger)

2005

C2504A Maserati Cambiocorsa (Vodafone)
C2505 Maserati Cambiocorsa
C2560 Peugeot 307 (Works)
C2561 Peugeot 307 (Works (Weathered))
C2577 Chevrolet Camaro (1969)
C2592 Opel-Vauxhall Vectra (Reuter)
C2593 Opel-Vauxhall Vectra (Frentzen)
C2594 Ford Taurus Nascar (Dewalt)
C2595 Ford Taurus Nascar (Sharpie)
C2596A BMW Mini Cooper S (NSCC)
C2597 Chevrolet Montecarlo (Dupont)
C2598 Chevrolet Montecarlo (Lowe's)
C2599A BMW Mini Cooper S (NSCC)
C2608W Porsche Boxster
C2609W Audi TT
C2610W Porsche Boxster
C2611W Audi TT
C2617W Audi TT
C2620 BMW Mini Cooper S (Electric Blue)
C2621 BMW Mini Cooper S (Astro Black)
C2630A Maserati MC12 (Works 2004)
C2632A Mercedes SLR McLaren
C2633 BMW Mini Cooper S (Range Presentation)
C2634 Dodge Viper
C2635 Batmobile (The Beginning)
C2636 Ford Crown (The Beginning)
C2639A Cooper Climax T53 (Jack Brabham)
C2640A Ferrari 156 Sharknose (Phil Hill)
C2641A Ferrari 330 P4
C2642 Ferrari 330 P4
C2648 Renault R24 F1
C2649 Renault R24 F1 (Alonso)
C2654 Chevrolet Camaro
C2655 Ford Gran Torino
C2657 TVR Tuscan (Synergy)
C2658 Lister Storm Lmp (Essex Invest)
C2660 MG Lola EX257 (Transvu)
C2661 Ford GT 2004
C2662 Maserati 250F (John Behra)
C2663 Vanwall (1958)
C2664 Porsche 911 GT3R (Gruppe M)
C2665 Porsche 911 GT3R (New Century)
C2667 McLaren MP4/16 (Juan Pablo Montoya)
C2668 McLaren MP4/16 (Kimi 2005)
C2669 Multi-Pack Batmobile & Police Car (Batman Begins)
C2670 Nissan 350Z (Pioneer)
C2671 Nissan 350Z (Alpine)
C2676 Ferrari F1 (2004)
C2677 Ferrari F1 (2004)
C2678 Maserati MCR 12 (Street Car)
C2682 Mitsubishi Lancer Evo 7 (Gwyndaff Evans)
C2682B Mitsubishi Lancer Evo 7 (NSCC)

C2683A Ford GT40 (Alan Mann Racing)
C2684 Opel-Vauxhall Vectra (Playboy)
C2685 Opel-Vauxhall Vectra (Valvoline)
C2686W BMW Mini Cooper S (John Cooper Challenge)
C2687W BMW Mini Cooper S (John Cooper Challenge)
C2688W Maserati Cambiocorsa (Racer)
C2689W Maserati Cambiocorsa (Racer)
C2691 Dodge Viper (Roe)
C2692 Holden Commodore (Super Cheap)
C2693 Ford Falcon (Betta Electrical)
C2694 Ford Falcon (Pirtek)
C2695 Ford Falcon (Caterpillar)
C2696 Chevrolet Camaro (Bob Jane)
C2697 Ford Gran Torino
C2698W Peugeot 307
C2699 McLaren MP4/16 (De La Rosa)
C2701W Nissan 350Z (Nissan)
C2702W Nissan 350Z (Nissan)
C6002 Honda Camel Pramac 2004 (Mako Tamada)
C6004 Honda Repsol 2004 (Alex Barros)
C6007 Honda Telefonica Movistar 2004 (Colin Edwards)
C6010 Aprilia Alica 2004 (Shane Byrne)
C6011 Aprilia Alica 2004 (Jeremy McWilliams)
C6012 Ducati D'antin 2004 (Neil Hodgson)
C6013 Ducati D'antin 2004 (Ruben Xaus)
C6014 Suzuki Rizla 2004 (John Reynolds)
C6016 Honda Repsol 2004 (Nicky Hayden)
C6017 Yamaha Fortuna 2004 (Marco Milandri)
C6018 Honda HM Plant (Rutter)
C6020 Yamaha Go!!!!!!! (Valentino Rossi)
C6021 Honda Movistar 2005 (Sete Gibernau)
C6022 Honda Repsol 2005 (Max Biaggi)
C6023 Ducati 2005 (Carlos Checa)
K2000/A Chevrolet Camaro
K2001/A Ford Focus
K2002/A Ford Mustang
K2003/A Mitsubishi Lancer Evo 7
K2004/A Porsche 911 GT3R
K2005/A Subaru Impreza
K2006 Ford GT40
K2007/A Ford GT40
K2008/A Mercedes CLK DTM
K2009/A Chevrolet Corvette Stingray
K2010/A TVR Tuscan
K2011/A BMW Mini Cooper S
K2012/A Caterham Seven (Gulf)
K2013 BMW Mini Cooper

2006

C2637 Nissan Skyline (Xanavi)
C2638 Nissan Skyline (Calsonic)
C2643 Ford Escort MK1
C2644 Aston Martin DBR9 (AMR)
C2645 Skoda Fabia (McRae)
C2646 Williams FW26 BMW F1 2005 (Webber)

C2647 Williams FW26 BMW F1 2005 (Heidfeld)
C2650 Dallara Indianapolis (Wheldon/Klein Tools)
C2653 Chevrolet Corvette Stingray (AIRT)
C2656 Ford Mustang
C2659 Maserati Cambiocorsa
C2666 Subaru Impreza (The Sun)
C2680 Maserati Cambiocorsa (Range Presentation)
C2703A Ferrari 156 Sharknose (Baghetti)
C2704 Seat Leon (Red Bull/Gene)
C2705 Seat Leon (BTCC - Plato)
C2706 Lola A1GP (UK)
C2707 Lola A1GP (France)
C2708 Lola A1GP (Netherlands)
C2709 Lola A1GP (Switzerland)
C2711/W Jaguar Trans Am (Rocketsports)
C2712W Nissan 350Z
C2713W Nissan 350Z
C2715/W Honda Bar (Button)
C2715/W Honda Bar (Button)
C2716 Honda Bar (Montoya)
C2717 Toyota Supra (Esso)
C2718 Toyota Supra (AU)
C2719 Honda NSX (Takata)
C2720 Honda NSX (Raybrig)
C2721 Nissan 350Z JGTC (Xanavi)
C2722 Nissan 350Z JGTC (Calsonic)
C2723 Renault F1 2006 (Alonso 2006)
C2724 Renault F1 2006 (Fisichella)
C2725 Williams FW26 Cosworth 2006
C2726 Williams FW26 Cosworth 2006
C2727 Ferrari 156 Sharknose (Von Tripps)
C2728 Maserati MC12 (Racing Box)
C2729 Cooper Climax T53 (Bruce McLaren)
C2730/W Porsche 911 GT3R (Sebah)

C2731W Porsche 911 GT3R (Flying Lizards)
C2732 BMW Mini Cooper S (Beautran)
C2733 BMW Mini Cooper S (Red Barons)
C2734 Ford GT 2004
C2734N Ford GT 2004 (NSCC)
C2735 Audi TT
C2736 Nissan 350Z (Drift Car)
C2737 Porsche Boxster
C2738 Dodge Viper (Foster Motorsports)
C2739 Ford Mustang (Troy Promotions)
C2740 Chevrolet Camaro (Behrens Racing)
C2741 Lola A1GP (New Zealand)
C2742 Lola A1GP (Canada)
C2743 Lola A1GP (Australia)
C2744 Lola A1GP (USA)
C2745 Lola A1GP (Italy)
C2746 Lola A1GP (Germany)
C2749 Subaru Impreza (Solberg - 2006)
C2750 Chevrolet Corvette Stingray (DX Sunray)
C2751 Ferrari F1 2006 (Schumacher)
C2752 Ferrari F1 2006 (Massa)
C2753W Mercedes SLR McLaren (McLaren)
C2754DW Porsche Boxster
C2755 Ford GT40 (Gulf)
C2756 Mercedes SLR McLaren (Pace Car)
C2757 Ford Escort MK1 (Colibri)
C2758/W Aston Martin DBR9 (Red Nose)
C2759 Chevrolet Camaro (Stubber)
C2760 Ford Mustang (Dan Furey)
C2761 Jaguar Trans Am (Cytomax)
C2765D Porsche Boxster
C2766 Ford Falcon (Russell Ingall)
C2767 Ford Falcon (Steve Johnson)
C2768 Holden Commodore (Greg Murphy)
C2769 Holden Commodore (Jason Richards)

C2776W Holden Commodore (Set C1190l)
C2777W Holden Commodore (Set C1190l)

2007

C2558A Multi-Pack McLaren M23 & Ferrari 312T (Hunt & Lauda)
C2710W Aston Martin DBR9 (Red Nose)
C2747W Ferrari 312 T2 (Lauda)
C2748W McLaren M23 (Hunt)
C2762 Seat Leon (Tom Coronel)
C2770A Ferrari 330 P4 (Twin Pack)
C2771W Ferrari 330 P4
C2772W Ferrari 330 P4
C2775 Ford Mustang (Allan Moffat)
C2780/D Renault F1 2006 (ING - Fisichella - 2007)
C2781 Renault F1 2006 (ING - Kovalainen - 2007)
C2782A Multi-Pack Maserati 250F & Ferrari 375 (Twinpack)
C2783A Mercedes SLR McLaren (Twinpack)
C2784 Maserati MC12 (Vodafone)
C2785 Jaguar Trans Am (Autocon Motorsports)
C2786 Porsche 911 GT3R (Jet Alliance)
C2787 Ferrari 330 P4
C2788 Peugeot 307 (Galli)
C2789 Subaru Impreza (The Sun)
C2790 Aston Martin DBR9 (DHL)
C2796 Chevrolet Camaro
C2797 Ford Mustang
C2798 Ford Escort MK1 (Shell Sport)
C2799 Ferrari 312 T2 (Regazzoni)
C2800 McLaren M23 (Villeneuve)
C2801 Nissan Skyline (Pennzoil)
C2802 Ford Focus ST RS WRC (Castrol - Gronholm)
C2803 Ferrari 375
C2804 Ferrari 430 (Scuderia Ecosse)
C2805 BMW Mini Cooper (Viper Stripes)

C2806/W/DW McLaren MP4-21 (Alonso 2007)
C2806D McLaren MP4-21 (Alonso 2007)
C2807 Mini Cooper (R. Aaltonen)
C2808 Range Rover Police Car
C2809 Audi R10 (Le Mans 2006 Winner)
C2810 Lamborghini Gallardo
C2811 Chaparral 2F
C2812 Porsche RS Spyder
C2813 McLaren MP4-21 (Pedro De La Rosa)
C2814 Mercedes 300 SLR (Fangio)
C2815A Ford GT 2004 (Range Presentation 2007)
C2815B Ford GT 2004 (NSCC)
C2816 Ford GT 2004
C2817W/D Honda 2007 (Button - Earth Livery)
C2818W Ferrari 430
C2819 Range Rover Street Car
C2820W BMW Mini Cooper (Zebra Roof)
C2821W BMW Mini Cooper (Chequered Roof)
C2822 Ferrari 430
C2823 Ford GT40
C2824W BMW Mini Cooper (Spider Web Roof)
C2825 Seat Leon (Thomson)
C2826AW Ferrari 375
C2827W Mercedes SLR McLaren 722
C2828W Mercedes 300 SLR (Moss)
C2829 Ford Falcon (Craig Lowndes)
C2830 Ford Falcon (Steven Richards)
C2831 Ford Falcon (James Courtney)
C2832 Holden Commodore (Mark Skaife)
C2833W Range Rover Police Car (Drift Car)
C2834W Lamborghini Gallardo (Drift Car)
C2835 Ferrari 430 (Sara)
C2835/(H) Ferrari 430 (Sara)
C2836A(H) McLaren M23 (Villota)
C2837 McLaren MP4-21 (Hamilton 2007)
C2838 McLaren MP4-21 (Pedro De La Rosa - 2006 Test Car)
C2839 McLaren MP4-21 (Raikkonen 2006)
C2840 Honda 2007 (Barrichello)
C2841 Williams FW26 Cosworth 2006 (A Wurz)
C2842 Eagle-Weslake 1967 (Dan Gurney)
C2843 Lotus 49 (Jim Clark 1967)
C2844 Nissan 350Z (Twinpack)
C2845 Mercedes 300 SLR (Le Mans)
C2846W Ferrari 430
C2847 Ferrari 430 (Twinpack)
C2848W BMW Mini Cooper (Chequered Roof)
C2849W Porsche 911 GT3R

2008

C2714 BMW 320SI (Andy Priaulx)
C2758D Aston Martin DBR9 (Red Nose)
C2774 Ford Mustang FR500C
C2853W BMW Mini Cooper S (After 8 Dark)

C2854W BMW Mini Cooper S (After 8)
C2855 BMW Mini Cooper
C2856 BMW Mini Cooper
C2857W Porsche 911 GT3R
C2860 Ferrari F1 2006 (Raikkonen)
C2861W Lamborghini Gallardo (Drift Car)
C2862W Lamborghini Gallardo (Drift Car)
C2863 Renault F1 2006 (ING - F Alonso - 2008)
C2864 Renault F1 2006 (ING - N Piquet Jr - 2008)
C2865 McLaren MP4-21 (Alonso)
C2866/D McLaren MP4-21 (Hamilton)
C2869 Fiat Cinquecento
C2871 Porsche 997
C2872 Porsche 997
C2873 Ferrari 430
C2874 Ferrari 430
C2875 Lamborghini Gallardo (Drift Car)
C2876 Lamborghini Gallardo (Police Car)
C2877 Range Rover Coastguard
C2879 Nissan 350Z (Greddy)
C2880 McLaren MP4-21 (Hamilton)
C2881 BMW Mini Cooper
C2882 Ford GT 2004 (Stillen)
C2883 Ford Focus ST RS WRC (Eddie Stobart)
C2884 Subaru Impreza (C Atkinson)
C2885 Peugeot 307
C2888 Ford Mustang FR500C (Roush)
C2889 Chevrolet Corvette Stingray
C2890 Ford Mustang
C2891 Chevrolet Camaro (Maurice Carter)
C2892 Chevrolet Impala - COT (Kellogg's - M Martin)
C2893 Chevrolet Impala - COT (Dupont - J Gordon)
C2894 Chevrolet Impala - COT (Lowes - J Johnson)
C2895 Chevrolet Impala - COT (AMP - D Earnhardt)
C2896 Chevrolet Camaro (1970-73 Jim Hall)
C2897 Peugeot 908 (Le Mans - Diesel)
C2898 Peugeot 908 (Test Livery)

C2899 Porsche 997 (Burgfonds - Huisman)
C2900 Porsche 997 (Morellato - Westbrook)
C2901 Lotus Esprit (James Bond)
C2902/D Ferrari 430
C2904/D Maserati MC12 (Sara)
C2905 Audi R10
C2906 Porsche RS Spyder
C2907 Dodge Viper (Naykid Racing)
C2908 Jaguar XKRS (Johnson Controls)
C2909 BMW 320SI (RAC C Turkington)
C2911 BMW Mini Cooper S (G. Nixon)
C2912 Seat Leon (Calciago)
C2913 Ford Lotus Cortina
C2914 Mercedes Le Mans Coupe
C2915 Ferrari 375 (A Ascari)
C2916 Chaparral 2F
C2917 Ford GT40 MKII (G Hill)
C2918 Ferrari 330 P4
C2919 Morris Mini Cooper
C2920 Ford Escort MK1 (Uniflo)
C2921A Morris Mini Cooper (Italian Job)
C2922A Aston Martin DBS (James Bond)
C2927 McLaren M23 (J Maas)
C2928A Ferrari 375
C2929 Maserati 250F
C2930A Aston Martin DBS (James Bond)
C2931 Morris Mini Cooper (Italian Job)
C2932 Morris Mini Cooper (Italian Job)
C2933 Morris Mini Cooper (Italian Job)
C2934 Fiat Cinquecento
C2935 Aston Martin DBR9 (Range Presentation)
C2935A Aston Martin DBR9 (NSCC)
C2936 Lamborghini Gallardo (Scalextric Club)
C2937 Ford Escort MK1 (Mexico)
C2938 Ferrari 430
C2940 Ford GT40 (Masters Racing Series 2007)
C2941A Ford GT40 (Le Mans 1966)

C2942A Ford GT40 (Le Mans 1966)
C2943A Ford GT40 MKII
C2949 BMW Mini Cooper (Red/Chequer Roof, Yellow Zebra Roof)
C2951 Ford Cortina (Bathurst 1964)
C2952 Ford Falcon (2008)
C2953 Ford Falcon (2008)
C2954 Holden Commodore (2008)
C2957 Chevrolet Impala - COT
C2958 Chevrolet Impala - COT (National Guard - D Earnhardt)
C2959(H) Aston Martin DBR9 (BMS Scuderia)
C2960 Aston Martin DBR9 (Gulf)
C2961 Porsche 997 (Dhl)
C2962 Ford Focus ST RS WRC (Abu Dhabi - Jm Latvala)
C2963A Alfa Romeo 159 (James Bond)
C2964 Lotus 49B (Gold Leaf)
C2983A Mercedes McLaren SLR 722 (Top Gear)
C2996/W Lamborghini Gallardo
C3006 Lamborghini Gallardo GT (Vitol)
C3009 Lamborghini Gallardo (Need For Speed)
C3024 Mercedes Coupe
C3029 Ford Escort MK1
C3030 Holden L34 Torana

2009

C2965 Aston Martin DBR9 (Gulf (Dirty Livery))
C2966 Ford Escort MK1 (Scalextric Club 2009)
C2967 Chaparral 2F (NSCC 2009)
C2968 Chaparral 2F (Range Presentation 2009)
C2969 Porsche 997 GT3 RS (Hornby Concessions)
C2970 Ferrari 250 GTO (Parkes)
C2971A Williams & McLaren (Monaco 1992)

C2972W Williams FW14B (Mansell)
C2973W McLaren MP4/7 (Senna)
C2974 Ferrari 308 GTB (Mat)
C2975 Chevrolet Camaro (Big Red)
C2976 Ford Mustang
C2978 Jaguar XKR GT3 2009 (Apex)
C2980A Morris Mini Cooper (50 Yrs Anniversary)
C2981A Ford (Alan Mann Twin Set)
C2982A Aston Martin DBS (Top Gear)
C2984A Ford GT 2004 (Top Gear)
C2992 BMW Mini Cooper
C2993 Alfa Romeo 159 (Carabinieri)
C2994 Aston Martin DBS
C2995 Ford GT 2004
C2998W Ford Escort MK1 (Alan Mann)
C2999W Ford Lotus Cortina (Alan Mann)
C3000 Ford Mustang FR500C
C3001 Chevrolet Camaro (1970-73)
C3002 Ford Mustang (Brut 33)
C3005 Chevrolet Camaro (1969)
C3007 Ferrari 430
C3012 Ferrari 430 (Scuderia Ecosse - Mansell)
C3018 Dodge Viper (Mopar)
C3019 BMW Mini Cooper S
C3023 Ford Lotus Cortina
C3025 Chaparral 2F
C3026 Ford GT40
C3027 Ford Escort MK1
C3028 Ferrari 330 P4
C3032 Eagle-Weslake Gurney Weslake
C3033 Ferrari 156 (Gendebien)
C3038DW Ferrari 430
C3039DW Ferrari 430

Useful websites

Official Scalextric Club http://www.scalextric.com/scalextric-club
National Slot Car Collectors Club http://www.nscc.co.uk
Slot Car Portal and pictorial reference library: http://www. ukslotcars.co.uk

http://www.slotcarcentre.co.uk
http://www.modelmotorracing.com

LEGO Color Guide
2010

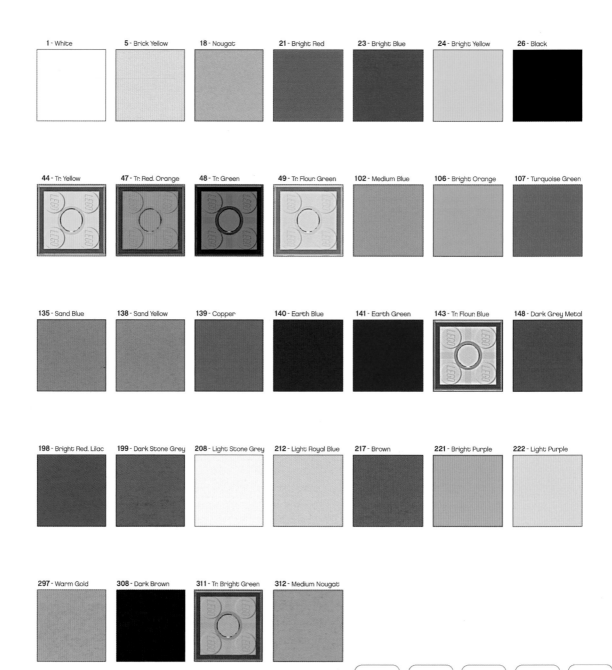

1 - White	**5** - Brick Yellow	**18** - Nougat	**21** - Bright Red	**23** - Bright Blue	**24** - Bright Yellow	**26** - Black
44 - Tr. Yellow	**47** - Tr. Red. Orange	**48** - Tr. Green	**49** - Tr. Flour. Green	**102** - Medium Blue	**106** - Bright Orange	**107** - Turquoise Green
135 - Sand Blue	**138** - Sand Yellow	**139** - Copper	**140** - Earth Blue	**141** - Earth Green	**143** - Tr. Flour. Blue	**148** - Dark Grey Metal
198 - Bright Red. Lilac	**199** - Dark Stone Grey	**208** - Light Stone Grey	**212** - Light Royal Blue	**217** - Brown	**221** - Bright Purple	**222** - Light Purple
297 - Warm Gold	**308** - Dark Brown	**311** - Tr. Bright Green	**312** - Medium Nougat			

28 - Dark Green

37 - Bright Green

38 - Dark Orange

40 - Tr. Clear

41 - Tr. Red

42 - Tr. Light Blue

43 - Tr. Blue

111 - Tr. Brown

113 - Tr. Med. Violet

119 - Bright Yel. Green

120 - Light Yel. Green
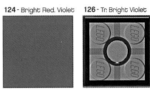

124 - Bright Red. Violet

126 - Tr. Bright Violet

131 - Silver

151 - Sand Green

154 - Dark Red

182 - Tr. Bright Orange

191 - Flame Yel. Orange
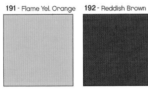

192 - Reddish Brown

194 - Med. Stone Grey

196 - Dark Royal Blue

226 - Cool Yellow

227 - Tr. Bright Green

232 - Dove Blue

268 - Medium Lilac

283 - Light Nougat

294 - PhosporentWhite
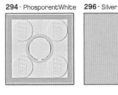

296 - Silver

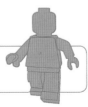

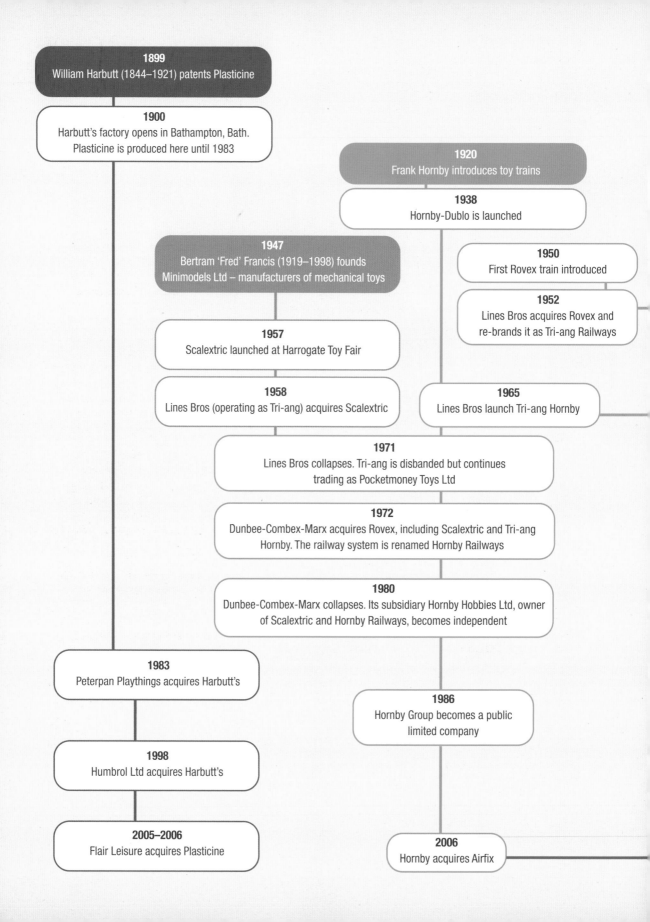

1899
William Harbutt (1844–1921) patents Plasticine

1900
Harbutt's factory opens in Bathampton, Bath.
Plasticine is produced here until 1983

1920
Frank Hornby introduces toy trains

1938
Hornby-Dublo is launched

1947
Bertram 'Fred' Francis (1919–1998) founds
Minimodels Ltd – manufacturers of mechanical toys

1950
First Rovex train introduced

1952
Lines Bros acquires Rovex and
re-brands it as Tri-ang Railways

1957
Scalextric launched at Harrogate Toy Fair

1958
Lines Bros (operating as Tri-ang) acquires Scalextric

1965
Lines Bros launch Tri-ang Hornby

1971
Lines Bros collapses. Tri-ang is disbanded but continues
trading as Pocketmoney Toys Ltd

1972
Dunbee-Combex-Marx acquires Rovex, including Scalextric and Tri-ang
Hornby. The railway system is renamed Hornby Railways

1980
Dunbee-Combex-Marx collapses. Its subsidiary Hornby Hobbies Ltd, owner
of Scalextric and Hornby Railways, becomes independent

1983
Peterpan Playthings acquires Harbutt's

1986
Hornby Group becomes a public
limited company

1998
Humbrol Ltd acquires Harbutt's

2005–2006
Flair Leisure acquires Plasticine

2006
Hornby acquires Airfix

TOY TREE

A potted history of the six toy-making companies featured in this book. From left to right: Plasticine, Scalextric, Hornby, Meccano, Airfix and Lego.

1901
Frank Hornby (1863–1936) patents 'Improvements in Toy or Educational Devices for Children and Young People' – or what would later become Meccano

1901
Mechanics Made Easy (the first version of Meccano) is launched

1907
Meccano Ltd is established

1934
Ole Kirk Christiansen (1891–1958) names his toy-making company Lego

1939
Nicholas Kove (1891–1958) founds Airfix – manufacturing inflatable rubber toys

1949
Lego starts producing plastic Automatic Binding Bricks

1952
Airfix make first commercial model – the *Golden Hind*

1953
Airfix make first aircraft kit – the Supermarine Spitfire

1953
Binding Bricks renamed Lego Bricks

1964
Lines Bros (owners of Tri-ang Railways) acquires Meccano Ltd including the Hornby brands

1958
Lego's famous stud-and-tube clutch system is patented

1969
Lego Duplo bricks (for younger children) are launched

1972
Airfix Industries acquires Meccano Ltd

1974
Lego Family Set figures introduced

1977
Lego Technic (the Expert Builder) series is launched

1978
Lego Minifigures launched

1981
General Mills acquires Meccano. Meccano Junior launched

1981
Palitoy acquires Airfix

1985
Marc Rebibo acquires Meccano from General Mills

1986
Humbrol Ltd acquires Airfix

1989
Dominique Duvauchelle acquires Meccano from Marc Rebibo

1995
Allen & McGuire acquires Hobby Products Group (including Airfix)

1996
Legoland Windsor is opened in the UK

2000–2006
In 2000 Nikko acquired a significant share in Meccano. Following various acquisitions, Meccano is now owned by Ingroup and Central Partner

1998
Lego Mindstorms launched

2001
Lego Bionicle launched

Further information

Plasticine official site http://www.flairplc.co.uk/pages/plasticine.shtml
Museum of Bath (historical collection of Harbutt's Plasticine)
   http://www.bathatwork.co.uk
Aardman film and television animation http://www.aardman.com/

Meccano official site http://www.meccano.com
http://www.users.zetnet.co.uk/dms/meccano/
http://www.internationalmeccanomen.org.uk/
http://www.nzmeccano.com/

Lego official site http://www.lego.com
http://www.hccamsterdam.nl/brickfactory/
The Unofficial Lego Builder's Guide http://www.apotome.com/inside.html

Bibliography

Plasticine
Bell Knight, C.A. *Harbutt's Plasticine: A Survey* (British Nostalgia
   Publications, 1983)
Blanchard, Albert V. Unpublished notes, 1963
The Plasticine People (Harbutt's Plasticine Ltd, 1972)
'Battle of Vimy – The Story of a Model' (*Daily Telegraph*, 1917)
Interviews with Terry Harbutt, 2009

Meccano
Brown, Kenneth. *Factory of Dreams: A History of Meccano Ltd* (Crucible Books,
   2007)
Gamble, Jim. *Frank Hornby: Notes and Pictures* (James G. Gamble, 2001)
Gould, M.P. *Frank Hornby: The Boy Who Made $1,000,000 With A Toy*
   (Meccano Inc, 1915)
Harrison, Ian, with Pat Hammond. *Hornby: The Official Illustrated History*
   (HarperCollins, 2002)
Love, Bert, and Jim Gamble. *The Meccano System and the Special Purpose
   Meccano Sets* Volume 6 (New Cavendish Books, 1986)
Love, B.N. *Meccano Constructors' Guide* (Model & Allied Publication Ltd, 1971)
Randall, Peter. *The Products of Binns Road: A General Survey* (New Cavendish
   Books, 1977)
Correspondence with Jim Gamble, 2009

Hornby
Brown, Kenneth. *Factory of Dreams, A History of Meccano Ltd* (Crucible Books,
   2007)
Clemens, Michael. *Steam Trails, The Withered Arm* (Ian Allen Publishing, 2007)
Ellis, Chris. *Hornby Book of Model Railways* (Conway, 2009)
Foster, Michael. *Hornby Dublo Trains* (New Cavendish Books, 1980)
Graebe, Chris and Julie. *The Hornby Gauge 0 System* (New Cavendish Books,
   1985)
Hammond, Pat. *Ramsay's British Model Trains Catalogue* (Warners Group, 2008)
Hammond, Pat. *The Story of Rovex* Volumes 2 and 3 (New Cavendish Books,
   1998 and 2003)
Harrison, Ian, with Pat Hammond. *Hornby: The Official Illustrated History*
   (HarperCollins, 2002)
Way, R. Barnard. *The Story of British Locomotives* (Methuen, 1953)
Tri-ang Railways: The First Ten Years... (Rovex Scale Models Ltd, 1962)
Interviews with Simon Kohler, 2009

Airfix
Price, Dr Alfred, and Paul Blackah. *Supermarine Spitfire Owners' Workshop
   Manual* (Haynes Publishing, 2007)
Ward, Arthur. *Airfix: Celebrating 50 Years of the Greatest Plastic Kits in the World*
   (HarperCollins, 1999)
Ward, Arthur. *The Boys' Book of Airfix: Who Says You Ever Have To Grow Up?*
   (Ebury Press, 2009)
Interview with Darrell Burge, 2009

Scalextric
Francis, Diana. Fred Francis obituary (The Ocean Cruising Club website, 1998)
Gillham, Roger. *Scalextric: A Race Through Time – The Official 50th Anniversary
   Book* (Haynes Publishing, 2001)
Green, Rod. *Scalextric: The Story of the World's Favourite Model Racing Cars*
   (HarperCollins, 2001)
101 Circuits for Scalextric Drivers (Minimodels Ltd, 1966)
Interviews with Diana Francis and Adrian Norman, 2009

Lego
Bedford, Allan. *The Unofficial Lego Builder's Guide* (No Starch Press, 2005)
Humberg, Christian. *50 Years of the Lego Brick* (Heel Verlag GmbH, 2008)
Interviews with Jørgen Vig Knudstorp and Jan Christensen, 2009

Acknowledgements

James May thanks the following for their help with his toy adventures, and with
the research for the text and sourcing the illustrations.

'Without all you lot it wouldn't have been possible or half as much fun…'

Anova Books, in particular Ian Harrison, Polly Powell, Fiona Holman,
John Lee, Matt Jones, David Salmo, Georgie Hewitt, Nichola Smith and
Laura Brodie.

Plum Pictures, in particular Vicki Bax, Abi Brooks, Paul Buller, Stuart Cabb,
Will Daws, Alex Dunlop, Jules Endersby, Ian Holt, Charlie Hyland, Nick
Kennedy, Rebecca Magill, David Marks, Sim Oakley, Martin Phillip, Lareine
Shea, Warren Smith, Graham Strong and Becky Timothy.

Also Component Graphics for the logo design, TV title sequence, book
jacket graphics and programme graphics; Caroline Allen, Simon Rogers
and Michael Wicks.

Plasticine
The inventor of Plasticine, William Harbutt; also Aardman; Jane Asher (Jane
Asher Party Cakes; www.janeasher.com); Paul Baker (3D Studios; www.3d-
studios.co.uk); BAPS Shri Swaminarayan Mandir; Judith Blacklock (The Judith
Blacklock Flower School; www.judithblacklock.com); N M Broadfoot; the
Chelsea Pensioners at the Royal Hospital, Chelsea; Lauren Green at Flair Leisure
Products plc; Chris Collins; Terry Harbutt; John Harford; Jane McAdam Freud
(www.janemcadamfreud.com); Naima JPS; Sake No Hana; Simon Kelly and
Stockwell Park School pupils; and the volunteers at the Ideal Home Exhibition.

Meccano
The inventor of Meccano, Frank Hornby; also Atkins, in particular Adam Miller
and Hayden Nuttall; Edwina Currie; Jim Gamble; Harry Kroto; Alistair
Lenczner (Foster + Partners); David Mackenzie; Michael Ingberg and Mattei
Théodore at Meccano France; Sue Barratt and Kristy Frost at Meccano UK; all
at North West Meccano Guild; Ian Mordue of North East Meccano Guild;
SkegEx (Geoff Brown and North Midlands Meccano Guild); University College
London, Department of Civil Engineering; and all the staff and students at the
University of Liverpool, Engineering and Architecture departments, in particular
Josh Woods, John Carroll and Danny Dobson.

Airfix
The inventor of Airfix, Nicholas Kove; also Poppy Boden (Cast For Life:
www.castforlife.co.uk); Darrell Burge and all at Hornby Hobbies Ltd
(www.hornby.com); Alex Medhurst and all the staff at RAF Cosford;
Roy Cross; Chris Ellis; Gateguards (www.gateguardsuk.com); Carolyn Grace
(www.ml407.co.uk/); James May (Senior – James's dad); Trevor Snowden;
Arthur Ward; Ken Wilkinson; and the staff, pupils and their parents from
Thomas Telford School.

Hornby
The originators of the Hornby, Rovex and Tri-ang railway systems, Frank
Hornby, Alexander Venetzian and the Lines Brothers; also Station Master's Café,
Barnstaple; Buffers Model Railway; Oz Clarke; Chris da Silva; Chris Ellis; Chris
Hughes; Simon Kohler and all at Hornby Hobbies Ltd (www.hornby.com); Paul
McGarry; and Coast and Countryside Services of the Tarka Trail.

Scalextric
The inventor of Scalextric, Fred Francis; also the Brooklands Museum; Diana
Francis; Tiff Needall; Adrian Norman, Paul Chandler, Victoria Reed, Martin
Ridge and all at Hornby Hobbies Ltd (www.hornby.com); Martin Toseland;
Simon Toseland; the companies now sited on the original Brooklands circuit
(Mercedes-Benz World, DWS Bodyworks, John Lewis, Trade City/Kier
Property, Marks and Spencer, Tesco, all the residents at Staniland Drive, The
Heights, Sony, Procter and Gamble, Gallagher); and the Locals and Pros who
raced the cars.

Lego
The inventor of Lego, Ole Kirk Christiansen; also Jane Asher; Neil
Thomas and Eva Wates at Atelier One; Oz Clarke; Denbies Wine Estate;
Christina Fallah (www.christina-fallah-designs.com); Barnaby Gunning
(http://barnabygunning.com); Jørgen Vig Knudstorp, Jan Christensen and
René Madsen at The LEGO Group (www.lego.com); Gill Mein; Connie
Robins; Louise Rogers; Gerald Scarfe; Nilu Izadi; Lightplan; Osram;
Encapsulite; Rodas Cleaning; and all the volunteers who helped
to build the house.

Picture acknowledgements

Airfix/Hornby Hobbies Ltd 134 (below), 135 (above), 139 (both), 140 (all), 141 (left), 142 (below), 143, 144 (all), 145 (all), 146 (above), 147 (above), 154 (above), 163, 253, 254, 255, 256, 257

Anova Books 59 (below), 66 (below), 96 (below), 97 (above), 102 (centre and below), 103, 104 (above), 137, 154 (below), 181; (photographer John Lee) 70–71, 77 (all), 100 (below), 101 (above and centre), 104 (above), 147 (below), 157, 173

Apex News and Pictures 122 (above)

Barking Dog Art 44–45, 125 (left), 165

Katie and Nigel Brecknell/Brooklands Museum 193 (above), 194, 197 (below), 198 (above), 201 (below), 205 (centre above)

The Bridgeman Art Library 36 (above) ('Sunflowers', 1888, oil on canvas, by Vincent van Gogh, 1853–90, National Gallery, London, UK); 36 (below) ('Flowers', w/c on paper, Emil Nolde, 1867–1956, Private collection, © Nolde Stiftung Seebuell); 64 (left) (The Eiffel Tower, 1889, colour litho by French School, 19th century, Bibliothèque Nationale, Paris, France/ Lauros / Giraudon); 65 (Great Exhibition of 1851, decoration of the transept by Owen Jones, 1809–74, Victoria & Albert Museum, London, UK)

Michael Clemens 113 (above), 125 (all)

Corbis 49 (Luke MacGregor/Reuters), 96 (above), (Hulton-Deutsch Collection), 214 (above) (Philip Gould), 214 (below) (Owen Franken), 216 (below) (Jean-Pierre Amet/Sygma)

The Daily Telegraph (photographer Martin Pope) 13 (left), 30, 41 (all), 46 (above and below right), 47 (all, top right and below)

Ebury Press © Arthur Ward 132, 133 (both), 134 (above), 135 (below), 136 (above), 142 (below), 146 (below), 252

Chris Ellis 108 (both), 110 (top three)

Christina Fallah (photographer Nilu Izadi) 226 (centre and below left), 227 (below), 230 (above right), 232 (below left)

Flair 29 (below), 32 (below), 243 (below)

Foster + Partners 88–89 (bird design by Alistair Lenczner and Rob Sims; photograph by Nigel Young)

Diana Francis (photographer Michael Wicks) 9 (below left), 174–176, 177 (above and centre), 180 (above), 196

Greg Frost 183 (below)

Jim Gamble (photographer Michael Wicks) 9 (above right), 51 (both), 53 (above), 54–58 (all), 60–63, 66 (above), 67 (below), 68, 73 (below); Carnegie Publishing 59 (above), 98 (below), 110 (below)

Getty 115 (above) (Hulton Archive), 115 (below) (Science and Society Picture Library), 170–171 (Popperfoto), 179 (Daniel Berehulak), 189 (above) (Hulton Archive), 194–195 (Popperfoto)

Barnaby Gunning 222 (all), 223

Darren Harbar 128–129

Terry Harbutt (Photographer Michael Wicks) 14–28, 29 (above), 238–242, 243 (above)

Edward Holman 217

Hornby/Hornby Hobbies Ltd 67 (above), 101 (top and centre), 109 (above), 136 (below); (photographer Thomas Neile) 94, 95 (both), 97 (below), 98 (both), 99 (above), 104 (below), 105, 106 (both), 107 (both), 109 (below), 111, 114 (above), 127, 248, 249, 250, 251

Matthew Jones 205 (centre below)

John Lee 9 (below right), 173, 188, 189 (below), 190 (above), 191 (both), 193 (below left, centre and below right), 197 (above), 198 (centre and below), 199, 200 (above left and right), 202 (left and right), 203 (both), 204 (all), 205 (above, far below and right), 206–207, 209 (right), 210, 221, 229, 230 (above left, below left and right), 231 (above left and right), 232 (above and below right), 234 (below), 235 (below), 236–237

LEGO® 211 (both), 212–213, 215 (all), 216 (above), 218 (both), 221 (above), 266–267

Mark Lewis (www.rooftop-photography.com) 228 (below right),

Liverpool Daily Post and Echo 86 (above right and below), 87 (right)

James May 38, 101 (below), 102 (top left and right), 179 (left), 244–247; (photographer John Lee) 2, 7, 9 (centre left), 92, 93, 197 (above); (photographer Michael Wicks) 48 (both)

Meccano 68 (below), 69 (all)

National Railway Museum/Science & Society Picture Library 90–91

Plum Pictures 10 (left), 31, 32 (above), 33 (all), 34 (above), 35 (above), 39 (above), 47 (centre), 74 (above), 75, 76 (above), 78, 80, 81, 116 (above), 123 (below), 124 (all), 153 (below), 155 (all), 156 (above and below right), 158 (below left and right), 190 (below), 192 (both), 200 (below), 201 (above and centre), 219 (below), 220, 224 (all), 225 (all); 226 (above left and right, centre left and right), 227 (above); Pawel Ambroziak 90, 112 (above), 114 (below left and right), 116 (below), 117 (all), 118 (both), 119, 120 (both), 121 (all), 122 (below), 123 (above), 170 (below left), 202 (centre); Abi Brooks 39, Lee Carus 50–51, 64 (above), 83 (both), 84–85 (all), 86 (above left and centre, centre), 87 (left); Jules Endersby 156 (left); Julian Fullalove 42–43; Charles Hyland 74 (centre and below), 112; Nick Kennedy 10–11, 13 (right), 32 (centre), 64 (below), 72, 73 (above), 141 (above right and below), 149, 150, 151, 152, 159 (all), 166–167 (second row, images 10, 11, 12, all third row and fourth row images, 9, 20, 21, 22 and 23); Henry Langston 9 (centre right), 131 (both), 153 (above), 160 (both), 161 (all), 162 (both), 164, 167 (fourth row, image 24), 168–169; Paul Lawrence 209 (left), 228 (above left and right, centre left and right, below left), 229 (below), 232 (below left), 233 (below), 234 (above and centre), 235 (above); Rebecca Magill 34 (below left and right), 35 (below), 37 (both), 158 (above); Lareine Shea 9 (above left), 40 (all), 82 (all), 166–167 (top row and second row, images 7, 8, 9)

Press Association 46 (below left)

Scalextric/Hornby Hobbies Ltd 178 (all); (photographer Thomas Neile) 170 (top left), 177 (below), 180 (below), 182 (both), 183 (above), 184–187, 258, 259, 260, 261, 262, 263, 264, 265

Gerald Scarfe 231 (Lego picture and cartoon)

The Times 53 (below)

Josh Woods 76 (below), 79 (all)

Index